CULTURE, PLACE, AND NATURE
Studies in Anthropology and Environment

K. Sivaramakrishnan, Series Editor

CULTURE, PLACE, AND NATURE

Centered in anthropology, the Culture, Place, and Nature series encompasses new inter-disciplinary social science research on environmental issues, focusing on the intersection of culture, ecology, and politics in global, national, and local contexts. Contributors to the series view environmental knowledge and issues from the multiple and often conflicting perspectives of various cultural systems.

Enclosed

CONSERVATION, CATTLE, AND COMMERCE
AMONG THE Q'EQCHI' MAYA LOWLANDERS

Liza Grandia

A Capell Family Book

UNIVERSITY OF WASHINGTON PRESS
Seattle and London

The Capell Family Endowed Book Fund supports the publication of books that deepen the understanding of social justice through historical, cultural, and environmental studies.

© 2012 by the University of Washington Press
Printed and bound in the United States of America
Design by Thomas Eykemans
Composed in Warnock, typeface designed by Robert Slimbach
16 15 14 13 12   5 4 3 2 1

UNIVERSITY OF WASHINGTON PRESS
PO Box 50096, Seattle, WA 98145, USA
www.washington.edu/uwpress

LIBRARY OF CONGRESS CATALOGING-IN-PUBLICATION DATA
Grandia, Liza.
Enclosed : conservation, cattle, and commerce among the Q'eqchi' Maya lowlanders / Liza Grandia.
    p. cm. — (Culture, place, and nature : studies in anthropology and environment)
Includes bibliographical references and index.
ISBN 978-0-295-99165-8 (cloth : alk. paper)
ISBN 978-0-295-99166-5 (pbk : alk. paper)
1. Kekchi Indians—Land tenure. 2. Kekchi Indians—Migrations. 3. Kekchi Indians—Economic conditions. 4. Culture and globalization—Guatemala. 5. Free trade—Guatemala. 6. CAFTA (Free trade agreement) (2005). 7. Guatemala—Economic policy. 8. Guatemala—Economic conditions. 9. Guatemala—Ethnic relations. I. Title.
F1465.2.K5G7 2011   330.97281—dc23   2011034987

The paper used in this publication is acid-free and meets the minimum requirements of American National Standard for Information Sciences—Permanence of Paper for Printed Library Materials, ANSI Z39.48–1984.∞

Cover photo: View of a cattle ranch on the road from Flores to San Andrés, Petén. Photo by Sam Moody, 2011.

In memory of Carlos Soza Manzanero, 1957–2003

A Petenero extraordinaire—xatero, conservationist, poet, teacher, honest administrator, scholar, civic leader, gardener, women's advocate, singer, storyteller, trickster, loyal friend, and fellow cancer victim—a true "hombre de maíz"

CONTENTS

FOREWORD

Liza Grandia has worked with Q'eqchi' Maya in their Guatemalan territories of Petén for nearly twenty years. She went there first as a conservation and development professional, returning a few years later as an anthropologist. Over the last two decades the region has suffered its newest form of enclosure, emerging as a protected area for the conservation of biological diversity and a zone of eco-commerce where carbon credits and sustainability industries reshape the material world and social fabric of the Q'eqchi' Maya.

It is perhaps not uncommon for studies in environmental anthropology to focus on the process and effects of displacement and dispossession. And we have come to expect such analysis from studies that take seriously the political economy of modern state formation, international commodity trade, and the effects of rising industrial consumption in the global north on the livelihoods and homelands of poor, often indigenous peoples, in the south. But decades of engagement allowed Grandia to develop an enviably deep understanding of Q'eqchi' Maya lives and to understand their own analyses of conservation activities. The resulting book has led her not so much to the effects of the current round of dispossessions, but to seek out and understand the series of dispossessions that have occurred in Maya territory, from the rise of industrial agriculture to the emergence of global-scale biodiversity conservation.

It is Grandia's insight that settlement and dispossession are processes that have been repeated with growing intensity and frequency during the last two centuries in Maya territories of Guatemala. She, however, does not stop there, but goes on to investigate, with care and precision, the ways in which each set of arrivals and conflicts unfolded. She narrates with passion and attention to detail the stories that bring to light both a critique of certain world historical processes and the ways in which Q'eqchi' Maya distinctly articulate them, so as not to simplify their lives or struggles into one or another version of a Manichean tale. One of the harder things to include in a historical examination of contemporary conflicts is the tension between divergent renderings of the past in varied sources, especially the historical memory of the people whose lives are being depicted. Grandia patiently works through the maze of remembrances and fashions a sympathetic scholarly account of how plantation agriculture, ranching, development projects, and conservation schemes created a cumulative set of constricting pressures on Q'eqchi' Maya society. In doing so she is able to trace how each historical period was viscerally experienced in the region and more abstractly represented abroad by the interested and affected parties.

Despite contents that are at times discouraging, this book does not tell a story entirely of despair or lost causes. Grandia sees hope and an opportunity to restore self-respect and livelihood to the indomitable Maya people who continue to strive for a place in the land they still regard as their homeland. She ends, therefore, not only describing ongoing struggles but also identifying the imperative to steward commons into the future. This wonderful book offers a meditation on the natural healing of social wounds that will have to occur in Guatemala and so many other places in the global south where indigenous people live and aspire to the peace and dignity that is the just pursuit of humanity.

K. SIVARAMAKRISHNAN
Yale University

On Conflicts and Conservation

First we were dispossessed in the names of kings and emperors, later in
the name of state development, and now in the name of conservation.
—Indigenous delegates to the 2003
Fifth World Parks Congress, Durban, South Africa

March 31, 1997. Days before Conservation International's Guatemala program, ProPetén, was to inaugurate a new biological station in Laguna del Tigre
National Park in the northwestern corner of the 1.6 million-hectare Maya Biosphere Reserve, sixty armed men in four motorized canoes arrived simultaneously from different sites on the Rio San Pedro. They burned the station to the
ground and held thirteen workers hostage for two days. In the months leading
up to this event, Guatemala's national park service, the National Council for
Protected Areas (Consejo Nacional de Areas Protegidas), or CONAP, had been
relocating communities settled illegally along roads a petroleum company had
built to its wells inside this same park. Among those involved in this orches-
trated attack on ProPetén's biological station were subsistence farmers who
feared eviction from two nearby Q'eqchi' villages established in the mid-1990s,
well after the park's opening in 1992.

Lacking the political will and authority to continue the evictions, the
CONAP director began negotiating usufruct concessions with the communities that had attacked the station, along with another dozen communities
occupying other parts of the park. In these negotiations, Ladino (mestizo)
squatters tended to emphasize their *need* for land, whereas Q'eqchi' communities emphasized their *moral* relationship to land as Maya people and their
customary right to plant corn for subsistence (N. Schwartz, pers. comm., 2010).

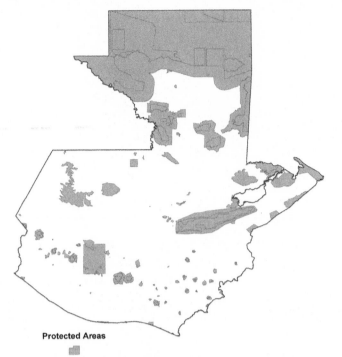

FIGURE P.1.
System of
protected areas
in Guatemala.
Source: Jason
Arnold and Daniel
Irwin, NASA/
SERVIR 2010

Protected Areas

One Q'eqchi' leader from these villages provocatively remarked to Conservation International's former vice president for Mesoamerica, "This is the Maya Biosphere Reserve, we're Maya, what's the problem?" (Nations 2001: 466).

This was not an isolated incident of indigenous communities in conflict with biodiversity conservation (for more cases, see, for example, Chapin 2004; Dowie 2009; Igoe 2004; West, Igoe, and Brockington 2006). From 1900 to 1960, the international conservation movement established almost a thousand protected areas. Multiplied a hundredfold, today there are at least 110,000 protected areas worldwide. Surpassing the World Parks Commission goal of protecting a tenth of the planet's territory, more than 12 percent of the earth is now under some protected status, an area of almost nineteen million square kilometers, equivalent to half the world's cultivated land (Dowie 2009: xx). A thousand indigenous groups once occupied about 80 percent of high priority ecoregions for biodiversity conservation identified by the Worldwide Fund for Nature (ibid.: 264–65). Some were allowed to stay in newly protected areas with restrictions placed on their resource use, but as many as fourteen million have been evicted from their ancestral homelands (ibid.: xxi).

Exceeding this worldwide trend, almost one-third of Guatemala's terri-

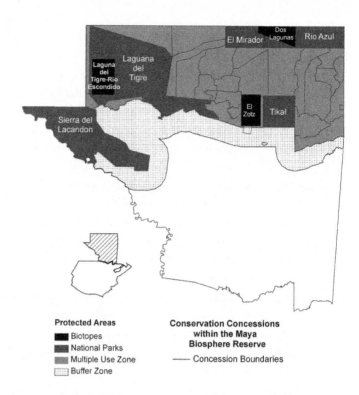

FIGURE P.2. Maya Biosphere Reserve, Petén, Guatemala. Source: Jason Arnold and Daniel Irwin, NASA/SERVIR 2010

Protected Areas
■ Biotopes
■ National Parks
■ Multiple Use Zone
▦ Buffer Zone

Conservation Concessions within the Maya Biosphere Reserve
—— Concession Boundaries

tory is now under protected status, thereby heightening the tensions between people and parks. Q'eqchi' people have had to contend with a disproportionate number of Guatemala's protected areas in their territory.[1] Constituting less than one-tenth of Guatemala's population, they nonetheless are surrounded by one-fourth (by number) and one-fifth (by area) of Guatemala's parks (Secaira 2000) (figs. P.1, P.2). Some Q'eqchi' communities were already legally settled in these regions before the parks were created in the 1990s. Others continued to arrive after it became illegal to settle there but before enforcement began. Many did so after the end of Guatemala's civil war in response to false rumors spread among indigenous communities that the 1996 Peace Accords authorized them to claim unoccupied land, regardless of its conservation status.[2]

Around that time, I was collaborating with ProPetén to design and raise funds for an integrated health and conservation program, Remedios (Remedies). My first project was with an indigenous women's medicinal-plant group in the Itzá town of San José (later described in Sundberg 1998). Conservation International's CEO had other ideas from Washington, D.C. He redirected our first grant to work instead with the two Q'eqchi' communities that had attacked the biological station, Macawville and Basilfield. Without road access, health conditions in their villages were precarious, and four mothers had recently died in childbirth in Macawville alone. Village leaders keenly wanted their wives trained in midwifery. Conservation International officials saw this as an opportunity to heal relations with communities they perceived as hostile to conservation.

Hence, one day in late April 1997, I found myself among a group of regional peasant federation leaders, biologists, foresters, and CONAP officials who descended on Macawville to negotiate a community land settlement. Most of us had traveled for more than six hours (by four-wheel drive, mule, and boat) while the officials arrived by helicopter. Despite the adversarial circumstances, the community had prepared a Q'eqchi' delicacy—spiced turkey soup—for the visitors. Afterward, we moved to a rustic schoolhouse for a long evening of speeches and bartering. The villagers boldly asked for ninety hectares per family. The CONAP director countered by asking how many had previously owned land. Only a few hands went up. Undercut by their historic landlessness, the villagers eventually received a usufruct right to forty-five hectares, the standard allotment for frontier settlement projects, on the condition that they collaborate with developing a natural-resource management plan for the agricultural concession.[3]

While some of Conservation International's staff biologists worried that my health project would attract new squatters to the area, over the next two years of organizing participatory health projects with Macawville, it became clear that all these Q'eqchi' families had settled in this remote, malaria-infested place for one reason only: land. I eventually passed this and other health projects to local leadership and left Petén for graduate school in anthropology. Still intrigued by what had driven so many indigenous people to occupy national parks, I returned three years later to the community as the first site of my research. Impressed by my new Q'eqchi'-language skills, however rudimentary, the people of Macawville began to reveal the secrets of what had driven them to settle there. I heard stories of massacres, cruel plantation bosses, corrupt officials, and bankruptcy caused by illness, among other unspeakable tragedies.

I also learned why they had burned down the biological station. Knowing the villagers feared eviction, an illegal logger had apparently incited them to burn down the station as a distraction as he smuggled out several truckloads of timber. A few people actively sought me out to apologize. They had not realized that our organization was different from the national park service, CONAP. Little wonder they were confused: during the building of the first station, leadership at Conservation International's headquarters forbade the

Guatemalan staff from interacting with squatters. The second time around, the Guatemalan director of ProPetén, Carlos Soza, defied these orders and rebuilt the station with locally raised funds. Emphasizing community involvement, he established a highly successful agroforestry training program that engaged local farmers in conservation activities.

The results were noticeable. One man had given up farming altogether to work full-time as an ecotourism guide, professing a deep fascination with wildlife. Invited to a workshop that my Remedios program organized with other healers from Petén, a Macawville elder had resumed treating patients with medicinal plants. Many others had planted extensive fruit orchards. A newly formed cooperative was sustainably harvesting "xate" palm fronds for export. One housewife even figured out how to domesticate a wild boar. The villagers had located a natural shrine to the *Tzuultaq'a*, their god of the hill and valley. Of course, everyone was also delighted about record harvests of corn cultivated on the ashes of primary forests. Nonetheless, with their livelihoods progressively intermeshed with the forest, the village was no longer outwardly hostile to biodiversity conservation.

Or so it appeared in my field notes. Cognizant that many large international nonprofits like Conservation International were growing increasingly hostile toward integrated conservation and development programs (Brandon, Redford, and Sanderson 1998), I was looking for evidence of "good" conservation behavior from the community that had once burned down a biological station. Although I had passed oral exams in political ecology, I was, quite honestly, still a committed "biodiversity conservationist" at the beginning of my research. I began searching for reasons that would explain why an indigenous group such as the Q'eqchi' had been compelled to settle in national parks such as Laguna del Tigre and degrade their own environment (cf. Blaikie and Brookfield 1987). Aware of my own history as health program coordinator for Pro-Petén, many Macawvillians were likely "greening" their conversations with me (cf. Conklin and Graham 1995). Harking back to my days leading the Remedios health program, for example, they invited me to give separate family planning workshops for all the men and women in the village during my time there as an independent anthropologist.

Nonetheless, I was reflexive enough to avoid continued potential conflicts of interest and planned a multi-sited research program that would build on my long experience working in the environs of the Maya Biosphere Reserve but then expand my geographic frame for understanding Q'eqchi' agrarian problems.[4] A serendipitous visit with the family of a Q'eqchi' colleague who had worked with me in Macawville (described in more detail in the introduction) led me to broaden my initial research question about the push-pull factors of migration into protected areas into a broader inquiry about the enclosures of Guatemala's last frontier.

Meanwhile, ProPetén was in the process of separating from Conservation International to become an independent Guatemalan nongovernmental organization (NGO) with a more autochthonous vision of environmental justice and ecologies of the poor (Guha and Martinez-Alier 1997). During my two years of concentrated field research for this book, I also served as secretary and then president of the board of directors for the new ProPetén. At the time, I was frustrated with how our protracted legal and financial disputes with Conservation International over the biological station and other issues (Grandia 2009c) took away my time with Q'eqchi' communities. In retrospect, I realize that this led me to begin questioning seriously the colonial politics of international conservation organizations that feel more comfortable partnering with corporations than with indigenous and local people. (See Haenn 2005 for another account of a former employee of a large conservation organization who turned critical environmental anthropologist during her field research.)

Perhaps this is why I became less interested in Q'eqchi' conflicts with protected areas than in their history of repeated dispossession. While environmental anthropologists rightly call for more studies about indigenous livelihood changes *after* displacement from protected areas (West, Igoe, and Brockington 2006: 252), I found I wanted to examine how *prior* livelihood changes caused by earlier displacements created the conditions for current Q'eqchi' evictions from parks. Focusing only on the conflicts with parks ignores the enduring history of enclosure of Q'eqchi' common lands from the colonial period through to contemporary neoliberalism—as well as the ongoing Q'eqchi' resistance to plantations, pastures, and development plans. Promising abundance and prosperity, this frontier has long fueled the imaginations of many actors—as cash for lumber barons, refuges for rebel guerrillas, havens for drug traffickers, garrison outposts for military men, enormous ranches for cattlemen, oil and mineral reserves for multinational corporations, living laboratories for tropical ecologists, spiritual fields for missionaries . . . and for landless families, an open territory promising a new start. They all needed to be in the picture.

This is not to deny that the declaration of several million hectares of protected areas in northern Guatemala since the 1990s has striking parallels to other enclosure movements, especially when managed by large international conservation organizations without adequate involvement from local communities and Guatemalan civil society. Purportedly preserving common land for the good of humanity, biodiversity conservation has taken over territory that indigenous people might have managed quite sustainably were it not for other land inequities and corporate enclosures. As I was concluding this manuscript, a conference declaration from a meeting of indigenous peoples, local communities, and Afro-descendants held in Yucatán arrived by e-mail. The long list of threats to indigenous land was striking: "During the past four decades our territories, rich in cultural diversity, biodiversity, traditional knowledge, endemism, and sacred areas, have been subject to repeated systems of colonial-like dispossession, expropriation, biopiracy, bioprospecting, alienation, declaration of protected areas, and megaprojects" (translation mine) (Tercer Precongreso 2010). Emphasizing the participants' commitment to Mother Earth, the declaration condemns not conservation per se but *top-down* programs such as the Mesoamerican Biological Corridor (Corredor Biológico Mesoaméricano), or MBC, the Puebla to Panama Plan (PPP [pronounced "peh peh peh"]), and Reducing Emission from Deforestation and Degradation (REDD) that exclude them from territorial autonomy while colluding with other threats like megaprojects.

Q'eqchi' people are certainly aware of hypocritical or selective enforcement of conservation rules. As Fernando Yat from Tamalton observed, "The 'licenciados' [college-educated professionals] tell us not to cut down the forest. But we see that the rich people cut down more [than us] and no one says anything. Look down the road. A congressman got [140 hectares] near here and didn't leave a single tree. People like him just plant grass and more grass [for pasture]." An exclusive focus on the poor in this book might reinforce stereotypes about the uneven responsibility for environmental change across classes (Haenn 2005: 107). It is only fair that I should also "study up" (Nader 1972) and include elites who seek to privatize and plunder Guatemala's frontier commons for capital accumulation. Even as I tried to write a clean opening story about Q'eqchi' people and parks, other actors, such as petroleum companies, ineluctably crept into my text. Were it not for the added pressures of plantation agriculture, cattle ranching, declining terms of trade, and other large-scale development projects, Q'eqchi' people, like the residents of Macawville, might over time develop a more amicable relationship to state-led conservation and/or develop their own autochthonous conservation initiatives.

When I returned to Guatemala in fall 2009 on a book tour for this ethnography in Spanish, I had dinner with an old conservation NGO friend, Anita, who had nursed me through my first bout of amoebas in Atelesville back in

1993. She now works as the Wildlife Conservation Society's community extension agent in Macawville. Having heard rumors that many Macawville residents had sold their negotiated farm concessions inside the park, I was eager to learn more. Obviously following orders to evade such questions, she instead told me a Disneyfied story of how environmentally sensitive the schoolchildren had become. As proof of this, she explained that they had painted animal murals on the doors of their homes with materials she had purchased for them with funding from the United States Agency for International Development (USAID). With ranchers, narco-traffickers, and other land speculators hovering to buy up their parents' land, this did not strike me as a particularly strategic environmental education project, but perhaps the children's sentiments were genuine.

The attentive reader may notice that I avoid any reified conclusions about the "ecological nobility" of Q'eqchi' people in this book. Instead, there are Q'eqchi' people of many different conservation persuasions across the Guatemalan and Belize border, whose relationship to natural resources has been profoundly shaped by a history of dispossession. There are opportunists who recklessly clear-cut primary forest in order to plant hybrid corn for commodity sale. There are also environmental stewards working in partnership with government to co-manage parks. Mostly, there are those who seek to escape brutal conditions of plantation labor by migrating to the frontier, often unwittingly into protected areas. Ultimately, I hope to have portrayed Q'eqchi' people as citizens of a complex world affected by an array of local and global factors that they both conform to and resist.

As people working for a living, they are not much different from you or me. Despite years of being disciplined into a docile corporate workforce, many people across the United States also resist working for "the Man." They are bored with the long commutes, unhappy with their ugly cubicles, exhausted from excessive and inflexible hours, concerned about job insecurity, and worried about the dwindling purchasing power of their paychecks—all the while knowing that corporate executives are collecting larger million-dollar bonuses each year. Perhaps these recalcitrant workers play hooky by faking a sick day, surf the Internet when they should be "industrious," doodle on notepads during meetings, linger too long in the coffee room, steal office supplies, gossip on the phone, or misplace work on purposely messy desks. . . . The techniques of foot-dragging and resistance to the corporate order are many.

Against more than a century of social conditioning, American workers still yearn to own the fruits of their own labor—to have respect and independence.

Regardless of the risks, every year, hundreds of thousands of ordinary people take the plunge and start their own small businesses, go back to farming, pursue their artistic dreams, or forge other noncorporate career paths. Perhaps you, gentle reader, are one of those resistant workers, struggling against a dehumanized, "Dilbert"-style wage-work system. If so, you may perhaps recognize a glimmer of your feelings in Q'eqchi' people's determination to find a piece of land where they can work for themselves with dignity.

ACKNOWLEDGMENTS

Preparing to depart Petén, Guatemala, in 1999 and move to Berkeley for graduate school, I read Marcel Mauss's *The Gift* for the first time. Thrilled by this new anthropological concept of "reciprocity," I exclaimed to my friend (and then boss) Carlos Soza, "Did you know there is no such thing as a 'free gift'?" "Of course, there isn't," he replied nonchalantly, much wiser than I about social structures. Since then, I have acquired many reciprocal debts, and while I cannot possibly repay them all, I do want to sincerely acknowledge some of the people who helped make this book possible. Many more are thanked in the Spanish-language version of this ethnography (Grandia 2009c).

Countless villagers opened their doors without reservation to this strange "gringa" (or *nimla ixq*, literally "big lady," as they called me in Belize) who wandered into their yards calling, *"K'ab'anuuu . . . ma waankex"*—"With permission, anyone home?" I never wanted for a bite of food, a gourd of steaming chocolate or a mug of sweet coffee, a stool or hammock for resting, or a place to lay my head at night. I hope I have done justice to their stories and that my publications may result in policy changes that make the lives of those who hosted this research a little easier.

All names in the book are pseudonyms, but I would like to acknowledge the families who provided room, board, and good spirits in different villages and their children, who adopted me with unconditional affection: Maria and Pedro Tzalam; Nina, Javier, and Antonia Xo; Sebastian Pan and Arcelia Xo; Antonio, Margarita, and Felicita Cholom; Iocone Williams and John Harris; José and María Coy; Domingo, Candelaria, and Rosaria Acte; Perfecto Makin and Melina Cuc; and Luis and Matilda Ishim. Others who conversed deeply with me and whose friendships I hold close to my heart include the Yaxcal family, the extended Cholom family, the Chayax siblings (Silveria, Irma, Nimfa, and Reginaldo), Reginaldo Gomez, Lotario Caal, Pedro Cucul, Alfredo

Tzalam, Gonzalo and Olivia Pop, Venancio and Gloria Rax, Raymundo and Jose Tot, Demetrio Bo, Eliseo Acuña, Marina Ansora, Victoria Winter and Manuel Maquin, Josefina Coc, Mateo Keh and Dominga Coy, Alfredo Choc, and John Ishim. Those in the cattle community who provided critical information and/or invited me for a pleasant day at their ranches include Julio España; Juan Rojas; Ruben Galdamez; Ruben, Angelina, and "Negro" Lopez; and Cristobal and Mirna Urrutia. I also hired occasional field assistants who provided translation, clarifications, transcriptions, and good gossip: Estela Cus, Eric and Oswaldo Cholom, Kensy Tesucún Chayax, Deborah Pinelo, Juan Pop, Lydia Keh, Alehandro Coy, Rosaria Acte, Orlando Paau, Clara Cucul, Albina Makin, Federico Sam, and Martha Ishim.

Since 1993, I have worked with ProPetén, led for a decade by Carlos Soza, to whose memory this book is dedicated. Without the loyalty and leadership of Rosa María Chan and Rosita Contreras, ProPetén surely would not have survived the loss of Carlos Soza in 2003. In addition to these fierce and graceful women whose friendship I treasure, the following colleagues have shared special insights, information, and camaraderie with me over the years: Manuel Baños, Christian Barrientos, Ivan Bermejo, Henry Cano, Marco Antonio Castellanos, Amilcar Corzo, Xiomara Dehesa, Miriam España, Sharon Flynn, Brian Gurr, Daniel Irwin, Orly Lam, Jim Nations, Conrad Reining, Gustavo Rodríguez, Faustina Rax Yaxcal, Lucky Romero, José Venancio Alvarado, Eric Mena, Ericka Moerkerken, Oscar Obando, Manuel Manzanero, Zucely Orellana, Andrew Soles, and Yadira Vanegas. A special thanks to Amilcar Corzo for always keeping me on my gringa toes.

Representatives from almost one hundred institutions shared their time in interviews and/or provided documents or access to their libraries (see Grandia 2009c for a full list). Those who were particularly charitable include Michelle Asturias, Jorge Cabrera, Emma Caddy, Victor Cal, Carlos Camacho, Alfredo Che, Greg Ch'oc, Cristina Coc, Erick Cuellar, Byron Garoz, Encarnación García, Rudy Herrera, Alfonso Huet, Francisco Leiva, Pedro Kukul, Bayron Milian, Rodolfo Negreros, Joseph Palacio, Ludwig Palacio, Marco Antonio Palacios, Luis Pantí, Filiberto Penados, Victor Hugo Ramos, Osmany Salas, Tania Tapia, Bartolo Teul, Ernesto Tzi, and Daniel Vogt.

I am gratified to have had the opportunity for many conversations with the following friends and researchers working in the region, not necessarily in relation to their institutions: Richard Adams, Tani Adams, Alberto Alonso Fradejas, James Anaya, Clara Arenas, Paz Cainzos, Jan Capps, David Carr, Jennifer Casolo, Julio Cambranes, Maia Campbell, Elin Danien, Sean

Downey, Chris Fagan, Ricardo Falla, Meredith Fort, Moira Gracey, Georg Grünberg, Rob Hamrick, Nora Haenn, Laura Hurtado, James Hutchins, Christopher Jones, David Kaimowitz, Eva Kalny, Tom Korczowski, Christopher Lutz, Peter Marchetti, Beatriz Manz, Jason Pielemeier, Sergio Romero, Leopoldo Sandoval, Estuardo Secaira, Luis Solano, Avrum Shriar, Finn Stepputat, Jim Stinson, Anthony Stocks, David Stoll, Juanita Sundberg, Ileana Valenzuela, Jacob van Etten, Paula Worby, David Wahl, Laura Wides, and Megan Ybarra. Among the many anthropologists now connected through the Q'eqchi' Scholars Network listserv I established in 2007, I have learned much from Abigail Adams, David García, Jon Schackt, Rick Stepp, Richard Wilk, and Becky Zarger. Like many others, I am indebted to Q'eqchi' linguist Rigoberto Baq, who, over cake and buckets of coffee, enthusiastically taught me the fundamentals of his language.

Jessica Lawrence enlivened my sad spirits after Carlos Soza's passing with a mid-fieldwork visit during which she endured, with extraordinary aplomb, ticks, sweltering August heat, muddy midnight treks, a wild hitchhike across the Northern Franja Transversal, and bedbug-infested inns with dangerous mattress springs. Other friends and colleagues who provided special feedback and encouragement at different stages of the writing process include Hoda Bandeh-Ahmadi, Jim Baird, Laura Bathurst, Addie Bentley, Halina Brown, Linda Coco, Monica Eppinger, Patty Ewick, Anita Fabos, Susan Fischer, Bill Fisher, Ellen Foley, Roberto Gonzalez, David Harnett, Chris Hebdon, Enrique Mayer, Tarek Milleron, Melanie Mintz, Jonathan Padwe, Analiese Richard, Liz Roberts, Beckley Schowalter, Jennie Stephens, and Michael Watts.

I am indebted in particular to two academic mentors. Norman Schwartz of the University of Delaware provided my first fieldwork training and imparted a lifelong passion for anthropology. Eighteen years ago, when I returned from my first excursion into the tumultuous politics of Saxb'atz village, he greeted me with surprise at the door of the ProPetén office, saying, "Congratulations, you made it back! Let's go get coffee at Las Puertas and you can tell me all about it." With me and other researchers in Petén, he established a collegial atmosphere of exchange—among not only foreign academics but also local scholars. He has exchanged hundreds of e-mails with me on Petén and sent generous critiques, comments, and suggestions about almost everything I have published over the years.

I am also fortunate to have been apprenticed to Laura Nader, who was the best adviser a graduate student could hope for. I regard her as one of the freshest and most independent minds alive today—perpetually blazing trails with new insights, making every conversation with her a thrill. Always accessible, she read the draft of this book and many other writings in great detail and offered astute commentary. For me, she demonstrates how one can build a career as an engaged public intellectual upon a rigorous base of scholarship—a mentor to emulate in every way.

My love and thanks to my family, Dwight, Jackie, and Tim Grandia, for their support, encouragement, letters, field supplies, humbling nicknames, phone calls on lonely nights, good humor about indoor pigs during village visits, financial support in the early years in Petén, understanding about culture shock upon my returns, rearranging family vacations to meet me in the field, and summoning guardian angels when necessary. My husband, Aaron Tukey, patiently listened to dull, nightly accounts of progress on the many versions of this book. He sacrificed a job in his beloved San Francisco for my academic career, bore my long hours and weekend workdays without remonstrance, and nursed me through three bouts of malaria and a long year of cancer treatment and recovery. The final joyful inspiration to finish came from my beloved daughter, Adelaide Rose, who patiently waited for me to revise this manuscript before starting her descent into this world under the harvest moon.

Finally, this research and writing were made possible by grants from the Berkeley Fellowship, the Dean's Normative Time Fellowship, the National Science Foundation, the Environmental Leadership Program, the Sarstoon Temash Institute for Indigenous Management, Clark University's faculty research funds, and, most especially, a postdoctoral fellowship at Yale University's Program in Agrarian Studies, led by the insatiably curious and intellectually vibrant Jim Scott and his delightful program administrator, Kay Mansfield. ProPetén provided significant in-kind support as well.

Thanks to an anonymous donor, Oxfam–Great Britain, the World Lutheran Foundation, and Oxfam International, which financed the translation, first and second editions of a 2009 Spanish version of this book, and a documentary film about Q'eqchi' dispossession in Petén, respectively. AVANCSO and ProPetén provided critical staff resources for these projects. Helvi Mendizabal, my lively editor at AVANCSO, also had a hawk's eye for detail and greatly improved that version of the manuscript. I am most grateful to Lorri Hagman and K. Sivaramakrishnan at the University of Washington Press for permission to publish first in Spanish and for their patience with delays due to cancer treatment. As a young author, I learned the value of working with a small and dedicated editorial team.

Inspired by the committed work of Inge Hatse and Patrick De Ceuster (2001a) and to show respect for the knowledge contained therein, I shall carry out a *wa'tesink*, a ritual Q'eqchi' offering of food, for this book in due time.

I beg forgiveness for anyone I have inadvertently forgotten. *Chaakuy inmaak.*

All errors and mistakes contained within are, of course, my responsibility alone. I welcome any feedback at liza.grandia@gmail.com.

LIZA GRANDIA
Worcester, Massachusetts

Q'EQCHI' LANGUAGE AND ORTHOGRAPHY

Linguistically, the Q'eqchi' language is more closely related to nearby highland Maya languages such as K'iche', Kaqchikel, and Mam than to other lowland languages like Itza or Mopan. The 2002 population census revealed that Q'eqchi' had become the second most popular Maya language in Guatemala (up from fourth place in the 1994 census). Of the four major ethnic groups (K'iche', Q'eqchi', Kaqchikel, Mam), those who identified themselves as Q'eqchi' also had the highest proportion of native speakers, at 84 percent (INE 2002).

While often spelled as "Kekchí" in Spanish texts, "K'ekchi'" in Protestant missionary materials, and "Ketchi" in the British/Belizean context, this book uses the Q'eqchi' orthography endorsed by the Academy of Maya Languages of Guatemala based on a thirty-two-letter alphabet: A, aa, b', ch, ch', e, ee, h, i, ii, j, k, k', l, m, n, o, oo, p, q, q', r, s, t, t', tz, tz', u, uu, w, x, y. All vowels (a', e', i', o', u') can also be accompanied by a glottal stop ('), which some linguists consider the thirty-third letter. Pronunciation is similar to English except for the letters *x* and *w*, which sound like "sh" and "kw" respectively. Q'eqchi' has no accent marks, as words are always stressed on the last syllable. Although Q'eqchi' pluralizes words only with *eb'* used as an article or a suffix, I have made some Q'eqchi' words plural by adding *s* to the end for the ease of English-speaking readers. All Spanish terms are enclosed in quotation marks, and Q'eqchi' words are in italics.

While I tend to favor the more neutral words "farmer" and "settler" in order to avoid the pejorative connotations sometimes associated with the word "peasant," Q'eqchi' people also refer to themselves as "indigenous" (*ralal ch'och'*), "Q'eqchi'" (*aj Q'eqchi'*), "countrymen" (*aj komon*), "farmers" (*aj awinel*), and "peasants" (technically, *aj k'aleb'aal*, but normally expressed in Q'eqchi'-fied Spanish as *aj kampesiin*) or merely as "poor" (*neb'a*). I substitute the Q'eqchi' term of respect for men and women (*Qawa'* and *Qana'*) with the better-known Spanish "Don" and "Doña."

NOTES ON MEASUREMENTS

Weight

1 quintal = 100 pounds

Currency

Q: quetzals (Guatemala)
Bz$: Belizean dollars
US$: U.S. dollars
Q7.75 = US$1 = Bz$2
Average daily wage in northern Guatemala was Q25 = US$3.25
Average daily wage in Belize was Bz$25 = US$13.50

Area

1 hectare = 2.4 acres = 1.43 "manzanas" = 10,000 square meters
1 "caballería" = 111 acres = 45 hectares = 64 "manzanas"

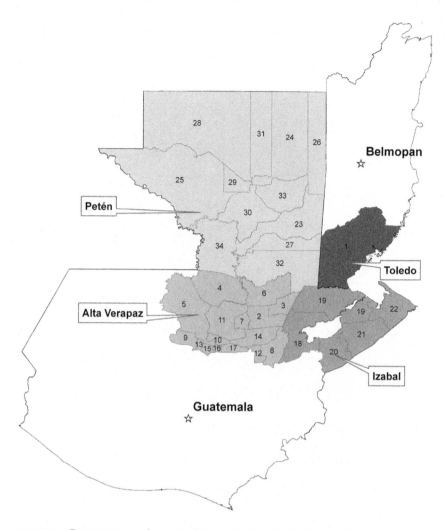

FIGURE 1. Departments and municipalities of Guatemala (Petén, Alta Verapaz, and Izabal) and the Toledo district of Belize. Source: Jason Arnold and Daniel Irwin, NASA/SERVIR 2010

1	Toledo	13	Santa Cruz Verapaz	25	La Libertad
2	Cahabón	14	Senahú	26	Melchor de Mencos
3	Chahal	15	Tactic	27	Poptún
4	Chisec	16	Tamahú	28	San Andrés
5	Cobán	17	Tucurú	29	San Benito
6	Fray Bartolomé de las Casas	18	El Estor	30	San Francisco
7	Lanquín	19	Livingston	31	San José
8	Panzós	20	Los Amates	32	San Luis
9	San Cristobal Verapaz	21	Morales	33	Santa Ana
10	San Juan Chamelco	22	Puerto Barrios	34	Sayaxché
11	San Pedro Carcha	23	Dolores		
12	Santa Catarina la Tinta	24	Flores		

FIGURE 2. Guatemala and Belize topographic map with department capitals and approximate location of communities. Source: Jason Arnold and Daniel Irwin, NASA/SERVIR 2010

Q'EQCHI' PSEUDONYM (IN 2009 SPANISH EDITION)	ENGLISH EQUIVALENT
1. Chimo' (by the scarlet macaws)	Macawville
2. Saxb'atz (by the spider monkeys, *Ateles geoffroyi*)	Atelesdale
3. Chipoch (by the steamed corn dumplings, "tamales")	Tamalton
4. Sehalaw (in tepezcuintle territory, *Agouti paca*)	Agoutiville
5. Chinapek (small rock)	Rockridge
6. Sehix (by the jaguars)	Jaguarwood

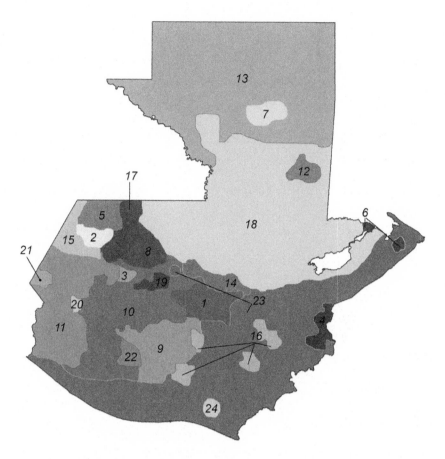

FIGURE 3. Linguistic areas of Guatemala. Source: Jason Arnold and Daniel Irwin,
NASA/SERVIR 2010

1	Achi	9	Kaqchikel	17	Q'anjob'al
2	Akateco	10	Kiche	18	Q'eqchi'
3	Awakateco	11	Mam	19	Sakapulteco
4	Ch'orti'	12	Mopan	20	Sipakapemse
5	Chuj	13	Non indigenous	21	Tektiteko
6	Garifuna	14	Pocompch	22	Tz'utujil
7	Itza	15	Popti'	23	Uspanteko
8	Ixil	16	Poqomam	24	Xinka

Enclosed

Introduction

THE commonness of the word "common" in our everyday language reveals how important this shared agrarian land arrangement once was to our culture. We speak a common language and try to reach common ground in our agreements for the common good. Something ordinary is commonplace. Friends and lovers share interests in common and expect common courtesies from one another. We still rely on common sense, privilege information that is common knowledge, and root our legal systems in common law. I happen to reside in the Commonwealth of Massachusetts (also the official title of the states of Kentucky, Virginia, and Pennsylvania), so named to emphasize governance by the people's will. My own university recently inaugurated a public library wing called the "academic commons."

The history of the commons and their enclosure also continues to resonate deeply with contemporary global social movements. Indeed, the idea of the commons has become a powerful iconographic image for struggles over shared access to global information and intellectual property via the Internet. Common Dreams is one of the most widely read alternative media sites. Experiments in "copylefting" by the Creative Commons organization are shaking up intellectual property rights. Wikimedia Commons has fundamentally transformed encyclopedic writing. Common Cause is an NGO that seeks to hold government more accountable to its citizens. Commonweal is another nonprofit working for a healthier and safer environment for all. And, with no other manifesto except to be an open, common meeting space, every year the World Social Forum brings together hundreds of thousands of people from around the world to discuss how to defend the "earth and people's common goods." In 2009, the Norwegian Nobel Committee awarded political scientist Elinor

Ostrom the prize for economics in recognition of her lifelong research on governance of the commons. In 2011, the Occupy Wall Street movement began seizing public parks and common areas across the country in protest against corporate greed. Against the relentless pressures of neoliberal privatization and the commodification of practically everything (land, air, water, genes, even human reproduction), the metaphor of "the commons" has emerged yet again as a revolutionary symbol for justice.[1]

The commons also happen to be linguistically significant for the Q'eqchi' Maya, Guatemala's second-largest indigenous group (numbering almost a million people), among whom I have conducted research since 1993. They use terms based on a loanword from Spanish ("común," meaning "common"), referring to another Q'eqchi' person as *aj komon*, describing their community as *li komonil*, and commencing any formal address or speech with *komonex*— the Maya equivalent of "you, the people" or, more succinctly, "y'all" (Romero 2008). As these words reveal, for Q'eqchi' speakers, the commons represent not just shared village lands but also the social organization necessary for managing collectively owned resources. In others words, commons are not only material places but also the relationship of an individual to his or her community. People regulate their commons, but their commons also regulate their interactions with one another and the world. To degrade or "enclose" common places endangers other social functions and what it means to be human, in the Q'eqchi' sense of that word.

"Enclosure" refers to the process of commodifying new aspects of human life in a way that catalyzes broader transformations in communities and social relations (De Angelis 2004). Historically, the term (also spelled "inclosure") referred to the privatization of common village lands. Although the idea of private landownership seems self-evident to Westerners today, to many indigenous people, and even not so long ago to Europeans, the idea was abhorrent. In the academic literature, the classic example of enclosure is the destruction of the English peasants' open-field system, which many political economists argue eventually gave rise to industrial capitalism. That case and Q'eqchi' experiences, among others, suggest that the enclosure or privatization of common resources is a recurring process that takes place in two steps (not necessarily in this order). First is a physical, legal, or political process, often led by states, to transform land or other aspects of life into private goods or, in Karl Polanyi's (1944) terminology, "fictitious commodities" that can later be bought and sold on the market.[2] Second is a cultural, social, and disciplinary process legitimating those enclosures so that they become normalized or simply forgotten. As Balzac put it in *Le Père Goriot*, "The secret of great wealth for which you are at a loss to account is a crime that has never been found out, because it was properly executed" (2004: 85). The first, usually more coercive, part of this process is generally easier to identify and resist, whereas the second part tends to be more consensual and slippery, residing in the netherworlds of culture.

Based on eighteen years of research, more than six in residence, this book explores the recurring enclosures of Q'eqchi' common lands in northern Guatemala and southern Belize. While most of the text focuses on the first part of this process—the repeated loss of Q'eqchi' territory to pastures, parks, plantations, and development plans—the concluding chapter explores how the same ideological framework behind the relentless privatization of commonly held Q'eqchi' lands is also degrading public and community resources in industrialized countries. In other words, this is not meant to be just another sad anthropological story about another beleaguered indigenous group. Rather, Q'eqchi' experiences of enclosure can teach us something about the consequences of privatizing our own public commons—not only land and public spaces, but also water, the atmosphere, educational systems, social services, even the human genome. Q'eqchi' tenacity in reclaiming land in order to maintain the independence of their farming livelihoods may, I hope, also teach us something about resistance to the excesses of corporate capitalism.

The Q'eqchi' people have faced the following challenges over the last five hundred years. Made famous in the sixteenth century as one of the few indigenous groups to resist Spanish military conquest, Q'eqchi' people eventually succumbed to Spanish missionary efforts led by Bartolomé de las Casas, a Catholic priest who had convinced Charles V to allow him to experiment with a new method of pacific, religious conquest. They were placed under Dominican rule and re-congregated into new towns, while most of their territory was acquired by the Spanish Crown. Unlike neighboring lowland Maya groups who were annihilated by conquest, the Q'eqchi' survived and managed gradually to rebuild their society both culturally and demographically until after independence from Spain. Then, during the Liberal reforms enacted at the end of the nineteenth century, they once again lost most of their highland territory to foreign planters in Guatemala's first coffee boom. Also suffering the first massacre of the Guatemalan civil war at Panzós, hundreds of Q'eqchi' communities were once more uprooted from their homeland during the last part of the twentieth century.

At the end of the long Guatemalan civil war, many indigenous and peasant leaders hoped that the 1996 Peace Accords might bring agrarian justice in a country where 2 percent of the wealthy own more than two-thirds of the land. Unable or simply unwilling to redistribute land, the Guatemalan government instead decided to embrace the new World Bank paradigm of "market-assisted agrarian reform" being implemented around the globe, which, in theory, would shift land control away from elites to the "invisible hand" of the market. As the laboratory for this experiment, the technocrats chose Guatemala's northernmost department of Petén, the last region of the country where poor and indigenous people could claim enough land to become independent farmers. Armed with a $31 million loan from the World Bank, between 1998 and 2008, the Guatemalan government mounted an ambitious land survey project ostensibly meant to help small landholders gain land tenure security by mapping and titling their parcels. Contrary to project expectations, Q'eqchi' small landholders are now selling (or being forced to sell) their plots to speculators. Cattle ranchers were the first to take advantage of the World Bank project to encroach upon Q'eqchi' land (Grandia 2006, 2009b). Since the turn of the millennium, African-palm planters, narco-traffickers, and other investors have joined in this voracious consumption of Q'eqchi' territory.

Over the centuries, Q'eqchi' people escaped state violence and the repeated loss of territory by migrating deeper and deeper into the northern forest frontier. Emptied during the colonial period after Spanish genocide of neighboring Maya groups, these lowland forests provided Q'eqchi' people with what Mexican anthropologist Gonzalo Aguirre-Beltrán (1979) calls a "region of refuge." Little by little, they transformed open-access forests into managed commons and expanded their territory fourfold over the centuries. Setting up hearth and home in these tropical forests was no easy task, but Q'eqchi' settlers proved to be highly successful migrants. Yet, when faced with modern enclosure by the World Bank, Q'eqchi' mobility has become an Achilles heel.

Believing that they will be able to claim land farther out on the frontier, many Q'eqchi' settlers sell the lowland homesteads they worked so hard to acquire only to find that the only "free" land left in Guatemala was turned into protected areas for biodiversity conservation during the 1990s or claimed by other large commercial interests. Determined to continue farming, Q'eqchi' peasants are now responsible for both the highest rates of private land occupations as well as the most numerous invasions of protected areas in Guatemala.[3] With the northern third of Petén now protected as the Maya Biosphere Reserve (see fig. P.2, p. xiii), no other frontier remains where Q'eqchi' peasants might flee, except perhaps as illegal migrants to the United States. There are few opportunities for return migration to their places of origin. The only other recourse for landless Q'eqchi' farmers is to invade private properties. The choice between confronting cattle guards armed with AK-47s or poorly paid, unmotivated, and unarmed park rangers is obvious. Consequently, government and NGO officials routinely characterize the Q'eqchi' as environmentally destructive, calling them derogatory names such as "leaf-cutter ants," "termites," and "nomads."

These new enclosures and Q'eqchi' resistance to them seem eerily reminiscent of prior expropriations. Yet this time, with the aid of a World Bank–funded land administration project, agrarian re-concentration is legal and permanent. Options for landless Q'eqchi' families will likely worsen under neoliberal programs such as the Dominican Republic–Central America Free Trade Agreement (DR-CAFTA) and the Puebla to Panama Plan (PPP). As Q'eqchi' farmer Sebastian Yaxcal described these pressures to me, "We're all caged" ("Estamos enjaulados"). A visit to the hometown of an old Q'eqchi' friend early in my research illustrated how various contemporary enclosures have imprisoned her family on their frontier homestead.

TWENTY HECTARES AND A TOUCAN

October 13, 2002 (the 510th anniversary of Columbus's arrival in the Americas). I had just returned to Guatemala and was studying Q'eqchi' for six weeks in the departmental capital of Alta Verapaz and the Q'eqchi' mountain heartland. Happy to escape Cobán's cold drizzly weather, I readily accepted an invitation to visit the family of a Q'eqchi' friend, Francesca Cuc, with whom I had worked in Petén. She had grown up in Rockridge, a steamy lowland frontier town about sixty kilometers north of Cobán. Throughout my twenty months of fieldwork, I continued to pass through this town to visit Francesca's family and cross-check patterns I observed in other places.

Founded as a small assembly of homes next to an oil field, Rockridge had grown to more than a thousand households with thirty-seven surrounding villages. Change was coming quickly to this region. In 2000, the government installed electricity; in 2001, it paved the road down from the misty mountains of Cobán, shortening the journey from twelve to two hours. As part of the PPP, it soon hoped to pave the road adjacent to the pipeline snaking through the town en route to an Atlantic port, carrying oil for export to the United States. The town also boasted a doctor's office, a dentist, a gas station, a computer school, a microlending NGO, and a high school for training elementary teachers. Outside of town, cattle ranches stretched as far as the eye could see.

Through dusty streets once quietly populated by Q'eqchi' families, Ladinos in cowboy hats swaggered with pistols holstered, and I tried to avoid their stares while walking to Francesca's new cinderblock house. In preparation for my arrival, her family had graciously prepared the traditional Q'eqchi' chicken soup, kaq ik, to thank me for arranging a scholarship for Francesca's niece, Marta, who was graduating that weekend. I noticed that, before serving the soup, they pulled out the meat to divide equally among the bowls and then poured back as much broth as each person wanted. Symbolic of the egalitarian ethics of Q'eqchi' land management practices, the best parts of the soup get divided equally, and everyone can have as much of the broth as they can hold.

We toasted Marta's graduation with a bottle of sparkling grape juice ("champagne," as they called it), while Francesca's sister-in-law, Johana, made jokes about her preference for Q'eqchi' moonshine (b'oj). Later that evening, the Cuc women put on their best woven skirts and traditional embroidered blouses to attend a community dance in honor of the graduates. Marta sweated to pull on her first pair of panty hose purchased for this special occasion. Western rock music blared from the community hall. Undaunted, Johana pulled me onto the floor to join her in some traditional Q'eqchi' folk dances to these unlikely rhythms. When some drunken Ladino cowboys began to harass me, we had to leave early.

The next morning, we visited Francesca's father, Don Vicente Cuc, and conversed about how and why he had settled in this place. He began by explaining that the only clothing he owned until he was twelve years old was a white sheath tied together at the waist with some string. He remembered his parents promising him that one day he would have pants with seven pockets. Vicente paused in the conversation to count his pockets—one, two, three, four, five, six . . . "exactly" (tzakal) seven, if he included his shirt pocket, he concluded with a laugh.

As a young man, Don Vicente decided to flee his impoverished life on this coffee plantation to seek better opportunities on another plantation in Panzós, a lowland region to the east, where Francesca was born. From there, during the presidency of Carlos Arana Osorio (1970–74), he heard that a government agency, INTA [Institute for Agrarian Transformation (Instituto para la Transformación Agraria)] was offering twenty-hectare plots in a remote place located more than two days by foot from Chisec, the nearest town to the south. Exploring the area, he discovered five or six houses spread out half a kilometer from one another under the forest canopy. Despite the isolation, this was the first opportunity in his life to own land, so he decided to bring his family to live in Rockridge. It took INTA nearly twenty years to formalize the land titles, so Q'eqchi' settlers were left to organize themselves and decide who would farm where. Relying on principles of customary land management passed down by their ancestors, they lived well, depending on the bounty of the rain forest and mutual solidarity networks. Although Don Vicente earned very little for his corn crop, which he sold downriver to middlemen, his children ate well off the farm ("milpa") and grew up healthy. Having learned the secrets of medicinal plants from the forest, his daughter Francesca would later decide to become a health worker.

When his children reached adulthood, Don Vicente made the unusual decision to subdivide his parcel, giving four hectares to each child and keeping a portion for himself. However, the children of most of his neighbors continued north to Petén after their parents sold their parcels to the cattle ranchers entering the region. Don Vicente recollected that since his Q'eqchi' neighbors had never held private property before and did not understand the value of their parcels, when the cattle ranchers offered to buy them out, many willingly accepted payments as small as $130 for a "manzana" of land (roughly an acre, or seven-tenths of a hectare) that he figured would be worth as much as $7,700 or more today.

The Q'eqchi' families who stayed in Rockridge found themselves gradually enclosed by parks and cattle plantations. In 1995, the government protected lands north of their village as part of the new Ceibal-Cancuen archaeological complex. Prior to that, cattle ranchers, many of whom were military officers, had used their power during the civil war to make enormous land claims through government colonization programs. For instance, stretching for miles across the road from Don Vicente's home was a plantation that once belonged to ex-president General Romeo Lucas García, now sold to another cattle rancher. Contiguous to Lucas's old property was another large cattle ranch, whose new owner has blocked access to a communal forest where Q'eqchi' families once collected firewood, water, and other forest products such as palm thatching for their homes. With cattle ranches on all sides and plot size dwindling each generation, the villagers had no other option but to cut the ranchers' barbed-wire fences so as to be able to travel to their milpas. Women sneaked through the ranch at night to wash their clothes in a stream by moonlight, hoping to avoid the ranchers' armed guards. Don Vicente recalled to me one particularly bitter loss of communal forest access when that rancher cut down many of the cohune palm leaves the villagers had used to thatch their homes. They petitioned him to salvage these leaves, but he demanded thirteen cents[4] per leaf (an exorbitant total amounting to five weeks' wages, since more than six hundred leaves are needed to thatch an average-size house). The villagers were clearly unable to pay this sum, so the rancher ordered his workers to burn the leaves.

At this point, Francesca's oldest brother, Miguel, joined the conversation to explain that because he was just sixteen when INTA gave out land, he was too young to apply and lost his opportunity to claim a parcel. With ten children of his own, he cannot make a living with the four hectares he received from his father. With some other neighbors, Miguel formed a cooperative to attempt to buy back some land from a rancher with help from one of the FONTIERRAS [Land Fund (Fondo de Tierras)] programs funded by the World Bank. Unfortunately, their bid failed because the rancher demanded such a high price ("Four million quetzals [$516,129]! Imagine that!" Miguel exclaimed). After that fiasco, Miguel tried sharecropping in Petén but realized that, with the travel costs, he was actually losing money on his milpa. His only other option was to work as a day laborer on the cattle ranches, weeding pasture. Lately he has been too ill for this sweltering work, because a few months before, his herbicide sprayer leaked and he got drenched with paraquat (a chemical highly regulated in the United States and banned in the European Union but which is still exported to Third World countries). Despite the risks, he is thinking of joining the peasant confederation CNOC [National Coordinator of Peasant Organizations (Coordinadora Nacional de Organizaciones Campesinas)], which has been organizing invasions of private property, much like the Landless People's Movement (MST) in Brazil. I recalled seeing homemade signs along the road from Cobán saying "CNOC vive!" (CNOC lives!), and Miguel's comment confirmed the organization's growing influence.

The next morning, the Cuc family took me up a steep, muddy path to show me a cave they had discovered a few miles outside of town. A Catholic catechist himself, Don Vicente had the opportunity to travel to the western highlands and train as a Maya priest, or "daykeeper" (aj q'ij), learning how to perform pan-Maya rituals that he practiced along with traditional Q'eqchi' ceremonies in a cave discovered decades before by villagers from Rockridge. When another rancher suddenly denied them access to their original cave, they began searching for another sacred area and discovered this new cave several miles south of their village. They organized a committee to request the site from the municipality as communal property but had made little headway and wanted my advice. I realized that, unfortunately, the sacred areas of living Maya people do not fit into any of the "right" legal categories in Guatemala: the cave is neither a biodiversity site nor an ancient Maya ruin. Still, I gave them some NGO contacts and promised to contribute suggestions for their proposal.

As there had been many radio announcements that weekend about Columbus Day, Don Vicente had one more question for me before I departed later that *morning: Were white people like me ("blancos") the same as the Spanish who had conquered Guatemala? And should he consider Europeans "gringos"? Little wonder that Don Vicente should be curious about foreigners in Guatemala. National elections were approaching, and on the ride back to Cobán, several of my fellow passengers were complaining about the privatization of the electrical utility by a Spanish-owned company, DEORSA. Customer service was appalling: power outages lasted days, sometimes even weeks at a time, but they were still expected to travel almost two hours to Cobán every month to pay their bills directly at DEORSA's regional office, often waiting three to four hours in queue. I was impressed by their clear understanding of the contradictions of foreign investment and neoliberalism. This led to another discussion about their fears that after the election, the new government would privatize more essential government services. Someone had even heard a rumor that the nearby archaeological ruins of Cancuen might be given away to foreigners under the PPP. [Field notes, October 13, 2002]*

Postscript: I later heard that Francesca's brother helped organize the village to confront one of the ranchers, but his family paid dearly for his courage. The rancher retaliated by having Francesca's innocent younger brother murdered while he was walking home from his post as a schoolteacher. A few months later, the family hoped their fortunes might change when Francesca's nephew Emilio won a scholarship to study at a community college in Iowa, but the United States embassy denied him a visa because another family member had been caught working illegally in the United States.

Dramatic processes of enclosure are afoot in Guatemala. Don Vicente's life embodies not only the history of the three main epochs of Q'eqchi' dispossession but also the continued resistance of Q'eqchi' people against these enclosures. First, as a living legacy of the Q'eqchi's spiritual conquest, Don Vicente is a Catholic catechist but continues practicing Q'eqchi' rituals and has become active in the pan-Maya movement. Second, like the descendants of so many other Q'eqchi' people displaced in the late nineteenth-century liberal reforms, Don Vicente was born into grinding poverty on a German coffee plantation but fled into the northern lowland forests and managed to claim land in Rockridge through the colonization process. Third, the Cuc's family's recent tragedies illustrate how Q'eqchi' people have been inadvertently caught in broader disputes over who shall control Guatemala's last frontier in a new age of neoliberalism. With land located along a new transportation corridor for global trade schemes, speculation in this region is rampant. As a corn commodity farmer, Miguel wrestles with increasingly unfavorable terms of trade. The family has made little headway in protecting the new sacred cave, because the mainstream conservation model promoted by transnational biodiversity NGOs fails to take into account indigenous cultural patrimony. Meanwhile, the family's need for generating cash becomes more acute as its members absorb the pressures of Western consumerism—to have "champagne," panty hose, and zinc-roofed houses. Seeing no future in farming, the Cuc family children and grandchildren all want to further their education, but scholarships prove elusive. In turn, their collective struggles with the Church, the coffee and cattle industries, conservation interests, corporate trade, and, finally, consumerism can help us understand something about the enclosure of commons writ large.

ENCLOSURES

Just as Q'eqchi' people have suffered and resisted repeated enclosures, so once did British commoners. The enclosure of the British commons, in fact, was so formative to the rise of industrial capitalism that rival political economists of different ideological persuasions have all narrated stories about it. These were no small theoretical debates, as they aimed to explain how, out of the historical dissolution of feudalism, the early bourgeoisie accumulated sufficient stock with which to start fueling the motor of capitalism. Even those laissez-faire theorists who asserted that capitalism later reproduces itself naturally by the workings of an invisible hand somehow had to explain the extra-economic forces required to jump-start capital. They also had to rationalize the inherent inequity of that process—that is, how the wealthy classes acquired sufficient capital to hire workers and why peasants were inspired to sell their labor to capitalists in unfair wage relations.

On the left, Karl Marx described the enclosures as a process of "primitive accumulation," a phrase that now serves in the academic literature as a shorthand description of the brutality and external political power wielded in the first outbreak of industrial capitalism (Perelman 2000). Marx felt that peasants would "sell their skins" only after they had been robbed of their previous livelihoods and ties to the land (1976: 873–76). Likewise, Karl Polanyi (1944) wrote a detailed historical narrative about this time period but portrayed enclosure as contested and incomplete. This is because he felt that society would never permit raw, unharnessed capitalism (what he called "the self-regulating market") because, long before that happened, people would push back to demand social and cultural controls on private enterprise.

Those on the right were less specific and historical in their arguments. While admitting that some extra-economic force was needed to jump-start capital, Adam Smith attributed the "accumulation of stock" to the greater division of labor in a society (2007: 212–13). Thomas Malthus used abstract mathematical reasoning to argue that while enclosures caused suffering, population growth would intensify scarcity and lead to even more suffering, thereby justifying the privatization of common resources and naturalizing the unequal distribution of land and wealth in society (2004).

Because the English enclosures so deeply informed early European political economy debates about capitalism, and, hence, continue to inform contemporary development plans, policies, and projects, we should briefly examine that history, so as to be able to recognize similar patterns in Q'eqchi' experiences of dispossession. To begin, common resources were essential to the survival of peasants in medieval England, as they continue to be for most indigenous groups around the world. Though tied to feudal estates, English peasants had rights to allow their domestic animals to graze and forage on open fields, hunt and collect wild foods and fuel from the forests, and glean the leftovers of the manorial harvest. Rather than farming square parcels as people do today, they farmed in long rows better adapted to plowing with draft animals. Later theorists such as Garrett Hardin (1968) mistakenly imagined the English commons as anarchic places of open access inexorably doomed to environmental "tragedy," yet historians such as E. P. Thompson (1991) show that the English commons were clearly governed (or "stinted") by community customs. For example, English villagers performed annual, ritual exercises, often on religious holidays, for the purpose of protecting the boundaries of their commons from encroachments (ibid.: 100; Hyde 2008)—much as Q'eqchi' communities still organize periodic workdays to clear common paths to their fields and maintain village grounds.

In England, the enclosure process took place in two phases—both highly contested and resisted by peasant commoners (E. P. Thompson 1991). With the disappearance of serfdom in the fifteenth century, many peasants had become free laborers or yeoman farmers (proprietors of their own land), but they were expropriated during the sixteenth-century Reformation when the Tudors seized monastery estates, roughly a fifth of England's arable land, and the nobility took land that peasants had cultivated for generations. With profits to be made in the wool trade, the landed gentry continued to encroach upon peasant common lands by aggressively extending their grazing pasture for sheep. "All this happened without the slightest observation of legal etiquette" (Marx 1976: 889).

The second phase of enclosures began in the eighteenth century, as nobles began to seek legal justification for their plunder through formal parliamentary acts of enclosure. John Clare described them in his poem "The Mores" (likely composed 1821–24) as "*lawless laws* enclosure" (1984: 169). Undermining the open-field system, new legislation compelled farmers to claim plots of contiguous land and build expensive gates and fences around them. Other laws allowed the state to "clear" estates, burn down cottages, and evict peasants from these newly consolidated properties (Marx 1976: 889). All told, between 1700 and 1850, parliamentary enclosure acts "extinguished" the open fields in approximately half of British settlements (Shaw-Taylor 2001). Nineteenth-century copyhold acts also allowed landlords to switch peasant holdings on manors from heritable and guaranteed tenant rights to more flexible and profitable tenure systems (leaseholds for which rent could be increased indefinitely).

There were "lawless laws" not only to justify enclosure but also to keep newly dispossessed peasants from reestablishing rural livelihoods. These included new legal restrictions on traditional gleaning practices, which previously had contributed as much as 10 percent of a peasant family's annual income and provided food security, especially for women—for example, a 1788 court case began requiring the poor to acquire prior permission to claim harvest leftovers (P. King 1989). A startling number of game laws (growing from six to thirty-three laws by the end of the eighteenth century) redefined peasant hunting as illegal poaching. Already by 1831, one-seventh of all criminal convictions were related to the game laws, and many of the "criminals" convicted of poaching during this time period were sent to Australia (Perelman 2000). While suppressing peasant hunting, parliament provided an exception for the gentry, allowing them to destroy subsistence crops while riding across farmers' fields during fox hunts (ibid.).

Other laws criminalizing beggary disciplined the poor by forcing them into the wage-labor system (Piven and Cloward 1993). For example, a 1572 statute enacted under Queen Elizabeth I prescribed flogging and iron branding of the left ear for any persons older than fourteen years caught begging; repeat offenders over the age of eighteen could be executed if no one agreed to take them into service; and three-time offenders would be subject to capital punishment (Marx 1976: 897–98). In 1785, only one of nearly a hundred people executed in London and Middlesex had been convicted of murder; the rest had been found guilty primarily of crimes against property, for example, pulling down fences (Thompson 1966; Andreasson 2006). That so many vagabonds still risked punishment in attempts to avoid factory labor should indicate something about the conditions of early industrial employment, so grimly depicted in the novels of Charles Dickens.

In other words, the enclosures were not an easy historical transition. E. P. Thompson (1991) and others wrote vividly about the protracted folk rebellion of peasants, poachers, and paupers against the British enclosures, epitomized by the mythical figure of Robin Hood, who rose to popularity during this time period. Like Q'eqchi' people today, English peasants generally preferred the leisure, community, and security of subsistence livelihoods to unfair wage labor. Outsiders might deride this as peasant "conservatism," but subsistence farmers recognize the economic and ecological efficiencies of small-scale household production, which they do not lightly abandon for the vagaries of wage labor. After all, what matters to a peasant household is not achieving record profits in one particular year but rather producing enough to eat decade after decade in order to keep the ghouls of famine at bay (Scott 1976).

As Niccolò Machiavelli (1950) noted long ago, state and legal force goes only so far. Methods of enclosure might initially be overt but eventually have to be stealthily legitimated. The public must forget the socialization of costs and the privatization of property-holding benefits. Rousseau argued that the propertied classes did this by turning clever usurpation into an inalienable right, writing, "The first man who, having enclosed a piece of land, thought of saying, This is mine, and found people simple enough to believe him, was the true founder of civil society" (1994: 42; see also Andreasson 2006: 3). In other words, to legitimate a new property claim, there must be a dynamic hegemonic interplay between possession and persuasion (Gudeman and Rivera 2002; see also Gramsci 1971 and Nader 1997). Hence, the enclosures were accomplished not simply by planting hedges but through fictitious fences constructed around people's minds so that they would forget what had been so rudely taken. Seizing land in and of itself would not create a new class of workers. Peasants had to be convinced to conceive of themselves with new working identities until their separation from the land was normalized, or at least no longer challenged (De Angelis 2004). As Karl Marx put it, capital accumulation needs its "Platitudinous Sancho Panza" (1976: 794).

As harsh criminal punishments proved insufficient to prevent recidivist "sloth," state agents experimented with new disciplinary techniques for creating a docile workforce. As described by Michel Foucault (1977), workhouses, hospitals, and prisons became places for the creation of new working identities among the poor, sick, and criminal (see also Federici 2004). An important part of this ideological reconditioning were transformations in the sense of time itself through the suppression of religious festivals and leisure activities enjoyed by pre-capitalist English peasants—for example, new laws against tending a home garden on a Sunday (Perelman 2000)—which also required a gradual shift in the display of wealth from public to private life (Mies 1986).[5] Above all, cleverly disguising this war of the propertied against the poor was new Liberal rhetoric about freedom, rights, progress, and, especially, "improvement."

The new theories of property that emerged from the British enclosures were far more important than the amount of physical land seized. Enclosure, after all, involved more than just erecting fences; it also required the destruction (or "extinguishment" in legal terminology) of common property rights and the ideological construction of private property as a superior legal form. As theorized by John Locke (1980), early English experiments with colonial rule in both Ireland and the United States served as a laboratory for new ideas that equated private property with improvement. Literally meaning to "make better," the word "improvement" ("mejoras" in Spanish) became synonymous with adding value to agricultural land (E. M. Wood 2002). Beyond the sense of simply harvesting more from the same amount of ground, "improvement" also came to mean the liberation of land from any customary practices and its transformation into a new, privatized form of property. Even though Native American ownership customs met Locke's definition of property (as mixing their labor with the land), he concluded that because they failed to generate recognizable profit, their claims were less valid than those of European settlers. Following this logic of Western superiority, the English colonizers could rationalize the seizure of Native land by claiming to add value to what they portrayed as "wasteland," "empty lands" (in legal terminology, *terra nullius*), or its Spanish equivalent, "baldíos." These theories traveled with European imperial expansion, justifying enclosure of indigenous lands for foreign profit.

This English history provides five lessons relevant to lowland Guatemalan Q'eqchi' peoples.

First, although the enclosures began as conflicts over land, they ultimately created struggles over labor. Just as the privatization of the British countryside served to produce workers for industrial capitalism, in Guatemalan history, the seizure of Q'eqchi' and other Maya lands has allowed elites to control indigenous labor for profit.

Second, in studies of common property, anthropologists point out that although outsiders may perceive customary management as opaque, confusing, or "illegible" (Scott 1998), commons are almost always well regulated by cultural traditions and social arrangements that are understood clearly in the local context (McCay and Acheson 1987). They also usually have embedded within them some internal mechanisms of appeal for addressing conflicts or perceived inequities. Contrary to the modern notion that private property is the clearest form of ownership, local people generally understand their own commons systems better than the "improved" bureaucratic rationalities imposed from outside (Scott 1998).

Third, the creation of a new industrial labor class in England was not predestined or conspiratorially planned; rather, the interests of the eighteenth-century English gentry happened to align and reinforce the interests of the emerging capitalist class. The English enclosure laws were feudal in intent (so as to reinforce the power of the nobility), but capitalistic in effect, as they served to create wageworkers out of peasants (Perelman 2000). The emergent bourgeoisie merely seized opportunities afforded them by the state to co-opt those aspects of previous economic systems that help to facilitate accumulation. As Q'eqchi' encounters with cattle ranching will demonstrate, a seemingly feudal land use can be simultaneously creating the groundwork for a new corporate order.

Fourth, enclosures do not happen naturally. In England, they began with brute force, eventually became coded in law, and continued to be supported by the state. As Rosa Luxemburg (1951: 351) points out, capitalism is fundamentally impatient to accumulate and thus "employs force as a permanent weapon, not only at its genesis, but further on down to the present day."[6] Or, as Hannah Arendt put it, "The original sin of simple robbery . . . had eventually to be repeated lest the motor of accumulation suddenly die down" (1973: 148; see also Retort Collective 2005). In Guatemala, elites also rely on force, trickery, chicanery, coercion, subsidies, and political maneuvering to acquire cheap Q'eqchi' land and labor for investment through even the most "modern" corporate trade agreements.

Finally, a series of corollary transformations to labor and social relations concurrent with the English enclosures contributed to the growing importance of markets to people's everyday survival. Put in anthropological terms, enclosure can either be a "synchronic" spatial process that weaves new geographic areas into the orbits of capitalism or a "diachronic" temporal process that deepens people's dependence on their wages (De Angelis 2004). In the

Q'eqchi' case, therefore, enclosure encompasses both the direct experience of land dispossession (undermining people's abilities to provide for themselves) and the indirect cultural transformations that follow (normalizing people's new relationships to markets).

All told, there is a critical difference between simple piracy of common resources for accumulation and more catalytic forms of plunder that establish new labor relations, property regimes, or processes of commodification. Because rural people depend so deeply on land for their livelihood and identity, changes to land tenure can often spark social change far beyond the farming sector. For this and other reasons, land activists and scholars regard with alarm the World Bank's recent foray into marketized approaches to land reform in Guatemala and many other poor countries.

BANKING LAND

Building on a series of projects launched in the 1990s, the World Bank published its first comprehensive statement on land policy since 1975, laying out a program of "market-assisted" agrarian reform (Deininger and Binswanger 1999; expanded in Deininger 2003). Those papers outlined a World Bank offensive aimed at nothing less than redefining the role of states in relation to their physical territories (Bobrow-Strain 2004; Mendes Pereira 2005a; Rosset, Patel, and Courville 2006), guided by three neoliberal assumptions: (1) states are not capable of managing land distribution, (2) the market can do it more efficiently, and (3) private enterprise, in turn, will help alleviate poverty.

Projects range from cadastre (topographic surveying) to titling and registry modernization and training for policy makers and technocrats. The number of loan approvals for land projects underscores the World Bank's increasing financial commitment to agrarian issues: growing from three projects during 1990–94 (amount not specified) to nineteen during 1995–99 ($700 million), to twenty-five during 2000–2004 ($1 billion). With loans spanning thirty-two countries, the World Bank first targeted, coincidentally or not, countries with a long history of agrarian struggle and the greatest land inequities in the world, including Brazil, Colombia, El Salvador, Guatemala, Honduras, the Philippines, and South Africa (Mendes Pereira 2005b). Experimenting with various names ("negotiated," "community-based," and "market-led" land reform), the World Bank eventually settled on "market-assisted" to describe its depoliticized approach to "land administration" (Rosset 2004).

To justify development intervention, the World Bank first rhetorically repudiates a state's sovereign right to design its own land policies and distributive mechanisms by criticizing those efforts as "coercive," "expropriative," "traditional," "discretionary," "conflictive," "supply-driven," prone to "corruption," and mismanaged by "bureaucratic behemoths" (Borras 2005; Mendes Pereira 2005a; Sydow and Mendonça 2003). While some state-led agrarian reform programs have indeed produced disastrous results, the Bank ignores other successful cases of redistributive land reform that led to quick economic development (e.g., in Japan, South Korea, and Taiwan) or to unusual increases in human development indicators (e.g., in Kerala, India, and Cuba). From the Bank's ideological perspective, top-down land redistribution is simply no longer a viable option. Rather, the state's role should be reduced to facilitating transactions between "willing buyer/willing seller" in an unfettered land market.

Next, in building its case for leaving land distribution to the market, the World Bank portrays private property as an evolutionary improvement over other possibilities such as collective or usufruct tenure (Garoz and Gauster 2002) because it prizes efficiency over equity (although some analysts argue that efficiency will also result in equity). By focusing on making land transactions easier, the Bank emphasizes the importance of the commodity value of land for sale or trade over other social protection or noneconomic values of land (Mendes Pereira 2005b). Above all, the Bank's focus is on enhancing tenure security of land that is already claimed but, notably, not on helping the poor secure *more* land.

Central to World Bank logic on agrarian reform is an argument made by Peruvian economist Hernando de Soto (2000), that without formal property titles and access to credit, the poor will not be able to prosper within a capitalist system. The proposition that people cannot make a profit without property is almost a mirror image of Locke's theory that without profit, people cannot claim property. Yet for many indigenous people, potential profit and access to credit contradict other, more important cultural values associated with land.

Moreover, critics maintain that by ameliorating some land problems but ignoring overall inequities, these World Bank projects eliminate the urgency of agrarian issues while giving the appearance of solving deep-rooted land problems. Case studies of World Bank projects around the world, especially in Brazil and Colombia, demonstrate that although World Bank programs on land distribution currently may have small geographic impact, their overall policy impact has been far more powerful (Mondragón 2005; Mendes Pereira 2005a, 2005b). In fact, entire paragraphs of World Bank one-size-fits-all policy papers have been reproduced in agrarian legislation around the world.

Of course, there is no monolithic World Bank logic; the institution is a hydra with its own well-intentioned internal critics. While there are certainly conscientious people at the Bank concerned about issues such as gender, indigenous rights, and the environment (Borras 2005), land administration projects nonetheless are evaluated through a technocratic operational culture (Goldman 2006) responsible for so many development failures (Danaher 1994). They are also beholden to a broader World Bank paradigm of "green neoliberalism." Fusing techniques of enclosure with belief in the "free market," green neoliberalism seeks to open nature and communities that depend on natural resources to outsiders—whether governments, NGOs, or foreign investors (Goldman 2006: 184). Welding two seemingly contradictory ideas, economic growth and environmental conservation, green neoliberal logic argues that the best way to save nature is to privatize it and let the market decide its value. If we want to save the atmosphere, we can supposedly just set up markets for trading emissions without addressing the continued extraction and burning of fossil fuels. In order to ensure clean water for urbanization, city users might arrange to pay communities that conserve watersheds while ignoring the many other related burdens cities place on the countryside. Watersheds could be saved if downstream users were to pay for the "environmental services" of upstream conservation.

The problem with such oxymoronic "win-win" alliances is that, in a conflict, business usually trumps the environment. In an age of corporate power, development benefits are also more likely to trickle up than trickle down. Politics, rather than science, tend to influence enforcement guidelines, making them difficult to monitor. Ecology is inherently unpredictable, and, thus, packaging nature into "things" to be sold on the market can lead to unforeseen outcomes. Finally, to many indigenous groups, the commodification of nature, especially land, is anathema. Indigenous people do not want just *any* land; they want specific, spiritually sacred homelands as well as the right to autonomous local governance and self-determination (Stavenhagen 2006).

Green neoliberal projects also tend to target environmental problems in out-of-the-way places that by their marginality, remoteness, and general quirkiness create friction for global capital (Tsing 2005). Unless natural resources and commercial infrastructure can be standardized and made legible to outsiders, doing business in the hinterland requires inordinate human and capital investment (Scott 1998). Hence, there is something slippery in the World Bank's land project methodology. In Guatemala and elsewhere, the World Bank is clearly experimenting with land market mechanisms *on the periphery*—postponing plans to replicate these projects in core national territory until it has normalized the idea that states should pass land control to the invisible hand of the market.

The first phase of the project started in Guatemala's northernmost region of Petén (1998–2007). Before evaluating the Petén work, the Guatemalan government accepted another World Bank loan of $62 million in December 2006, which it is using to expand the project to six other departments, including all the rest of Q'eqchi' territory in Alta Verapaz and Izabal. Eventually the Guatemalan state plans to expand these land administration techniques to the whole country. Thus, what happens at the margins of a Q'eqchi' frontier settlement offers clues about new structures developing in the middle.

PLACES AND METHODS

The third-largest Central American country, Guatemala is approximately the size of Ohio or Tennessee. The country is divided into twenty-two departments that are administered by appointed governors but do not have the legislative power of states in the United States' federal system. With twenty-one or twenty-two Maya languages (depending on who is counting) plus two other non-Maya indigenous groups (Garifuna and Xinca), Guatemala is majority indigenous. Guatemalans refer to the nonindigenous minority, people of mixed-race backgrounds, as "Ladinos" instead of the term "mestizos" commonly used in other Latin American countries. Although Guatemala's elite are counted as Ladinos in government censuses, they nonetheless consider themselves whites, or "blancos." Guatemala was once a majority Catholic country, but with many syncretistic Maya customs. Evangelical Protestant groups, who gained a strong foothold in Guatemala during the civil war, have reached numerical parity with Catholics.

For a relatively small country (109,000 square kilometers), Guatemala hosts extraordinarily diverse ecosystems: highland mountain ranges ("el Altiplano") with rich volcanic soils, fertile plains along the Pacific and Atlantic coasts ("la Costa Sur" and the Motagua Valley), an arid eastern region ("el Oriente"), the cloud forests of Verapaz, and the subtropical, dry, broadleaf forests of the north. Q'eqchi' communities have migrated and adapted to an extraordinary variety of highland and lowland ecosystems. Residing across four Guatemalan departments (Quiché, Alta Verapaz, Petén, and Izabal) plus the Toledo district of Belize, Q'eqchi' people inhabit the largest territorial area of any Maya group, numbering about 852,012 in Guatemala and 12,366 in Belize. In the past, they referred to themselves as "Q'eqchi' speakers" (*laa'o aj Q'eqchi'*) but not necessarily as a cultural group with a strong identity outside of language (Wilson 1995). The 2002 census in Guatemala was the first opportunity for Maya groups to self-identify as an ethnic group, and at least one hundred thousand people who did not learn Q'eqchi' as a mother tongue did so.

The Q'eqchi' highland homeland lies in the cloud forests north of Guatemala City. Separated from the western highlands by the Cuchumatanes mountain range, Alta Verapaz lacks a direct connection with the Pan-American Highway. For these geographic reasons and others, Q'eqchi' people do not share as much of a pan-Maya identity as do the eighteen other Maya groups located in the western highlands. Alta Verapaz is the wettest area of the country, so Guatemalans joke that it rains thirteen months a year there (Dillon 1985; Collins 2001). In fact, they have a special word for the steady drizzle—"chipi chipi" in Spanish and *yoo chi mus mus hab'* in Q'eqchi'. Blanketed by moisture, the region is home to epiphytes, ferns, mosses, natural springs, abundant caves, and nests of the elusive quetzal, Guatemala's national bird, commemorated in the name of the national currency. The Verapaz mountains gently slope down into the Polochic Valley to the east, into Ixcán to the west, and northward into the green ocean of Petén's tropical forests.

Because the central Q'eqchi' highlands and the urban regions around Cobán have been so well studied (e.g., Wilson 1995; Hatse and De Ceuster 2001a, 2001b; Parra Novo 1997; Pacheco 1992; A. E. Adams 1999; Cabarrus 1974), I decided to focus on the rural, lowland hinterlands, tracing Q'eqchi' migration routes across four regions: north-central Petén, southeastern Petén, and Izabal in Guatemala and the Toledo district in Belize. I deliberately chose a mix of five villages of different sizes (table 1) at different stages of pioneer settlement and with different relationships to protected areas that were connected in some way by kinship or migration history. Per anthropological custom, I identify these villages with English-language pseudonyms, but all other Spanish place-names (e.g., for towns, departments, and districts) are real.

In some communities, I visited every household (Atelesdale, Agoutiville, Jaguarwood), while in others, I relied on samples based on kinship stratification (Macawville and Tamalton) and conversations with key informants. From every village studied, I took day-trips to neighboring communities for comparison. Befriending Q'eqchi' ranch workers, small Ladino cattle owners, cowboys, and ranch administrators enabled me to gain insights into the operations of nearby ranchers. Some of my best information came from my practice of hitchhiking on cattle and corn-buying trucks, whose drivers were always so

TABLE 1. Village Profiles

ENGLISH PSEUDONYM	Q'EQCHI' PSEUDONYM	REGION	FOUNDED	POPULATION CIRCA 2002	PROTECTED AREAS	LAND TENURE AND PERCENT SOLD	INFRA-STRUCTURE	LENGTH OF RESIDENCE
Atelesdale	Saxb'atz (By the Monkeys)	Northern Petén	1977	300 families, about 60% Q'eqchi'	In the Multiple Use Zone of the Maya Biosphere Reserve	Usufruct or "possession rights" (half sold)	Accessible by dirt road; potable water and electricity inaugurated in 2002	15 mos. since 1993
Macawville	Chimo' (Alongside the Scarlet Macaws)	Northern Petén	1920s, resettled by Q'eqchi families 1995	111 Q'eqchi' families, 99% Q'eqchi'	In a nuclear zone of the Maya Biosphere Reserve	Usufruct or "possession rights" (none sold to non-Q'eqchi' people)	20 km by foot from nearest village when resettled; dirt road built in 2000	4 mos. since 1997
Tamalton	Chipoch (Place of the Corn Dumplings)	Southeastern Petén	1950s	>200 families, 95% Q'eqchi'	n/a	Private parcels, awarded by FYDEP (half sold)	Dirt road built in the 1960s	1 mo. in 2003
Agoutiville	Sehelaw (In Tepezcuintle Territory)	Izabal	1880	87 families, 82% Q'eqchi'	Near a proposed protected area in the Santa Cruz mountains	Collective title from INTA, later subdivided into private parcels (70% sold)	River access; dirt road built a decade ago; irregular electricity; potable water inaugurated 2003	6 mos. in 2003, 2007
Jaguarwood	Sehix (By the Jaguars)	Toledo, Belize	Est. circa 1900, Q'eqchi' families arrived around 1912	49 families, 96% Q'eqchi'	Adjoining the Sarstoon Temash National Park	Communal land management (none sold, one-third have leases)	River access only until road inaugurated in 2002	3 mos. in 2004

startled to see a gringa walking through the countryside that their curiosity impelled them to give me a ride.

While some anthropologists deride applied work, I found that my long-term engagements with conservation efforts and agrarian rights campaigns in this region helped me situate this village research in a broader context. For four of my six-plus years in residence in Petén since 1993, I worked with the Guatemalan environmental organization ProPetén to expand the typical conservation package of forest and park management into new arenas such as health and family planning, organic agriculture, gender and ethnic equity, opposition to petroleum extraction, and agrarian reform. The institutional affiliations and community friendships I formed through this NGO work provided me extraordinary access to information after I became an anthropologist. In addition to thousands of meetings and informal conversations with conservation and development professionals during my years of NGO work, I formally interviewed as an anthropologist more than a hundred people in the agrarian sector and explored government and NGO archives in many different cities. Although town research was illuminating, my first anthropology mentor, Norman Schwartz, long ago encouraged me to maximize my time in the villages, because it was something so few ethnographers actually did. There is always another seemingly important meeting or conference, and those certainly should be a part of a fieldwork plan, but long stretches of relaxed time with one's village subjects must also take priority. Over two uninterrupted years (2002–4), I dedicated most of my time to participant-observation in the five villages described briefly below and then reintroduced in text boxes in successive chapters.

Organized into twelve municipal jurisdictions, the department of Petén covers one-third of Guatemala's territory but holds less than 5 percent of the overall population. Northern Petén is generally flat with thin tropical soils on top of large beds of limestone marked by depressions and sinks, forming waterholes, caves, and underground lakes. The climate is generally hot and humid, with an average daytime high temperature between 80 and 90 degrees Fahrenheit, sometimes exceeding 100 degrees in the hottest months of May–August. The contrast between the rainy (June–December) and dry (January–May) seasons is quite pronounced. In fact, the scarcity of groundwater plus the abundance of other discomforts (poisonous snakes, malaria, dengue fever, leishmaniasis, intestinal parasites, and skin pests such as ticks, black flies, and chiggers, to name a few) dissuaded Q'eqchi' colonists and others from settling in northern Petén until land scarcity elsewhere compelled them to do so.

Unlike other areas of Q'eqchi' territory, which have significant urban and professional populations, Q'eqchi' settlement in Petén is basically rural and poor. The oldest areas of Q'eqchi' settlement are in the southernmost municipalities of Sayaxché and especially San Luis. Today, however, the focus of Q'eqchi' migration is shifting to municipalities north and northwest of Lake Petén Itzá, where I started my research. I chose two communities located inside the Maya Biosphere Reserve, Atelesdale and Macawville, in which I had already lived for a year and which I had visited regularly since 1993. Moving south, I then traced Q'eqchi' migration from those communities back to Tamalton, a village in a much older area of Q'eqchi' settlement in the San Luis municipality.

Next, I moved to a Q'eqchi' community previously unknown to me near the border between the departments of Izabal and Petén. Just northwest of the lively Atlantic shipping centers of Puerto Barrios and Rio Dulce are dozens of fairly isolated Q'eqchi' communities nestled in the fertile valleys and ecologically rich mountain ranges of the Sierra Santa Cruz and the Cerro San Gil in the Livingston municipality. Established in the nineteenth century, these are among the oldest lowland Q'eqchi' settlements in Guatemala. Agoutiville, the community I chose here (my favorite, if anthropologists are allowed to say so), was the most ritually active of the five villages studied but also the most endangered by cattle encroachment.

My fifth and last community was Jaguarwood, located less than a day's journey from Agoutiville, to the east across Guatemala's border with Belize, which Q'eqchi' people cross unrecognized by either government. (Of course, I took a circuitous route to enter Belize through an official border post.) As the first anthropologist to do comparative research among the lowland Q'eqchi' in neighboring Belize and Guatemala, I found that while the two countries have remarkably different political histories (Belize won its independence from Britain only in 1981), their agrarian challenges are quite similar. While the sociopolitical history of Belizean Q'eqchi' people is beyond the scope of this book (though ably described in other works such as Berkey 1994; G. Jones 1997; Schackt 1986; Wainwright 2008; Wilk 1987, 1997; and C. Wright n.d.), this cross-cultural comparison was critical for my conclusions about Guatemala. Working in collaboration with the Sarstoon Temash Institute for Indigenous Management (SATIIM), a Q'eqchi' conservation NGO, between November 2003 and April 2004, I carried out a study on traditional environmental knowledge among the elders of four Q'eqchi' communities bordering the Sarstoon Temash National Park, staying longest in Jaguarwood, the village profiled in this book. Any lingering preconceptions I had of Q'eqchi' people as being anti-conservation were shattered by the extraordinary environmental stewardship demonstrated by Q'eqchi' communities in southern Belize. It was here that I began to recognize the intimate relationship between the material and social Q'eqchi' commons.

Having directly witnessed how Belizean Q'eqchi' so deeply love the rain forests, I wondered how Guatemalan Q'eqchi' had come to be viewed as opposing biodiversity conservation efforts? The first half of this book addresses this question by delving into the history, migratory patterns, and agro-ecology of Q'eqchi' people as background for understanding contemporary threats to their landholdings. The second half then describes lowland Q'eqchi' struggles to defend their commons against both the cattle industry and a broader enclosure movement driven by transnational trade, infrastructure development, and neoliberal property reform.

CHAPTER OVERVIEW

Chapter 1 provides background for three critical periods of Q'eqchi' land enclosure via religion, business, and modernity, namely, (1) the sixteenth-century Spanish conquest of Mesoamerica, which partitioned lands among the Crown, military leaders, and the Catholic Church; (2) the 1870s coffee boom, when the Guatemalan government gave away communal indigenous lands to foreign investors and instituted a series of laws turning Maya people into serf labor; and (3) the design of colonization programs as part of the military's counterrevolution following the 1954 coup, sponsored by the Central Intelligence Agency (CIA), against Guatemala's first democratically elected president. The historical material in this chapter illustrates an important theoretical point: that beyond the mere control of land, elites were equally interested in coercively maintaining cheap indigenous labor during each of these three historical moments.

Chapter 2 explores the causes and consequences of Q'eqchi' territorial expansion and explains why we might characterize them as the "gringos of the Maya world." Since at least the colonial period, Q'eqchi' people have migrated into the northern lowland forests in response to land conflicts and elite attempts to control their labor. Almost half the population has left the mountains for the lowlands and, over time, has adapted remarkably well to the new ecosystems. Stories of the tragedies, epic journeys, and aspirations of Q'eqchi' pioneers convey the human dimensions of their migration.

Chapter 3 discusses the challenge of agricultural intensification for lowland Q'eqchi' farmers. Concerned about massive deforestation in the wake of frontier colonization, biodiversity conservationists in Petén worry whether Q'eqchi' "slash-and-burn" farmers will intensify their agriculture fast enough to remain ahead of the demographic momentum that otherwise pushes them to become squatters in national parks. Their focus on the ecological limits of the region clearly invokes neo-Malthusian discourse on the tragedy of the commons. In response, this chapter focuses on the social and environmental logic of the traditional Q'eqchi' system of milpa agriculture. While population growth may accelerate deforestation, the greater problem is the "property trap" in which Q'eqchi' settlers are caught. Cross-country comparison shows that the pressures of private property have compelled Guatemalan Q'eqchi' to erode their environment, while Belizean Q'eqchi' have adapted more sustainably to their lowland rainforest habitat through customary land management.

Land administration programs promoted as a market-based agrarian reform have been funded by the World Bank and other multilateral donors across Guatemala and Belize, as described in chapter 4. Despite the claim that these projects will slow the advance of the agricultural frontier into protected areas, the research presented here shows that instead many peasant beneficiaries are selling their land to ranchers as soon as their parcels are legalized and then moving farther north, often into national parks.

Although cattle ranching is the driving force behind deforestation and Q'eqchi' dispossession, it has been overlooked in the conservation literature on Petén. Chapter 5 fills this gap by providing a historical overview of the expansion of the beef industry into the northern Maya lowlands. Although tropical range ranching is not particularly profitable, the beef industry fulfills other social and speculative purposes by providing a physically powerful way for elites to control both land and labor until they can be profitably transformed into export-led agribusiness and other extractive activities. In the meanwhile, cattle ranching serves as both a biologically and an economically flexible tool of enclosure that constricts the pulse of local labor opportunities.

A century after the original Liberal reforms uprooted hundreds of highland Q'eqchi' communities, neoliberal programs of trade and investment are once again dispossessing hundreds of lowland Q'eqchi' communities, as described in chapter 6. One such program is the PPP, a $50 billion infrastructure portfolio designed to facilitate foreign investment and transportation in southern Mexico and Central America. Many of its megaprojects crisscross Guatemala's northern lowlands, intensifying speculative pressures on Q'eqchi' territory.

Land concentration will be further compounded by grain price disruptions expected under the DR-CAFTA.

The concluding chapter explains how the recurring dispossessions of Q'eqchi' people can deepen our understanding of other contemporary struggles to defend the commons and everyday life against corporate enclosures. Although much of this book has a grim focus on historical repetitions, it ends on a hopeful note. If enclosure is permanent, then so, too, will be societal responses to processes of enclosure. Recognizing enclosure as a perpetually contested process gives us a multitude of alternatives in the *here and now* not only for defending the material commons but also for strengthening the social commons of democracy.

1

Liberal Plunder

A RECURRING Q'EQCHI' HISTORY

> Pilar Ternera let out a deep laugh, the old expansive laugh that ended
> up a cooing of doves. There was no mystery in the heart of a Buendía
> that was impenetrable for her because a century of cards and experi-
> ence had taught her that the history of the family was a machine with
> unavoidable repetitions, a turning wheel that would have gone on
> spinning into eternity were it not for the progressive and irremediable
> wearing of the axle.
>
> —Gabriel García Márquez, *One Hundred Years of Solitude*

> Progress, far from consisting of change, depends on retentiveness. . . .
> Those who cannot remember the past are condemned to repeat it.
>
> —George Santayana, *The Life of Reason*, vol. 1

O N a recent flight to Guatemala, seated to my left were two middle-
aged gringos dressed in overalls who appeared to be on a volunteer
trip to build a church. In front of me was a group of young men with
military haircuts planning some kind of expedition; in fact, "kaibiles," soldiers
from Guatemala's special operations force, met them at the airport's baggage
claim. Seated behind were a couple of businessmen intently discussing strategies for the newly privatized telecommunications system in Guatemala. Like
the recurring characters in García Marquez's epic novel *One Hundred Years of
Solitude*, my three sets of neighbors on this plane seemed like a reincarnation
of the original Spanish invaders—missionaries, military conquistadores, and
colonial officials.

As the conquistador Bernal Diaz once described it, their goals were "to bring light to those in darkness, and also to get rich, which is what all of us men commonly seek" (quoted in Farriss 1984: 29). Regardless of which outsiders happen to hold power, the everyday lived experiences of Maya people have changed little (ibid.). Indeed, for the average Q'eqchi' farmer, the experience of dispossession has been remarkably consistent over the epochs. Through multiple conquests in the name of God (Christianity), gold (commerce), and glory (civilization) (Hecht 1993), outsiders have repeatedly sought to enclose Q'eqchi' territory, not only for the value of its fertile land, but also for the corollary control of the labor of its people (Taracena 2002). These interlopers consolidated and replicated their agrarian power during the three key moments in Guatemalan history preceding neoliberalism that are described in this chapter—colonialism, Liberalism, and developmentalism[1] (table 2). While the repetitive nature of these multiple histories of enclosure may make them seem inevitable in retrospect, Q'eqchi' people also repeatedly resisted their dispossession.

FIRST ENCLOSURE: CONQUEST BY CHRISTIANITY

Before the Spanish conquest, Q'eqchi' people likely lived around a 1,500-meter altitude in the elongated valleys between (present-day) Tactic and San Cristóbal and between Cobán and San Pedro Carchá. Located in a strategic zone between the northern lowland forests, the Atlantic ocean, and the densely populated western Guatemalan highlands, Q'eqchi' people took advantage of their geography by working as highland-to-lowland traders from at least the early Classic period (300–600) (Wilk 1997). Early writings by Spanish conquerors comment on Q'eqchi' involvement in long-distance commerce in cotton, chocolate, and annatto (*Bixa orellana*), and other forest and agricultural products, all of which traveling Q'eqchi' merchants ("Cobanero" salesmen) continue to trade today. Little else is known about precolonial Q'eqchi' political organization except that it was less hierarchical than more powerful city-states such as those ruled by the K'iche' and other western highland groups; this may help explain why the Spanish found the Q'eqchi' so difficult to conquer.

By the 1530s, the Spanish had established dominion over most of Guatemala except for territories belonging to the "unconquerable" Lacandón, Acalá, Mopán, Itzá, Manché Ch'ol, Pocomchi', and Q'eqchi' peoples (fig. 1.1).[2] Spanish conquest broke down these boundaries—either through forced resettlement or through mutual Maya resistance and flight—and leveled America's diverse mosaic of civilizations into a single category of rural "Indians" (Bonfil Batalla 1996). The people perceived to be "the Q'eqchi'" today were clearly influenced by their cultural and

TABLE 2. Summary of Q'eqchi' Enclosure by Epoch

EPOCH	POLITICAL ECONOMY	ROUGH PERIODIZATION	INTEGRATION	MECHANISMS OF ENCLOSURE
Colonialism	Mercantilism	Conquest (1523 or thereabouts) to independence from Spain in 1821	Localized, municipal control	Royal allotment of land to the conquerors for tribute collection and labor extraction
Liberalism	Rise of agricultural bourgeoisie and export-led capitalism	Struggles back and forth between Conservatives and Liberals (1821–73) through six decades of Liberal dictatorships (1873–1930s); some overlap with Ubico	Regional	Development of export crops on the best soils of the highlands for coffee and the south coast for other plantations; colonization plans for the north
Developmentalism	State-led modernization	Caudillo: Ubico dictatorship (1931–44)	National integration	Penetration and colonization of Guatemala's hinterlands; military terror and genocide, shaped deeply by Cold War politics
		Civilian, democratic: the 1944 October Revolution through the fall of the Arbénz administration in 1954		
		Military, authoritarian: Castillo Armas to Vinicio Cerezo (1954–86), but note that the Guatemalan civil war does not formally end until the 1996 Peace Accords		
Neoliberalism	Corporate capitalism	Roots in the structural adjustment policies of the 1980s and free trade policies from the 1990s onward	Transnational	World Bank market-assisted land reform coupled with international trade and infrastructure intended to promote corporate investment (the PPP and the DR-CAFTA)

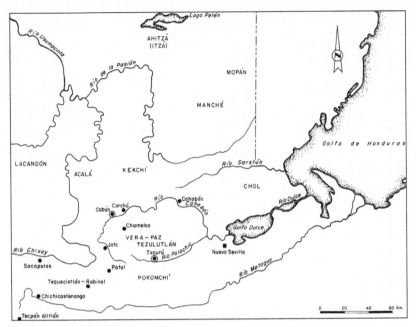

FIGURE 1.1. Ethnic groups, circa 1550. Source: André Saint-Lu, "La Verapaz, Siglo XVI," in *Historia General de Guatemala*, vol. 2: 628, illustration 175. © Fundación Herencia Cultural Guatemala, Archivo 1359

linguistic interactions during the colonial period with other neighboring groups, particularly the Manché Ch'ol and Acalá. The Spanish coveted Q'eqchi' territory, in particular, as a staging ground for taking control of the expanse of forest that stretched from Chiapas, across Petén to Belize, and down into part of the Verapaz and Izabal departments between the Sierra de Chinajá in the west and the Motagua Valley in the east (Sapper 1985). After several failed forays into the Q'eqchi' region, the Spanish retreated and renamed this frontier the Land of War, or Tezulutlán. The Spanish inability to conquer Q'eqchi' and surrounding lowland peoples militarily sparked the interest of Fray Bartolomé de las Casas (1474–1566), a farmer turned Dominican priest.

De las Casas had gained fame as the first Spaniard to chronicle and condemn the atrocities of conquest he witnessed as a Hispaniola settler. Traveling back and forth to Spain for religious and legal study, he advocated before the pope and King Charles V for more humane treatment of the native peoples of the Americas and proposed "peaceful" religious conversion as an alternative means of conquest (Todorov 1984).[3] Returning to the Americas in 1535, de las Casas accepted the challenge of Guatemala's Spanish rulers to prove his theories in the Land of War. According to a fellow Dominican priest named Remesal (for other histories, see Pedroni 1991; Gomez Lanza 1983; Biermann 1971; and Dillon 1985), de las Casas purportedly initiated his peaceful conquest in 1542 by teaching a musical poem about the life of Jesus to four traveling K'iche' merchants whom he sent into Q'eqchi' territory with the usual Spanish trade goods (axes, machetes, pots) and trinkets. These singing bards sparked the interest of local rulers, or "caciques," who invited the Dominican priests to visit. Leading the delegation, Bartolomé de las Casas convinced the caciques to convert to Christianity through baptism by offering them the privileges of Spanish nobility and protection from Spanish settlers (Biermann 1971: 467).

By 1545, Dominican priests claimed to have pacified Tezulutlán. Through papal bull, de las Casas became bishop of this new Episcopal province along with Chiapas. Renaming the region Vera Paz (Land of True Peace) in 1547, Charles V granted the Dominicans control of the area and banned Spanish settlers from claiming landed estates known as "encomiendas." Elsewhere, these land allotments included not only the right to use the soil but also exclusive rights to enslave local indigenous labor; as Severo Martínez observed in his history of Guatemala, "Indians were part of the landscape" (Mauro and Merlet 2003: 7).

Having consolidated political control over the region, Dominican friars began resettling Q'eqchi' and neighboring lowland Maya groups into forced resettlements, what they called "reducciones" (literally, "reductions"). By 1574, they had established fifteen nucleated towns, separated by approximately a day's travel on foot (A. King 1974), which remain the municipal centers of contemporary Verapaz. Invented by Guatemala's Bishop Francisco Marroquín, forced resettlement became a common colonial administrative practice for facilitating indoctrination of the indigenous population, tribute collection, and seizure of native lands—a concept akin, one might argue, to the so-called model villages established by the Guatemalan military in the early 1980s.

Though portrayed as a peaceful means of religious conversion, this resettlement process almost always required violent enforcement to prevent Q'eqchi' families from fleeing back to their villages (A. King 1974). Spanish captain Tovilla described how he assisted one Dominican raid: "We burned all their houses. We took all the corn the carriers could bring. We destroyed the milpas. . . . So they are well punished and will be obliged to be peaceful, unless they want to die because we didn't leave them anything to eat or any metal tools with which to cultivate the land again" (Scholes and Adams 1960: 166). Although the Dominican order forbade friars to inflict corporal punishment, they called upon Spanish authorities to administer lashings and organize forays into the un-Christianized northern hinterland (Biermann 1971). Historians applaud de las Casas for a 1541 decree prohibiting the forcible relocation of native peoples to unfavorable climates, but, in practice, Dominican priests did not always respect this policy (Sapper 1985, 2000). They also transformed the Q'eqchi' economy in order to fill Church coffers. Emulating Spanish conquistadores, the Dominican priests started demanding tribute in 1562 (Cahuec del Valle et al. 1997) and reorganized the Q'eqchi' into religious brotherhoods ("cofradías") for this purpose (Scholes and Adams 1960). Although the brotherhoods eventually became a potent symbol of Maya identity in the twentieth century, Q'eqchi' people initially resisted the economic burdens of organizing the required religious festivals. Dominican priests also wrote about their frustrated attempts to get their Q'eqchi' subjects to plant foreign fruit trees such as oranges, citron, lemons, peaches, and quince (A. King 1974)—foreshadowing the complaints of contemporary development agents about Q'eqchi' disinterest in agroforestry projects.

In addition to such everyday forms of resistance, there were regular armed uprisings in the Dominican forced resettlements. When the priests temporarily left the area, Q'eqchi' people burned down the first church de las Casas had built in Cobán (A. King 1974). The denial of a 1799 Q'eqchi' petition to remove the names of dead people from the tribute rolls provoked another revolt in Cobán in 1803, which led to the assassinations of the mayor, the military commissioner, the governor, and a prominent merchant (A. E. Adams 1999; Bertrand 1989). The most common form of Q'eqchi' resistance to tribute requirements was to flee into the forest, making it difficult for the Dominicans to maintain accurate census records.

Q'eqchi' flight may also have been an escape from epidemics of European diseases. Unfortunately, the real scope of the demographic collapse of the Q'eqchi' and other lowland groups will never be known, as the Spanish conquerors burned pre-Columbian Maya books and records. Nonetheless, most historical demographers estimate that nine-tenths of Native American peoples died within a century of European contact from disease, violence, and ecological devastation (Crosby 1972). Perhaps 90 million native peoples had perished by 1600, making it the greatest relative holocaust in the recorded history of humanity (R. Wright 1992: 14). Recognizing that European diseases might have been spread through Spanish military forays along the Belize coast in 1507, up to Lake Izabal in 1508, and through to Petén in 1525 (G. Jones 1997), George Lovell and Christopher Lutz (1995) estimate the combined population of Verapaz and Petén at 208,000 people immediately preceding contact. Just three decades later, the figure had fallen apocalyptically by three-quarters to 52,000 in 1550 and continued to plummet. Once Dominicans established a permanent presence, the census of "tributaries" (probably referring to male heads of household) in Alta Verapaz fell again by half, down from 7,000 households in 1561 to just 3,535 in 1571. That community and ritual life survived at all reveals the resilience of Maya traditions (Nations 2001: 463).

In other ways, colonial life under the Dominicans was comparatively easier for the Q'eqchi' than for other Maya groups under direct Spanish rule. Due to the emphasis on religious conversion, the Dominicans provided education for both boys and girls, and many nineteenth-century travelers' reports commented on the unusually high rates of urban Q'eqchi' literacy. The Dominicans ended forced resettlements in the 1760s, allowing families to live on their farms most of the year so long as the men returned to town for religious festivals and tribute payments (A. King 1974). Not until Guatemala's recent civil war did the Q'eqchi' area become significantly re-urbanized, as people fled violence in the countryside for more anonymous and safer urban residences.

Although their entire territory technically belonged to the Spanish Crown, Q'eqchi' people were able to maintain their traditional, community-based land management under Dominican rule. This would have grave unforeseen consequences for the Q'eqchi' in the late nineteenth century, when the Guatemalan government decided to reassert its claim over untitled land. Unlike highland Maya groups, who began using the judicial system to protect their community lands from Spanish settlers in the 1500s, Q'eqchi' people had no legal experience defending their territory and were, therefore, disproportionately hurt by government land expropriations starting in the 1870s. Nonetheless, another peculiar fact of colonial history also provided many Q'eqchi' with an escape—migration into the northern Maya lowlands.

Although the Dominicans pacified the Verapaz region by the mid-sixteenth century, the northern hinterlands remained both spiritually and militarily unconquerable. Neither from the north (from Yucatán) nor from the southeast (from Comalapa) could they manage to convert or conquer lowland Maya populations across this thickly forested region. Considering Manché Ch'ol resistance to be less "ferocious" than that of the Mopán, Lacandón, and Acalá peoples, the Dominicans made regular expeditions into Ch'ol territory in the early seventeenth century. By 1633, they had converted some six thousand Ch'ol "souls," but Ch'ol people continued to flee back to the forest (Sapper 1985), while other unconquered groups repeatedly attacked the newly pacified settlements.

Exasperated by this lowland resistance, in 1692, the Council of the Indies issued a final and definitive order to conquer and convert the lowlands and sent troops from Huehuetenango and Chiapas to undertake the task (A. King 1974). During a five-year campaign culminating in 1697 with the conquest of the Itzá in Petén, the Spanish rounded up Mopán peoples from southern Belize and resettled them around Lake Petén Itzá (G. Jones 1997). They resettled the Ch'ol in Urrán, a distant and inhospitable valley above the Motagua River, where they died of disease and starvation (Sapper 1985). Lacandón and Acalá prisoners were moved to Cobán, eventually losing their identity and language to Q'eqchi' cultural assimilation (ibid.; Cahuec del Valle et al. 1997).

In addition to cultural jumbling in the urban resettlements, there was significant intermixing among remnant groups in the forest frontier, especially between eastern Q'eqchi' people and the Manché Ch'ol. Based on evidence from Otto Stoll, J. Eric Thompson (1972) suggests there were two different "stocks" of Q'eqchi' people: those from the highland Cobán region and those he calls "Q'eqchi'-Ch'ol" people from the lowland Cahabón area. One elder and his wife from a Q'eqchi' village in southern Belize told me a story of having given lodging about fifty years ago to a "Ch'ol" man who came to visit them when he got lonely in the forest (Grandia 2004b; for other stories, see Wilk et al. 1987; Schackt 1981; Danien 2005). While it is unlikely that any unconquered Manché Ch'ol people survive today, the depth and breadth of Q'eqchi' people's contemporary knowledge of hunting, fishing, agriculture, and especially healing with medicinal plants in the Atlantic coastal region certainly indicate that they had a long history of interaction with northeastern forest people (cf. G. Jones 1986).[4] The astonishing migration of Q'eqchi' people into Izabal and Belize all the way to the Atlantic coast in response to their next enclosure certainly suggests that the Q'eqchi' had some prior knowledge from the Manché Ch'ol about this lowland rain forest and ocean habitat.

SECOND ENCLOSURE: CONQUEST BY COMMERCE

After Guatemala gained independence from Spain in 1821, a protracted struggle commenced between Conservatives, who wanted to uphold the power of traditional colonial elites, and anticlerical Liberals, who felt it was necessary to undermine the power of the Catholic Church in order to transform Guatemala into a modern, capitalist economy (A. E. Adams 1999). These terms are capitalized here to emphasize that Conservatives were conservative not in the contemporary, *political* sense of wanting to uphold traditional religious and personal ethics but in the nineteenth-century sense of hoping to maintain the traditional *economic* power of estate owners along with Catholic authority and landholdings. Likewise, Liberals defined themselves not in the contemporary, progressive sense but rather as members of the ruling elite who felt that foreign investment and immigration were the ideal path to modernization. Put another way, Conservatives wanted to rule by caste, Liberals by class. Unlike other regions of Latin America where leaders sought to assimilate the rural, indigenous populations, Guatemala remained ethnically stratified—with indigenous land and labor subordinated to elites, both Liberal and Conservative (Weaver 1999).

When Liberals seized power briefly after independence, they attempted to expropriate indigenous common lands as well as Catholic Church properties so that they could reward foreign investors with large land grants. They passed an 1824 law inviting "all foreigners that may wish to come to the United Provinces of Central America . . . to do it in the terms and the way which may best suit them," including free land grants and tax exemptions (Fuentes-Mohr 1955: 27). In order to speed the pace of European settlement, President Mariano Galvez (1831–38), for example, concessioned more than half of Guatemalan territory—including 6.4 million hectares in Alta Verapaz, Petén, and part of Izabal—to English, British, and Guatemalan entrepreneurs (Weaver 1999), with additional perks if the immigrants married the "aboriginal inhabitants . . . or coloured people" of Guatemala (Fuentes-Mohr 1955: 27). Aggravated by a cholera epidemic, these and other land issues sparked a major peasant rebellion led by Rafael Carrera (1851–65), which brought the Conservatives back into power for the next two decades. The Conservatives reinstated the colonial Laws of the Indies and saw themselves as feudal "protectors" of "the Indians."

When coal tar dye substitutes caused the world market for cochineal to fall in the 1850s, many of the rising agricultural bourgeoisie began investing in coffee, which had been introduced to Guatemala in 1743 by the Jesuits. While cochineal as an export crop had little need for land or labor (even at its height, the total area under cochineal production was only 3,781 acres [McCreery 1983]), coffee was a high-maintenance crop and prospered in temperate areas belonging to indigenous peoples. Small-scale commercial cultivation began in the 1830s, and a Swiss businessman, Carl Rudolf Klee (the largest cochineal exporter of the mid-nineteenth century, with a last name still associated with the Guatemalan elite), set up the first coffee trading houses that same decade (Cambranes 1985; A. King 1974). His work sparked the interest of German trading firms in Hamburg and Bremen that soon took over the industry. The U.S.

Civil War briefly disrupted international trading networks, but afterward coffee production and marketing continued to expand in two suitable climatic areas: on the Pacific Coast and in Alta Verapaz. By 1871, coffee already constituted half of Guatemala's exports (McCreery 1983).

With this economic shift, Guatemala's agricultural elite brought the Liberals back to power for seven decades (1873–1944), and a second conquest by commerce unraveled the Q'eqchi' world. Beginning with Presidents Manuel Garcia Granados (1871–73) and Justo Rufino Barrios (1873–85), the Liberals restructured Guatemala's economy, inviting foreign investment by lifting the export tax on coffee, awarding preferential land grants to foreigners, and enforcing compulsory labor laws. During this same period, Barrios strengthened the army and established a national military academy, the Escuela Politécnica, in part to enforce these legal subsidies to investors (Campbell 2003; R. N. Adams 1993). He even ran ad campaigns in Europe to attract coffee investors (Wittman and Saldívar 2006) and once remarked to a German diplomat that "100 foreign families were worth as much as 20,000 indians" (Cambranes 1985: 302).

The first commercial coffee growers came mostly from England, France, Spain, Ireland, and Belgium (de la Cruz Torres 1982), but German immigrants soon dominated the coffee trade. North Americans were involved in other ways, such as running pack-mule teams that transported goods to and from the sea, and two men, William Champney and Robert Hempstead, acquired significant landholdings in Senahú and Cahabón (Reep 1997; Grandin 2004), municipalities that would later become the most important sources of outmigration to Petén. The first German investor was Heinrich Dieseldorff, a surname almost synonymous with coffee in Alta Verapaz today. Like many planters who followed, Dieseldorff began work as a trader-exporter but soon acquired land near Cobán.

In Cobán, Germans established a special chamber orchestra, imported street lamps, sent their children to private schools with teachers brought over from Germany, and eventually organized Nazi political events (A. King 1974). One of the reasons that Alta Verapaz, in particular, was subject to German and other foreign investment was its location, which was easily accessible from the sea. Ships could enter through the Río Dulce and travel down to Lake Izabal, leaving only a short distance (ninety kilometers) to transport goods by pack mule to Cobán (Collins 2001). So important was access to the Atlantic that, in the mid-1890s, German settlers raised 1.5 million marks among themselves to build a railroad along most of this overland route. Because no road yet existed from Guatemala City to Cobán, Alta Verapaz had, in many ways, closer economic ties to Europe than to the rest of Guatemala (A. King 1974). The linkage between investment and infrastructure continues to be relevant in Q'eqchi' territory through the PPP.

Many wealthy Guatemalans invested in coffee as well. The local Alta Verapaz government encouraged coffee production by exempting large growers from military service. In addition, the government provided free coffee seedlings to foreigners and Guatemalan Ladinos, who consisted mostly of elite whites, or "criollos" (Cambranes 1985). Short depressions in world coffee prices occurred at different periods (e.g., in 1898 and 1928), but, overall, the market continued to expand dramatically during the twentieth century, attracting further investment by foreigners and Guatemalan elites alike. The Guatemalan government occasionally worried about its monocrop coffee economy and sought to promote other crops such as rubber, quinine, cacao, bananas, and cardamom (A. King 1974).[5] However, it was primarily coffee that led to an 1877 law allowing the Barrios administration to confiscate communally managed, indigenous lands and award them to private investors.

As Q'eqchi' communities had never secured title to their lands, all their territory reverted immediately to the state as "baldíos," or national "wastelands." Between 1871 and 1883, the government declared more than 404,687 hectares in Q'eqchi' territory available to private investors (Comisión de Apoyo 2002). Any foreigner or citizen who wanted these new state lands simply had to make a public claim ("denuncio") to an area and pay to survey it. In theory, indigenous communities could dispute these claims and were eligible to purchase their own land, as some western highland Maya groups did (McCreery 1994). Most Q'eqchi' people did not because they were unfamiliar with the titling system, lacked the literacy skills to navigate the government bureaucracy, or simply were outbid at auction by wealthier foreign investors (Schmolz-Haberlein 1996; Grandin 2004). As a result, in Alta Verapaz by 1910, forty-seven outsiders (Ladinos and Germans) had acquired extensive plantations, while only six indigenous communities had protected their land through this process (Schmolz-Haberlein 1996). Other communities lost their land when they defaulted on tiny debts or through other indirect manipulations of the law (Wilk 1987). In 1888, ninety-seven indigenous residents of Verapaz had farms large enough to be registered as "plantations" in a government census; by 1930, only nine did; and by 1949, there were none (Grandin 2004: 26).

The foreign seizure of virtually all the arable land in Alta Verapaz was swift. Practically overnight, the Q'eqchi' were made into feudal labor in their own territory. In 1879, most Q'eqchi' people lived in free villages, but by 1921, almost

40 percent of the population lived on the coffee plantations as a kind of permanently indentured sharecropper known in Guatemala as a "mozo colono" (worker-serf). In Cahabón in the 1930s, one foreign planter held one hundred thousand acres that covered seventeen communities and employed half the entire municipal population (Grandin 2004: 26.).

Historians still disagree on exactly how much land Germans were able to claim, as the Germans quickly intermarried with Guatemalan families and fathered many children out of wedlock.[6] By 1900, four German companies had consolidated most of the coffee trade and also held the largest plantations (A. King 1974). Calculations from data published by Sapper in 1897 show that German holdings (158,760 hectares) amounted to almost one-fifth of the Alta Verapaz jurisdiction and a much higher percentage of its arable land. One firm alone held 36,000 hectares (Wagner Henn 1996, citing Sapper). Cambranes (1985) describes even higher concentrations of foreign landownership, calculating German holdings in Alta Verapaz by 1900 to be almost 300,000 hectares. By 1924, Germans controlled 45 percent of the coffee cultivation and 80 percent of the trade in all of Guatemala (A. King 1974).

As early as the 1880s, writers began commenting on the rampant land speculation occurring in the Q'eqchi' region. The Alta Verapaz political chief (a person appointed by the executive branch, somewhat akin to a governor) wrote in 1892: ". . . it is common knowledge that the land distribution program in this Department has been designed to satisfy a hungry few. I don't know how, but one person can claim fifty, one hundred, even five hundred caballerías of land, which were principally occupied by Indians in their capacity as tenant farmers" (Cambranes 1985: 198). In gross contrast to the massive land grants given to foreigners, the same political chief assigned one to ten "cuerdas" (one-tenth of an acre to one acre) to peasants made landless by these seizures—a small consolation prize indeed.

Although land acquisition was important, the German coffee barons also needed access to cheap labor. As far back as the colonial period, King Ferdinand V wrote in 1512 that the real wealth of the Indies was "the good use of Indians" (Cambranes 1985: 49–50). Three hundred years later, little had changed; as a German planter wrote: "He who wanted to establish a finca had first of all to find a set of lands which not only had the right climate and soil, but also an Indian village from which he could get the necessary labour-force. Without a labour-force close to the land, the enterprise had not a chance" (ibid.: 300–301). The average coffee plantation needed at least twenty resident families, but forty to sixty was ideal (Reep 1997).

So although the rapid agrarian transition to foreign ownership appeared to be about land (and it certainly was, on some level), the displacement of thousands of indigenous farming families also ensured a steady supply of cheap labor for the new agricultural bourgeoisie, otherwise known as planters, or "finqueros" (Cambranes 1985). From the 1860s onward, coffee was instrumental in transforming Guatemala's feudal and colonial mercantilism into a "modern" capitalist economy (McCreery 1994), guaranteeing a steady supply of indigenous labor to landowners while freeing them of many of the non-market, patron-client obligations customary in the colonial period. Specifically, in the late nineteenth century, Guatemala passed a series of laws supporting labor drafts, or "mandamientos," for public and private works and military service, debt peonage, and the punishment of "vagrants." Draft laws allowed municipal mayors to require all indigenous people to work as much as two weeks a month—often far away from home—for government or private owners (A. King 1974).[7] Howard (1977: 27) describes a 1912 piece published by a French count criticizing these labor drafts in the Q'eqchi' area, which sent men to work without pay more than a hundred kilometers from their homes in order to satisfy "the malice of some District Officer who arranges in this manner to aid a planter in need."

Debt operated as the system's linchpin. Unlike other Latin American countries in which debt servitude was an informal practice, in Guatemala it was a "fully legal system, mandated, regulated, and enforced by the state for the creation and manipulation of a rural labor force" (McCreery 1983: 742). Landowners commonly asked the help of a mayor or a governor in distributing "advance wages" that villagers would be forced to accept. In Cobán in 1889, the Ministry of Development even organized a special court that forced Q'eqchi' people to work on the coffee plantations (A. King 1974). According to an 1894 law, peasant debt service to private landowners took priority over labor conscription for public works or military service. Racism was built into the system, as the same law also exempted "Indians who know how to read and write and are abandoning their traditional dress" (McCreery 1983: 743).

Under this state-private system, there were two classes of laborers: day laborers ("jornaleros") who contracted with landowners on a temporary basis, and worker-serfs who lived permanently on the plantations and were given small plots to farm in exchange for their labor. Although day laborers earned slightly more than worker-serfs (ten Guatemalan cents a day, compared to eight cents a day in 1935), wages for both were ridiculously low. Landowners could bind both kinds of workers to the plantation by running monopoly company stores that charged exorbitant prices. By paying wages insufficient to purchase food staples for one person, let alone for a whole family, plantation owners kept workers in permanent debt. (The great interest that Q'eqchi' people manifest today in setting up rural dry-goods stores likely is a rebellious legacy of this debt history.) Plantation owners, furthermore, had the right to pursue, jail, or whip any laborer who attempted to flee and then add the cost of capturing the runaway to the worker's debt (Grandin 2004). If coffee prices fell, plantation owners simply stopped paying wages and would only credit the money due workers against their debts. Though technically illegal, planters or their agents would often force a man's family to fulfill his debt if he was ill, had fled, or was deceased (McCreery 1983).

In late nineteenth-century municipal registries from Izabal, Q'eqchi' men were automatically described as "day laborers," while the Ladinos' profession was written as "farmer" ("agricultor"). Not until the mid-twentieth century did municipal workers also begin to describe Q'eqchi' men as farmers. Were labels not sufficient to reduce the Q'eqchi' to permanent plantation work, local governments continued to assist landowners in their quest for a permanent reserve of cheap labor. Well into the 1960s, the Estor municipality in Izabal extracted a one-quetzal "rental" fee per month from all the Q'eqchi' families living on land given in a concession to Explotaciones Míneras Izabal (EXMIBAL), a subsidiary of the Canadian International Nickel Company. The municipality conscripted into plantation labor any Q'eqchi' people unable to pay the fee. Instead of directly paying these Q'eqchi' workers their rightful wages, plantation owners paid municipal authorities until all the contrived rental fees were settled (Carter 1969: 5).

Vagrancy laws passed in 1878 and expanded in the 1930s reinforced this system of debt peonage by requiring landless peasants as well as those with small landholdings to prove regular employment of at least 100–150 days a year (Schmolz-Haberlein 1996; Brockett 1998). The last of the Liberal dictators, President Jorge Ubico (1931–44), introduced a bureaucratic innovation requiring each worker to carry a booklet ("libreta") in which his boss would record work obligations and debt. Elites also enforced debt slavery through a law requiring all people seeking employment to present a letter of recommendation from a former employer explicitly stating that the worker had no outstanding debts.[8] If a landowner was discovered to have not asked for this letter, he could be fined (Cambranes 1985).

Often compared to Porfirio Díaz of Mexico, President Ubico was a modernizer aligned with both the military and the plantation elite. The godson of Justo

Rufino Barrios, Ubico aimed to integrate the indigenous population into the national economy and shift control of indigenous labor from plantation owners to the state (Grieb 1979). In this sense, his leadership was critical to Guatemala's transition from nineteenth-century Liberalism to modern bureaucratic state formation. Infamous as a micromanager, Ubico made legendary "inspection" trips into the interior to settle work and land disputes. He became the first Guatemalan president to travel to Petén, on an aerial inspection visit to assess potential highway routes (ibid.). His forays into Q'eqchi' territory have become so mythologized that many people believe he was a Q'eqchi' orphan (A. E. Adams 2001).

These new methods of state record-keeping also led to great abuses by landowners who could write whatever they wanted in the booklets of their largely illiterate employees. "An employer thus could keep a laborer on indefinitely by neglecting to balance his accounts or by refusing him a 'licencia' (ticket of leave)" (McCreery 1983: 746). If a worker's debt became too large, a landowner could force a contractual change from day laborer to permanent worker-serf. Particularly loathed were the labor contractors ("tratistas") who indebted the indigenous population with store loans or credit and then tricked them into signing work contracts that could be auctioned off to the highest-bidding planter (ibid.). Another labor agent, the facilitator ("habilitador"), coerced villagers into accepting advance wages that bound them to a plantation.

In addition to providing labor for plantations, peasants had to contribute to Ubico's zealous road-building program, designed to integrate Guatemala's hinterlands into the national economy. Intensifying policies established by previous Liberal regimes, Ubico sponsored a 1933 road law requiring every adult male between age eighteen and sixty-five to contribute unpaid road labor and provide his own food for two weeks every year (Schmolz-Haberlein 1996). Governing Guatemala during the Depression and renowned for his thrift and dislike of corruption, Ubico sought the least expensive but most labor-intensive construction designs—building, for example, bridges out of wood rather than steel or concrete. Many road projects were built and inaugurated and then repaired and re-inaugurated several times over (Grieb 1979), all with free indigenous labor.

If not for fear of peasant rebellions, Guatemala's elites might have forced the "lazy" indigenous people to work year-round, as suggested by this quote from a German planter: "Conditions still prevail which permit the Indian to meet all his needs and those of his family after no more than 60 days of easy work and it will be necessary to pressure them to work on the plantations a part of the remaining 300 days of the year. . . . The truth is, that if it were entirely up to the Indians, they would not work at all" (Cambranes 1985: 203–4). Lest indigenous people decide to work independently, the planters wanted to limit their educational opportunities, as stated by Erwin Dieseldorff, Verapaz's largest coffee baron: "We've learned from experience that the Indians who have learned to read and write are no longer useful as agricultural workers" (Grandin 2004: 36). A fellow coffee planter emphasized that the wealth of Alta Verapaz was not in the "soil but the low wages of our laborers" (ibid.: 38). The state even worked to prevent Q'eqchi' autonomy by regulating the size of milpas; for example, J. Eric Thompson (1930: 41) mentions a law enforced in Cahabón that prohibited the planting of cornfields larger than 2.8 hectares. Landowner labor requirements took priority over Q'eqchi' food security. As German planter Richard Sapper suggested, Q'eqchi' worker-serfs could attend to their own milpas, but only "in return for working on the plantation [one to two] weeks a month" (Cambranes 1985: 235–36).

Liberals argued that coercive labor was necessary for the development of agriculture and "progress" itself. In a fascinating letter to the minister of the interior in 1879, the Izabal political chief justified sending Q'eqchi' peasants a long distance to work on coffee plantations, writing: "It is true, Your Excellency, that, in support of agriculture and commerce, the general population of these villages are being forced to work, but without these efforts, agriculture and commerce, the source of wealth in this Republic, would suffer and this would produce unemployment which would be detrimental to the interests of the private sector and the public treasury" (Cambranes 1985: 187). In a similar vein, Erwin Dieseldorff remarked in 1889, "These lands were earlier inactive and paralyzed, and to thousands of families who not so long ago were decimated by abandonment and misery there are the valuable *fincas* which in the name of progress suddenly sprouted in what once were but barren deserts of Alta Verapaz" (ibid.: 306).

Seeing themselves as agents of progress, Liberals were often surprised by Q'eqchi' resistance to foreign investment, land dispossession, and labor requirements. Melchior (Jorge) Yat led a major Q'eqchi' revolt in 1864 against commercial coffee production (de la Cruz Torres 1982). Three more revolts followed, in 1879, 1885 and 1906. Around 1900, a shaman-prophet figure started a nativistic movement near Chamelco. Many nameless others resisted by setting fire to plantations, killing cattle, writing petitions, signing multiple contracts with different plantations, complaining to local offices, even murdering foremen and planters (Cambranes 1985). Throughout the 1930s and 1940s, a

Q'eqchi' political leader, José Angel Icó, traveled widely—as far north as San Luis, Petén—to organize villagers against forced labor practices (Grandin 2004). Finally, perhaps the most common method of Q'eqchi' resistance was migration north, east, and west into the Maya lowlands, where they could continue subsistence agriculture, competing with state-led plans to incorporate these hinterlands into the national economy.

THIRD ENCLOSURE: CONQUEST BY COLONIZATION

By the early 1940s, the Ubico dictatorship had grossly overextended its power, and a group of military and academic dissidents organized to overthrow him in the 1944 October Revolution. Almost a decade of political freedom, with municipal elections, more open media, and allowances for union organizing followed. Also known as Guatemala's "ten years of spring," this period was led by two democratically elected presidents, Dr. Juan Jose Arévalo (1945–51) and Colonel Jacobo Arbenz (1951–54). While the academic and military dissidents who overthrew the Ubico dictatorship despised his political despotism, they nonetheless continued to pursue his aim of integrating the northern territories into national transportation networks.

In this new democratic context, the 1950 agricultural census documented in undeniable statistics the country's shockingly inequitable land distribution: just 2 percent of the population controlled at least 72 percent of Guatemala's arable land (Handy 1988), 75 percent of which lay idle (Manger-Cats 1966: 236). Put another way, less than two dozen of Guatemala's richest estate owners controlled more land than the poorest 249,169 small landholders combined (Brockett 1998). Indigenous farmers averaged less than 3.2 hectares each, while the median for Ladinos was 24.6 hectares (Handy 1988: 707).

Although the new 1945 constitution prohibited excessively large landholdings ("latifundios"), Guatemala's land reform process began slowly (Brockett 1998). Among his preliminary reforms, President Arévalo began awarding titles to people who had worked their land at least ten years, required landowners to rent land to the poor, limited sharecropping fees to just 5 percent of the production value, and revoked vagrancy laws. He also established an ambitious colonization experiment in 1945 for Poctún (now Poptún), a tiny village in Petén's most temperate region, populated then by a handful of Q'eqchi' and Petenero families. Here, Arévalo wanted to establish Guatemala's first National Agrarian Colony, to be named after the mythic Tecún Umán. Calling them "soldiers of the reconquest," he sent more than four hundred workers, military officials, doctors, and engineers to design a modern city with commercial, industrial, sports, and residential zones. The goals of the colony were to expand the scenic landscape of the country; diversify its crops; provide parcels to landless farmers, thereby reducing congestion in the tired and overpopulated regions of the southern and eastern regions of Guatemala; and recover and defend Guatemalan territory from neighboring countries (Brockett 1998; Manger-Cats 1966; Municipio de Poptún n.d.; Presidencia de la República 1950: 17). Although the Poptún experiment was abandoned under the subsequent Arbenz administration, leaving only a military base, Arévalo sparked the national imagination with the idea of state-led colonization as a method of land reform. Many historians tend to divide Guatemala's twentieth-century history into pre- and post-coup periods in order to emphasize U.S. intervention, but there was a continuity of ideas about modernization and development across these political shifts.

Building on Arévalo's nascent reforms, President Jacobo Arbenz made agrarian transformation a national priority soon after he assumed office in 1951. His Agrarian Reform Law (Decree 900, approved by Congress on June 17, 1952) abolished debt servitude and allowed the government to expropriate and redistribute land from three sources: (1) idle land on the largest plantations (explicitly exempting those with less than 90 hectares), (2) unclaimed national lands ("baldíos"), and (3) German estates seized after World War II and declared "national plantations." Over eighteen months (January 1953–June 1954), working through decentralized local committees, Arbenz's administration gathered an astounding 884,000 hectares for redistribution—equivalent to about 17 percent of privately owned land in Guatemala (Brockett 1998). Arbenz even expropriated 1,700 acres from himself (Oliver 2004)! To the dismay of many elites who perpetually underreported the worth of their landholdings, the expropriations were compensated at the owner's last self-declared property value for tax assessment (Handy 1988). About a third of total expropriated land came from areas settled by Q'eqchi' people, who represented only 10 percent of the national population at that time (Manger-Cats 1966).

With striking fairness and efficiency, the state distributed parcels ranging in size from 3.5 to 17.5 hectares per family to one-fifth of the landless population (Brockett 1998). One-third of the estimated 100,000 beneficiaries of the Arbenz reform were former plantation employees, many of whom were Q'eqchi' worker-serfs from Verapaz coffee plantations. In less than two years and without expansion into frontier lands, the Arbenz administration distributed more land (750,000 hectares) than subsequent military regimes would through two decades of colonization programs (only 538,917 hectares between 1954 and 1974) (figures compiled from Brockett 1998, Manger-Cats 1966, McPherson 1996, and IDS 1961). Arbenz's land reforms showed that, given sufficient political will, the land system could be rapidly reorganized, even without the benefits of sophisticated Global Positioning System (GPS) technology and computer databases. Beyond the actual land distributed, the 1952–54 land reform, in the words of Arbenz himself, brought "an earthquake in the consciousness" of Guatemalans about their agrarian rights (Handy 1988: 709).

Unfortunately, Arbenz provoked Cold War controversy when he attempted to expropriate still-idle lands awarded back in 1894 to the United Fruit Company. As with other expropriations, the Guatemalan government offered to compensate United Fruit with government bonds at the company's self-declared tax value of $1.2 million. When the Guatemalan government refused United Fruit's demand for $16.5 million (Brockett 1998: 103), the company began a campaign painting Arbenz as a backdoor Communist threat to the United States. Not incidentally, U.S. secretary of state John Foster Dulles and CIA director Allen Dulles, John's brother, both had large investments in firms with a stake in United Fruit; U.S. president Dwight D. Eisenhower's personal secretary happened to be married to United Fruit's press director; and the U.S. ambassador to the United Nations at that time owned United Fruit stock (Schlesinger and Kinzer 1982; Grandin 2004). In August 1953, President Eisenhower authorized the CIA to overthrow President Arbenz in an operation named PBSUCCESS (Schlesinger and Kinzer 1982; Grandin 2004).

After Arbenz stepped down on July 27, 1954, the CIA propped up the coup's leader, Colonel Carlos Castillo Armas, trained by the U.S. military at Fort Leavenworth, Kansas (Grandin 2004), the first in a long line of puppet dictators friendly to U.S. interests. Within a month of the coup, the military junta began reversing Arbenz's agrarian reforms by returning expropriated land to former owners and demanding payment from peasants who had received credit from the Arbenz administration. It squelched resistance by jailing more than five thousand peasant organizers and killing at least two hundred leaders (Brockett 1998), many of whom had been identified from a list of some seventy thousand Guatemalans considered "subversive" by the CIA. Next, the junta reestablished the plantation peonage system by allowing landowners to provide workers with sharecropping plots, instead of wages (Manger-Cats 1966). Within a year and a half, 99.6 percent of Arbenz's peasant beneficiaries had either fled their holdings or been "reconditioned" (to use the government's word) as plantation workers. These policies deeply affected the Q'eqchi', who had disproportionately benefited from Arbenz's land reforms. Several elders whom I interviewed in Izabal and Petén vividly remembered the swift counterreform.

With the aid of U.S. advisers (International Development Services, Inc.), the military-led government launched a new land policy (Decree 559) in 1956 that emphasized the comparative advantage of private landownership.[9] In contrast to Arbenz's redistributive strategy, the new law effectively revoked taxes on idle land by basing them on a landowner's testimony of soil quality. U.S. advisers also encouraged the Guatemalan government to look toward northern colonization as a safety valve for continued agrarian pressure and also as a way of bolstering the export economy via cattle and timber. In many ways, these plans simply extended the modernization aspirations of previous administrations, but with U.S. support, colonization took on an authoritarian tenor in the context of the Guatemalan civil war. CIA opinion was that Guatemala was not "ready" for a democracy and, instead, should be ruled by a modestly dictatorial regime friendly to U.S. military and business interests, even if this ultimately required complicity with genocide. U.S. advisers developed a kind of mini–Marshall Plan (Vargas 1984), with much of this foreign aid directed to colonization of the northern lowlands as a means of reversing the tremendously effective agrarian-reform process of the early 1950s.[10]

In colonization plans for the region, U.S. advisers were also fairly explicit about the importance of creating a rural labor force to assist with extractive activities (timber, oil, minerals) and possible industrial development along the Northern Franja Transversal (Franja Transversal del Norte), both of which would save them from "primitive, subsistence-type farming," as one 1968 CIA memo put it (George Washington University, National Security Archive, 00370). Following U.S. advice, the military-led Guatemalan government launched two ambitious colonization projects in the late 1950s: the National Institute of Agrarian Transformation (Instituto para la Transformación Agraria), or INTA, and the Company for the Promotion and Development of the Petén (La Empresa para el Fomento y Desarrollo de El Petén), or FYDEP, a state company. Meant to reduce the threat of peasant protest, they resembled other colonization programs across Latin America (J. R. Jones 1989) run through expensive and paternalistic bureaucracies,[11] as described below.

INTA, the National Institute of Agrarian Transformation

Through INTA, the Guatemalan government first promoted colonization of the southern Pacific coast for the production of export crops. By the late 1950s, this coastal zone was saturated and land speculation had become rampant. Unable to accommodate a growing influx of landless farmers, INTA looked to the north for new colonization lands rather than addressing these problems on the south coast.[12] The story of Don Rodolfo García illustrates this south-to-north colonization shift. A fifty-two-year-old Ladino owner of a cattle ranch in Fray Bartolomé de las Casas, Don Rodolfo was born in Tiquisate on a homestead his father had purchased from another south coast colonist. By the time Don Rodolfo turned twenty, the economy of the south coast had changed and, as he said, "There was little work there. It was all industrial plantations; they didn't need [to employ] people." Because his father sold the family's parcel to a sugar company, Don Rodolfo's family became one of the first forty families (mostly Q'eqchi' but with a smattering of Ladinos like him) to settle in a village located in the middle of INTA's first northern colonization zone, the Northern Franja Transversal, a belt stretching 8,500 square kilometers from Huehuetenango to the Caribbean (fig. 1.2).

For colonization purposes, INTA divided the Franja Transversal into five regions from west to east: Ixcán, Lachua, Sebol, Livingston, and Modesto Mendez (Gobierno de Guatemala 1964). These were all connected by a highway initiated in the 1970s, parallel to a 235-kilometer oil pipeline constructed by Basic Resources. In practice, INTA focused most of its attention on the central section of Sebol (Grandia 2006) and then expanded into the Ixcán in the 1970s and 1980s. Military officers staked such extensive land claims (typically around oil wells, along roads, and in zones of guerrilla combat) that the Franja Transversal came to be known as "the Generals' Strip." General Romeo Lucas García, the Guatemalan dictator (1978–82) responsible for most of the massacres of Maya communities during the civil war, owned an estimated eighty thousand hectares, almost one-fifth of the private land in the Sebol and Lachua sectors (Falla 1980; Solano 2000; Grandia 2006).[13]

Landless settlers were also eligible to apply for individual plots amid the large ranches claimed by military officers and other elites. In regions where the land was difficult to measure or held by preexisting Q'eqchi' communities, INTA sometimes awarded the land with common title, either as a collective agrarian patrimony or as a cooperative agrarian community enterprise. Constant—and perhaps purposeful—changes to land titling programs exacerbated INTA's bureaucratic disarray and Q'eqchi' vulnerability to corrupt state agents. Discrepancies between INTA records and peasants' accounts of what they paid for the land were routine. Disreputable INTA workers gave colonists fabricated provisional receipts and then pocketed the payments. Reflecting on

FIGURE 1.2. The Northern Franja Transversal plus Petén colonization zones.
David Eitelberg, 2011

that period, Felipe Canté, a colonist in Ixcán, remarked, "I don't know, perhaps it was the policy of the government to leave us without documents, without titles, so they could take the land away from us later on" (Manz 2004: 73). According to INTA's own records, its agents managed to emit provisional titles ("escrituras") for less than 15 percent of the land allotments assigned between 1959 and 1982.

While some small landholders benefited from INTA's colonization program, the slow titling process discouraged many, who then sold their claims via the informal economy. Others found their parcels too small (nine hectares on average) to subdivide for their children, and many moved farther north into Petén. While INTA had granted parcels to 4,887 families by 1962, the number of landless agrarian families grew to 140,000 in that same time period (Brockett 1998). In order to meet the demand for land, the Guatemalan government looked north, intending to colonize the vast forests of Petén through a new government agency, FYDEP, whose directors unabashedly aimed to grant land for agribusiness, cattle ranching, and timber management.

FYDEP, the Company for the Promotion and Development of the Petén

Petén has long been treated as another world in Guatemala—a mysterious land filled with beauty, danger, and hardships. Because of its size (larger than the country of El Salvador) and remoteness, many policy makers have advocated that Petén ought to have its own special programs for colonization, health care, environmental protection, land legalization, and social science research. Even Arbenz's land reform program did not attempt to touch Petén. Aiming to integrate Petén into national life, FYDEP portrayed the department as a "sleeping giant" that needed to be awakened carefully (Rodríguez de Lemus 1967; Casasola 1968).

Of the 2,200 properties allotted in Petén prior to 1950, only 56 were officially purchased and registered; the rest was held in usufruct or shared as communal forests (Manger-Cats 1966; Schwartz 1990). With the creation of FYDEP in 1959, the state divided Petén's untitled territory into two categories, roughly equal in size, for agriculture and forest reserves. The 1,530,017 hectares for agriculture were registered as two giant plantations (nos. 253 and 292), to be subdivided through colonization projects. The forest reserve established in the northern third of Petén allowed for new commercial timber concessions and continued extraction of non-timber forest products such as chicle, "xate" palm leaves, and allspice from permanent forest camps like Macawville (see pp. 52–53).

MACAWVILLE, "ALONGSIDE THE SCARLET MACAWS" (*CHIMO'*)

Alligators breed less than a kilometer downriver, adding a thrill to this anthropologist's morning ablutions in the natural springs bubbling up around the village. Flocks of endangered scarlet macaws fly regularly overhead, and howler monkeys awaken villagers every morning. Situated on the corner of a natural park, Macawville seems very much a wild place, but if one looks more closely, the remnants of previous epochs reveal a different history—of repeated dispossessions, relocations, and reconstructions.

Cycles of booms and busts began in Macawville more than a millennium ago. Located a few miles from the village center, the archaeological site Waka' (El Peru) was once a critical trading site aligned with Tikal at the center of lowland Maya power. After Waka' betrayed this alliance through a royal marriage with the rulers of Calakmul to the north, it fell into rapid decline.

Swallowed by the forests for nearly a thousand years, this area rose to prominence again as the base for a logging camp in the late nineteenth century, during the Liberal period, for the export of mahogany and Spanish cedar down the San Pedro River. By the 1920s, it had become a camp for harvesting "xate" (a palm frond) for export and chicle (a resin purchased by Wrigley for making chewing gum) from the *Manilkara zapota* tree. With an airstrip suitable for DC-3 planes, Macawville became a boomtown as large as Petén's central area at that time (Fagan 2000; field notes). Around

1978, the military cleared the camp as part of a counterinsurgency campaign to remove potential sympathizers who might aid guerrilla forces operating in the area. Were it not for the remains of a concrete tank left from a failed water-bottling scheme, the relentless regrowth of the forest might have obscured the depopulated village's vibrant economic history.

Macawville was completely uninhabited until the early 1990s, when it began to receive a trickle of Q'eqchi' migrants that became a steady stream after the 1996 Peace Accords. Most had escaped brutal labor conditions on coffee plantations, and all were in search of land. At least one family had been involved with the guerrillas, and many others had fled massacres during Guatemala's civil war. Unbeknownst to them, the area had been declared part of Laguna del Tigre National Park in 1992. By the late 1990s, the national park service began to establish a presence in the region, and ProPetén built the aforementioned biological station a few miles down the river from Macawville. I first traveled to Macawville in 1997 to establish a training program for midwives and health care promoters (fig. 1.3) as a member of a multidisciplinary team whose aim was to help the community write a land management plan and develop more sustainable alternatives to extensive corn cultivation for sale to urban markets (fig. 1.4)

By 2002, when I returned to Macawville as an anthropologist, the village had 112 households officially registered with the government, all but one of which were Q'eqchi'. Alongside the treacherous Sacluc swamp, a new road, inaugurated in 2000, had shortened travel to town from ten hours to three, but other village infrastructure remained rudimentary.

FIGURE 1.3. Macawville health post, 1998. Photograph: Liza Grandia

FIGURE 1.4. Macawville corn harvest, 2002. Photograph: Liza Grandia

Both a dependency of the presidency and administratively tied to the military (from 1966 to 1970), FYDEP was a peculiar bureaucracy that functioned like a "state within a state" (Schwartz 1990: 252). Its broad mandate ranged from archaeological conservation to land adjudication to general economic development of the region. In practice, this meant that FYDEP built infrastructure; promoted investments; controlled, taxed, and marketed forest products; and zoned land resources. By generating 50–75 percent of its budget from taxes on timber and non-timber forest extraction, land payments, and tourism fees, FYDEP held a substantial degree of financial autonomy (ibid.). Unlike the leaders of many government agencies who left with each election, the FYDEP director outlasted many presidential administrations.

Colonel Oliverio Casasola, who became FYDEP's third director in 1962 (Rodriguez de Lemus 1967), was a charismatic, albeit controversial, figure in Petén's settlement. Casasola's writings demonstrate familiarity with other colonization experiences in Italy, Brazil, and Bolivia and even with anthropologist Oscar Lewis's *Life in a Mexican Village*. Albeit conscious of the peasants' desperate need for agricultural land in Guatemala, he made clear in his book *The Grandeur and Miseries of Petén* (Grandezas y Miserias de Petén) that the landless poor were not welcome in this department, writing: "Petén is Guatemala's great business potential and not a political or social adventure. To believe that this should be a place of agrarian reform is a national crime. We have nothing to reform here, nothing to redo, but everything to make, everything to form" (Casasola 1968: 61). Worried that "paralyzing poverty" would overrun Petén's rich natural resources, he feared the "human storm to Petén" would "contaminate an organism that must remain healthy" and, in turn, "infect the health of the rest of the country" (ibid.: 44, 47).

Although formally mandated to promote small-farmer settlement, FYDEP remained institutionally uninterested in the work of agrarian colonization. Casasola wanted skilled and capitalized businessmen to develop Petén, not landless peasants. Not until the mid-1960s did FYDEP reluctantly accept a congressional order (Decree 354) to establish a department of colonization and organize peasant cooperatives along the border with Mexico. The idea was to create a "human defensive barrier" (Millet 1974: 51) against a planned Mexican hydroelectric dam that would flood vast portions of Guatemala's side of the Usumacinta watershed (an idea that resurfaced four decades later in the PPP).

As more colonists poured into Petén with the inauguration of an all-weather dirt road in 1970, FYDEP continued to discriminate against poor settlers. Beginning in the 1960s, FYDEP awarded logging concessions in

50,000-hectare blocks (Fagan 2000). Colonization guidelines initially allowed cattle ranchers to claim up to 675 hectares each, a figure later reduced to 225 hectares—that is, the same size parcel awarded to foreign investors by the Barrios administration in the 1870s (Manger-Cats 1966). Local and national elites often registered land in the names of different kin (wives, daughters, etc.), allowing them to combine parcels and build estates that exceeded the legal limit (Schwartz 1987, 1995, 2001). Landless peasants, by contrast, were limited to parcels of 23–90 hectares. Though the cost of land was the same for both, it was more difficult for small farmers to gain title because the prices for agricultural land and the associated survey costs were disproportionately more expensive for them (Schwartz 1987). In the end, metropolitan and local elites and military officers benefited disproportionately from the colonization process (Schwartz 1990)—in terms of both land acquisition and associated investments in tourism and commerce.

AGAIN?

While both colonization agencies focused on the regions where landless Q'eqchi' had been settling since the late nineteenth century, neither welcomed indigenous colonists into their programs. INTA aspired to recruit acculturated and Spanish-speaking colonists who could integrate "into a national Guatemalan cultural identity." Leading FYDEP's explicit condemnation of Q'eqchi' settlement, Casasola (1968: 45) did not mince words in blaming Petén's growing illiteracy rates on "Q'eqchi' migrations to the municipality of San Luis caused by the economic and agricultural failure in Alta Verapaz, colonization without roads, reckless fires, erosion, and land exhaustion." Well into the 1980s, the legacy of his opposition to Q'eqchi' settlement was evident in FYDEP: "The presence of these peasants is damaging Petén's vegetation because their system consists in advancing and advancing as they go burning forests to convert land for agricultural production. Because the productivity of these soils is limited, the deforestation logically advances in gigantic proportions" (FYDEP report, quoted in Góngora Zetina 1984: 113–14). FYDEP's recurrent criticism of Q'eqchi' milpa production also implicitly condemned traditional Petenero agriculture, which had operated for centuries on similar land-use principles.

Yet, Q'eqchi' settlers tenaciously continued migrating into the lowlands and claiming as much land as they could. The most recent census puts Petén's indigenous population (virtually all of whom would be Q'eqchi') at 31 percent; the actual percentage is likely higher because the Guatemalan census consistently undercounts indigenous peoples. Overcoming language barriers, Q'eqchi' settlers steadily pressed land claims with the colonization programs. A common practice for monolingual communities was to hire a bilingual Q'eqchi' leader who could negotiate with government agencies. When formal claims failed, they developed their own system of real estate valuation and documentation in order to purchase use rights or the estimated value of land improvements from other settlers. In this way, thousands of Q'eqchi' pioneers managed to acquire parcels. One-fifth of indigenous migrants to Petén even won title to the coveted "caballería" (45 hectares), sufficient land to give them a chance at becoming middle-class farmers (Grandia et al. 2001; Schwartz 2001). News of their success, in turn, served to intensify and accelerate the migration of thousands more Q'eqchi' families into this lowland region, but their fates were not so lucky.

Though some Q'eqchi' settlers did manage to establish better lives for themselves on the frontier, many commentators foresaw this process as "a second conquest" (Schwartz 1990; Peckenham 1980; Góngora Zetina 1984) because the colonization plans were so clearly designed to benefit elites. As states pull frontier commons into their national economies, they undermine the subsistence and natural economies that originally made these lowland regions attractive to landless peasants. In other words, because frontier development strategies are designed to operate within the existing socioeconomic structures of the nation-state, they tend not to foment agrarian justice but to replicate the very same land inequalities that led peasants to migrate in the first place (see also Schwartz 1987; Peckenham 1980; R. N. Adams 1965).

Certainly, both INTA and FYDEP were driven by an economic system focused on growth of the gross domestic product. Inspired by Mexico's oil bonanza and fueled by the petroleum embargoes and the world energy crises of the 1970s, the Guatemalan government awarded exploration contracts across Petén and the Franja Transversal to a long series of U.S. and other foreign oil companies; in 1975 alone, more than fifty oil companies solicited concessions (Falla 1980). Colonization planners similarly welcomed national and foreign logging interests in Petén and nickel mining operations in the eastern Franja. Even though soil studies repeatedly showed that little land in the northern lowlands was suitable for agriculture, project planners were determined to dedicate the best lands available to cattle with an eye to boosting beef exports. Although program evaluators knew as far back as 1971 that colonization grants for cattle ranching were often awarded to absentee landlords, no major changes were ever made (Millet 1974).

Like that of their colonial and Liberal predecessors, the vision of colonization planners was economistic (increasing income), urban-centric (developing towns and diversifying the workforce), integrationist (connecting hinterlands to the national economy and, in turn, connecting Guatemala to the rest of the world through exports produced in colonization zones), obsessed with roads and infrastructure (for facilitating investment), and, above all, determined to privatize indigenous lands and other natural resources—themes that all reappear in the neoliberal period today. In other words, globalization is nothing new to the Q'eqchi'. Since the Spanish conquest, they have had to contend with many different kinds of national and foreign intervention in their lives. What has gradually changed for Q'eqchi' people over the past five hundred years is the scale of national integration and the degree to which international forces impinge upon everyday life, as reflected in table 2 (see p. 31).

As far back as 1549, the king of Spain ordered the colonial tribunals to prohibit Spanish settlers from pressuring the natives to sell their land and to return "to the Indians that land which they had taken from them in exchange for a shirt or an arroba of wine" (Cambranes 1985: 50). The legacy of such usurpations lives on, however. Four and a half centuries later at the Alta Verapaz land negotiation table, I witnessed a community lose its land to a descendant of a German coffee planter who had tricked a drunken Q'eqchi' leader into signing over the village land in exchange for a bottle of wine.

From the colonial period through Liberal rule, modernization, development, and colonization, outsiders have repeatedly used religion, military power, economics, law, bureaucracy, and state planning to claim both Q'eqchi' land *and* labor. Over and over again, the Q'eqchi' have suffered enclosure of their common lands. With a migration outlet to the north, however, the Q'eqchi' people could escape deeper and deeper into the northern forests after each historical epoch of dispossession—that is, until foreign environmental interests made human settlement illegal in these forests by protecting them as national parks. The forests themselves became the next mechanism of Q'eqchi' enclosure, as their penchant for migration and swidden agriculture brought them into conflict with biodiversity conservationists.

2

Maya Gringos

Q'EQCHI' LOWLAND MIGRATION
AND TERRITORIAL EXPANSION

ISCUSSING Q'eqchi' migration, another anthropologist once remarked to me, "Oh, I like the Q'eqchi'. They are like the gringos of the Maya world!" Some say that anthropologists unconsciously gravitate toward studying people in whom they see reflections of their own cultures and personalities. Like gringos, the Q'eqchi' exude pragmatic confidence about their territorial expansion. Traveling to distant, even foreign lands, "the enigmatic Q'eqchi', in one sense, are quite 'worldly'" (Collins 2001: 327), yet many other outsiders (as well as other Maya groups) regard the Q'eqchi' as conservative, backward, even reactionary.[1] The Q'eqchi', in turn, consider all non-Q'eqchi'-speaking outsiders—whether they be Ladinos or gringos—as *aj kastiil* (Spanish speaker) or *kaxlan winq* (literally, "chicken men," probably originating from the Spanish introduction of domesticated fowl).

Despite nearly five centuries of spiritual, political, and economic domination, Q'eqchi' people have managed to expand their territory to approximately 2.5 million hectares (Secaira 2000), an estimated fourfold to fivefold increase that is quite astonishing in comparison to the territorial losses of most other indigenous peoples across the Americas since the colonial period. This chapter explores the reasons for the remarkable cultural resilience of Q'eqchi' people in establishing a diaspora unparalleled in the Maya world.[2]

HISTORICAL MIGRATION PATTERNS

Aside from scattered reports from the Spanish, little is known about Q'eqchi' migration patterns in the colonial period except that Q'eqchi' people regularly faded into the northern forests to escape taxes, tribute, and forced labor.

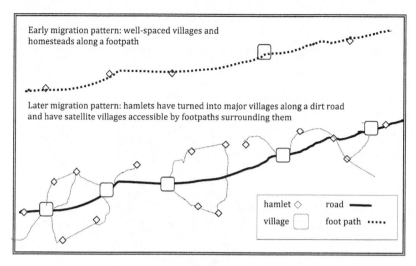

FIGURE 2.1. Leap-frog migration pattern

Q'eqchi' lowland migration re-intensified from the end of the nineteenth century onward in response to major agrarian crises in highland Alta Verapaz. Following a kind of leapfrog pattern, the first wave of migration produced sparse lines of settlement stretching hundreds of kilometers from Cobán (see Sapper 1985). Then, over a certain number of years, the migration stream thickened and took on a life of its own—what migration scholars call "cumulative causation" (Massey 1990). Through natural demographic momentum, hamlets grew into villages or towns, from which satellite settlements began to branch off (fig 2.1).[3]

As seen in figure 2.2, Q'eqchi' lowland migration began mostly in a northeasterly direction. Since the nineteenth century, there have been three notable surges pushing Q'eqchi' settlers deeper into the forests. Following the coffee boom, Q'eqchi' people ventured as far as San Luis, Petén, and out to the Atlantic coast of Belize. During the Ubico dictatorship, Q'eqchi' migrants made more substantial forays into Petén and Belize. During and after the Guatemalan civil war, Q'eqchi' migrants fanned out to the northwest toward Ixcán and also northwestern Petén.

Coffee

Although Q'eqchi' people had likely fled into the lowlands after the Spanish conquest in the sixteenth century, the first incident of more contempo-

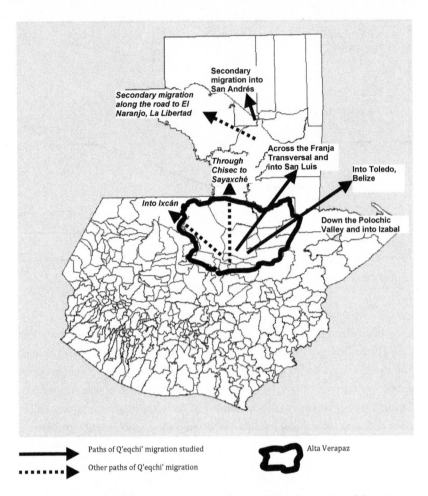

FIGURE 2.2. Q'eqchi' migration streams. Source: Macro International, Inc., in collaboration with L. Grandia (from survey data, 2001)

rary Q'eqchi' lowland migration documented in the academic literature was a movement to Senahú in response to the first Liberal reforms of the 1830s (Reep 1997). A new wave of eastward migration followed in the 1860s, in response to the first generation of coffee investors. With the return of Liberal rule in the 1870s, Q'eqchi' migration quickened. In 1879, the Guatemalan government's political chief in Izabal reported that peasant families were "roaming through the mountains headed to the north of the lagoon in that department [Izabal] because of hardships imposed by the authorities" (Cambranes 1985: 187). An 1880 government report stated that many highland Q'eqchi' villages were unable to continue planting because of "lack of manpower" due to the "huge wave of Indian migration to the Department of Izabal" (ibid.: 188).

These first lowland Q'eqchi' migrants were primarily political and economic refugees—fleeing the hardships of life as plantation worker-serfs under foreign coffee investors who had usurped Q'eqchi' lands with the blessings of the Guatemalan government. Waves of Q'eqchi' migrants then passed through the Polochic Valley like "migratory birds," staying a period and then moving eastward into Izabal or north toward San Luis, Petén, and beyond (de la Cruz Torres 1982: 52; Pedroni 1991). By 1921, the census showed a considerable number of villages in lowland municipalities, but with decreasing population density according to their distance from the highland Q'eqchi' heartland of Cobán.[4]

Beyond this stepwise settlement, some Q'eqchi' migrants continued as far as Toledo, Belize. One group joined the organized return to Belize in 1886 of a Mopán community whose ancestors the Spanish had forcibly relocated to Petén in 1697. A prominent German coffee planter, Bernard Kramer, brought other Q'eqchi' families to his plantation in southwestern Toledo shortly thereafter. In 1892, the political chief of Alta Verapaz also mentioned that after foreign coffee planters seized more than 200,000 hectares of land, "a large number of families [had] gone to live in Punta Gorda in the Colony of Belize" (Cambranes 1985: 198–99). Subsequent Q'eqchi' migration to Belize has been a slow seepage of families across the border, punctuated by peaks that correspond with political and economic repression in Guatemala.

Roads

After the late nineteenth-century coffee exodus, the second major wave of Q'eqchi' migration occurred in the 1930s and 1940s in response to Ubico's new vagrancy legislation and corvée labor brigades that every male citizen had to join for two weeks a year, contributing free labor for public works, or pay a fee. Plantations or villages that would benefit from nearby road projects had to provide free labor indefinitely—a practice perpetuated in the present day by NGOs and government donors that require voluntary community labor as "participation" or "matching contributions." For large road projects, the state reported hiring about half its labor at the official rate of twenty-five to fifty cents a day (Grieb 1979). Q'eqchi' workers, however, may have been chronically underpaid, as several of my informants remembered wages of only three to five cents a day; Don Francisco Cac recalled that not until the democratic Arévalo administration did they receive fifty cents a day. Because many of the road projects aimed to integrate Alta Verapaz and then Petén into the national economy, Q'eqchi' people probably bore a disproportionate burden of roadwork. Several elders I met described Ubico's roadwork as the cause of their flight into the lowlands. Shamans and healers fleeing to Belize to escape being persecuted as "witches" by Ubico made up another subset of the northward waves of Q'eqchi' migration during this period.

Though officially outlawed after the October Revolution in 1944, there are reports of Q'eqchi' communities being tricked into providing labor for the state as late as the 1980s. Don Miguel Pop, a farmer now living in Macawville, recalled how his father had been forced into helping to build the road from Fray Bartolomé de las Casas to Chahal with nothing but axes and stones for tools. Years later, Don Miguel found himself in a similar predicament. As late as the 1970s, municipal workers in Chahal forced him and his neighbors to provide one week of hard labor a month building roads for the municipality as well as doing personal work for Ladino municipal employees, such as repairing their homes or planting fields. When someone eventually informed them that their village actually belonged to another municipality and these work brigades were illegal, he and other village leaders went to the town hall to investigate. Along the way, they somehow got thrown in jail but were able to escape into the mountains when they were temporarily released to buy their own provisions for prison. They regrouped and returned to town, where an INTA colonization worker encouraged them to take their case to the departmental governor in the city of Puerto Barrios, more than a day's journey by foot. Luckily, after their long journey, the governor resolved their complaint and the Chahal municipality never bothered them again.

Also beginning during the Ubico period, some Q'eqchi' men traveled deep into Petén as specialized laborers to work in chicle or "xate" harvesting camps, such as Macawville (discussed in ch. 1), and later as workers for petroleum companies. Others were brought up by large landowners in short-term labor brigades for clearing forest for cattle or agriculture. These Q'eqchi' men either married in Petén to women of other ethnicities or subsequently brought their families to join them permanently. When working in Ladino settings, like chicle camps, individual Q'eqchi' men tried to assimilate, but as more Q'eqchi' moved into the region, many abandoned their jobs as forest harvesters and rejoined Q'eqchi' agricultural communities. Quite a few families descended from Q'eqchi' chicle tappers still live in towns like San Andrés and have maintained distinctly Q'eqchi' surnames, but their children speak only Spanish and consider themselves Ladinos (see also R. N. Adams 1965; J. R. Jones 1990).

Civil war

The third peak in lowland Q'eqchi' migration occurred from the late 1960s to the 1980s in response to the Guatemalan civil war (fig. 2.3). A long line of military dictators, distinguished only by their increasing brutality toward Guatemala's indigenous and poor, followed the 1954 CIA-sponsored overthrow of President Arbenz. In 1960, a group of junior military officers led an unsuccessful coup that evolved into an armed guerrilla uprising across the country. Nearly four decades of civil war in a country of just 13 million people left an estimated 150,000 people dead, 50,000 more "disappeared," 200,000 children orphaned, 1 million internally displaced, 50,000 international refugees, and 40,000 widows.

While many Q'eqchi' acquaintances initially told me they had migrated to Petén in search of land, after they knew me better, they began to confide that they had come to escape the killing elsewhere, especially during the early 1980s. Doña Magdalena Choc first said she had followed her siblings to Petén when she was orphaned at age eighteen, but as we continued talking, she revealed that she had fled her home village during Lucas's regime in the late 1970s after

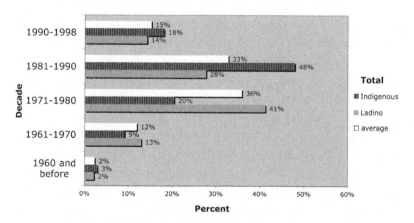

FIGURE 2.3. Decade of arrival by ethnicity. Ladino migration to Petén peaked in the 1970s, but indigenous (mainly Q'eqchi') migration did not peak until the 1980s. In the 1990s, Q'eqchi' people represented the highest percentage of migrants. Source: Grandia et al. 2001

witnessing the military murder her parents. In other instances, allusions to the violence were very subtle. For example, in telling his life story, Don Mariano Baq commented obliquely that his birth village had once been quite large but "one by one they left fleeing and disappearing." I later learned from neighbors that Don Mariano had joined the insurgency as a result of those massacres.

Though not as hard hit as the departments of Quiché and Huehuetenango, which suffered 344 and 88 massacres respectively, Alta Verapaz was the site of 61 massacres, as documented by the United Nations, roughly 10 percent of the national total. Because of the delicacy of talking about the Guatemalan civil war, the numbers of Q'eqchi' who moved because of political violence are likely still undercounted in published research as well as in my field notes and survey data. Since the overwhelming number of migrants came to Petén in search of land, migrants fleeing the war could simply blend in with the rest. Though Petén might seem a "lawless" or "Wild West" frontier to outside observers (e.g., Perera 1993), the anonymity of remote Petén settlements and comparably fewer massacres gave Q'eqchi' refugees a relatively safer place to live.

EXPANDING TERRITORY

The overwhelming reason Q'eqchi' settlers give today for their lowland migration is, like the generations before them, the search for land. My Petén-wide survey showed that 80 percent of indigenous migrants to Petén stated that the search for land was their primary reason for migration; adding those who stated that they came as children with their parents (who were probably also looking for land) brings this figure closer to 90 percent (Grandia et al. 2001). Many of those looking for land were young couples starting their married lives, but Q'eqchi' people of all ages made the move. Sometimes the male head of household or an older son would make a reconnaissance journey to assess the region and identify a destination, return home to discuss the move with the family, and be quizzed by his wife or mother, "Is there water? Is the hunting good? Will the harvest be good?" Indeed, many Q'eqchi' men told me that their wives were the ones who really propelled their families to migrate. While Q'eqchi' women might appear bashful to outsiders who do not speak their language, anyone who speaks a modicum of Q'eqchi' will find they are gregarious, inquisitive, outspoken, and as able as their husbands as pioneers.

Some migrants came specifically because they wanted agricultural land that did not require fertilizers. Several people, in fact, mentioned that they had abandoned exhausted land where only grass would grow. Quite often people mention having received such poor-quality land (too hilly, too rocky, too waterlogged, too sandy, etc.) from the government colonization agencies that they decided to sell it and move north in search of better-quality soils still covered with primary forest. Some went farther north into the forest, hoping to improve their opportunities to fish and hunt in addition to practicing agriculture. Others lost, sold, or simply abandoned land, because of trickery by Ladinos or family quarrels over dividing land after the death of kinfolk.

The Q'eqchi' desire for land stemmed not from some abstract wish for property ownership but, as migrants routinely explained to me, "to find a place to work." As one settler elaborated, "Oh yes, I came here to work. Anyone who comes [here] from somewhere else wants a place to work—to plant his beans, his root crops, his banana trees." No longer willing to accept the exploitation of life as worker-serfs on coffee plantations or sharecroppers on cattle ranches, they emphasized that they wanted to work *for themselves.* Dozens told me stories about exploitation on the fincas—having to work from sunup to sundown for just a few cents a day and barely finding time to plant their own crops. Rape of indigenous women by landowners was common in plantation life. Don Mariano Baq put it to me this way: "The person who can stay there is the one who can endure [hardship]."

As Don Sebastian Cucul recounted: "The life of a poor man is hard if a rich man takes away his land . . . it's because of the rich that we had to come here." Don Sebastian was born on a Verapaz plantation that measured sixty "caballerías" and employed two thousand men. He described the owner as a German "millionaire" who paid them a mere thirty-five cents a day (in the 1950s) and permitted them less than a third of a hectare of land and just one week off a month for planting their own crops. Around 1960, at the age of thirteen, Don Sebastian set off for Petén wearing only the clothes on his back and with barely enough bus fare in his pocket, eventually finding land in the San José "ejido," common lands administered by the municipality. Asked if he ever went back to visit his birthplace, he replied, "What would I do that for? I have nothing, nothing there." Besides, he explained, everyone else had left; he estimated that there were 1,200 or 1,400 families from that plantation who were now "scattered across Petén."

Don Benjamin Coc related a similar story of the hardships of finca life. Born into a worker-serf family on Cubilwitz, a well-known German-owned coffee plantation outside of Cobán, he began working a full day's labor at the age of twelve; the plantation did not provide any schooling. Because his parents could not afford to buy him pants, he wore only a white shift tied around the waist with a cord until he reached puberty, like most Q'eqchi' boys of that generation. He was forced to work for the plantation two weeks out of every month, making fifteen cents a day. His family was so poor that the only shoes he ever had were homemade sandals. When he was cutting chilies one day, he accidentally sliced open his foot with a machete, leaving a three-inch scar that is still clearly visible half a century later. At age twenty, he decided to travel to Petén, "which was famous for making a dime," and became a muleteer in the chicle camps. He eventually settled down as a farmer in Macawville.

Some recounted having migrated because of a conflict with a plantation boss. Don Manuel Coy explained that he accidentally crossed the boundary on the coffee plantation designating his land for sharecropping and the owner wanted to put him in jail. He had heard that land in Petén was free and went to explore. Observing that the land was fertile (*mas q'emal li choch*), he went back, sold everything, and brought his wife with him to a village in San Luis. Others moved simply because they wanted a better life for their children. Indeed, for Don Manuel Aq's father, the exploitation of his children was the last straw that drove him to leave the German-owned coffee plantation where he had grown up. The owner gave them only fifteen days off each season for their own work, so there was never enough time to cultivate their own crops. Worse yet, they were never paid for work on the coffee plantation. Don Manuel Aq's father was a humble man who could not read and write. He endured these oppressive conditions for years, but when the plantation owner tried to put his children, the youngest only ten years old, to work picking up the coffee seeds that fell on the ground, Don Manuel's father decided to take the whole family to Petén.

As they fled plantation labor, Q'eqchi' families followed fairly predictable paths. Although most popular references to Q'eqchi' lowland migration describe it as "spontaneous" or anarchic, well-defined patterns become visible under closer analysis. Q'eqchi' settlers initially followed behind the colonization programs—filling in previously settled areas in the Northern Franja Transversal, including the municipalities of Fray, Chisec, Chahal, Livingston, and especially the region around Sebol. Richard Adams (1965) reported that Izabal was at that time the department with the largest relative increase in indigenous population over the previous fifty years, but later it would become a major source of further migration into Petén. Survey data (Grandia et al. 2001) also show that many migrants to Petén came from colonization zones of the Franja Transversal (fig. 2.4). Later, a distinct movement northward in Petén is evident as the southern municipalities (such as San Luis, Poptún, and Sayaxché), in turn, began to expel settlers toward the northernmost munici-

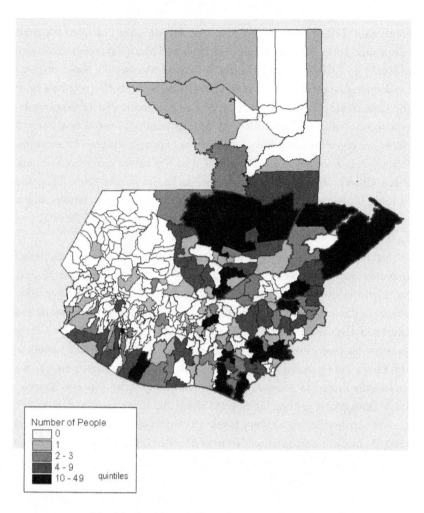

FIGURE 2.4. Municipal residence before migration to Petén. Source: Maps designed by L. Grandia and L. Montana at Macro International, Inc., for Grandia et al. 2001

palities of Petén (mainly La Libertad and San Andrés). This pattern of repeated Q'eqchi' dislocation points to the failure of the colonization programs to provide stable land claims to settlers.

Both village and municipal data sets clearly show that Q'eqchi' people generally moved in clumps and developed networks among a small group of villages. For example, a set of neighboring villages in southeastern Petén (Tamalton, Chapayal, and Seamay) moved to Atelesdale over a couple of decades, whereas another set of villages from Izabal (Guitarra, Arenales, and Searranx) and from east-central Petén (San Lucas Aguacate, Poité, and Machaca) preferred to move gradually to Atelesdale's neighboring village of Macawville. Some of these block migration patterns go back several generations and often originate from the same coffee plantations where settlers' grandparents and great-grandparents were born in highland Alta Verapaz. Interestingly, many new lowland places are given the same Q'eqchi' names as highland villages—for example, Finca Actelá from Senahú is reincarnated as the village Actelá in San Luis, Petén. Others take on biblical names, such as La Nueva Eden (New Eden) and El Buen Samaritano (Good Samaritan), or simply express the settlers' hopes for a better life, including La Esperanza (Hope), La Bendición (Blessing), and La Gloria (Heaven).

Just one keystone family was sufficient to set in motion a multigenerational migration pattern between several villages. For example, Doña María Caal, an elderly widow from Atelesdale, and her late husband initiated a migration stream of a much larger group of kin and their "compadres" (godparents) and effectively founded three major Q'eqchi' villages in the lowlands; over three generations, they traveled from a plantation in Cahabón, started a hamlet in the Franja Transversal, proceeded to Tamalton, in San Luis (see pp. 69–70), and finally moved to Atelesdale, in San Andrés. Q'eqchi' people who never knew Doña María continue to migrate along this string of villages. Don José Cux of Macawville, whose story is told in chapter 4, is another pioneer who started a block migration pattern from a Cahabón plantation to a village in San Luis and on to another new settlement in San Andrés.

Pioneers who start block migration patterns are exceptional. Most Q'eqchi' people will follow previously established migratory patterns rather than embark on new ones. However, as Q'eqchi' farmers become more desperate for land and have access to more information sources, their settlement patterns may become more chaotic. For example, the population of Macawville (settled with precarious land claims in Laguna del Tigre National Park) has far more diverse migration origins than the longer-established community of Atelesdale located roughly forty kilometers to the east. Among 220 migration histories of Atelesdale residents, almost half of the settlers originated from one set of neighboring villages in San Luis over the past twenty years. A closer analysis, however, reveals an intriguing trend: the older migrants tend to come from a similar set of places, but newer migrants have more diverse places of origin.

In a few cases, too, people went out of their way to explain that they just felt like moving and wanted a change of scenery. A common refrain in Q'eqchi',

TAMALTON, "PLACE OF CORN DUMPLINGS" (*CHIPOCH*)

Having lived for a year in Atelesdale, a bi-ethnic village north of Lake Petén Itzá (see ch. 4) in the early 1990s, I was curious about the migrants' place of origin, Tamalton in San Luis, Petén. Doña María Caal, the widowed mother of my host family in Atelesdale, always spoke with such nostalgia of Tamalton, where her daughter still lived, that I invited her to accompany me for a visit in 2003.

Romeo Lucas García (who later became president of Guatemala) built a road through the village in the 1960s, connecting his personal cattle ranch to the highway to Guatemala City. This brought many migrants from the Cahabón and Lanquin area and fostered a land conflict with a nearby Q'eqchi' village. It also brought a dozen or so Ladino shopkeepers and ranchers who often serve as godparents to Q'eqchi' families.

As luck would have it, we arrived for a multiweek stay on the eve of a three-day *mayejak* to celebrate the change of "mayordomos" (*chinams*), deacons in the Catholic Church. Over two days and one sleepless night, members of the Catholic church held a ceremonial vigil with traditional music (fig 2.5), prayers, processions, fireworks, and multiple meals of steamed corn dumplings with beef stew made with a steer slaughtered for the whole congregation. The rituals, which filled the air with smoky incense, were straightforward and egalitarian; the point seemed to be the simple joy of being together.

Not to be outdone by the Catholics, a Protestant farmer invited me to visit a sacred cave in his parcel where he said others went to hold ceremonies and which he admitted he also believed was alive, although his pastor might disagree. In addition to these small caves, the community reveres an outcropping in which they believe their village *Tzuultaq'a* resides (fig. 2.6).

FIGURE 2.5. Traditional instruments played at a *mayejak*, Tamalton, 2003. All night, these visiting musicians played homemade instruments (violin, harp, guitar, drum, and flute). The food offerings on the floor in front of the harp were meant to consecrate the music. The Pepsi bottles served as a seat for the percussionist drumming the hollow part of the harp. Photograph: Liza Grandia

FIGURE 2.6. Tamalton's largest hill with a sacred cave high above the road, 2003. Doña María Caal is pictured here. Photograph: Liza Grandia

With undulating hills reaching as high as a thousand meters, abundant rainfall, cooler temperatures, and a large number of creeks and rivers, the geography of San Luis feels more like highland Verapaz than hotter, drier areas north of Lake Petén Itzá. Several Tamaltoners asked Doña María and me when we had come "from Petén"—even though we were still technically *in* Petén. Living in San Luis, they considered themselves to be in what was rightfully Q'eqchi' territory.

Nonetheless, facing language and literacy barriers, most received plots from FYDEP that were one-tenth the size of parcels awarded to Ladino ranchers. Having now subdivided and sold portions of their land, most families in Tamalton own less than ten hectares today. To survive, they sharecrop or rent small parcels each season from the Ladinos. Many spoke candidly with me about being poisoned by the pesticides they use to make their small plots more productive.

I began to understand why so many decided to move farther north, to "Petén."

conveying dissatisfaction or weariness with a place, was "I got bored there" (*Xin titz*). There are, of course, always some people in any society who like to travel and yearn for adventure; however, given the financial difficulties associated with migration, these stories of boredom may mask other reasons for moving, such as land conflicts or general land scarcity. To some degree, these are two sides of the same coin, since scarcity will usually lead to increased conflict, which sometimes gets expressed through accusations of witchcraft.

Before the government built roads into southeastern Petén, Izabal, and Belize, people entered the region via extensive footpaths and trading networks set up by Q'eqchi' pioneers. Even in the most far-flung areas of the Q'eqchi' diaspora, the few consumer goods required by Q'eqchi' households can always be acquired from those quintessential traveling salesmen known as "Cobaneros," who carry their wares in large bundles on their backs (for early reports of "Cobaneros," see Thompson 1930, Howard 1977, and Sapper 1985). Emanating from the central highland Q'eqchi' towns of Cobán, Chamelco, and especially Carchá, the "Cobaneros" bring skirts and blouses, garlic, plastic items, toys, flashlights, radios, men's and children's clothing, jewelry, books, shoes, cacao, incense, and tools to rural Q'eqchi'. They sleep wherever a family provides them a hammock and receive their meals at low or no cost from any woman willing to cook for them. Sometimes they take special orders, delivering the goods within two months on their next circuit. Improved bus transportation to town markets has reduced the number of "Cobaneros" in Petén and Izabal, but in remote villages that lack roads (especially in Belize), traveling "Cobaneros" can be seen several times a week.

Aside from provisioning remote villages, "Cobaneros" carry messages among distant kin and bring information about new places, thereby facilitating migration. For example, writing at the beginning of the twentieth century, Karl Sapper describes a conversation with his research assistant, who had once been a trader and maintained a desire to return to the lowlands to settle permanently. Speculating that these long-distance merchants stimulated lowland colonization, Sapper writes, "His and similar stories by other traders must have excited the migration fever of his ethnic companions" (1985: 43). Besides traveling salesmen, other people serving as information conduits include chicle harvesters who first traveled to Petén by airplane to work in the chicle camps and likely brought back stories to the Q'eqchi' heartland about the availability of land farther north; hunters introduced to new lands on their extended hikes through the forest; evangelical preachers who are usually reassigned every few years to a new village; military conscripts posted to different regions; roving NGO or government workers; and perhaps even the itinerant anthropologist.

Don Juan Choc, a key leader from Macawville, was one such scout. He was born to a poor Q'eqchi' servant whose bosses raped her; each of his three siblings has a different father. His own father was a rich Ladino who rejected his son when Don Juan attempted to make contact at age sixteen. Reflecting on his childhood working in a coffee plantation, Don Juan said, "Life was so hard. . . . We only had twenty-five pounds of corn a week to eat." He remembered when they ran out of food entirely for a fortnight and had to eat tortillas made from plantains. When he was twenty, he began to learn to read and write at the Baptist Bible Institute in Cobán, but lacking money for food and uniforms, he had to quit school shortly after learning the alphabet. Working as a bus driver's assistant on the Cobán–Guatemala City route, he ate well for the first time in his life, and his coworkers helped him expand his literacy skills. By then, his mother had moved to Fray Bartolomé de las Casas, and he joined her, finding work with the Ministry of Health's malaria prevention division. After six years, he moved to Ixcán and worked with the governor's office in community organizing; later, he found employment with an NGO, Schools without Borders. Next he was offered a job as an elementary-school teacher with the bilingual government program National Community-Managed Program for Educational Development (Programa Nacional de Autogestión para el Desarrollo Educativo), or PRONADE, but moved to Petén to escape marital problems. After settling along the road to El Naranjo in La Libertad, he became a leader in the region and eventually moved to Macawville, bringing several families with him. He recently sold his land and moved back to Cobán to open a hardware store. Throughout, Don Juan provided information across regions to many different people. Whether they moved once or six times like Don Juan, there are certain cultural dispositions that have made the Q'eqchi' people successful migrants.

Egalitarian social structure

Because the Q'eqchi' have a highly egalitarian social ethic, new lowland communities composed of a melting pot of unfamiliar families from different places—with more people continually moving in and out—are nonetheless able to reorganize themselves and develop strong social cohesion. They form work groups several times a year for collective village tasks, including clearing common areas and paths and building needed infrastructure such as schools, churches, and development projects; any man who does not contribute labor must pay a fine. In addition to these formal work groups, families assemble smaller groups of kin and friends to help one another with tasks ranging from building houses to planting corn.

Under customary systems, because everyone is expected to participate in these networks of mutual cooperation, potential village members are carefully interviewed before being granted admission to a community. In some cases, in recognition of the benefits they will accrue by joining an already established village, newcomers must pay a fee to the general community coffer (from $25 up to $250 per family in some Belize villages). In turn, this payment grants them access to communal forests, agricultural land, and village infrastructure. Before Don Pablo Botzoc could gain admission to Jaguarwood, he was grilled at a public village meeting, getting questions like: "Why do you want to come here?" "Did you murder someone in Guatemala?" "Exactly why don't you have a wife?" He explained humbly that his wife had been ill and that he had lost all his money and his land while seeking a cure for her. After hearing his saga, the villagers agreed to let Don Pablo join Jaguarwood, and he soon became the most devoted member of the Catholic Church and a godfather to many children as a way of expressing his gratitude for being accepted into the community.

Don Pablo's story illustrates that everyone has the capacity to become a leader or an elder in Q'eqchi' villages. In contrast to western highland Maya groups who have specialized spiritual leaders—*aj q'ij*, known as daykeepers or Maya priests—in Q'eqchi' communities, any four elder men and women can perform the planting and religious rituals and participate in a council of elders that traditionally makes important community decisions, like choosing an *alcalde* (village mayor). Men and women typically begin their service as elders after the age of sixty; however, if there are not enough people who fit this criterion (often the case in younger migrant communities), the definition of "elder" is flexible.

Q'eqchi' rituals are led by a group rather than a single expert. They are relaxed, even informal events, with the group of elders discussing among themselves what the next step should be. That makes organizing ceremonies a highly egalitarian and easily replicable practice. Likewise, any adult (usually a man, though sometimes a woman) can be elected as a "mayordomo," who is in charge of organizing ceremonies and festivals as well as maintaining church facilities. Traditionally, seven people should serve the village as "mayordomos," but in practice, there is some leeway, and many lowland villages just have one or two people in this leadership role.

Nor do Q'eqchi' communities necessarily employ other village specialists like midwives, because Q'eqchi' women usually give birth alone, with the aid of their husbands, or, for the first child, with the additional help of their mothers or mothers-in-law.[5] There is nevertheless a valued role for healers (*aj ilonel*) in Q'eqchi' communities, although today they must be careful to avoid accusations of witchcraft from newly converted evangelical Protestants.[6] Anyone who feels he has a calling and has the money to study may become an apprentice to a healer in his own or any other village. As opposed to the more open healing traditions of other Maya groups, such as their Itzá neighbors, Q'eqchi' healers guard their knowledge with great secrecy, but they have a clear training process for developing new generations of healers who can provide medical services in even the most remote migrant villages.

Whatever the Q'eqchi' people may lack in material wealth is compensated for by their extraordinary social intelligence, based on concepts of balance, equity, and respect for others. Although harmony ideology was perhaps imposed by Christian missionization (Nader 1990), it is also important for the cohesion of Q'eqchi' communities. In any village, there will always be some kind of internal conflict—squabbles with neighbors, personality differences among leaders, religious disagreements, and so on. When these small conflicts become entrenched and potentially violent, one or both of the disputing parties usually migrate so as to avoid a serious feud. This was especially true in Guatemala during the civil war, when the military could execute without investigation people who might have been falsely accused of being guerrillas by their neighbors. Don Antonio Tiul, for example, left a conflictful situation in a San Luis village and moved farther north to Atelesdale. A military officer helped him make this decision by giving him this advice: "Why are you going to argue over this land? There is so much land in Petén . . . just leave that land behind." By keeping their internal conflicts private, Q'eqchi' communities have been able to present a unified front to the external world, which in turn has helped protect them from the intrusion of state authorities.

Flexible spirituality and subsistence strategies

Q'eqchi' faith includes many elements of Christianity. It revolves around respect for the earth and the cosmos, manifested through the figures of the *Tzuultaq'a* (literally, "the mountain and below"), which anthropologists usually translate as the Gods of the Hill and Valley. Some Christian Q'eqchi' now see the *Tzuultaq'a* as one facet of a monotheistic God, perhaps akin to the Holy Spirit. Others see the *Tzuultaq'a* as a separate but complementary force alongside a Christian God, something like the Western concept of Mother Nature. For many Catholics, the *Tzuultaq'a* and their helpers (e.g., Lord Thunder, or *Qawa' Kaq*) fit easily among the medley of saints and apostles to be worshipped, and they believe the smoke of burning candles and incense will also help carry the message of their supplications. While most Protestant converts condemn belief in the *Tzuultaq'a* as paganism, when hard pressed, many avid evangelicals admitted that they continue to believe the mountains are alive (*yoo yoo li tzuul*), even though they no longer participate in the traditional, collective Q'eqchi' ritual known as a *mayejak* (see also A. E. Adams 1999).

Faith in the *Tzuultaq'a* varies widely across families, communities, and regions, but certain core beliefs about the *Tzuultaq'a* nonetheless serve to unite a Q'eqchi' identity across the diaspora. Q'eqchi' people say that the *Tzuultaq'a* live inside the mountains, more specifically in caves, which they call "stone houses" (*ochoch pek*). Although the karstic landscape of northern Guatemala and southern Belize lacks large mountains, Q'eqchi' settlers in these regions still find sufficient hills to maintain their spiritual practices. As Pedro Coc explained, the principal mountains are located around Cobán (see also Wilson 1995); they are like the grandparents of a family with many descendants in the lowlands and other places (see also A. E. Adams 2001). Another Belize elder, Santiago Asij, explained it this way: the hills close to their lowland villages have less powerful *Tzuultaq'a* who can send messages to the larger mountains around Cobán. In other words, the *Tzuultaq'a* are connected, like family, and stay in touch with one another.

Every village or town must identify its own sacred spot where the *Tzuultaq'a* lives. If for some reason the lowland area does not have a cave, a village may look for a large stone near a water source and name this as a sacred site. The elders of Jaguarwood, Belize, narrate how they discovered a sacred place for their village, a set of mysteriously large boulders in a round depression in the forest, hidden from view unless one stumbles onto them. Before they found this site, Jaguarwood elders made pilgrimages to other caves in Izabal, including in Agoutiville. On one of these occasions, the Agoutiville elders told their Jaguarwood friends about a dream they had received from the *Tzuultaq'a* advising the Jaguarwood leaders to cease their pilgrimages to Guatemala and, instead, find their own sacred place in Belize. Following these instructions, the people of Jaguarwood searched far and wide for weeks; finally, an old man happened upon a place that looked exactly like the spot in the elders' dream. They named it Santa María Mayejal (Place of Offering to Santa María). There was much rejoicing, for this gave the people a new sense of belonging to Jaguarwood.

Typically, the *Tzuultaq'a* are named after nearby bodies of water, animals, crops, people, Catholic saints, and/or the village itself—and vice versa. Some are female figures, but most manifest themselves as men. They may be referred to as "you, my father" (*at inna'*) and "you, my mother" (*at inwa*), which reflects the duality and complementarity of gender roles in Q'eqchi' culture (Secaira 2000). They have personalities, just like any human being; some are kind, but others are angry and vindictive. Nevertheless, the *Tzuultaq'a* are said to be more approachable than the Christian God, and a skilled elder can talk to them with ease, as someone might speak to a friend. Stories abound about people miraculously taken into the mountain and invited to dine with the *Tzuultaq'a*, to be given instructions on organizing Q'eqchi' ceremonies and sacrifices. The *Tzuultaq'a* also enjoy music and raise domestic animals; many villagers say that upon entering a cave, one can hear a guard dog barking or music filtering up from the depths.

In addition to ceremonies held at the site of their local *Tzuultaq'a*, most devout Catholics make regular pilgrimages, ideally on an annual basis, to a larger sacred site. Because a trip to the mountains of Cobán can be prohibitively expensive, some lowlanders have started traveling instead to see the Black Christ at the Catholic church in Esquipulas in eastern Guatemala (de Borhegyi 1954) or to ancient Maya ruins, such as those at Tikal. This shows that the destination does not matter as much as the act and ritual of pilgrimage, allowing Q'eqchi' people to reinvent their spiritual practices in each new place to which they migrate.

Moving with little more than the clothes on their backs, clay griddles for baking tortillas, grinding stones, machetes, sleeping mats or hammocks, and perhaps a few other tools, early Q'eqchi' pioneers adapted quickly to their new forest environment. Through their frugality and the simplicity of their everyday existence, they found freedom. One elder woman, Doña María Caal, related the story of how she and her husband founded the village of Boloncó in the middle of the forest. Lacking even pots when they arrived, she made holes in the ground and lined them with banana leaves so that she could cook her corn. For most Q'eqchi' settlers, fulfilling the dream of owning land makes the initial hardships of pioneer homesteading more bearable. Compared to life on a coffee plantation or cattle ranch, almost any opportunity for subsistence agriculture seems dramatically better. Despite prevalent stereotypes in Guatemala and Belize of the Q'eqchi' as rigid, monocrop corn farmers, given sufficient land and appropriate market incentives, many have diversified their crops.

Through indigenous agronomic science involving trial and error over generations (Nader 1996), the Q'eqchi' people identified and settled along lowland soil belts best suited to their agriculture. They developed what James C. Scott (2009) characterizes as "escape agriculture," emphasizing root crops and smaller swiddens, also relying on hunting and harvesting of wild species. In fact, if one overlays a map of the best soils in the Toledo district of Belize, these locations coincide almost perfectly with Q'eqchi' settlements. Whereas neighboring Mopán preferred larger settlements in hilly regions or uplands, Belizean Q'eqchi' established small settlements usually located on lower, swampier land and/or hillsides (Wilk and Chapin 1990). When the walking distance to shifting fields grew too long, either families moved their houses closer to the fields or the village splintered (Wilk 1997). In the isolated Toledo lowlands, many communities were born, grew, shrank, and disappeared back into the forest; some were never recorded in the census at all. Like many Americans, Q'eqchi' people were willing to move whenever they began spending too much time getting to work. In all lowland Q'eqchi' regions, there is a strong cultural preference for settling alongside rivers, which provide water, transportation, and silt fertilization for riverside farms. Unfortunately, this also leaves Q'eqchi' farmers vulnerable to the interests of cattle ranchers who covet those same rich soils.

Strong kinship

Commonly, Q'eqchi' migrants learn about new places through their relatives. In the Q'eqchi' kinship system, the nuclear family, parents, and grandparents are the most important, followed by siblings, brothers- and sisters-in-law and then everyone else. Relationships with siblings are particularly important, as illustrated by the different terms used to describe "older sibling" (*as*) versus "younger siblings" (*itzin*), as well as a special word for eldest sister (*chaq'na'*), honoring her role as a secondary mother figure. Interestingly, there is no word in Q'eqchi' for "cousin." Although the words for "aunt" and "uncle" are occasionally used, the corresponding words for "nephew" and "niece" are not commonly known. Nonetheless, any and all of these kin can be called upon for help when settling in a new village. Of those who had migrated to Petén, about 33 percent said a family member helped them get established, another 15 percent got help from a friend, 5 percent were aided by other sources, and 48 percent received support from no one (Grandia et al. 2001).

Other ritual or de facto kin who may provide migration support derive from the Catholic system of "compadres" chosen for a child's birth, first communion, and marriage. While parents might choose the same couple for some or all of these life passages, they would generally wish to maximize their child's ritual kinship relations to as many other families as possible. Although exclusively a Catholic tradition, newly converted Protestants usually continue to refer to their "compadres" as such or substitute the term "brothers" ("hermanos") for fellow church members.

Because kinship is strong, but not binding, Q'eqchi' migrants in search of land are willing to leave their extended families for years at a time, if not forever. Over the course of my fieldwork, many people confessed to me with teary eyes that they had no idea whether or not family members they had left behind were still living. In the migration histories I collected, quite a number of people said that they had moved after becoming orphaned or were taken to a new place by a surviving parent. Released from family obligations, as adults these orphans were free to move as they chose.[7] In fact, nearly one-third of the seventy migration stories narrated to me in Atelesdale referred to the death of a loved one, either a parent or a spouse, as the catalyst for a move (see also Adams 1965 on the phenomenon of orphan migration).

Another kinship factor influencing migration is the flexibility of residence after marriage. A marriage partner may come from the same village (endogamous) or from another village (exogamous). Decisions about residence tend to be practical—a choice between the two extended families based on the availability of land or the support they will offer. In olden days, either a girl was "asked for" (*tzamanb'il*) and went to live with the boy's family, or the boy "entered" (*oksinb'il*) the girl's family. Either way, the boy's parents would have to visit the girl's parents and negotiate the arrangements. Generally, if the girl's family is poor, if her mother is widowed, or if she has few or no brothers, the boy will be asked to live and work with the girl's family. Otherwise, it is more common for the girl to live with the boy's family. If neither family has land to offer the young couple, they may move somewhere else entirely. Even if they do live with one set of parents initially, a young couple will usually try to set up an independent household after their first child is born. Survey data show the average age of arrival to Petén of Q'eqchi' residents in 1999 as 22.5 years old, suggesting that young couples are the primary demographic in search of land (Grandia et al. 2001).

Put another way, migration occurs not only in individual, personal, and historical time but also in family time in response to certain life transitions such as attaining adulthood, getting married, growing old, or being left an orphan (cf. Chayanov 1986). Indeed, one of the most common themes in Q'eqchi' migration histories is that young couples or individuals moved north because private property systems had unraveled the community safety net and their parents did not have enough land to share with them. As in most gringo families, young Q'eqchi' people are expected to make their own way in the world after a certain age.

Marriage and the search for land to sustain one's present and future family are clearly among the most important factors driving Q'eqchi' migration. One of the underlying reasons for Q'eqchi' territorial expansion may therefore be their high rate of natural growth—with a rural fertility rate of 8.9 children, well above the national rate of 5.0 and the Petén average of 6.8.[8] Not only has the Q'eqchi' population grown threefold since the 1964 census, but there has also been a proportional, internal shift toward the lowlands. In fact, relative to the total Q'eqchi' population, the percentage of lowlanders has grown steadily from an estimated 6 percent in 1893 to 40 percent in 2002 (for more details, see Grandia 2009c).

Cultural confidence

A final reason for the resilience of Q'eqchi' people is less tangible than the others but is nonetheless quite powerful. Perhaps because of their colonial isolation in Verapaz under Dominican rule, Q'eqchi' converts developed strong cultural cohesion. An anthropologist who had done comparative work among many indigenous peoples of the Americas, Anthony Stocks (2002), found the Q'eqchi' to be "amazingly confident" and with an "expansive culture."[9] Certainly it required courage to move into a new ecosystem in which they could not speak the dominant language. As Don Vicente Cuc described, when he first arrived to Petén seeking work, he did not even know the Spanish word for "tortilla." He and his companions remained hungry until, on their third night in Petén, a vision came to him in a dream as to how he should order tortillas, and they were able to make themselves understood at a local diner.

There is remarkable cultural continuity between highlanders and lowlanders in food tastes, manners, folklore, dream interpretation, dress, and religious beliefs—all despite the fact that lowland Q'eqchi' may grow up, form a family, and live to a ripe, old age without ever having traveled to the Q'eqchi' capital of Cobán. While first-generation lowlanders tend to maintain their dialectical differences, younger lowland populations have begun to speak what might be considered a new dialect, with words borrowed from Spanish and English in Guatemala and Belize, respectively (Romero 2008). Historically, linguists from the highland Q'eqchi' area described two dialects centered around Cobán and Cahabón (Bac 2000; DeChicchis 1986), but there may be as many as four today (Bac, pers. comm., 2002). While all these dialects are mutually intelligible, Cobán's remains the prestige dialect or, as many lowlanders put it, "the real Q'eqchi" ("el mero Q'eqchi'"). For instance, a local schoolteacher in Macawville explained that the people laughed at his Cobán accent when he first settled in the village but are now interested in having him teach the Cobán dialect to their children.

Since the late 1970s and 1980s, Q'eqchi' people have been developing, in tandem with the rise of the pan-Maya movement in Guatemala and Belize, a sense of shared ethnic identity beyond their linguistic cohesion (see, e.g., Warren 1978, 1998; Wilson 1995). Before the 1980s, many Q'eqchi' people identified principally with their village communities. Then, during the civil war, they began referring to themselves as *laa'o li neb'aj* (we, the poor) and subsequently began saying *laa'o li Q'eqchi'* (we, the Q'eqchi') (A. Huet, pers. comm., 2002). Richard Wilk observed a similar shift in Belize, where the Q'eqchi' once referred to themselves simply as *winq* (people) or *kristianeb'* (Christians). Today, Belizean Q'eqchi' people have equally strong senses of being citizens of Belize *and* Mayas.[10] Although I did not detect any particularly strong geographic Q'eqchi'-Izabaleño identity, the very strong Petenero identity developed by mestizos is creeping into Q'eqchi' consciousness. For instance, Don Domingo Ba, using a mix of Spanish and Q'eqchi', described himself "puro Kobaneer" (pure Cobán-born) and his wife as "pura Peteneer" (pure Petén-born), which, in his mind, gave her an authoritative claim to land in the Maya Biosphere Reserve. Although many lowland Q'eqchi' defer to their "elder cousins," the Itzá, as the original inhabitants of Petén, other Q'eqchi' leaders have surmised that because the Itzá are so few in number (around 1,500 people, mostly concentrated in San José) and use very little land, they, the Q'eqchi' cousins, are welcome to settle in this region (N. Schwartz, pers. comm., 2003).

In terms of social organization, there are several pan-Petén Q'eqchi' groups, mostly involved in land rights advocacy. Some of the density of lowland Q'eqchi' organizing in Petén may be a result of the NGO boom in this region in the 1990s as well as the ripple effect of returned refugee communities. It may also be that because of high migration rates, there is weaker identity at the community level but, conversely, greater ease with organizing into pan-ethnic groups (A. Huet, pers. comm., 2002). As Alexis de Tocqueville observed so long ago of North Americans, among Q'eqchi' lowlanders, rugged individualism does not preclude gringo-like enthusiasm for the organization of groups (for an impressively thorough description of lowland Q'eqchi' organizations, see Macz and Grünberg 1999).

MIGRATING THEORY

The scholarly literature on Guatemalan migration has tended to focus on more traditional categories of migration such as urbanization, political displacement caused by the civil war, and seasonal migration to coastal plantations (Micklin 1990), with comparatively less attention paid to *rural-to-rural* migration or the unusual *urban-to-rural* migration among the Petén Q'eqchi' (Ybarra et al. forthcoming) stemming from internal displacement due to poverty rather than politics. Additionally, most scholarship on migration and the environment is dominated by aggregate modeling of economic variables and analyses of causality (push and pull factors). These tend to focus on how certain crises (environmental, economic, or demographic) motivate small decision-making groups (individuals and households) to move.

While in some sense Q'eqchi' people were and are "choosing" to move, there are also strong "structural conditions that make certain choices possible" (C. Wood 1981: 339). If the rural poor and landless are culturally and historically inclined to oppose wage labor, migration may be not a choice but their only option for cultural survival. Classic migration theory often gets caught in a structure or agency bind by insisting on distinguishing between "innovating" migrants who want something new in their lives and "conservative" migrants who, in response to a threat to their current circumstances, move in order to retain their way of life in another locale (Massey 2001). For Q'eqchi', these are not mutually exclusive categories.

Moreover, Q'eqchi' migrants make decisions not based on a thought-out plan of frontier settlement but in response to immediate constraints and opportunities. In doing so, they tend to follow existing paths. Over time, Q'eqchi' migration streams seem to develop a momentum and life of their own. Simply put, "migrants tend to be people who have migrated previously" (Anthony 1990: 904). That is not to say that Q'eqchi' people move with the idea of moving again. To the contrary, most migrants hope to stay where they first settle. Nonetheless, the experience of having moved once makes it easier to muster the courage to move again.

Still, the decision to migrate always involves serious risks with serious consequences. Aside from daring pioneers who move repeatedly, most Q'eqchi' families will move just once, if at all, during their lifetimes and usually in response to individual and/or collective crises such as falling ill, having a poor harvest, becoming involved in a conflict with a neighbor, defaulting on a loan, being tricked into selling one's land for a bottle of liquor, finding oneself inadvertently living in a protected area, fleeing violence, and the like. Q'eqchi' lowlanders would like to stay in one place and have a nice house, just like any Guatemalan, but economic realities have denied them and their children such stability.

Powerful actors such as the World Bank continue to use negative images of Q'eqchi' "nomadism" to justify hollow claims that land privatization will somehow slow the expansion of the northern agricultural frontier. As one government official affiliated with this project said to me, "[Otherwise] the Q'eqchi' are never going to develop . . . they have a nomadic culture." Worldwide, nomadic or migratory peoples (from the Roma to Amazonian tribes to African desert pastoralists) have been repeatedly stereotyped as lazy, uncivilized, criminal, or worse. Beyond the implied racism of such remarks lies another double standard. It is acceptable for the wealthy, educated, and urban to move for employment or business reasons. Cattle ranchers may buy and sell property across the region. Transnational corporations making investments under the DR-CAFTA or the PPP are allowed to come and go. When Q'eqchi' people migrate, they put down roots and embed themselves into their new environment. In contrast, when transnational businesses move, they expect the people to adapt to *them*. Poor people may move only if they are willing to be temporary wage laborers but not if it might lead to permanent residence or upward mobility. Yet sometimes a bold move such as migration is the only option, and as Donald Sawyer (1984) reminds us, "desperate and determined people" cannot be held back by barbed wire—much less by invisible or poorly enforced park boundaries.

3

Commons, Customs, and Carrying Capacities

THE POPULATION AND PROPERTY TRAPS
OF THE PETÉN FRONTIER

S ATELLITE images reveal that within three and a half decades of colonization, forest and natural savanna cover in Petén dropped from approximately 90 percent to less than 50 percent (fig. 3.1). Seemingly in an inverse
relationship, Petén's population grew from less than 50,000 to approximately
500,000 in that same time period (fig. 3.2) (Grandia 2000). Meanwhile, farmers
and meteorologists have observed dramatic reductions in total precipitation
as well as the number of days with rainfall. The longer dry season, in turn,
has provoked severe forest fires in Petén almost every year since 1998. Farmers
complain of additional symptoms of climate change such as decreased yields,
invasive weeds, pests, and even plagues of locusts.

In Malthusian tones, many biodiversity conservationists have blamed these
environmental problems on population growth and swidden, or shifting, cultivators, more pejoratively described as slash-and-burn farmers. By definition,
swidden agriculturalists use long fallowing periods, shift fields over a large
area, and rely on fire to control weeds and provide nutrients for the soil. To
an outsider, burned milpas may appear unsightly and disorderly (Dowie 2009:
136), but the practice helps farmers avoid the use of poisonous herbicides and
petrochemical fertilizers. Despite these environmental advantages, conservationists and government land managers still perceive extensive agriculture
as a threat to protected areas and criticize Q'eqchi' agriculture as "anarchic,"
"nomadic," "wandering," or "economically backwards . . . like Cuban commu-
nists!" Some have even argued that the Q'eqchi' are an impervious cultural

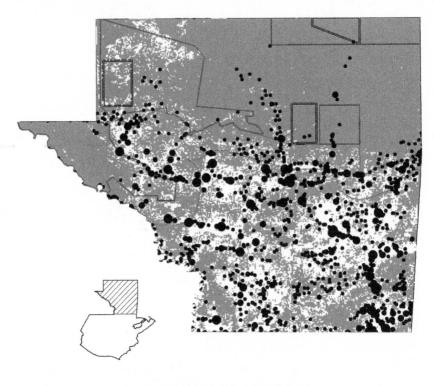

Settlements & Population

- •   < 300.00
- •   300 - 400
- •   400 - 900
- •   900 - 1200
- •   > 1200

Landcover

 Forested

 Deforested

FIGURE 3.1. Map of Petén deforestation in relation to the Maya Biosphere Reserve. Source: Jason Arnold and Daniel Irwin, NASA/SERVIR 2010

group with "impoverished" and "inappropriate" environmental cognition (Atran et al. 2002: 437). Over the past decade, they have spent millions of dollars, to little avail, trying to convince Q'eqchi' swidden farmers to convert to sedentary agriculture and diversify their crops.

Having worked with conservation organizations in Petén for more than a decade, I also used to worry about Q'eqchi' swidden agriculture and population growth as an environmental problem. Through conducting comparative anthropological research in Guatemala and Belize and by reading critical analyses about the founder of demography, Thomas Malthus (Ross 2000; Lohmann

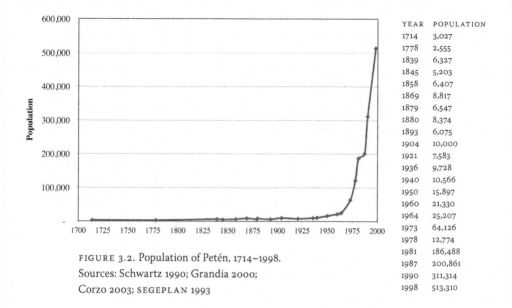

FIGURE 3.2. Population of Petén, 1714–1998.
Sources: Schwartz 1990; Grandia 2000;
Corzo 2003; SEGEPLAN 1993

YEAR	POPULATION
1714	3,027
1778	2,555
1839	6,327
1845	5,203
1858	6,407
1869	8,817
1879	6,547
1880	8,374
1893	6,075
1904	10,000
1921	7,583
1936	9,728
1940	10,566
1950	15,897
1960	21,330
1964	25,207
1973	64,126
1978	12,774
1981	186,488
1987	200,861
1990	311,314
1998	513,310

2003), however, I came to realize that Petén's environmental problems were a result not simply of population increase in swidden cultivators but also the displacement of Q'eqchi' farmers by private property.

The tensions between property and population may be better understood by returning to the ideological source of the confusion: the writings of Thomas Malthus and one of his most influential followers, Garrett Hardin. Because environmentalists guided by these thinkers have so maligned Q'eqchi' relationships with the environment, this chapter examines the many socio-ecological advantages of Q'eqchi' customary land management over private landholdings in the karstic soils of the northern Maya Guatemala lowlands. Where customary management has been lost among Q'eqchi' people in Guatemala, the private property system fosters environmental degradation, which is further compounded by population growth. While there are certainly environmental consequences to Petén's exponential demographic explosion, agrarian inequity and the destruction of indigenous commons have thus far been equally, if not more, responsible for the diminished carrying capacity of the lowlands.

SPECTERS OF MALTHUS

Writing at the height of the English enclosures, Thomas Malthus concluded in his 1798 *Essay on the Principle of Population*: "The power of population is indefinitely greater than the power in the earth to produce subsistence for man. *Population, when unchecked, increases in a geometrical ratio. Subsistence increases only in an arithmetical ratio.* A slight acquaintance with numbers will show the immensity of the first power in comparison of the second. . . . This implies a strong and *constantly operating check on population from the difficulty of subsistence"* (2004: 7) (emphasis mine). Malthus penned these famous words during a period of political upheaval in England following the French Revolution. There were heated domestic debates about the international grain trade and the revision of welfare reforms in response to the widespread poverty that followed the enclosure of the commons, which turned a quarter of England's common cultivable land and open fields into private property between 1750 and 1850 (Ross 2000: 3).

Although Malthus's name would later become synonymous with family planning methods, he actually disapproved of limiting family size (ibid.). Instead of reducing the number of poor, Malthus wanted simply to reduce the moral obligation of the rich to the poor by arguing that the suffering of the poor was the inevitable result of mathematical laws of nature instead of social patterns of inequity. Empowered by the warm reception of his first treatise, in the second edition, Malthus more boldly called for shifting the burden of raising children onto the individual so as to punish freeloading. If parents had not shown "moral restraint" in determining the size of their families, the children had no legitimate demand upon the common good for land. The poor, Malthus argued, would learn frugality and discipline only after they recognized that they had no communal subsistence rights or any God-given right at all to live.

As a defender of the interests of the wealthy, Malthus eventually inspired a revision of England's Poor Laws in 1834, which made welfare relief conditional on labor in the brutal workhouses that Charles Dickens's novels would so vividly condemn. Although this aspect of his treatise may seem ruthless in retrospect, the more important question is why his narrative about population and subsistence has persisted so tenaciously. For indeed, while Malthus's writings merely grew arithmetically, responses to his work over the centuries have grown geometrically. Neo-Malthusian narratives continue to shape the policy advice of pundits such as Homer Dixon on environmental security, Robert Kaplan on the planet's anarchic future, and Thomas Friedman on globalization. Organizations such as Zero Population Growth (renamed Population Connection) implicitly blame the suffering of the Third World poor on overpopulation without ever examining the underlying causes of their poverty (Lohmann 2003).

Malthus's treatise also deeply shaped influential thinking behind the modern environmental movement that emerged in the late 1960s, including Paul Ehrlich's *The Population Bomb* and Garrett Hardin's influential essay "The Tragedy of the Commons" (both published in 1968). In what became one of the most cited articles of the twentieth century, Hardin returned to the example of the English commons, arguing that pastoralists would keep putting more livestock out to graze and inevitably degrade the collective pasture, purportedly because it cost them nothing extra to do so. Presenting this tragedy as a universal phenomenon, Hardin argued that the only solution for saving the environmental resources of the commons was to place them under government ownership or allow individuals to pursue resource extraction under the clear rules of private property.

As with Malthus, context is critical for understanding the full meaning of Hardin's thesis. Saturated with Cold War ideology, Hardin essentially treats "commonism" as equivalent to "communism" and fears that the poor might be attracted to these doctrines because of their own overbreeding or a desire to profit off the work of the industrious (Ross 2000). Like Malthus, who was a devotee of both David Ricardo and Adam Smith, Hardin viewed state regulation as anathema, leaving privatization as the favored solution. While Malthus focused explicitly on population but argued implicitly for private property regimes, Hardin wrote explicitly about property but expressed an underlying concern about population growth. A 1975 quote from Hardin further echoes Malthus's idea of applying eugenics to the poor: "If each human family were dependent only on its own resources; if the children of improvident parents starved to death; if, thus, overbreeding brought its own 'punishment' to the germ line then there would be no public interest in controlling the breeding of families" (quoted in Ross 2000: 9). His 1968 essay suggests that the planet is a global commons in which no individual suffers for adding another child, thereby leading to overpopulation and environmental destruction.

As Nobel laureate Elinor Ostrom and others have argued, the fundamental problem with Hardin's argument is that he mistakenly equates the idea of common property with a free-for-all of purely self-interested actors. To the contrary, common-pool resources are governed by trust and reciprocity (Basurto and Ostrom 2009). They are usually well managed through custom, culture, collective decision-making, planning, and dispute resolution for the benefit of present and future generations. Moreover, customary land management usually involves a mix of open-access and quasi-private areas (Ostrom et al. 1999). When politicians decide to nationalize or privatize commons, it can be challenging to re-create such complex community structures and "get the [new] institutions" right (Ostrom 1990). Hence, ecological ruin often results not from the "tragedy of the commons," as Hardin would have us believe, but from the "tragedy of enclosure" (Martinez-Alier 1991).[1]

In response to these and other criticisms of his article, Hardin eventually clarified that he was writing about open-access resources, not managed commons (1998). Unfortunately, the rhetorical damage was done, as "the tragedy of the commons" had already become "one of the modern world's most dangerous myths" (Monbiot 1994: 1). Indeed, Hardin's portrayal of communal lands as "anarchic" and poorly managed and the depiction of local farmers as inherently lazy have inspired decades of technocratic, neocolonial development interventions that have destroyed the common property management of indigenous peoples and others. In the environmental community, Hardin's fairy tale has taken on almost biblical stature for "green business" advocates, who insist that the privatization of nature is the only way to save it. In the case of Petén, the World Bank has employed Hardinian arguments to insist that the privatization of the frontier is the only way to save the parks. In addition to dismantling the remnants of Q'eqchi' customary land management, this logic has facilitated the privatization of other common property in Petén such as "ejidos," settler claims inside parks ("agarradas"), and cooperatives—all to the benefit of ranchers and wealthy elites eager to buy these lands.

If Malthus and his disciples were writing not merely demographic treatises but political economy texts about property regimes during processes of enclosure, we would need to rethink the "population-environment" issues at stake in northern Guatemala. In turn, this might lead us to see the Q'eqchi' countryside as not just being squeezed by population but also caught between two modes of property organization: a well-managed commons tradition led by local people versus a new private titling regime led by the World Bank. While the customary Q'eqchi' land system is perfectly transparent to its community members, the bureaucratic state process of land titling seems opaque, chaotic, and unjust to them. The reverse is true for technicians working for state agencies: their own system seems objective and fair, while indigenous customary land management seems bizarre or simply "illegible" (Scott 1998). With the aid of the World Bank, the state viewpoint is achieving hegemony, channeling Q'eqchi' families into a land titling system contrary to their cultural preferences and the social and ecological logic of the milpa system still being practiced in places like Jaguarwood (see pp. 89–90).

JAGUARWOOD, "BY THE JAGUARS" (SEHIX)

Jaguarwood is the oldest of the southern Toledo villages, founded at the turn of the nineteenth century by hunters from Poptún, Guatemala, traversing the region via Dolores, Belize (TMCC and TAA 1997). Most of Jaguarwood's fields and forests are located on the former Kramer estate (established by a coffee baron family from Cobán), long since converted to Indian reserve or national lands, with a few leases scattered throughout. The population of Jaguarwood has fluctuated dramatically over the years—from about 50 people in 1912, up to 162 in 1931, and then down after the 1937 famine and 1945 hurricane to just 75 in 1952. After growing rapidly to 300 by 1959, many people left when a citrus development project failed, bringing the total back to 133 in 1966. The population grew again to 222 by 1980 (Schackt 1986) and was about that size when I arrived in 2004.

In collaboration with SATIIM, a Q'eqchi' NGO, I had the good fortune to work with the charismatic elders from Jaguarwood, as well as three nearby villages, to document their natural-resource use in relation to the Sarstoon Temash National Park, a couple of miles to the south. Through this project, I began to appreciate the ecological sense of customary Q'eqchi' land tenure. After hearing only theoretical discussion of the "old ways" of farming in Guatemala, in Jaguarwood I witnessed the continued compatibility of this land tenure system with "modern" life.

As shown in figure 3.3, abundant forests surround the village, protecting incense groves to the north and a sacred site to the south where the people go to pray and make offerings to the *Tzuultaq'a*. Unlike Guatemala, where most protected areas have been invaded by agriculture and cattle, here, the people respect the boundaries of the national park, traveling there only occasionally to hunt, fish, and collect non-timber forest products for crafts and construction. Most farmers maintain several small plots in different stages of fallow along with one more permanent plot for the second milpa along the river. The majority, those affiliated with the Catholic church, make collaborative decisions about where each family will sow and help one another with corn planting and harvesting.

Some of those who converted to Protestantism no longer participate in this system of labor exchange, opting instead to plant alone or manage the cattle herds the Mennonite missionaries helped them start, about two hundred head among ten families. Some Protestants had applied to the government for private leases in prime areas around the village and along the roadside, some of which overlapped with the fruit orchards and corn fields of the farmers in the customary system. Those who followed customary traditions had to walk up to seven kilometers from the village to reach their fields.

Cattle ranching had clearly intensified the religious factionalism described by Jon Schackt (1986) two decades earlier. After a series of conflicts and serious threats of violence, the two groups reached a compromise. Those with lease

FIGURE 3.3. Overflight view of Jaguarwood village center.
Source: Sean S. Downey 2007

land could continue where they were but would not claim additional lands. Those participating in the customary system would each get an acre of prime land left along the road for planting cacao to sell to Green & Black's, a British fair trade company operating in Belize. They would coordinate their milpa agriculture to ensure that swidden fires would not threaten the orchards. Meanwhile, some were contemplating tourism-related businesses and collaborating with SATIIM in developing a comanagement plan for the park.

ECOLOGICAL AND SOCIAL EFFICIENCIES OF THE "WANDERING" Q'EQCHI' MILPA

Contrary to stereotypes, Q'eqchi' customary land management has an order and logic based on the concept of usufruct rights, meaning the land is for those who use it. If someone clears a piece of high forest, other members of the community will respect that usufruct claim even when the land lies fallow. In other words, under a collective system, families can claim and retain plots over long periods of time in an arrangement that resembles the private property system. Nonetheless, others may request to borrow a fallow field ("guamil") from the person who cleared it. Even in Q'eqchi' villages with private property, farmers continue to borrow and swap land at unusually high rates. Each family is responsible for its own agricultural work and reaps its own harvests. The system is collective in that community members make group decisions about how land should be distributed among households; no one may sell his or her individual plots without the consent of the whole village. When someone dies, the land usually reverts back to the community. Hence, youths are not dependent on their parents for land but rely on their own good standing in the community.

Under the customary system, members are precluded from taking more land than they will actually use, so the system tends toward equity rather than accumulation. Q'eqchi' labor practices of mutual aid also have various, indirect economic leveling functions and conservation effects. Q'eqchi' farmers almost always prefer to plant (and sometimes to harvest) in groups, but the rest of agricultural labor tends to be organized within the family. Q'eqchi' women will sometimes accompany their husbands to their fields for specific tasks such as the corn harvest (*q'olok*) or bean picking (*michok kenq'*), but men generally carry out the bulk of subsistence agriculture, and land is usually designated as belonging to a family led by a male farmer. The farmer benefiting from the group labor is expected to make proper ceremonial arrangements, provide breakfast and lunch, and return the favor to those who helped him. As farmers must plant according to both the moon cycle and the start of the rainy season, scheduling labor groups becomes a logistical challenge. Hence, the amount of land a Q'eqchi' farmer can plant is regulated by the number of men he can recruit for the planting and the amount of work he can perform himself while reciprocating the help others have given him, all in this short period of time.

Communities usually reserve prime lots close to the village for their weaker members, such as elderly, disabled farmers or female-headed households, so as to shorten the distance they must travel to their fields and ease the hauling of crops back home. If someone is unable to plant (due to illness, for example), the community will often clear and plant a small farm on that person's behalf. Even in villages with private land, community members may still borrow or rent land and collectively cultivate a corn crop that will be sold to underwrite the *mayejak* ritual or other shared expenses. All in all, the system emphasizes equity, such that every family is able have a field of corn for basic subsistence. No one gets rich, but no one starves either, because customary land management reinforces systems of mutual aid.

Depending on variations in geography and village leadership, each community may manage its land in a slightly different manner in order to allow farmers access to different ecological niches. For small farmers, the *total amount* of land controlled is often less important than the *ecological variety* of the land, which allows farmers to take advantage of both the wet and dry seasons. Especially fertile land (for example, silted riverside plots) will be distributed equally in small plots. With a communal system, farmers can cultivate two or three small fields in different locations in a way that maximizes their crop yields. The year's first milpa (*k'at k'al*) does better on high, dry ground, while the second (*saqiwa* or "matahambre") does better on lower, damper soils. If crops from the previous year were poor, farmers can also plant a third crop, called the "milpa de San José" (also known as *payapak* or *junxil k'al*), on swampy soils. For this reason, in terms of labor per unit of production, milpa cropping can be far more productive than sedentary agriculture on rigidly divided private land.

In contrast to private property, which gives owners exclusive rights over large blocks of land, the customary system allows for multiple and shared uses of different ecosystems and forest resources used for hunting, fishing, gathering, and collecting non-timber forest products. For example, Q'eqchi' copal harvesters will care for clumps of trees over the long term, as if they were private property. Whenever farmers travel to their milpas, they take advantage of other forest resources in some way—collecting a medicinal plant, checking traps, gathering fuelwood, finding vines for lashing a haul, or perhaps just admiring some birds along the way. In contrast to a European forestry model that separates forest and field (Scott 1998; Fay and Michon 2003), the Q'eqchi' treat the two as a continuum (fig. 3.4) or as integrated "agrarian environments" (Agrawal and Sivaramakrishnan 2000).

Working in Toledo's Aguacate village, Richard Wilk (1997) found that farmers hunted 70 percent of their game meat (by weight) during daily walks to the milpa and not on special hunting trips. In turn, farmers support wild animals by planting extra maize seeds for them and anticipating a certain amount of crop loss. In that sense, deer fattened in the milpa are both "wild" and quasi-domesticated (N. Schwartz, pers. comm., 2003; and for similar archaeological conclusions, see Reina 1967; Nations and Nigh 1980; and Fedick 1996). Moreover, the availability of edible forest plants and wild meat and fish greatly decreases the size of the milpa a farmer must plant in order to meet his basic cash needs. Hence, Q'eqchi' farmers living in a densely forested village like Jaguarwood, Belize, plant smaller milpas than do farmers elsewhere. All in all, there is an ecologically positive synergism between farm and forest in traditional Q'eqchi' land management (cf. Li 1999).

Since the devil is often in the details, one might wonder then, how do the

FIGURE 3.4. Field and forest continuum, showing Agoutiville's milpas nestled next to the Sierra Cruz mountain range, 2003. Source: Liza Grandia

Q'eqchi' divvy up the land? There are two steps to choosing a field. The first is a private process of asking the *Tzuultaq'a* for permission to clear a certain amount of land for subsistence needs. This may be done through a family ceremony or, better still, a collective village ceremony called a *mayejak*—a multi-day affair involving nighttime vigils with sacred harp music, sexual abstinence, special foods, a pilgrimage to a cave or other ritual ceremony, and a church ceremony.[2] The second is a visible measuring process that makes known publicly where one intends to plant. Customarily in a Q'eqchi' village, the four principal male elders (*cheekel winq*), in order of their hierarchy and usually at a community meeting, will announce the dates and areas they plan to clear for their own fields. After the elders have commenced their work, younger men are free to choose their fields and schedule labor groups. Traditionally, land was demarcated with measurements that reflected the days needed to prepare the soil or the amount of seed needed to plant it.[3] A farmer might claim an area by marking it with posts, unusual plants, or trees or by clearing a fire lane around the perimeter (Collins 2001). Anyone who is unsure about the ownership of a particular field is expected to ask around the village before clearing, although most men know where all the others intend to plant. In the rare case of a dispute, the village mayor (*alcalde*), elders, or the entire community may mediate.

Despite being typecast as excessive monocroppers, Q'eqchi' farmers plant root vegetables, beans (running up the cornstalk), squashes, chilies, cooking herbs, tomatoes, okra, pineapples, and bananas in and among the first milpa (planted in April/May) and sometimes the second (planted in December) (table 3).[4] In addition to these cultivated crops, people take advantage of volunteer plants such as greens (*ichaj*), mushrooms (*okox*), and different leaves for cooking tamales (e.g., *ob'el* or "Santa Maria" and *mox* or "moxán"). All told, I documented some eighty crops, fruits, herbs, and wild plants cultivated in Q'eqchi' milpas in Belize plus at least another twenty food species harvested from nearby forests and fallow fields (Grandia 2009c: appendix). Many of these crops reproduce annually; thus, what may look like an abandoned fallow field may still be a productive area to which farmers return to collect foods.[5]

For the second, or dry-season, milpa, plots tend to be more stable and function more like private property. Where surface waters are abundant, farmers may maintain smaller, semipermanent riverside plots that are flooded annually with silt. The beef industry poses a threat to this system because cattle ranchers seek control of riverbanks, where they water their herds. When riverside land is not available, Q'eqchi' farmers may maintain a more permanent plot for the second milpa by sowing a nitrogen-fixing velvet bean (*Mucuna* spp.) that will be cut and mulched in November before they plant corn (see also Bourque 1989). A third, less permanent, option for farmers is to plant their second milpa in the same field as the first milpa, using the corn stalks from the first milpa as mulch.

Long-term research in Petén, Guatemala, shows that forests regenerate faster in small fallowed milpas than in large clearings such as pastures (Ferguson et al. 2003; Schwartz 1990; Shriar 1999). If a small plot is cropped for two years but remains surrounded by forest, it can become productive again after a four- to seven-year fallow period.[6] However, if large areas are deforested (either by too many contiguous milpa plots or by extensive cattle pastures), soil renewal through reforestation may take as long as fifty years. While outsiders may criticize the "wandering" milpa system, that quality is one of its primary ecological advantages.

If Q'eqchi' farmers were restricted exclusively to square, twenty- or thirty-hectare milpas, they would likely clear more contiguous land. They would also lose access to many necessary forest resources and/or the different soil types required for good crop returns. Indeed, one of the reasons cited by small farm-

TABLE 3. Lowland Q'eqchi' Milpa Cycle

JANUARY	Clear underbrush Plant beans
FEBRUARY	Clear underbrush, fell big trees, and/or clear low fallow fields
MARCH	Continue clearing Cut green corn Harvest beans
APRIL	Finish harvesting beans Burn Begin planting corn and rice (midmonth) Plant other crops Beware that corn stores are scarce
MAY	Burn (if not completed in April) Harvest the second milpa Continue planting corn, rice, and other crops
JUNE	Perform other maintenance tasks (house building, fishing, hunting, building storage house for corn, etc.)
JULY	Continue other tasks Rest while the rains begin Plant bananas and plantains
AUGUST	Plant beans Weed corn crop Beware that corn stores are scarce Cut green corn Organize ritual dances
SEPTEMBER	Cut rice and begin harvesting the first corn crop (*k'atk'al*) planted in April Plant black beans
OCTOBER	Continue harvesting the first milpa and/or the rice
NOVEMBER	Clear brush for the second milpa Organize a *mayejak*
DECEMBER	Plant the second milpa Harvest black beans

ers in Guatemala for selling their surveyed land to speculators is that they were given only swampy land and could not grow a good first milpa or, conversely, that they received only hilly land and the second milpa did poorly.

Figure 3.5, based loosely on Jaguarwood, illustrates the inequities arising from a transition to private property by comparing land distribution under a customary land management system (left) with a private property system established through typical government surveying practices (right). In the customary system, each farmer claims a small amount of land next to the road for permanent crops, shares river access for the second milpa, and may plant as much land for the milpa as he can muster labor to work it. Albeit messy, the system has a logic and tends toward equity. In contrast, divide the same landscape into blocks as in map B, and one lucky farmer monopolizes river access, while others receive plots of unusable swampy land. A young farmer might acquire a plot close to the village, and an elder would be left to walk two hours to his field. An herbal healer could lose the right to harvest patches of rare forest plants for his patients, and everyone in the village has to walk farther for firewood. Almost all lose road access for transporting cash crops to market. Although the private property system may look ordered on paper, it disorders village relations.

VILLAGE VARIATIONS

Generalizations aside, customary Q'eqchi' land management is not a monolithic system in which every community continues to observe the same timeless indigenous practices. The Q'eqchi' in Belize remained isolated for almost a century, protected from interference and large landholders and, thus, were able to maintain sustainable land-use traditions that were eroded in Guatemala by agrarian inequity. The model described above is based on four Belizean villages surrounding the Sarstoon Temash National Park (Grandia 2004a, 2004 b, 2004c). Guatemalan Q'eqchi' communities have adapted in different ways to historical, political, and economic constraints.

Villages in northern Guatemala such as Macawville and Atelesdale, both located inside the Maya Biosphere Reserve, practice extensive corn commodity production, focusing mostly on the first (burned) milpa and leaving the second (mulched) milpa for cultivating products for home consumption. Having received a concession from the National Council for Protected Areas (Consejo Nacional de Areas Protegidas), or CONAP, they were channeled into private parcels with a usufruct "right of possession" but were allowed to maintain a communal forest reserve. Land is currently abundant enough (forty-five hectares per family) that they should be able to postpone the intensification crisis until the next generation. Nonetheless, there are already signs of ecological strain. Once consistently high, yields are now erratic; drought, fires, crop theft,

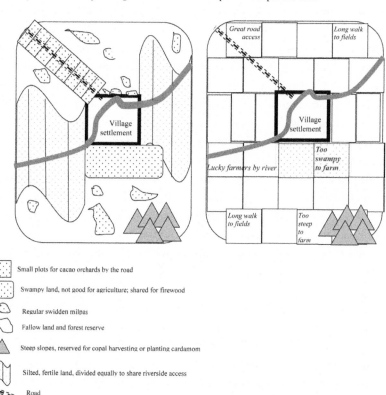

Map A—customary management   Map B—with private land

| | |
Great road access | Long walk to fields
Village settlement
Lucky farmers by river | Too swampy to farm
Long walk to fields | Too steep to farm

Small plots for cacao orchards by the road

Swampy land, not good for agriculture; shared for firewood

Regular swidden milpas

Fallow land and forest reserve

Steep slopes, reserved for copal harvesting or planting cardamom

Silted, fertile land, divided equally to share riverside access

Road

FIGURE 3.5. The landscape of customary management versus private parcels

and pests are common problems. In 2003, Atelesdale farmers reported harvests ranging from as little as four hundred to as much as seven thousand pounds per hectare. Reflecting on this variability, Roberto Tiul remarked, "here they plant who-knows-how-many-[hectares] and still don't make any [money]." In lieu of alternative markets or more off-farm employment in ecotourism, farmers in both these villages continue to meet their cash needs by planting the crops the truckers are willing to buy—dry corn, beans, squash seeds, and occasionally chilies and rice. This is not to say that these Q'eqchi' farmers lack interest in better land management. Before they migrated to Macawville, many of them had planted a nitrogen-fixing bean (*Mucuna* spp.) that replenishes soil fertility organically; once ProPetén made seeds available, the number of farmers planting this green mulch more than doubled within a year. Some have also begun investing in fruit trees and other agroforestry crops, again with ProPetén's help.

In the lush, rolling hills of southeastern Petén and Izabal, villages such as Tamalton and Agoutiville are more densely populated. The region was parceled by colonization agencies and has already suffered the effects of agrarian privatization; agricultural land has grown scarce. Because many families have sold their parcels to cattle ranchers and/or subdivided them for their children, the average-size parcel here is much smaller than in northern Guatemala. These villages also have a disproportionately high number of renters and sharecroppers, who pay around $35 a hectare per milpa (almost two weeks' wages). Because of this land tenure insecurity, many Q'eqchi' farmers focus on planting more corn for the second (mulched) milpa, which tends to command better market prices and requires less land than the first (burned) milpa.[7] Renters obviously lack incentive to improve their soils with green mulches, and many have turned instead to chemical fertilizers. Despite the agrarian squeeze, they have maintained an active ritual life and highly value group labor, often with modern variations (fig. 3.6). As Sebastian Yaxcal commented after their annual three-day *mayejak*, "We people in Izabal give offerings and sacrifices; we do it with our indigenous knowledge. But I've been to Petén—there in Petén they don't know anything . . . they no longer practice our customs." Overall, there appeared to be more interest in crop diversification and intensification among farmers in southeastern Petén and Izabal than in northern Petén, partly because of greater respect for elder knowledge but also because of greater opportunities for marketing produce in nearby towns.

Moving east into Belize, sustainable Q'eqchi' natural-resource management systems are even more in evidence in southern Toledo communities such as Jaguarwood and neighboring Orchardon that border the Sarstoon Temash National Park. In the northern part of the Toledo district and in western border areas with Guatemala, Belizean farmers are more oriented toward cash crops of red beans, rice, cacao, or whatever the market demands. To the south, however, many Q'eqchi' communities have maintained diversified subsistence production through customary land management. Wild meats and plants are central to their diet, and villagers (especially children) in this part of Belize are notably taller and better nourished compared to Q'eqchi' in Guatemala. Though they have a higher cash income than the average Guatemalan peasant, the people in Jaguarwood eat remarkably less junk food like chips and soda; as Carmen Asij remarked, "I would rather spend my money on meat." Because of the difficulty of transporting products to and from market, most Belizean farmers plant relatively smaller milpas intercropped with foods they want

FIGURE 3.6. Group labor for planting corn. Three Agoutiville generations plant corn together following full ritual customs but not excluding occasional cell phone interruptions, 2007. Photograph: Liza Grandia

for home consumption (root vegetables, beans, bananas, pineapples, chilies, cilantro, onions, tomatoes, and herbs). Women cultivate home gardens of fruit trees and especially the highly prized annatto, which provides a paste used for seasoning the traditional Q'eqchi' meat stew, *kaqik*. Those who farm as their primary occupation (less than half the village) are almost all Catholic and form reciprocal work groups for planting.

Although the Toledo villages have a strong subsistence economy, they are by no means static. Many residents are well educated, and Jaguarwood boasts several schoolteachers and an elementary school library larger than the public library for all of Petén. Many have abandoned farming altogether and earn wages from woodcarving. Some want to move into tourism. A few have invested in cattle with support from British agriculture extension agents and religious missionaries. Other cash-earning opportunities have ebbed and flowed over the years. Jaguarwood residents grew bananas in the 1920s and 1930s, tended orange plantations and raised pigs in the 1950s, worked with oil companies in the 1970s, cultivated red beans and rice in the 1980s, and planted cacao groves as well as market gardens in the 1990s. Contrary to modernist discourse, Q'eqchi' people have demonstrated a dynamic ability to move in *and* out of "capitalist" structures whenever the conditions are right (Wilk 1997).

For example, in the early 2000s, after the government opened a road to Orchardon, Martha Bolom, like other elder women (*chekel ixq*) in the village, began to travel to Punta Gorda town twice a week to sell traditional Q'eqchi' milpa foods. She expanded her market potential by planting a complex orchard of fruit trees in her backyard. By 2004, she was grossing $20–30 on a typical day, from which she subtracted $3.50 for bus fare, $3–5 for food, and $1 for a tax on her market spot, thus earning $12.50–22.50, comparable to national wages. These new market opportunities have, in turn, changed village practices as deep-rooted as the ownership of large pig herds, which is a favorite Q'eqchi' method of "banking" extra corn (Wilk 1981). Because of the damage animals cause to home gardens, however, Orchardon decided to ban free-range pigs, cows, and horses.

The sustainable practices of Jaguarwood and Orchardon contradict the stereotypes of Q'eqchi' farmers that are common in Guatemala. As these Belize villages show, the Q'eqchi' are not ignorant of complex lowland agricultural systems or agroforestry techniques.[8] Q'eqchi' farmers can and do practice sedentary, intensive agriculture on river plots or mulched fields. Q'eqchi' agriculture is deeply flexible in terms of crops and geography; given the right marketing system and transportation access, both male and female Q'eqchi' farmers diversify their production and adopt long-term, environmentally friendly crops. In response to a guaranteed fair trade market for cacao, hundreds of Belizean farmers invested in this tree crop even without secure land tenure. When Punta Gorda opened a farmers' market, Q'eqchi' women avidly expanded their roles in agricultural production through home gardens and orchards. In turn, these economic activities provide women higher status in the community; for example, Jaguarwood elected its first female chairperson in the last election. Also, Q'eqchi' families are equally (if not more) interested in non-farm alternatives (such as tourism and woodcarving) as in agricultural intensification. Q'eqchi' parents deeply value education. In Jaguarwood, several adults commented with pride that a schoolchild from their village had recently won the regional spelling bee. Because of the greater availability of reading materials from village libraries in Belize, one can observe people of all ages reading in hammocks in the afternoon, a sight not typically seen in Guatemala.

This is not to romanticize Belizean forest communities, but on the whole, they have maintained a stronger tradition of environmental stewardship than their Guatemalan neighbors and continue to rely on forest materials for housing, hunting, gathering, crafts, and spiritual purposes (Grandia 2004c). Although they might tell outsiders that they are ashamed of eating wild foods, they actually enjoy these ingredients in traditional comfort meals. They tell delightful stories to their grandchildren about forest spirits (Grandia 2004b). Families leave patches of forest between their houses for aesthetic and sanitary purposes. They love the beauty of their natural surroundings and might even build a two-story house just so they can watch the Temash river meander by on a quiet evening.

All told, the variables most closely correlated with the more sustainable practices exemplified by Jaguarwood (planting smaller milpas, more diversified cropping practices including agroforestry, and participation in forest management)[9] are, first and foremost, the ability to maintain customary land management, followed by longevity of settlement, continuation of group planting practices (usually associated with Catholicism), and access to fair markets. Lacking roads until a few years ago, Belizean Q'eqchi' villages remained relatively isolated and protected from government interference. Because the British colonial government rarely allowed them to apply for leases, they continue to practice swidden farming and forest management according to customary norms. Unlike their Guatemalan neighbors, they escaped the fate of plantation agriculture and were able to maintain more of their traditional agricultural and forest knowledge. Comparing these two different national groups offers insights into the property and population traps in which Guatemalan Q'eqchi' farmers have been caught.

THE PROPERTY TRAP

Why is there such a startling difference between the two countries? Because of the way Guatemala's peculiar agrarian history eroded customary land management practices, Q'eqchi' communities have been forced into inappropriate private property regimes, thereby creating a variety of negative feedback loops leading to environmental degradation. Without the appropriate repertoire of tools and knowledge to adapt sustainably to these new land regimes, Q'eqchi' farmers get caught in a property trap. Having lost the ecological and social efficiencies of the traditional system, they have not yet adapted to the economic and environmental constraints of more sedentary agriculture on private parcels. This stalled transition between one property system and another is exacerbated by several cultural factors: erosion of traditional knowledge, misperceptions of a limitless frontier, and confusion about inheritance.

Erosion of traditional knowledge

As the daughter of Alabama vegetable farmers, I had been totally flummoxed as to why Guatemalan Q'eqchi' families did not plant more vegetables even though they obviously relished these foods and purchased them when available. Asked why they did not diversify their crops, farmers would tell me they did not know how, which seemed odd, since they earned their living from the land and were accomplished corn farmers. It was not until Alfredo Chun in Jaguarwood, Belize, explained about "getting knowledge" of different crops that I finally understood. Every crop is thought to have its secrets, and farmers must learn the right time for planting, the correct rituals to perform, and the right prayers to say. All this must be learned from an elder, preferably not one's father, because, as Pablo Botzoc explained, a man would feel "naked" if he revealed all his agricultural wisdom to his son. Traditionally, a young couple would visit a neighboring elder to "learn how to live." Alfredo Chun and his wife had done this as newlyweds, but he thought he was the only young man in Jaguarwood to have done so. Education, migration, nuclear family organization, and a general secularization have all taken their toll on intergenerational dialogue in Q'eqchi' villages.

After being dispossessed of their own land, Guatemalan Q'eqchi' were forced onto plantations, where the bosses limited the size and diversity of crops so that laborers would remain dependent on their wages. Over the generations, these plantation workers lost much of their agro-economic knowledge. Young farmers today have had to rely on what they can easily observe from others (extensive hybrid-corn cropping) and rarely experiment with older, more diversified crops and techniques. Many who grew up in sharecropping or plantation contexts are likely to have observed that their fathers probably had only the time and land to plant a basic corn crop with little frills. For these and other reasons (such as aggressive marketing of new hybrid-corn varieties), heirloom crops and multiple corn varieties are rapidly disappearing from the landscape. Conservationists may criticize the Q'eqchi' for their extensive monocropping of hybrid corn, but this is a consequence of Guatemala's agrarian history and certainly not an inevitable facet of Q'eqchi' culture.

Moreover, as Agoutiville farmer Sebastian Yaxcal commented, much of the "technical assistance" they receive is culturally inappropriate: "The technical expert, the one that studies, is very deceptive. He wants to earn his salary. Every-thing is political now. The knowledge of the ancestors is over. With a high school education, a technical education, the youth want to eat easy, to pass an easy life. That's what has stained the community." For example, he disagreed with agrono-mists who advised him to put pesticides in his family's corn bin to protect hybrid corn from insects. He knew from the elders that local varieties of corn were less susceptible to infestation and that sprinkling cacao-infused water, lime powder, or allspice leaves in the corn bins would keep out weevils. Leaders in other vil-lages are similarly skeptical about advice from development workers about how to manage their land. At a village meeting called to inform cacao farmers of a change in their extension agent, Mariano Asij of Jaguarwood challenged the NGO worker, asking, "Will the next agent know how to tell us to plant our cacao with the moon?" Poor farmers know all too well that they alone bear the risks of change and innovation. In a context of uncertainty and hardship, Q'eqchi' pio-neer settlers tend to fall back on conservative, tested farming methods that may or may not be appropriate in the new ecosystem (J. R. Jones 1989).

Instead of providing more culturally appropriate agricultural extension services to Q'eqchi' people in their own language, the ministries of agricul-ture in both countries help owners of medium to large farms diversify crops for export and leave poor farmers to produce the country's basic grains. The conversion of lowland forests by Q'eqchi' settlers to the production of basic grains has helped subsidize the shackling of poor workers in export-driven plantations in other parts of the country. Most Q'eqchi' farmers in Guatemala continue to plant only corn and beans mainly because these are the crops the truckers from Guatemala City will buy from them. When NGOs like ProPetén started providing agronomic advice in Q'eqchi' about primary grain crops, farmers proved eager to learn new techniques such as the use of natural pes-ticides. In other regions, Q'eqchi' farmers are planting cardamom, annatto, sesame seeds, even "xate" palms in commercial quantities. Clearly NGO proj-ects have an impact—whether or not they are worth the overall dollar invest-ment is another question.[10] Mostly though, the Q'eqchi' need better market opportunities; when given the right outlets, they figure out among themselves how to grow the desired crops.

Frontier optimism

Now that most policy makers, especially environmentalists, have access to geographic information system (GIS) maps, it becomes easy to assume that everyone shares a Western, technologically enhanced bird's-eye view of the limits of natural resources. In Guatemala, the biodiversity conservationists doggedly collect expensive satellite imagery on forest cover, which gives them a keen perception of the "closing" of the frontier, yet the average Q'eqchi' villager has never flown in a plane, much less been taught such abstract mapping skills in school. Nor have most of them had the opportunity to travel extensively and get a feel for the limits of the lowland Petén landscape or to even know where park boundaries actually lie. Locating agricultural land that will provide for his family's survival is the utmost priority for a Q'eqchi' farmer. A land search by trial and error—making their way through a maze of topographic, military, and governmental obstacles—is a common thread in many of their migration stories. For people traveling on foot and/or public transportation, the Maya lowlands may feel vast, never ending.

As Don José Cux explained, when his family was evicted from a share-cropping arrangement on a cattle ranch in southern Petén, he heard about "free land" in an abandoned place known as Macawville in northern Petén. After traveling with his father-in-law via public bus to the nearest village and then walking twenty-two kilometers for three days through a swamp in the middle of the rainy season, they finally reached an abandoned village. Seeing the empty homes, Don José sat on the banks of the San Pedro River with mosquitos swarming around him and wept. "What am I doing out here?" he wondered to himself. Still, he observed that the land was fertile and unoccupied; he did not yet know or understand that it was located in a national park. When he returned home after this exploratory trip, his wife asked him excitedly, "Is there really a river? Is it true there are fish and deer to hunt? Let's go then!" Don José and his wife were alone in Macawville that first year; both became ill with malaria, and his wife died. Don José said he cried a lot in those early, lonely days, repeatedly wondering, "Why in the world have I come to this place?" But soon his extended family came to join him, and others filled the village. Within about five years, he had welcomed one hundred households. Don José counted his blessings, saying, "We have a river, forest, a new road to the village, *and* our land." His extended family had been able to claim nine "caballerías"—as large as the cattle ranch they had left behind in San Luis, he explained with glee. Clasping his hands, he exclaimed to me, "We're in heaven [here]!" (Estamos en la Gloria!).

As the pioneers in the United States once believed, Q'eqchi' settlers such as Don José Cux maintain faith in the abundance of the frontier—that there will always be land and more forests farther north. This is not to say that Q'eqchi' people do not appreciate the forests, but as people who rely on the forests for their subsistence, they have a different perspective on nature. While Westerners prize large tracts of untouched wilderness at a comfortable distance, rural Q'eqchi' people prefer to have forests close by so that they can *use* them. While Westerners depict the tropical forests as "fragile," for people living next to them, like the Q'eqchi', the forests seem resiliently abundant. As one man heard his neighbors remark when they sold their parcels, "Is this the only land? No, there is land everywhere" (ProPetén 2009). They never imagined that the forests might one day disappear or that there might not be more free land farther north.

With their lush forests, the lowlands may have appeared more fertile to the Q'eqchi' than the thin tropical soils actually proved. Farmers often reminisced about the abundance of wildlife, good rainfall, and bountiful crops when they arrived in the lowlands. Asked to explain the change, almost invariably the reply was a taciturn "It just ended" (*Ki osok*). Christopher T. Fagan (2000: 22) recounts a conversation with a Macawville farmer who recalled, "San Luis had a forest like here (Macawville) when we arrived there, but when we left there wasn't any forest." Fagan asked what had happened, and the man replied, "We cut it all [down]." Even when they see that the corn harvest is bad, the forests are stressed, or wild animals are growing scarce, Q'eqchi' farmers tend to attribute such misfortunes to their failure to pay sufficient ritual respect to the *Tzuultaq'a* rather than to general environmental stress or climatic patterns. Like evangelical Christians, they see their ecological problems as a consequence not of their own behavior but of a lack of prayer. They believe that because the *Tzuultaq'a* are angry at human irreverence, they are guarding the animals deep within the sacred caves and refuse to release them for the people's benefit.

One wonders what kind of autochthonous, bottom-up Q'eqchi' environmentalism might have emerged in Petén had a top-down, Western, park conservation paradigm not been imposed on their landscape. Since the Spanish invasion, the Q'eqchi' have experienced only two categories of land: village lands managed communally and privately held plantations (*acieen*, the Q'eqchi' modification of "haciendas").[11] From a Q'eqchi' perspective, the concept of preserving forests through the creation of parks is another foreign idea. That is not to say that Q'eqchi' people do not appreciate the forest or lack environmental spirituality.[12] Although they may demonstrate little interest in *commercial* extraction of non-timber forest products, Q'eqchi' people do greatly enjoy *subsistence* extraction of products like copal, food, housing materials, and so forth (see also Secaira 1992). They also assiduously conserve the forests around their sacred caves and mountain shrines. Is valuing the forest for one's daily survival or for religious reasons somehow inferior to valuing the forest for ecological reasons or the aesthetic pleasures of biodiversity?

International conservation planners effectively divided Petén into two unequal parts— a series of deforested villages clumped together in the south and a vast contiguous block of protected areas in the north—and it has cost a lot of money to keep these parts separate. Perhaps instead of a 1.6-million-hectare Maya Biosphere Reserve, Q'eqchi' leaders might have planned a smaller park but added to it a mosaic of a thousand village forests (see Fedick 1996 on the "managed mosaic" of ancient Maya agriculture and Zarger 2009 on contemporary Belize mosaics).[13] The same amount of flora and fauna might have been conserved, but the benefits would have been distributed more equitably.

Inheritance confusion

As a people who have traditionally received land from their community, and not necessarily from their parents, the idea of family inheritance embedded in Western private property regimes is as puzzling as the idea of protected areas to Q'eqchi' families. With nucleated households and average fertility rates of almost nine children per family, when a father's older children reach marriageable age, he may still be responsible for several younger children. A father's economic burdens would, therefore, prevent him from dividing his parcel formally with an elder son or daughter (if her mate lacks land). If single, an elder son usually continues to work with his father, but they might plant separate areas within the same field. Sometimes fathers and sons or sons-in-law share the work of a corn crop but plant other secondary crops separately. They may do each other favors in cultivating their separate crops, but when a young man is married, he generally becomes solely responsible for his family and plants all his own crops. If his father cannot help him with land, the son must seek his own way in the world.

For farmers without social security, elders never really retire. One elder in Atelesdale, nearly blind, still travels daily to his milpa even though he fears he might not see snakes due to his poor vision. In a village down the road from Jaguarwood, William Ical, now well into his nineties, continues planting each year. At eighty-six, Don Vicente Chub farms with some help from his grandsons—and could still muster energy to dance longer than me at an all-night *mayejak* in the Catholic church. Don Vicente is bequeathing his land to one grandson, as his own children long ago sought their fortunes elsewhere.

The lack of clear father-to-son inheritance poses less of a problem in customary Q'eqchi' systems. A community simply sets aside a certain area for the younger generations; when a farmer dies or can no longer work, his land returns to the community to be redistributed to any young person who needs it. In the Western system of private parcels imposed on Q'eqchi' communities, however, obvious problems arise. A farmer cannot endlessly subdivide and still maintain adequate fallow land, so only some children or grandchildren are lucky enough to inherit land. Others are left to fend for themselves by moving elsewhere. In many cases, parents told me they planned to sell their land in order to avoid fights among their children.

In a frontier context, parents tend to encourage the younger generations to search for new land rather than intensifying production and subdividing the land they have. Indeed, the desire to acquire new land for one's children is a major factor driving migration northward. Many Q'eqchi' people explained that although they had some land in their place of origin, it was insufficient for their children. So long as the frontier appears open, it makes economic sense for rural Q'eqchi' families to claim new land before intensifying production on what they have.

These inheritance problems are compounded in communities inside parks, where there are no long-term property guarantees; the national park service simply concessions farm parcels for a period of twenty-five years. As Mario Mo, an energetic young Q'eqchi' farmer in Atelesdale with five children, explained, "CONAP gave me one forested caballería, but I have it almost all cleared. In five years I could finish a caballería and go on to the next! If only they'd given me two parcels." After finishing the backbreaking labor of clearing the forest, this young man was perfectly willing to sell the usufruct rights to his parcel to a cattle rancher and then claim another piece of forest for himself—never worrying about where his children might one day farm.

What is perhaps most worrisome about parcel sales inside the national parks is the frontier logic driving them. People displaced multiple times and driven to the edge of the agricultural frontier into illegal settlements inside parks still somehow believe there may be land farther north for themselves and/or their children. Roughly half the farmers in Atelesdale have no plans to leave land to their children, and soon there may be another landless generation inside the parks. Alicia Acal from Atelesdale, who holds a formally titled parcel outside the reserve, said she was planning to ask CONAP for another parcel inside the community concession because her titled land has degraded into weeds ("puro zacate ahora"). Many people in Atelesdale and Macawville expressed something like "Ask CONAP, and you shall receive." They figured CONAP would someday give their children land. Clearly the government has not conveyed to settlers that usufruct farming concessions awarded in protected areas will have to be subdivided for future generations. Were that policy made explicit and further immigration to the Maya Biosphere Reserve prevented, the sheer pace of population growth might nonetheless lead to serious agrarian pressure *within* protected areas, not to mention in the rest of the rural lowlands where average Q'eqchi' fertility is almost twice the national average.

THE POPULATION TRAP

As politically charged and uncomfortable as the topic may be, a discussion of swidden agriculture cannot ignore the question of population growth. Although Marxist-influenced political ecologists typically prefer to explain land degradation as a consequence of distributional rather than demographic factors, both play a part. Bringing population back into the equation is not to deny that militarization and overconsumption in industrialized countries are *the* critical environmental issues of our day (Guha 1997). Nor does it take responsibility away from economic elites (both national and foreign) who set in motion local environmental degradation by constructing roads into lowland forests for the extraction of timber, minerals, oil, and other forest resources and by squeezing peasants off the land, thereby pushing them to migrate.[14] Rather, it is to recognize that the stakes are so high—the irreversible loss of biodiversity, the poisoning of the planet, and countless lives destroyed or wasted through environmental injustice—that no part of the context can be left out. The challenge, therefore, for scholars sympathetic to the environmental problems of the poor is to explain how the tempo and distribution of population growth work as reinforcing links at a local and regional level without reducing environmental degradation exclusively to a matter of population (Arizpe, Stone, and Major 1994).

One could certainly argue that inequity generates most environmental problems globally, but that in certain local and regional contexts like Petén, population growth may also be a compounding factor. Scholars must guard against manipulating population rhetoric for political ends other than the health and well-being of women and their families. Still, to shy away from the question of population and resource use because of a kind of political correctness may lead to other ill effects. For progressives to remain silent on the issue is to surrender public debates to hard-core Malthusians (e.g., Kaplan 1994) who want to maintain a status quo of coercive family planning programs or to religious fundamentalists who would deny women access to reproductive-health services.

While customary Q'eqchi' methods of extensive swidden agriculture are eminently suitable to lowland ecology if sufficient land is available for fallowing (as in Belize), at higher densities, the same methods may not be as appropriate (as in Guatemala). Historically, the Q'eqchi' have proved to be resilient farmers, but they face an uphill battle in the need to innovate and adapt to more intensive methods of farming on smaller and smaller parcels, the shrinkage due partly to inequitable land distribution and also to high birthrates. Doña Maria Caal's family (fig 3.7) provides an example. Although she and all her children and grandchildren had fewer offspring than average for Petén, her family has grown substantially. Some have land, but most are renting or borrowing parcels from others in Saxb'atz.

Both they and policy makers in charge of Guatemala's agricultural planning have yet to anticipate what demographers refer to as the "momentum" of a young population structure. In rapidly growing countries like Guatemala, roughly half the population is under fifteen years of age. So even if Guatemala were to reach replacement-level fertility tomorrow, the country would still experience significant population growth because so many people have yet to reach their reproductive years. Moreover, marrying or mating young (as they do in Petén, at an average of 17.5 years, significantly younger than the national average of 19.4 [INE 1999]) also adds momentum to population growth. Both these factors explain why the population of China continues to expand long after its government imposed a draconian one-child policy.

The problem of population momentum is somewhat like the cautionary tale about the scalded frog. According to the story, if you drop a frog into a pot of boiling water, it will jump out, but if you put a frog in a pot of cool water and gradually raise the temperature, it will stay in the water until it boils to death. Like the frog in the pot, policy makers find it mathematically and socially difficult to fathom the problem of demographic momentum because of the built-in time lag of population growth. The regional government ministers participating in a demographic training workshop I held in Petén in 1999 found this by far the most challenging concept. However, once we started plotting out the number of new schools, clinics, and other public infrastructure they would be responsible for building, they began to understand the meaning of exponential population growth. In a best-case scenario (with the fertility rate drop-

FIGURE 3.7. One extended pioneer family, 1995. When I took this photograph of Doña María Caal with some of her grandchildren and great-grandchildren, the family marveled at how numerous they had become; after struggling as frontier pioneers, they simply did not anticipate they would be this demographically successful. Photograph: Liza Grandia

ping magically overnight from 6.8 to a replacement level of 2.1 and no further in-migration), we calculated that the population would still more than double within twenty five years because so many young people would be reaching reproductive age during that time period. Our more realistic predictions in that workshop for Petén's population in 2020 ranged from 1 million to almost 1.8 million.

Nor do highly paid World Bank land planners seem to understand demographic momentum. They divvied up all of Petén outside the national parks into private parcels of forty-five hectares per family. With the fertile, volcanic soils of the highlands, this would be more than enough land, but given the karstic soils of Petén, the average family needs at least twenty to thirty hectares just to survive. Although Guatemala has the highest fertility in Latin America, the World Bank developed no contingency plans for future generations. Many technocrats continue to believe the presumption that rural people *want* to have enormous families in order to have more hands in the fields. Yet there is no relation between family size and land (cf. Sutherland, Carr, and

Curtis 2004), nor do women want to bear the high number of children they currently average.

Land and family size

After asking hundreds of Q'eqchi' farming families about potential relationships between their family size and land use, I concluded that while children may provide extra help with family labor, especially with raising younger siblings (Kramer and Boone 2002), they also represent extra mouths to feed, clothe, and send to school. Male children as young as six years old may begin accompanying their fathers to the milpa but do not begin to contribute significant labor until they are eight or nine and only if they drop out of school. Rural youth often marry during their teenage years and are free to move elsewhere. In light of children's own family commitments, the ability to recruit adult labor among friends, kin, and neighbors is far more important for Q'eqchi' farm productivity than household (child) labor (Carter 1969). The wealthiest farmers seem to be those who can mobilize extensive ritual kin networks (the "compadrazgo" system) for communal planting or who can afford to pay for day laborers to plant more acreage (Fagan 2000).

Furthermore, data from a thousand-household, Petén-wide survey found no association between crop productivity and family size (Grandia et al. 2001).[15] Further testing this hypothesis, data on fertility in Macawville and Atelesdale compared with milpa size show a tendency for families with older children to have slightly larger milpas; however, the older children in these villages are attending school rather than helping in the fields. Hence, it appears that families do not become larger in order to claim larger farms but plant more land so that they can provision their larger families. Already on the cusp of desperate poverty, only the rare farmer is going to reduce his milpa size because he is planning to leave sufficient soil fallow for his children, much less his children's children, in a hypothetical ten to fifteen years. The idea of "planning" one's family in relation to available land is not a luxury available to the poor.[16] In the end, what farmers decide to plant varies far more according to personality than family size (cf. Reina 1967).

Women's reproductive desires

While Q'eqchi' families are being forced into a private system of landownership that requires long-term generational thinking about family size and land availability, they lack access to appropriate reproductive-health services. Hence, there is an extraordinary gap between desired and actual family size in northern Guatemala. Parents ideally wanted four children (two girls and two boys) but had an average of almost nine (Grandia et al. 2001). Many women told me, "Enough already!" (*Tzacal!*). Only in rare instances (for example, infertile women or newlyweds) did a Q'eqchi' woman express the desire for another baby. Some women responded by invoking a generic religious statement such as "However many God gives me," but if I paused for a moment, many would then inquire, "Is it true there is really a pill not to have any more children?" When given information in their own language that honestly addresses the false rumors they have heard about family planning methods, these same Q'eqchi' women quickly become interested in spacing their births.[17] Generational differences were even more striking: young Q'eqchi' mothers commonly told me they would be happy with just one or two children, citing the high cost of shoes, medicines, food, and school materials. A few even expressed concern about land scarcity as a reason for family planning. Doña Dominga Choc of Atelesdale, for example, had begun using the Depo-Provera contraceptive injection after her third child because "Where are they going to find land to make milpa to feed their own children one day?" While previous generations may have had more children with the intention of increasing the family labor supply or providing security or companionship in their old age, this is clearly no longer the case.

Vaccines, antibiotics, and other primary health medicines began to lower mortality rates many decades ago in Guatemala, but rural people have only recently gained access to basic family planning services for various reasons. Guatemala's conservative Catholic oligarchy was able to block public reproductive-health programs for many years. Meanwhile, donors like the United States Agency for International Development (USAID) get more bang for the buck by investing their dollars in urban clinics rather than serving the most remote rural poor in places like Petén. Few government officials ever really talk to rural women, much less indigenous women who do not speak Spanish, about what the women themselves want. In any case, women's health has always been treated as a lower priority than infant and child health, despite tomes of public health research irrevocably linking the two. Whether or not family planning would have been of interest to rural farming families decades ago is unknown because the services were simply not there.

While Q'eqchi' families still rely on reproductive and inheritance patterns from a more flexible system of customary land management, the World Bank and the Guatemalan state keep trying to push Q'eqchi' families onto square pieces of land, hoping they will somehow intensify their production and learn a kind of Malthusian "moral restraint." While forcing the Q'eqchi' into a private property regime, the state fails to give them a means of planning their families or any indication of how to improve and sustainably intensify their agricultural production in preparation for subdividing the land among their children.

CARRYING CAPACITIES

Caught in dual property and population traps, Q'eqchi' farming families cope with agrarian stress in different ways, as theorized in the broader academic literature on peasants. When landholdings and/or agricultural production are insufficient to maintain their households, peasants may turn to other strategies, such as the following:

- Belt-tightening: Reducing household consumption and/or making goods previously purchased with cash
- Self-exploitation: Intensifying production in a sustainable way on the same amount of land (diversifying into organic crops or using natural fertilizers)
- Resistance: Occupying land or protesting in other ways
- Environmental exploitation: Intensifying unsustainably and exhausting their land (e.g., reducing the fallow period, applying chemical fertilizers or commercial herbicides and pesticides)
- Proletarianization: Hiring out their labor power for wages (working for large landowners or moving into nonfarm labor such as urban construction)
- Displacement: Selling their land and moving elsewhere

Because there is little governmental and nongovernmental support for the first three strategies, Q'eqchi' families tend to resort to the other three, which, over the long term, will undermine the autonomy they desire as independent peasant producers. Meanwhile, conservationists worry that peasants may soon surpass, if they have not already surpassed, the carrying capacity of the region.

Archaeologists have also long wrestled with the question of how many people the Petén can support. They estimate that 1 million to 1.5 million people lived in the lowlands at the height of the late classic Maya civilization (600–850) (Whitmore and Turner 2001), more than double today's population.

Ancient Maya were able to sustain that population on poor karstic soils by combining swidden milpa with other more intensive forms of cultivation (terracing, arboriculture, raised beds, and drained swamp fields, among others) (ibid.; C. Wright n.d.; Fedick 1996; H. S. Carr 1996). Archaeologists influenced by Malthusian notions of scarcity once hypothesized that problems associated with population growth led to a sudden Maya demise, but new evidence suggests that the collapse was more of an uneven and prolonged unraveling than a sudden cataclysmic event (Demarest, Rice, and Rice 2004; M. Canuto, pers. comm., Feb. 2010). A more complex set of factors—population included, but also drought, deforestation caused by the harvesting of materials needed for building and sustaining cities, and social inequity—provoked general environmental deterioration that resulted in food shortages, extensive warfare, and political chaos in dozens of Maya cities at the end of the first millennium. Maya people lost faith in their rulers and forsook their cities, but they never "disappeared"; rather, they continued to live in villages away from the urban ruins, in much the same way that Q'eqchi' pioneers melted into the forest to escape political strife during the colonial period, the Liberal reforms (1880s–1930s), and the Guatemalan civil war (1960s–90s).

Based on archaeological evidence alone, we know there is no set carrying capacity (à la Fernside 1986) for the lowlands. While the concept of sustainability is somewhat nebulous, carrying capacity implies "a sense of calculability and precision" (Sayre 2008: 120). Garrett Hardin even endows the concept with biblical meaning, writing that "for human populations as for others, the prime commandment must be Thou shalt not transgress the carrying capacity" (quoted in ibid.: 131). Following an impressive genealogy of the term from its origins in shipping to its applications to ecology, Sayre then asks, Is carrying capacity fixed or is it dynamic? Is it natural or subject to technology and adaptation? And we might ask, How exactly does it take into account the ubiquitous problem of inequity?

The number of people the Maya lowlands can sustain obviously varies depending on the equity of resource distribution, the quality of the environment, the productivity of agriculture, and, perhaps most important, the suitability and flexibility of the property regime in relation to local cultures. The very idea of a set carrying capacity, which always seems implied in conservation discussions about agricultural intensification, may be a distraction from what is really happening with power and property.[18] In the overall scheme of things, which is the greater problem: Shifting (milpa) cultivation or the shifting (displacement) of Q'eqchi' farmers? Population growth or property inequity? Regional carrying capacity for agriculture or for cattle?

In conservation planning meetings, I never once heard anyone criticize cattle ranching as a land use, much less suggest that there might be a "cow carrying capacity" (Grandia 2009b), although there are at least as many cattle as people in Petén. Instead, conservationists wring their hands about Q'eqchi' swidden agriculture, all the while eating beef at their luncheon meetings.[19] Ranchers can control vast acreage with very low stocking rates and a handful of well-armed guards, but depressingly little local labor. Occupying more space than swidden agriculture, the cattle industry provides far less employment. For this reason, a cattle economy will reach its carrying capacity long before there are too many people for a regional economy based on subsistence agriculture. In turn, Q'eqchi' communities chopped up into private parcels will reach population saturation long before communities that manage their territory with more flexible customary practices based on the sharing of forest resources. In short, there are many different carrying capacities for Petén, dependent largely on the equity of land distribution. To be sure, sustainability depends on some kind of forest conservation, both for the intrinsic and use values of biodiversity for subsistence farmers and for stabilizing regional climate and rainfall. The question is, how much forest and how should it be territorially portioned— as large blocks or thousands of smaller forest patches connected by corridors? Many local conservation leaders feel that had the parks been designed smaller, they could have been more easily protected.

With half of Petén now devoted to large protected areas and the remaining half being taken over by pastures and palm plantations, very little arable land remains on which Q'eqchi' farmers and other smallholders may earn a living. Indeed, were it not for the large tracts of fallow land being converted to pasture for cattle, Q'eqchi' milpa production could remain relatively sustainable for a long time to come. This would allow for the gradual introduction of alternatives such as new agroforestry systems or fair trade products that would encourage genuine farmer participation and leadership. As it stands, Q'eqchi' farmers are the ones being blamed for not changing fast enough. Yet, given the precariousness of peasant production and the almost permanent subsistence crisis that farmers face year to year (Edelman 2005), it is unrealistic to expect that they will suddenly abandon basic grain production. Laura Nader rightly asks: "How has it come to be . . . that anthropologists are more interested in why peasants don't change than why the auto industry doesn't innovate, or why the Pentagon or universities cannot be more organizationally creative? The conservatism of such major institutions and bureaucratic organizations probably has wider implications for the species and for theories of change than does the conservatism of peasantry" (1972: 289). Rather than focusing on the "conservatism" of Q'eqchi' farmers, perhaps we should discuss the conservatism of multilateral donor banks and problems with their formulaic approach to land legalization and biodiversity conservation, which end up leaving the Q'eqchi' at the mercy of land speculators, cattle ranchers, and foreign investors.

4

Speculating

THE WORLD BANK'S MARKET-ASSISTED LAND REFORM

> As much as guns and warships, maps have been
> the weapons of imperialism.
>
> —J. Brian Harley, historian

WHEN asked if they own a parcel, frontier settlers frequently reply with macabre humor: "The only land I'll ever have is in the cemetery." Or, as a father from Atelesdale said in fatalistic response when questioned about what land his children might inherit, "Poor we were born, and poor we will die." Although the Q'eqchi' people have little hope of owning land in their lifetimes, they consider themselves intransitively *owned* by land.[1] Imagining land as simultaneously feminine and masculine, they often refer to it as "Our Father, Our Mother" and, as indigenous people, describe themselves as "children of the earth" (*laa'o laj ralch'och'*). Emphasizing their spiritual relationship with the soil, the Q'eqchi', for example, almost invariably prefix the adjective *loq'laj* (sacred) to the word *ch'och'* (land). In Spanish, Q'eqchi' settlers describe their parcels as "trabajaderos" (places to work). In either language, land is something not merely to be acquired but to be labored.

In contrast, the oligarchy that has ruled Guatemala since colonial times has regarded land as property and also as an idiom of power. It has maintained one of the most profoundly inequitable land regimes in the Western hemisphere. Beneath the beautiful tapestry of immaculately tended slivers of land like those shown in figure 4.1 lies an ugly patchwork of agrarian inequity. The existence of the latifundio, or large landholding, depends on the existence of the minifundio, or microparcel (a plot smaller than what a farming family requires for basic subsistence), and vice versa, in a system of polarizing greed and oppression.

FIGURE 4.1. Verapaz minifundios, 1993. Note the small size of corn parcels in highland Verapaz. Photograph: Aaron Tukey

Data from government agriculture censuses (1950, 1964, 1979, 2003) show that land concentration in Guatemala has changed little over the last half century. Roughly 2 percent of landowners controlled 60 percent of the land in 1950. Statistics from the 1979 census revealing that 2.6 percent of farms controlled 65 percent of Guatemala's agricultural land provoked so much outrage that the government simply stopped carrying out the survey until 2003. Opening up the northern frontier to landless peasants did little to improve Guatemala's overall land distribution. To the contrary, the 2003 agricultural census showed the top 3.2 percent of Guatemalan landowners still control 66 percent of the land. Much of these large landholdings remain idle; in fact, less than 40 percent of arable land in Guatemala is actually cultivated (Saldívar and Wittman 2004). Since 1979, the number of minifundios actually *increased*, especially in the Q'eqchi' department of Alta Verapaz, which is caught in a downward spiral of subdivision into smaller and smaller plots.

Despite five major attempts at land reform since independence from Spain (table 4), Guatemala's land distribution remains locked in this pattern of rigid extremes. Although the Liberal governments representing Guatemala's new merchant class managed to expropriate large tracts from the Catholic Church

TABLE 4. Phases of Land Reform in Guatemala

PHASE	INITIATED	CHARACTERISTICS	BENEFICIARIES
First	Late nineteenth century	Seizure of lands held by indigenous peoples and the Catholic Church	Foreign investors
Second	1950s	State-led expropriation and redistribution of land, preempted by U.S. intervention	Peasants
Third	1960s	Counterreform, colonization	Elites, military, cattle ranchers, some peasants
Fourth	1980s–90s	Land banks as "market-assisted land reform" under structural adjustment	A limited number of landless families
Fifth	1990s onward	Emphasis on juridical security through a national cadastral registry	Remains to be seen

at the end of the nineteenth century, they passed these on to wealthy planters and foreign companies for the development of export crops. U.S. intervention prematurely halted Guatemala's second attempt to expropriate large plantations and redistribute them to the poor in the early 1950s. The third counter-revolutionary phase attempted to diffuse agrarian pressure through frontier expansion, but to little avail, because military officers and other elites simultaneously claimed large plantations from the colonization agencies. Like many of its Latin American neighbors, Guatemala began its fourth attempt at land reform under the dual constraints of structural adjustment and civil war. From the late 1980s to the early 1990s, USAID and other donors promoted various "land bank" projects intended to facilitate land purchases on the open market. Without adequate price subsidies to help the landless poor, these projects fell far short of satisfying demand.[2]

Following Guatemala's drift to market-oriented land reform, the World Bank further steered the country toward establishing a more efficient national land registry. Under this paradigm, the government's new role would be to facilitate and record transactions between "willing sellers and willing buyers," in World Bank terminology. The state might verify the juridical and cadastral accuracy of land sales but should leave distributive outcomes to the dynamics of the market. Carlos Cabrera, a World Bank consultant and eventual director of the Guatemalan agency administering the loan, vigorously promoted this idea in the early 1990s, but it gained little traction at first (Gould 2009).

However, the presence of international donors during the Peace Accords negotiations that ended Guatemala's civil war in 1996 reinvigorated Cabrera's idea, which garnered support from strange political bedfellows, both left and right. One might ask why guerrilla leaders, after having fought a long civil war to rectify Guatemala's agrarian inequity, abandoned the cause of land redistribution and so uncritically accepted the World Bank framework? First, we must remember that emerging from a Cold War–shaped context in which any public discourse about agrarian reform could get someone labeled a Communist and "disappeared" by the military, the World Bank admittedly helped leftists put land reform back on the negotiation table, albeit minimally (Rosset 2004). Apparently, many on the left also hoped that the World Bank's technical approach to land reform would depoliticize the process and clean up corruption (Hernández Alarcón 1998a) and that information from a national land registry might help them achieve other goals such as resolving land disputes, creating a platform for designing other land reforms, helping to foment public planning and infrastructure development, making farmers eligible for credit with land security as collateral, and providing the necessary information for taxing idle land and large landholdings.

Members of the right-wing oligarchy—represented by the Coordinating Committee of Agricultural, Commercial, Industrial, and Financial Associations (Comité Coordinador de Asociaciones Agrícolas, Comerciales, Industriales y Financieras), or CACIF, and the National Council of Farmers and Ranchers (Coordinadora Nacional Agropecuaria), or CONAGRO—recognized that the World Bank's technocratic approach would help them solidify and perhaps even expand their holdings and preempt expropriation. Legally mapped titles would undoubtedly help them maintain vigilant control of their plantations and take swift action against squatters (Williams 1986). Others simply saw it as a necessary part of agro-development. Guatemala was the only country in Latin America without a reliable national land registry, a condition made worse during the civil war when the military seized control of national cartography. Of all the titles in the General Property Registry (est. 1887), 60 percent had never been updated since the first inscriptions in the late nineteenth century, and by 1993, 18 million documents in the registry lacked appropriate signatures (Chacón Véliz 2003). Failure to maintain the registry has resulted in so many competing and overlapping land claims that Guatemalans joke that their country has "three floors" (Hernández Alarcón 1998a).

Unfinished colonization projects in northern Guatemala exacerbated this chaos. Having completed only 5,000 titles over three decades, FYDEP passed 29,479 land claims to INTA, of which only 7,044 had gone past the first application stage. With only one topographer for all of Petén, INTA made little progress with the backlog (Kaimowitz 1995). By the time FONTIERRAS inherited these claims at the turn of the century, the stack had grown to 40,000 files (Schwartz 2001). Consequently, many settlers have waited more than twenty years for their titles. Boundaries overlap, municipalities dispute territory, multiple people claim one parcel—conflicts abound. Hence, many hoped that the World Bank might bring some order to this Wild West of pioneer claims.

Albeit the largest lender and hegemonic leader, the World Bank was certainly not the only donor institution influencing Guatemala's shift to market-based responses to land problems. As far back as 1968, USAID had financed a land survey project via Guatemala's National Geographic Institute. In another study carried out in the early 1980s, USAID suggested that the government create a land bank for selling property and providing credit to farmers. In 1991, the U.S. Department of Defense helped improve aerial photography of the country. European donors began to support various pilot projects across Guatemala.[3] In Belize, the Inter-American Development Bank (IDB) financed a similar land management project. Every donor wanted to sell its own agrarian model, technical package, and experts.

Two Guatemalan agencies established immediately after the 1996 Peace Accords were given responsibility for coordinating and implementing these various donor-driven initiatives. The purpose of FONTIERRAS was to help peasants purchase land on the open market through what became known as access projects. A quasi-state agency called the Legal and Technical Unit/Protierra (Unidad Técnico-Jurídico/Protierra), or UTJ—later renamed the Cadastral Information Registry (Registro de Información Catastral), or RIC—took charge of survey projects for setting up a national property registry.[4] UTJ was tasked with helping peasants gain title to their land by providing technical assistance with "territorial ordering," that is, cartographically measuring and registering the parcels through geographic information systems. FONTIERRAS was then supposed to handle the "regularization" process by providing technical and legal assistance with all the paperwork and fees required to adjudicate land by Guatemalan law. When necessary, the Presidential Dependency for the Resolution of Conflicts (Dependencia Presidencial para la Resolución de Conflictos), or CONTIERRA, a special executive branch agency (later transformed into the Secretariat of Agrarian Affairs), was supposed to help mediate or resolve land disputes. In practice, the lines between these and other agencies blurred. Subcontracting most of the work on the ground to foreign businesses compounded the confusion.

Plagued by long waiting lists, corruption, clientelism, poor technical assistance, speculative pricing, and high foreclosure rates, FONTIERRAS had lost most of its external donor funding by 2004. As one foreign consultant put it to me, the agency was "a black hole." However, UTJ's cadastral work for establishing a national property registry, otherwise known as the National Survey, marched on. My research focused on the largest of these cadastral projects, the Land Administration Project (LAP I) in Petén (1998–2007), financed by a $31 million World Bank loan. This ambitious project aimed to survey and register all land in Petén, approximately one-third of the country. Due to the project's large size and geographic scope, it profoundly influenced the government's approach to land administration in other parts of Guatemala and deeply shaped the design of the 2005 national Cadastre Law.

SURVEYING THE SURVEY

While an accurate cadastral registry is certainly important to any process of agrarian reform, the Peace Accords committed the Guatemalan government to improving nine other aspects of its agrarian policy: (1) conflict resolution, (2) training, (3) information systems, (4) public financing for land, (5) productive projects, (6) infrastructure for rural development, (7) credit, (8) legal reform, and (9) land taxes. To a certain degree, World Bank support for the National Survey motivated the government to strengthen its competence in two of these areas, training and information systems (nos. 2 and 3 on the list), but little to nothing has been done to address the other seven. In fact, many elements described as necessary for establishing free land markets in the World Bank's own conceptual papers seem to be missing in Guatemala, such as initiatives to avoid price distortions and unproductive land use, access to information on land availability and prices, the development of rural infrastructure and services to meet market demands, and, perhaps most important, sufficient macroeconomic stability to avoid having landownership serve as a guard against inflation (Garoz and Gauster 2002).

Without public financing for land (no. 4), it is unlikely that the poor could buy land, however accurately surveyed, or that the rich would consider selling their holdings. As the World Bank itself noted, large landholders tend not to sell land to smallholders "for fear that these actions could augment the demand for land redistribution, or the invasion of properties" (Hernández Alarcón 1998b, citing a 1994 World Bank report).[5] Without state-supported mortgages for the poor, land goes to those who can afford to pay in cash (Strasma and Celis 1992). Highly desirable plots will rarely enter the general market; instead, they are sold by word of mouth to family, friends, or acquaintances. Landowners are worried about kidnapping threats, and few are willing to advertise property for sale to the general public. High real estate transaction costs (lawyer fees plus a 12 percent sales tax on the total) also impede formal land sales among the poor. Rural infrastructure is so scarce that land prices tend to be based more on access than arability (Garoz and Gauster 2002). Finally, given that demand so far outpaces supply, a fair land market is unlikely to develop in Guatemala under current conditions.

Although World Bank documents rhetorically mention the collection of land taxes (no. 9) as a potential benefit (Mendes Pereira 2005b), the application of a progressive tax on idle and large landholdings (as outlined in the original INTA laws) has disappeared from the Guatemalan political agenda. The congress attempted to reform the tax code in 1998 by including a tax on idle lands on large plantations but revoked the law after what many political analysts describe as deliberate manipulation of peasant and public opinion by powerful landowning interests.[6] Land reform, when treated as a technical process, provides no enforcement policies for recuperating idle land or resolving historic agrarian conflicts (no. 1). Without the political will to give citizen groups access to the archives, improved land information systems (no. 3) will be meaningless.

Coordination for integrated agrarian development remains elusive, with no less than a dozen government agencies involved, many with overlapping mandates. Contrary to World Bank rhetoric about the efficiencies of structural adjustment, the "streamlining" of the land reform process has actually contributed to bureaucratic state-building. With numerous private contractors added to the mix, one employee confessed that she thought it would be practically impossible for an individual to wade through the complex bureaucracy and legalize a parcel oneself or on behalf of one's community.

Even were farmers to acquire greater tenure security through the National Survey, they might still suffer from low agricultural prices and lose the land they put up as collateral for production loans. As Nigel Smith explained in reference to the sale of half the TransAmazon lots by 1981: "It is not enough to open up frontier areas with highways, divide the land into parcels, provide credit, and expect largely illiterate farmers with few capital resources to flourish. . . . Along the TransAmazon, many settlers soon fell victim to a biased and inefficient credit system, a poor selection of crops, infertile soils, and isolation from large markets" (1993: 147). True agrarian reform must address the entire structure of rural areas—from strengthening rural education and health care, to improving the working conditions of agricultural laborers, bettering the terms of credit and loans, building transportation networks designed for small producers rather than foreign investors, and helping farmers access better markets and prices in addition to offering the usual range of technical assistance for agricultural production, processing, and storage. Budgets are not without limits. Hence, we must assume that monies loaned to Guatemala for titling are public funds otherwise unavailable for other productive projects (no. 5) and rural infrastructure (no. 6).

Finally and perhaps of most significance for the Q'eqchi', although a National Survey might appear to be a neutral measure of property claims, hidden within cadastral maps is a long cultural history privileging private property over collective, indigenous forms of land management. To borrow a word from Anna Tsing (2002), the survey has contributed to the "aura" of private property, as "maps reflect the interests of those who draw them" (Dowie 2009: 193). Although customary land management and communal tenure are supposedly protected by the Guatemalan constitution and reinforced by Peace Accords commitments, the National Survey as designed by the World Bank is overwhelmingly biased toward securing individual, private property. Fetishizing the objectivity of GIS technology, project leader Carlos Cabrera claimed he could manage a "chemically pure" national survey (Hernández Alarcón 1998a: 11). He and other managers emphasized that their goal was neither to give nor to take away property but merely to measure the existing situation with technical expertise—without questioning whether the current land distribution was right or just. Imagining that Petén was free of indigenous claims and that they could easily build on several pilot projects from the Petén environmental sector, the Guatemalan government chose this region as its first target for a World Bank loan (Gould 2009).[7]

GREENING THE SURVEY

As the World Bank was mobilizing national support for a land survey, the environmental sector in Petén was also experimenting with land titling projects, hoping this might stabilize the agrarian sector and slow further migration into the national parks. After the Guatemalan government established almost 3 million hectares of protected areas in the 1990s, tens of thousands of poor settlers with homesteads in those same areas suddenly found themselves threatened by land restrictions, leading to a flurry of conflicts and organized peasant revolts. In response, the government and several NGOs began delimiting peasant lands in the buffer zones and multiple-use zones in the parks. In the mid-1990s, CARE-Guatemala launched a titling program, with support from USAID and the IDB, to legalize almost four thousand landholdings in the buffer zone of the Maya Biosphere Reserve. The aid agency German Technical Cooperation (Deutsche Gesellschaft für Technische Zusammenarbeit) sponsored a similar project around protected areas in southern Petén through its Proselva organization. Although CARE failed to finish titling the whole buffer zone and conflicts stalled Proselva, these experimental efforts provided valuable lessons for carrying out projects on a larger scale.

Picking up the idea that a land survey in Petén might slow the expansion of the agricultural frontier by eliminating informal land markets and giving settlers long-term tenure security, planners of LAP I hoped that "cadastral surveying, conflict resolution, titling, and registration services would induce a series of behavioral changes among rural landholders; many of these would be environmentally positive, such as: i) longer-term land management, ii) reduced deforestation to prove use and possession, or from land invasions, iii) private reserve establishment, and iv) appropriate intensification of agricultural land use" (World Bank 2006b: 4). Although many researchers had data to the contrary (D. L. Carr 2004; Grandia 2004c; Gould 2001; Shriar 1999), the Bank's hypothesis was that without land titles, farmers would not invest in sustainable agricultural techniques such as planting tree crops. Bank planners also accepted FYDEP's presumption that residents of Petén wanted private property and ignored timely advice from its own expert consultants that the land survey needed to develop methodologies that would respect and protect various types of communal land management for both social and ecological reasons (Schwartz 1998).

Despite its many environmental justifications, much of the project loan initially went to titling urban lots in Petén's municipal towns. Fairly uncontroversial, the urban work helped land agencies gain public consent for the more complicated rural survey and titling efforts that followed. For the urban work, UTJ coordinated with municipal governments, but for the rural part of the project, the World Bank subcontracted with private businesses. Small Guatemalan companies such as Arbora, Geotecnica, Teca, and ATP initially received contracts, but when the World Bank began requiring bidders to hold at least a million dollars in capital, only private international companies qualified for subcontracts. A Spanish company, Novotécnica, became the main implementing agency. Other groups, including the Catholic Church land pastorate, peasant organizations, and environmental NGOs, served as community advocates or village "accompaniers." Later, some of these civil society groups began accepting subcontracts for legalizing parcels in certain jurisdictions. Working to maximize their bottom line, however, the private contractors brought a different spirit to the work than their nonprofit counterparts. Orlando Romero, who worked for more than a decade with development and conservation NGOs, was surprised by the change in institutional culture when he got a job with a private World Bank contractor, explaining, "We weren't allowed to get interested in side problems [or do favors for the villagers]—just had to legalize the land, period."

Wherever a settler's claim had stagnated under FYDEP, the subcontractors were to help him or her complete the process to title. If claimants could prove eligibility, collect a variety of certificates from the municipal jurisdictions in which they had lived, and, most important, prove no conflicts with neighboring claims, they could proceed to have their land surveyed and the soil analyzed. Once blueprints were drawn and approved through public legal declaration, claimants might then make a 10 percent down payment plus pay another 20 percent in taxes, legal fees, and closing costs. At that point, with provisional title ("escritura") from the government, they might begin to pay for their land in installments over nine years or all at once. Once payment was complete, they would have to get three state agencies to coordinate the inscription of the title in the National Property Registry in Guatemala City. Though the government had removed some of the more onerous paperwork (such as health verification by a doctor) required by FYDEP, the process could take the average farmer dozens of trips to town and thousands of quetzals in legal and administrative fees over many years (see Grandia 2009c for more details).

The World Bank loan to the Guatemalan government through UTJ subsidized many of these costs by supporting the travel of government workers and subcontractors to the rural areas where they could legalize entire communities all at once. Although parcels were legalized privately, the land agencies took advantage of community infrastructure and civic spirit for much of the organizational work (village meetings, messages passed among neighbors, consultation with elders, etc.). Claimants had to pay for the survey (about $600 per parcel) and the land itself, but the World Bank project covered the rest in Petén. The subcontractors were paid for a quota of *finished titles*, which means that they could keep any additional profit for lands in their region that were already adequately titled. A Novotécnica employee estimated that half the land claimants in Petén had initiated at least some of the paperwork; the other half were just informal claims that had to be taken through the entire legalization process from scratch.

Beneficiaries were supposed to be small landholders, but neighboring large landowners could slip into the process because the subcontracts were designed for average holdings. For example, Novotécnica held one subcontract to title 45,000 hectares, which were to be distributed, in theory, among a thousand families. However, as Orlando Romero confided, this obscured a wide range of ownership size. According to my own archival analysis, that subcontract benefited just six hundred families, averaging 74 hectares each. The standard deviation was an astounding 118 hectares, with parcel sizes ranging from 3 to 1,335 hectares, far in excess of the standard parcel size (45 hectares) awarded by FYDEP.

Working quickly, the subcontractors have little incentive to give advice to communities, to explore historical or contradictory land claims, and, much less, to worry about the future. Rather, as one of the project architects put it, they work to "reaffirm what was already done." In many cases, they are formalizing lands that exceed amounts allowed by colonization laws. For example, one landowner in the Melchor region, "Doña María," had falsely claimed 180 hectares (four "caballerías") in addition to her already substantial 540 hectares. The titling technician, Orlando Romero, decided to award these 180 "excess" hectares ("excesos") to her neighbors, but Doña María insisted that she had "improved" the land with pasture and asked to be compensated almost ten dollars a hectare. Though portrayed as a cut-and-dried measurement process, survey agents regularly encounter these kinds of problems but lack any formal negotiation procedure for resolving them. In this instance, the neighbors willingly compensated Doña María for the pasture, but Orlando or his company could have just as easily decided to let her keep her illegal encroachments.[8]

According to the colonization rules, if land recipients failed to move to Petén or abandoned their parcels for more than six months, the state could rescind their titles.[9] Moreover, land could not be bought and sold without the explicit permission of one's spouse, but colonization agencies did little to support women's co-ownership and inheritance. Land recipients were also required to leave 20 percent of their parcels as forest reserves, to protect watersheds, and to respect a right-of-way for any road—rules that were virtually ignored, especially by cattle ranchers. As one land activist exclaimed, "If big ranchers can violate those laws so publicly, imagine what they do to campesinos!" Although

FIGURE 4.2. For god, for country, and for the cadastre. The RIC flag was placed next to the flags of Guatemala and Guatemala's national university at a 2009 conference for land technicians. Photograph: Liza Grandia

FIGURE 4.3. The business of survey equipment. Trade representatives display their survey equipment at the 2009 land technicians' conference. They dominated the program and were allotted more time than social scientists reporting on the impact of the project. Photograph: Liza Grandia

the Peace Accords recapitulated the state's authority to rescind such illegally acquired properties, survey contractors have little incentive to do so.

The titling agencies protest that such enforcement is beyond their power and technical scope of work while ignoring the administrative procedures directly under their institutional control. For example, in 2003, FONTIER-RAS-Petén had yet to develop an adequate system to cross-check beneficiaries, to see if they had received land elsewhere or if their spouses had also received land. Moreover, the agency was rubber-stamping the land-use studies required for titling. Files show that many of the soil analyses were fraudulent, and most reveal serious contradictions between recommended and actual land use. Yet, rather than putting temporary liens on the land until landowners rectified the problematic land uses (such as reforesting steep slopes instead of grazing cattle on them), FONTIERRAS approved them pro forma.

A promotional poster for the project, ubiquitous around Petén in 2003, emphasized that to "compile information about boundaries, ownership, possession . . . requires technical specialists with equipment and technology," one of many examples of how project managers depicted the deeply political process of land reform in falsely neutral technical terms (see also Gould 2009). Perhaps the most troubling aspect of the technomanic nationalism (figs. 4.2, 4.3) surrounding the Petén survey was that virtually no project staff, much less peasants, had any idea of how the title beneficiaries would eventually bequeath their parcels to their children. Spending millions on land titling without making clear provisions for updating the registry to record sales or inheritance seems a recipe for disaster. True, the subcontractors were supposed to list beneficiaries, but often they cut corners by eliminating children who lacked valid or easily locatable birth certificates. Although private property may seem a straightforward land regime to World Bank economists, in practice, land sales and inheritance problems quickly complicate the process. Kevin Gould (2009) reports that so many parcels had changed hands in the long delay between the cadastral survey and the awarding of title that some project managers were arguing in favor of starting over again.

Surveyed parcels may look good on paper—in other words, "legible" to the state (Scott 1998)—but have no correspondence with real ecological boundaries and run contrary to lowland farming logic. Perhaps earlier land administration programs lacked the agility to allow settlers to claim multiple sites with different agro-ecological niches or combine their individual forest reserves into contiguous community blocks, yet new GPS technology ought to facilitate creativity in land-use planning and allow the state to develop culturally and environmentally friendly mosaic landscapes. Instead, the technicians continue to turn Petén into a permanent checkerboard of deforested, rectangular private plots, both outside and inside protected areas, as happened in Atelesdale (see pp. 130–31).

CUSTOMARY, NOT COMMUNAL

Many project managers and fieldworkers assert that Q'eqchi' people prefer private title, while anthropologists and other Q'eqchi' leaders argue the opposite (Ybarra 2011). Undoubtedly, the dominant national ideology about the rightness of private property has penetrated Q'eqchi' culture in many ways. Obviously drawing on their history of servitude as worker-serfs to large landowners, many Q'eqchi' fathers refer to their sons-in-law and sometimes their own sons as "my worker" (*inmooz*). As many ethnographers have noted, the Q'eqchi' have projected the political authoritarianism of Guatemala onto their gods, who are described as capricious, despotic, angry, and vengeful (Wilson 1995; A. E. Adams 1999; Kahn 2002; Hatse and De Ceuster 2001a). Because the Q'eqchi'

ATELESDALE, "PLACE OF SPIDER
MONKEYS [*ATELES GEOFFROYI*]"
(*SAXB'ATZ*)

I began my work in Petén in 1993 in the
bi-ethnic (Q'eqchi' and Ladino) village
of Atelesdale as a community volunteer for Conservation International, or
CI, and ProPetén. Two weeks earlier, a
group of angry farmers, afraid of being
evicted, had run employees of CONAP,
the national park service, out of town,
threatening them with guns and stones,
and setting fire to their guard post.
Founded in 1977 on a campsite where
forest harvesters used to water their
horses, Atelesdale grew to 85 families by
1985, to 140 by the time I arrived in 1993,
and doubled again to 300 households in
2003. Everyone there had come in search
of land, though a few were also likely
hiding from the law. With a legendary
number of murders, shoot-outs, and
witchcraft feuds, Atelesdale was known
as one of the most dangerous places in
the Maya Biosphere Reserve, but I lived
there for a year and visited at least once a
year for a decade, so it had become a second home for me. While Ladinos once
dominated village politics, by the turn of
the millennium, two-thirds of the village
and almost all the leadership positions
were occupied by Q'eqchi' settlers, primarily those who had immigrated from
Tamalton.

Settlers in Atelesdale, situated just
south of the old FYDEP forest reserve,
were once free to claim land under the
rules of the colonization program. With
the unexpected establishment of the
much larger Maya Biosphere Reserve
in 1992, Atelesdale residents suddenly
found themselves living inside the Multiple Use Zone where farming is prohibited. This led to several years of conflict
until CONAP agreed in the mid-1990s to
award Atelesdale residents agricultural
concessions of forty-five hectares per
family and hired a private company to
prepare cadastral maps of each parcel.

While their land tenure was insecure,
most farmers opposed anything related
to conservation. Once awarded a quasi-
secure concession from CONAP, however, they began to demonstrate interest
in learning about organic agriculture
and agroforestry from ProPetén in the
late 1990s. In some ways, Atelesdale
seemed a textbook case of the neoliberal
hypothesis arguing that farmers must
have secure tenure plus the added pressure of population growth before investing in agricultural improvements.

Then something happened that none
of the technicians predicted. Based on
mere blueprints, cattle ranchers began
buying parcels by the dozens. Politically
weak, CONAP failed to enforce the
terms of the Atelesdale concession, and
the illegal sales continued. Within two
years of receiving land possession rights
from CONAP, in 2003, approximately
a quarter of the residents had sold their
usufruct parcels to cattle ranchers. Only
14 percent of Q'eqchi' families had sold,
but another third were contemplating
doing so. Although they themselves
knew the suffering associated with being
landless, most had no plans to subdivide
their land to bequeath it to their children, figuring that their children would
have to move elsewhere inside the park
and acquire new land.

Most of those who sold remained in

the village, renting parcels from others. Firewood is growing scarce. Forest harvesters who cut "xate" for export can no longer make a living. Once abundant, game meat has become a luxury. Spider monkeys are now a rare sight. Uncontrolled forest fires from swidden, arson, and pasture planting rage across village lands almost every dry season, threatening the nearby Zotz and Tikal National Parks.

Back in the village in 2003, I heard rumors of landless Atelesdale farmers planning to invade yet another section of Laguna del Tigre National Park. Contrary to World Bank models showing that land tenure security would help Petén's protected areas avoid invasion by peasants, cadastral surveys seemed to be propelling more people into them.

people consider the *Tzuultaq'a* to be the true owners of the forest and its wild animals, they must take care to honor and petition the gods for a "license" for planting or hunting—using a word, *liceens*, that is clearly borrowed from the Spanish word "licencia," a term derived from the legal consent sharecroppers or worker-serfs needed in order to leave the estate to which they were contractually bound. Throughout the lowland Q'eqchi' world, people describe the *Tzuultaq'a* as old white men whose cave homes deep inside the mountains offer banquet tables of food and other magical images of luxury (such as snakes holding their hammocks in place).

Q'eqchi' views on landownership are clearly shaped by their experiences with pale foreigners in the colonial and Liberal eras. They have also been influenced by the more recent history of their interactions with colonization agencies. Prior to the arrival of government land programs, Q'eqchi' villages created a managed commons out of an open-access frontier with a customary system that included a mix of small family usufruct claims and shared community resources. In other words, they shared decision-making and designated some common places, but the land was not "communal" per se. Yet, when the moment came to formalize their collective claims, the two colonization bureaucracies channeled Q'eqchi' settlers into square individual parcels that ignored community needs and social processes. Sensing that the most expedient, inexpensive, and safest path to land security was through individual ownership—especially in the context of a civil war in which the military was overtly hostile to collective organization—many Q'eqchi' farmers consequently sought private plots.[10] This move should not be confused with a genuine or exclusive desire for private property. When faced with a choice between an individual parcel and no parcel at all, Q'eqchi' farmers logically opted for the individual parcel; however, if some kind of collective land management had been part of the formal FYDEP repertoire of land adjudication, that likely would have become the choice of many Q'eqchi' communities.

Following the concept of usucapion, a Roman law allowing acquisition of property by possession, FYDEP's emphasis on improvements as the means for proving landownership resembles, in a way, Q'eqchi' notions of usufruct use. Under FYDEP's rules, even after final sale, the state maintained "tutelage," meaning that without the state's permission, land recipients could not sell, mortgage, divide, or trade the parcel for twenty years. Consequently, a parallel land market arose in which settlers claimed, held, and sold land based on usufruct rights. Settlers found their own mechanisms of land valuation and documentation and often appealed to village presidents or municipal mayors to witness or stamp property transfers. Such transactions were technically illegal, but other settlers respected them. What might have appeared to outsiders as a wild frontier was actually ordered and legitimated by de facto customary law (cf. Schwartz 1998).

In contrast to FYDEP, INTA tended to be more receptive to Q'eqchi' customary management, for example, awarding communities land titles known as Collective Agrarian Patrimonies that left internal land distribution to village leaders. INTA later organized Associated Peasant Businesses, through which each household received an individual family parcel, but agreed to participate in some collective labor such as processing and marketing (Deere and León 1999). Q'eqchi' communities took full advantage of the flexibilities and ambiguities of these alternative tenure regimes to continue their own customary land management.

When channeled into private property, many Q'eqchi' people fell through bureaucratic cracks and lost or abandoned their claims for almost ridiculous reasons. Many, especially women, cited the lack of national identification cards as a barrier to legalizing their claims, a problem affecting 10–25 percent of the rural population (Campbell 2003). One farmer resignedly told me he would not be able to get a titled parcel because he accidentally left his national identification card ("cédula") in his pocket and his wife washed it, ruining the ink. Others lamented that they had been absent—for example, visiting relatives the week colonization officials conducted a community census—and missed getting on the list.[11] Another man believed he would never get land because the municipality where he was born had burned down and his birth certificate had been lost. Don Samuel Mucu went so far as to say that he regretted marrying his wife just because she was from a different municipality that was so far away they could not travel there for her papers. Others lacked money on hand for the cadastral measurement and thought that, because of this, they would have to renounce their claims.

Of course, for a literate person with some savvy about the functions of government agencies, many of these problems were imminently rectifiable. For example, one afternoon in Atelesdale, the Ixim family was gathered to de-grain their corn harvest and invited me to join them for lunch. Afterward, they asked me about a parcel they had abandoned in a village in southern Petén. Although it was degraded and infested with weeds, they hoped their daughters might use it one day for pasture. They had left the paperwork with a caretaker, who apparently tried to resell it after cutting down the timber for himself. I suggested that they check with FONTIERRAS to see if the land had been registered and request another copy of their papers. While the sons listened politely, I heard their mother mutter under her breath in Q'eqchi', "We don't have money for that." I explained that there was a new regional office nearby, and they could take the bus there and back in half a day. The son-in-law explained to this unrealistic gringa that to make any kind of movement ("movimiento") through bureaucratic red tape requires a lot of money. Q'eqchi' peasants have been so abused by the corruption and immobility of government agencies that they may over-anticipate the hassle involved in completing any paperwork, giving up rightful claims that might have been resolved if they had citizen power or oversight.

Added to that is the problem of racism, language barriers, and general discrimination against the poor. An activist with the Association of Indigenous Peasant Communities for the Integrated Development of Petén (Asociación de Comunidades Campesinas Indígenas Para el Desarrollo Integral de Petén), or ACDIP, Rigoberto Tec, recalled visiting the FONTIERRAS office after returning from a village. He was dusty from the bus ride, and the staff left him waiting in the reception area *for four hours* until he revealed his organizational affiliation. He decided to go incognito another time, wearing sunglasses, and, thinking he was a regular peasant, FONTIERRAS staff denied knowing anything about his case. They were going to send him on a wild goose chase to another office until he revealed he was from ACDIP, and then they suddenly "started to scurry." Aside from overt disrespect, institutional discrimination is also manifested through a subtle lack of attention to details with Q'eqchi' files. For example, when I noticed that a disproportionate number of Q'eqchi' files in the FONTIERRAS archives had been misplaced because staff had misspelled Maya surnames or had put the files under similar-sounding names, I pointed this out to the archivist, but he simply shrugged.

The World Bank's main justification for forcing indigenous people into private parcels is that it enables them to access credit, using their land as collateral. While microcredit programs have transformed millions of lives worldwide, in a country like Guatemala where elites have used coercive debt to force indigenous people to labor on their plantations since the colonial period, the invocation of credit as a justification for land reform raises suspicion. Unless the farmer has adequate technical assistance with the process—from production to marketing—and a sure means of paying back the loan, credit may serve more to dispossess him or her than to aid development (Dozier 1969: 214). Indeed, many small farmers in Petén are credit averse, and understandably so (Gould 2001; Ybarra 2008b). Q'eqchi' settlers relate many stories about being displaced because of failed or coercive credit endeavors. Two examples stand out:

Case A: In Atelesdale, Ricardo Bolom once took out a bank loan to expand his corn crop. After the harvest, someone stole forty sacks of corn from his field trough, leaving him $800 in debt. He did not want to default on the loan, since he considered that to be "stealing money from the bank." Knowing he would otherwise lose his parcel as collateral, he decided to preemptively sell to a cattle rancher for $1,500 and use the money to pay off his loan. That was fifteen years ago, and he heard that the rancher who bought his parcel later resold it for $66,666 to a larger ranch now valued at $200,000. With much regret in his voice, Don Ricardo emphasizes that he had sold his land, not because he wanted to, but "because of necessity." He considers that to be a turning point in his life from which "we could never recover," and his family is resigned to "dying without land." Perhaps, he ponders, they could have fought to get another parcel, "but why would we make our lives so difficult to own a piece of land?"

Case B: Before they moved to Agoutiville, Lorenzo Cac's family had been part of a cooperative of twenty-five families near Rio Dulce for whom a government agent had arranged a loan so that they could plant cacao for export. Unfortunately, this technician failed to anticipate that the cacao would not produce seeds until the sixth year but the village loan would come due after three years. To pay off the penalties for not making the loan payments on time, the villagers were forced to sell their land, about 160 hectares, for $53,000 to a neighboring landowner who cut down their cacao and established an industrial pine plantation on the land. Lorenzo explains the technician's mistake: "Well, they bring a different ideology from other countries and other climates. They have their analysis in theory and on paper . . . [but the reality in Guatemala is different]."

Megan Ybarra (2001: 19) also found that farmers in her Q'eqchi' field sites were disinterested in credit. As she puts it, "They saw it as irresponsible to risk their land as collateral when they owe it to their children." Were the staff of development agencies or the agencies themselves, instead of individual farmers, held accountable for failed loan programs, perhaps there would be fewer credit schemes foisted on the poor. Ironically, most of the contemporary titling fieldwork still takes advantage of the strength of Q'eqchi' community organization, but the land institutions miss the opportunity to use this same process to develop community-based collateral systems, such as those created by the Nobel Peace Prize–winning Grameen Bank.

Reflecting previous historical epochs of intense private titling, a final problem for Q'eqchi' people is the pace at which colonization agencies and, later, World Bank subcontractors passed through their communities. According to Greg Grandin (2004: 410), in the late nineteenth century, surveyors working for wealthy outsiders moved with such speed through the Polochic Valley in Alta Verapaz that they measured land in triangles rather than squares in order to save time. Today, World Bank–funded field technicians, anxious to complete their contracts, press farmers to make decisions quickly. Kevin Gould (2009: 160) observed one Petén land technician advise a Q'eqchi' community, "This is a fast project and if you don't participate, you are going to end up with nothing to show. Take advantage of this opportunity!" The technicians unscrupulously lead peasants to believe that their parcels must be surveyed immediately and legalization costs paid within a year and a half, which is untrue. If settlers do not survey with World Bank subcontractors, their land claims remain valid; they simply lose the free legal support being offered through the project. In other words, while communities cannot refuse the cadastre, they can refuse to pay for the legalization process.

Customary management may not be the first choice for all Q'eqchi' communities. If, however, villages were given sufficient time to deliberate on an array of options—protecting sacred sites such as caves and incense groves, selecting multiple parcels in different agro-ecological niches, establishing forest reserves, saving land for future generations, maximizing water and river access for everyone, and so forth—they might opt for communal titling arrangements more conducive to environmental conservation and social equity. Farmers know their lands best. Giving them decision-making power could produce creative and entrepreneurial ideas—for example, funding development projects by collecting dividends for carbon-sequestration from village forests. In the end, villages might still opt for dividing everything up into private parcels, but that should be *their* decision.

Q'EQCHI' RESISTANCE

After having their customary practices repeatedly ignored by those implementing the cadastral survey, many Q'eqchi' groups have taken matters into their own hands through land occupations, projects to re-communalize their land holdings, and even international human rights appeals for territorial autonomy.

Peasant organizing and land occupations

Mostly dormant during the civil war, peasant organizing has resurged since the 1990s. The dominant organization nationally is the National Coordinator of Peasant Organizations (Coordinadora Nacional de Organizaciones Campesinas), or CNOC, composed of a coalition of regional organizations, with some of its most powerful member groups from the Q'eqchi' area: the National Peasant and Indigenous Coordination (CONIC); the Verapaz Union of Peasant Organizations (UVOC); the Cahabón Peasant and Indigenous Unity (UNICAN); and ACDIP.[12] Through its land pastorates, the Catholic Church is the other major player in grassroots agrarian politics. Understanding the power of civil disobedience, these grassroots organizations have repeatedly taken over major highways across Guatemala to protest land laws, the PPP, and the DR-CAFTA. On any given day, CNOC and its member groups can mobilize tens of thousands of members to block ports and highways or even close down traffic in the capital. Like landless people's movements elsewhere, they have begun using occupation or threats of occupation to reclaim land and gain stronger negotiating power in formulating national policy. As a result, the Q'eqchi' region, especially Alta Verapaz, is now Guatemala's epicenter of agrarian conflict, with the largest number of occupations of both protected areas and private plantations. According to research conducted in the late 1990s, 20 to 40 percent of the country's land conflicts were in the three departments of Q'eqchi' settlement (Hernández Alarcón 1998b). A database of 501 cases being mediated by CONTIERRA in 1999 showed that an astounding 61 percent were in the Q'eqchi' region (MAGA 1999).

While many Q'eqchi' land occupations have resulted in violent evictions, quite a few have succeeded in forcing the owner to sell and/or the state to legitimate the claim. Connecting land reclamation with historical injustices, peasant leader Rigoberto Tec explained, "While the government has failed to recuperate illegally acquired parcels, we have forced them to be rescinded through organized occupations." A FONTIERRAS worker made a similar admission, explaining that when land applications surpass staff availability, workers pay more attention to cases in which there is "conflicto fuerte" (strong conflict) and often those in which an advocacy group like CNOC, CONIC, or UNICAN has intervened.

Q'eqchi' leaders insist that their occupations are not politically motivated but are historically based efforts to recover lands previously stolen from them. They also invoke moral and spiritual rationales for their land occupations. "How can we be expelled from this land if we are the earth's children?" asked one peasant leader in Purulha. As another group occupying land in Carchá said, "We are children of this land and we don't understand how it can have an 'owner' now" (Caal Xi 1992: 3). Whatever the rationale, Q'eqchi' leaders are rapidly learning how to phrase their demands in ways that enlist support from academics, donors, and NGOs sympathetic to their agrarian struggles.

Bio-cultural mosaics

In another corner of the Q'eqchi' region, the grassroots NGO Association for Harmony in Our Community (*Sa Qa Chol Nimla K'aleb'aal*), or APRO-BASANK (also known as SANK), has taken a less confrontational strategy of working *within* the system to gain flexibility for different forms of communal ownership and comanagement of cultural heritage sites.[13] In this case, a French hotel owner appropriated the ancient Candelaria caves of Chisec, Alta Verapaz, as his private ecotourism domain. With the intervention of an applied anthropologist funded by USAID and with support from the Peace Corps, the Ministry of Culture reclaimed this archaeological site from the French hotel and, in a surprising move, in 2003 entrusted it to the surrounding communities for comanagement (Ybarra 2008a). APROBASANK trained the villagers in the use of GPS technology and thus did not have to hire expensive private technicians to demarcate the communities. Each village then developed a unique natural-resource management plan for protecting the forests around the caves. They all reserved communal areas for firewood, medicine, and hunting, and some also considered saving arable land for future generations. Otherwise, they divided land for agriculture according to knowledge of local soils and family preference (Stocks 2002).

After the government offered secure title to these communally managed lands, village leaders began expressing interest in conservation efforts. They managed to convince FONTIERRAS that the land they were going to maintain as forest around the Candelaria caves should be sold to them at reduced cost (10 percent the price of agricultural land) and eventually bought it for the symbolic price of a few cents. The communities also secured permission to plant crops such as shade coffee, cardamom, and cacao under the forest canopy and collaborated with a jaguar conservation corridor project (Pielemier 2004; del Cid and Garcia n.d.).

The APROBASANK experience showed that although communal management may not have been the first choice of these Q'eqchi' communities, in the right context, "the ability to base community management of resources on a common moral framework reappeared as an important part of the cultural repertoire" (Stocks 2002: 17). Beyond establishing a new legal precedent for indigenous comanagement of cultural patrimony, the project's other key achievement was to move beyond simplistic and polarizing debates about communal versus private land. By harnessing the advantages of both systems, APROBASANK and the communities constructed management plans suited to the ecology of each place. Moreover, they explicitly built in a pricing structure that encouraged conservation and discouraged speculation by reinforcing the capacity of communities to protect themselves from outside interests, which, as historian Michael Bertrand (1989) argues, has been the central advantage of customary land management since the colonial period. This process was by no means perfect; there is always the danger that future generations may not respect the commitments made to conservation. Eventually there may also be a problem reminiscent of the Mexican "ejidos" in which outsiders and children of the original land beneficiaries may develop a secondary landless status in the communities (Haenn 2005). Nonetheless, it is a prime example of using the legalization process to achieve both economic and conservation goals—instead of just getting the communities through the paperwork as fast as possible.

A Belizean Maya homeland

A thorough analysis of the Belizean land situation is beyond the scope of this book, but a particular Q'eqchi' victory in the Belize Supreme Court deserves mention. Having been more successful than their Guatemalan neighbors at maintaining their customary land management systems, two pan-Maya groups (the Toledo Maya Cultural Council and the Toledo Alcaldes Association) mobilized against concessions awarded on their land to Malaysian logging companies in the mid-1990s (TMCC and TAA 1997). Together they filed a lawsuit (with legal support from the Indian Law Resource Center based in Washington, D.C.) before the Organization of American States (OAS) for human rights violations and built momentum for a broader territorial claim. After signing the Ten Points of Agreement with the government in 2000, they also secured a commitment that the government would impose a ten-year moratorium on land sales for two miles on each side of the newly paved southern highway to Toledo. Eventually winning a symbolic victory in the OAS case in 2004, they nevertheless remained stalemated in negotiations with the Belizean government for real territorial autonomy. Meanwhile, a new threat emerged in 2002 when the IDB suggested expanding the Land Management Project, a cadastral initiative similar to Guatemala's National Survey, from Belize's northern districts into Toledo.

With support from the leadership of two newer organizations (the Maya Leaders Alliance and the Julian Cho Society) and a team of lawyers from the University of Arizona's Indigenous Peoples Law and Policy Program, two Toledo villages (the Mopán community of Santa Cruz and the Q'eqchi' community of Conejo) filed a joint claim in the Belize Supreme Court for the constitutional right to maintain their traditional land management systems. Various academic witnesses (historians, geographers, and anthropologists, including myself) provided expert testimony in support of the communities' claim (Grandia 2009a). On October 18, 2007, the Belize Supreme Court handed down a historic ruling in favor of the Maya plaintiffs of these two villages. In a subsequent verdict announced June 29, 2010, the court extended its decision to more than thirty Maya villages covering almost the entire Toledo district.

SPECULATIVE CONCLUSIONS

On the other side of the border, thousands of Q'eqchi' farmers remain in limbo with the land titling process in Petén. Despite millions of dollars poured into the Petén survey, UTJ and the subcontractors were unable to finish titling lands in Petén, even with a two-year extension through 2007. Like FYDEP and INTA before it, the project left thousands of applications only partially finished. Many of those who did receive title have fallen prey to land speculation and profiteering. Peteneros, some Ladino migrants, and especially Q'eqchi' smallholders are now selling their land. As far back as 2003, Susana Fernández, a titling contractor employee, estimated that approximately 10 percent of the awarded titles had already been sold. Another technician working in the San Luis region, José Jolom, estimated that between one-fourth and one-third of the six hundred titles legalized by his agency had been immediately sold for prices as low as $800 to $1,200 per "caballería" (45 hectares), which was roughly 10–15 percent of the average value in that area. Alberto Alonso Fradejas and Susana Gauster (2006: 35) estimated that 20–25 percent of beneficiaries in Petén and the Verapaces sell their land as soon as they receive the title. The World Bank itself reports that one-fourth of the 538 land parcels entering the market in Petén in 2004 had been resold (aka "circulated" in World Bank terminology) (2006c). Based on my own observations and interviews, the percentage of sales is, without a doubt, far higher today.

Worse yet, some people are selling even *before* they have legalized titles, as a result of the technocratic implementation of the project. For every family who cannot pay several hundred dollars for the measurement and legalization process (however subsidized it may be), there is a cattle rancher or someone else to pay the fees in exchange for part of the property. In some regions of northern Petén, villagers are ceding their claims for as little as $133 a "caballería," that is, *one-fifth of 1 percent* of current land values in Izabal and southern Petén. Land technician José Jolom recalled one poor Q'eqchi' father with seven children who, lacking the money to get birth certificates for his children, decided, "Perhaps it's better I sell." José encouraged him not to sell, but the father insisted, "A rich man is going to buy it from me." The next time José returned to that village, the man had indeed sold the parcel for $400, a pittance. Now, José reflected sadly, "his children will get nothing."

As these projects are being implemented, there is no social or educational process to help communities discuss the value of their land, nor are there any legal mechanisms to compel individuals to think twice about their decision to sell. To the contrary, such land sales translate positively into World Bank bureaucratese as "increased dynamism in land markets" (2006c: 70). Yet the more land people sell in these "dynamic markets," the more prices seem to be driven up, such that the repurchase of land becomes impossible. This contradicts a central theory behind the World Bank's market-assisted land reform, that as survey projects increase market sales, they will somehow also drive prices down. According to internal World Bank documents (2006c), upon titling, the cadastre project in Petén increased rural land values by 17 percent and urban lot prices by 35 percent.

In this heated speculative economy, World Bank titling programs become de facto subsidies to cattle ranchers and others with capital to purchase land. In Belize, similar speculative pressure is at work, but more from expatriates buying real estate, citrus plantations, and ecotourism businesses. Everywhere it seems that large landowners are enthusiastic about land titling because it so dramatically increases land values. In fact, the ranchers in a large village west of Agoutiville are so confident about purchasing opportunities they foresee resulting from the legalization process that they themselves are subsidizing legal support for titling village land, investing more than $11,000 each for a private lawyer and inviting community members to join along for $260. That ranchers are willing to pay so much up front means they must feel certain they will profit later.

Even without speculation, the World Bank project serves to formal-ize and freeze past inequities, as the Q'eqchi' received smaller parcels dur-ing the colonization process. In a sample of land applications from the San Luis municipality, Ladino families had applied for 30 percent more land dur-ing the colonization period than did Q'eqchi' families (an average of 52.9 and 40.1 hectares, respectively). In another data set of six hundred parcels legalized between 1999 and 2003, the average size claimed by Ladinos was 74.2 hect-ares versus just 44.2 hectares for Q'eqchi' parcels (see Grandia 2006 for more details). Floricelda Mo remembered clearly the inequities under FYDEP: "In San Luis, the rich people—the ones that know the system—got their parcels first and when everything was almost distributed, we Q'eqchi' people received the remainder. So it was mostly the ranchers and the southerners (sureños) who got land. Since a Q'eqchi' person doesn't know how to enjoy [private] land, we can be easily tricked" (field notes, 2003). While land privatization solidifies historical injustices, it also undercuts the possibility of future demands by the landless (Sydow and Mendonça 2003) and obliterates the possibility of restor-ing customary land management.

No one knows how much the Petén titling project contributed to land con-centration because the World Bank has yet to commission an evaluation of the project. While citizens and NGO groups might make use of the informa-tion, the archives remain almost as secret as they were during the civil war. Computer technicians working for UTJ (now RIC) do have this data at their fingertips, but no higher authority has requested such an analysis. Beyond land concentration, the project had less obvious, but equally important cultural impacts. In Petén, none of the project technicians bothered to ask Q'eqchi' communities about their incense groves, caves, shrines, and medicinal patches.

Without any options for protecting these places as cultural patrimony, village elders understandably feared revealing the locations to unknown Ladino project technicians. If denied access to their sacred places by the new owners, Q'eqchi' community cohesion, environmental stewardship, and spiritual life will undoubtedly suffer.

Despite serious concerns about project methodology and outcomes in the first phase in Petén, World Bank managers inexplicably decided to move forward with their original plans to expand the land survey to the rest of Guatemala. In December 2006, the World Bank approved a second phase of the Land Administration Project (LAP II), doubling the loan budget to another $62 million over six years for expanding the survey and titling programs to seven other departments (fifty-five municipalities), including all the rest of the places Q'eqchi' people live. Reducing the scope of the project to a cadastral survey, the Bank removed support for resolving conflicts and helping peasants with the legal process of titling their land after the blueprints are made. World Bank managers hope to cover territory more quickly without these social encumbrances, eventually reaching up to 80 percent of the country. Once again, the project plans to outsource the surveying work to private businesses and externalize the costs of associated social problems to "parallel initiatives" funded by other donors. Only in rare instances in which surveyed parcels are free of conflict might LAP II technicians consider helping peasants complete titling and registry. Because the cadastral survey will far outpace the legal work, smallholders will quickly receive maps of their claims but have little prospect of ever getting the parcels legally registered as titled property in their lifetimes. Many will likely sell—and sell cheap.

Were the World Bank managers who approved the second loan aware of mounting evidence of land speculation in Petén?[14] Or was this decision an unwitting consequence of an institutional culture that bases staff promotion on the dollar amount, rather than the social quality, of a manager's loan portfolio? Although the average World Bank project cycle lasts more than nine years, typically more than 60 percent of original project managers change positions within the bank in just two years (Goldman 2006). The Petén LAP I was headed by no less than a half dozen managers over a decade of planning and implementation. As a later manager summarized his inherited work to Kevin Gould (2009: 131), "I have to do my diligence which means making sure the document process is okay, making sure the financial management of the project is okay, making sure the development objectives and the specific objectives of the project are being reached on time and that the budget estimated in the documents [is complied with] so this is basically . . . my work is a task team leader." Noticeably absent from this list of administrative responsibilities is any concern about the long-term social and environmental impact. Foreseeing rapid turnover, project managers are apt to put their own career advancement ahead of a genuine curiosity about the consequences of a troubled project.

Whatever the internal reason, the external consequences are clear. Despite a desire for "chemically pure" management, the Petén land survey has exacerbated the division between large landholders and masses of rural landless workers. New globalization processes such as the PPP and the DR-CAFTA will only intensify this reconcentration of land into the hands of a few. The World Bank created a better investment context for national and transnational elites by establishing a neoliberal framework of secure property ownership that simultaneously produces a willing labor force of landless peasants. Was this intentional? One can only speculate.

5

From Colonial to Corporate Capitalisms

EXPANDING CATTLE FRONTIERS

A DAM Smith's metaphor of the market's benevolent "invisible hand" remains one of the most powerful narratives buttressing neoliberal economics today. Q'eqchi' people, however, see other kinds of invisible hands working behind the scenes, as illustrated by their folktales about an immortal, malevolent creature, *Laj Seleeq*, which they believe works secretly for the landlords surrounding their villages:

> Laj Seleeq *is a kind of dwarf, the size of a child but with its feet facing backward, so it can sneak up on people. Born from a cow (with which a worker was forced to have sexual relations), the baby* Seleeq *must be caught right from the birth canal so it cannot escape into the forest. The rancher must then whip the creature until it recognizes him as master, promising, "Father, I will obey your orders."*
>
> *Perhaps, they say, the rancher is an absentee landowner who lives in a nice house in town. At sunset, he'll order the* Seleeq, *"Go out to my pasture to see that no one is stealing the cattle." In the space of a whistle, the dwarf can travel several hundred kilometers to visit the owner's fields and report back moments later. The* Seleeq *also has the power to transform itself into other animals, and Q'eqchi' laborers swear they have heard the* Seleeq's *mysterious whistle right before a cat or some other animal suddenly appears to monitor their work performance like a foreman. If a rancher needs a guard, he can go to a special plantation where, for a high premium, he can buy a* Seleeq *that can tell the difference between the ranch workers and other trespassers.*

If the owner needs money, he can send his Seleeq to rob the bank—even
if there are a hundred locks inside, this dwarf-animal can get through. It can
steal chickens, pigs, even babies for the ranchers. Perhaps unconsciously allud-
ing to how the military "disappeared" so many innocent Guatemalans during
the civil war, the stories about Laj Seleeq now highlight their ability to kidnap
people. People say that the Seleeq has the ability to freeze a person cold, such
that he or she cannot escape or cry for help. (field notes, 2003, 2007)

Such magical stories are one way that Q'eqchi' people attempt to explain the inexplicable wealth of the ranchers who control so much land around them.[1] The symbolism resembles that of South American stories documented by other anthropologists about the devilish nature of capitalism and the expression of human relations through money or things, what Karl Marx called "commodity fetishism" (e.g., Taussig 1980). Undermining the idea of the free market, they assert a striking awareness of the use of labor subsidies, stratagems, and trickery as tactics for generating wealth.

The steady encroachment of cattle and export plantations onto lowland Q'eqchi' territory provides a compelling illustration of the techniques employed by elites to assert control over land and, as the *Seleeq* stories indicate, the underlying desire to control indigenous labor. As such, cattle ranching also serves as a generative subject for thinking more broadly about political economy and historical continuities of power. Because enclosure and economic change happen so quickly and dramatically in frontier regions like northern Guatemala, they are excellent places for witnessing the collusion of multiple kinds of capitalism—from the feudalistic management of the frontier ranching economy to the development of modern agribusiness alongside transnational superhighways following the old cattle routes. While there are many excellent studies on cattle across Latin America (Downing et al. 1992), and especially in neighboring Chiapas (e.g., Bobrow-Strain 2007; Collier and Quaratiello 1994), the conservation literature on Petén thus far has largely ignored ranching's environmental impact on the northern lowlands (Grandia 2009b). Finally, as the cattle industry has been the primary agent of Q'eqchi' dispossession in the lowlands, exploring in more detail how ranchers acquire land from smallholders can help in anticipating the speculative methods of new economic actors entering the region, such as African-palm planters, narco-traffickers, carbon traders, and oil and mineral companies.

For historical reasons dating to the colonial hacienda system, cattle ranching is a preferred and predominant land use in the Americas (Hecht 1984). It allows for fiscal flexibility (herds can contract or expand in relation to cash flow needs), requires little labor, benefits from significant state subsidies, and serves as an economic activity compatible with high social status (Chevalier 1963; J. R. Jones 1989). In fact, the main land measurement still used in Petén (a "caballería," equivalent to forty-five hectares) was the area around which a Spanish gentleman might ride leisurely on a horse ("caballo") in an afternoon. More than just a business, cattle ranching is a lifestyle.[2]

Across Central America, the scrawny cattle descended from Spanish colonial stock became known as "criollo," or creole breeds. The first cattle to enter Guatemala likely came from the Canary Islands and Santo Domingo between 1520 and 1560 (Alvarado Pinetto and Gonzalez Alvarado 1981). Albeit relatively small animals that matured slowly (taking up to five or six years before they could be brought to slaughter), these colonial cattle were fairly resistant to disease and drought. Creole cattle required little supervision, could subsist on wild grasses, produced both milk and meat, and essentially managed themselves. For these and other reasons, creole breeds were well suited to the "hoarding" logic of premodern cattle production (Williams 1986).

Although most ordinary Peteneros devoted themselves to subsistence agriculture, cattle and horses raised for trade with Mexico dominated Petén's cash economy from 1710 to 1850. By the end of the nineteenth century, Petenero businessmen turned to the extraction of timber (primarily mahogany and Spanish cedar) and non-timber forest products (chicle, "xate," and allspice). With the rise of a profitable forest economy, the cattle sector went into decline by the end of the nineteenth century, with only a handful of elite families maintaining herds totaling a few thousand head (Schwartz 1990). Several subsequent colonization schemes (in 1834, the 1870s, 1919, the 1930s, and even 1952–54 under Arbenz's agrarian reform) failed to entice additional ranchers to the region (ibid.; Corzo 2003; Fuentes-Mohr 1955). Albeit unsuccessful, these colonization plans nonetheless managed to keep alive colonial aspirations of turning Petén into cattle country.

Not until the mid-twentieth century were conditions right for the expansion of Guatemala's beef industry into the northern lowlands, mostly as the result of events in the United States. Postwar prosperity, industrial food processing, suburbanization, and other dietary changes had·led to dramatic increases in annual per capita beef consumption, which nearly tripled from 63 pounds in 1950 to a 150 pounds by 1976 (Williams 1986; Tucker 2000). Faced with heightened demand, the fast-food industry needed to find alternative sources of beef close to home. Additional breakthroughs in refrigeration technology and shipping improvements meant that a steer eating grass on Guatemala's Pacific coast could, within a week, become a North American hamburger. Beyond geographic proximity, Central America had the added attraction of being free from hoof-and-mouth disease. The establishment of export-packing plants approved by the U.S. Department of Agriculture (USDA) across Central America in the 1960s catalyzed improvements in breeding, pasture management, and transportation (Williams 1986). Under the auspices of the Cold War–driven Alliance for Progress, the United States increased Central American beef quotas and continued to raise them through the latter half of the century.

Guatemalan cattle production consequently exploded from a 1 percent annual growth rate in the 1950s to a 5.4 percent growth rate between 1965 and 1981 (Alvarado Pinetto and Gonzalez Alvarado 1981). Landowning families took advantage of the boom by turning their idle holdings into pasture. Cattle ranchers expanded their landholdings in the 1960s from Guatemala's fertile Pacific coast up through the Motagua River Valley into what Guatemalans call the "East," or "Oriente" (Brockett 1998; T. M. Adams 1982). In this process, many poor Ladinos lost their land, and some of them (about five hundred) joined a guerrilla insurgency that led, in part, to the civil war (Schwartz 1990).[3] Others joined the first wave of landless colonists traveling to Petén, whom ranchers would soon follow.

Around the same time, U.S. and other foreign advisers to Guatemala's two colonization programs (INTA and FYDEP) encouraged the spread of cattle ranching from eastern Guatemala into Petén.[4] In addition to road construction, the colonization programs rewarded ranchers with vaccination and deparasitization campaigns, donation of registered bulls to improve stock, and tractor machinery with which to dig watering holes. Although the World Bank did provide some loans in the 1970s, credit was less critical to cattle ranching in northern Guatemala than in other parts of Latin America (Kaimowitz 1995). By far the most important state subsidy to cattle ranching was preferential land granting under the colonization programs.

While poor settlers in Petén could claim between twenty-two and forty-five hectares, cattle ranchers were initially eligible to receive more than a thousand hectares each (Schwartz 1990). Ranching concessions to military officers, in particular, included highly arable land and/or plots with speculative commercial value near roads or oil installations. For these reasons, people nicknamed the Northern Franja Transversal the "Generals' Strip" and a fertile savanna in east-central Petén the "Valley of the Stars" (referring to military insignia).

Although FYDEP later lowered the cattle ceiling to 225 hectares, ranchers still received five to ten times more land than peasants. Knowing that cattle ranchers were receiving up to 225 hectares, Don Antonio Caal from Tamalton decided to request 90 hectares from FYDEP. At his application interview, the FYDEP officer asked skeptically, "How many head of cattle do you own?" None, Don Antonio replied but then insisted, "I have a right [to land] because I have children." The officer cackled and said, "Well, then you'll get twenty-three hectares [like other Q'eqchi' peasants]." Don Antonio retorted, "People have five senses. Do cows have five senses?" The officer asked, "What kind of question is that?" Don Antonio countered that his children deserved as much land as a cow, saying, "Well, to get fat, people have to work the land, but cattle get fat without working." Tired of arguing, the FYDEP officer said, "You're full of sh**, but I'll give you a bigger plot if you don't tell anyone else." Most of Antonio's Q'eqchi' neighbors, however, received only twenty-three hectares.

Partially because of bad press about the so-called hamburger connection linking rain forest destruction to U.S. fast food (Nations and Komer 1983), but mostly because of pressure from the U.S. cattle lobby to change import quotas, the Central American cattle industry reached a plateau in the 1980s (Edelman 1995). In Guatemala, however, government land subsidies continued to encourage cattle ranching. Some production remains destined for Mexico and the United States, but demand from Guatemala's growing urban population now drives the beef industry.[5] According to Bank of Guatemala statistics, the percentage of beef destined for national consumption grew from 57 percent in 1990 to 84 percent in 1996. Guatemalans ruefully note, though, that they get left with the worst grade ("cutter") meat from old cows (and in some cases, herbicide-contaminated meat that fails USDA standards [Edelman 1987]), while higher-grade steers are reserved for export.

Cattle production in northern Guatemala reflects these heterogeneous markets. As a general rule, lowland cattle production takes about two years. Small producers (with less than thirty head) raise calves ("crianza"), which requires less start-up capital. Meanwhile, large producers (with more than one hundred head) dominate the fattening ("engorde") stage because it requires extensive pasture and, hence, significant capital investment. Large producers also have a monopoly on exports, breeding bulls, purebred registered cattle, and new technologies such as artificial insemination. The entrance of more large ranchers to Petén has flipped the earlier calving/fattening equation. Through the 1990s, the Petén region was producing calves to be fattened later on more mature ranches on the south Pacific coast (Kaimowitz 1995), but today ranchers from the south coast and as far away as Nicaragua are sending their calves to Petén for final grazing.

Sometimes large and small producers work with each other as partners ("a medias") while other ranchers conglomerate and claim land under the names of different family members in order to evade colonization regulations, but overall, cattle production tends to be a solitary business. Surprisingly, small and medium producers resent the large, capitalized, and absentee ranchers as much as dispossessed Q'eqchi' farmers do. I recall Don Chevy Lopez, a big-hearted rancher from Atelesdale who had used his own labor to build up his herd from a few steers to a hundred head, sneering at the new investment ranchers from Jutiapa arriving in his village. While they might have the economic prowess to buy up forty to fifty "caballerías," he warned gleefully that "they had yet to see a Petén summer [dry season]."

Petén's cattle herd has grown geometrically, roughly in tandem if not slightly ahead of human population growth—reaching at least 500,000 today (though some estimates run as high as 1.5 million head) (fig. 5.1). One study reported 4,000 ranches in Petén (SEGEPLAN 1993); ten years later, the 2003 agricultural census showed almost twice that number (7,100 landowners with pasture). The vast majority (70 percent) of Petén ranchers own less than 10 head, while the largest producers have herds that number upward of 15,000. So while average cattle holdings are low (just 13 head), a much higher standard deviation (a factor of 20 head) indicates that ownership is highly skewed (Grandia et al. 2001). Although there is little reliable data on conversion of forest to pasture, David Kaimowitz (1997) calculates that pasture had grown from 32,000 hectares in 1964 to 300,000 hectares in 1991. These figures roughly concur with the 2003 agricultural census that reported 376,319 hectares in pasture, or 36 percent of total cultivated land in Petén. One must interpret these official statistics with caution, since some ranchers may be reluctant to provide honest numbers about their herd sizes and landholdings due to fear of expropriation (if the landholdings were illegally granted through colonization programs) and involvement with narco-trafficking, among other factors. Nor do official numbers take into account pasture rented from other landholders or located in protected areas. Hence, in addition to the official government data, two other proxy indicators are useful for estimating the scope of land converted to cattle.[6]

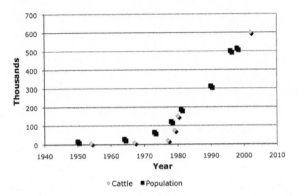

FIGURE 5.1. Cattle compared with population growth in Petén. Population sources: various, in Grandia 2000. Cattle sources: 1957–64, Schwartz 1990, citing Latinoconsult 1968 (6,000); 1967, Rodríguez de Lemus 1967 (10,000); 1977, Schwartz 1990 citing FYDEP data (21,000); 1979, ibid. (75,000); 1980, Schwartz 1990 citing Zetina O. (150,000); 2005, Schwartz 2001, Grandia fieldwork (500,000–700,000)

Branding registries ("fierros") tally the number of ranchers located in a given municipality (fig. 5.2). Not everyone participates, but the registries are nonetheless useful measurements of the relative maturity of a cattle district. While the registries continue to grow each year in northern municipalities such as San Andres, they have stabilized in Petén's more southern municipalities, which experienced their first cattle boom in the 1980s. In no municipality, however, are the registries decreasing.

Soil studies provide another perspective. Land applicants register a parcel by submitting a soil and land-use study to the National Forests Institute (Instituto Nacional de Bosques) (INAB). An analysis of the 652 soil studies approved between 1999 and 2003 shows that cattle ranchers hold significantly larger parcels (by more than 50 percent) than do farmers. In a region predominantly owned by military officers (the aforementioned Valley of the Stars), more than 90 percent of the best soils were found on landholdings larger than two hundred hectares. Moreover, the data set showed that more than half of the parcels legalized between 1999 and 2003 were at least partially devoted to cattle, and a quarter were devoted exclusively to cattle with no agricultural production at all. Based on these sources, plus estimates from ranchers and cattle truckers, an estimated half of Petén's land outside protected areas has been converted to pasture.

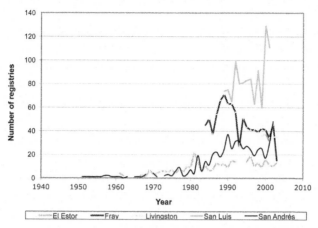

FIGURE 5.2. Cattle branding registries in the Northern Franja Transversal and Petén by municipality

TECHNIQUES OF ENCLOSURE

Following Lockean notions of private property, under the rules of the colonization programs in northern Guatemala, settlers and ranchers had to prove to the state that they had made improvements on the land. One of the clearest ways to stake a claim, therefore, was to deforest and then fence the parcel. As a way of anticipating future opportunities and preempting claims by small settlers, ranchers frequently cleared far more land than they had the capital to maintain. Today, in order to prevent invasions by the landless poor, cattle owners tend to invest in pasture expansion rather than take steps to intensify production.

The actual work of converting forest to pasture with axes and machetes is extremely labor-intensive, so ranchers take advantage of peasant labor for the task, often through sharecropping. One Q'eqchi' leader described the process with a rhyme, "We go along clearing. They come along fencing" (Vamos descombrando. Ellos vienen alambrando). The story of Don José Cux illustrates a typical sharecropping arrangement:

> Born as a laborer on one of the largest German coffee plantation in highland
> Verapaz (measuring some four hundred caballerías), at age sixteen, Don José
> set out walking to Petén with no shoes, no hat, not even a bag to carry—even if
> he had a bag, he had nothing to put in it, he remembered, "I was so poor. . . ."
> In southeastern Petén, he found a cattle ranch where the owner liked to have

*Q'eqchi' families live for a time to clear the forest for agriculture; in exchange
for use of the land, the rancher expected the Q'eqchi' families to plant pasture
after harvesting two corn crops. For the rancher, it was an inexpensive way
to clear forest. For the families, it was the first time they had sufficient land
to plant their corn. Reflecting on his first sharecropping experience, Don José
exclaimed, "Oh, I liked it a lot! . . . It was almost like I was the owner . . ."*

*Two years later, when he returned home to visit his mother, he was wearing
blue jeans and shoes and had bought himself a watch and a radio, too. His family was so impressed that they decided to follow him back to Petén and worked
on the ranch with twenty other Q'eqchi' families for fifteen years, planting corn
for themselves and grass for the ranch owner. The day arrived, though, when the
whole plantation had been converted to pasture, and the owner simply kicked
them out. Don José said to me, "There I was again with the same problem I had
in the coffee plantation—no land! But this time I had children I was responsible
for!" He decided it was better to look for his own land farther north and ended
up in Laguna del Tigre National Park.* (Field notes, 2002)

In Don Jose's case, the rancher allowed the Q'eqchi' families to clear and cultivate as much land as they wanted in exchange for planting grass among the
corn. In other sharecropping arrangements, the rancher requires half the farmer's labor time (usually two weeks of work a month) or half the land cleared (i.e.,
if the farmer wants to plant a hectare of corn, he must clear a second hectare
of forest for the owner).

If a rancher wishes to put in pasture quickly and avoid patron-client relations
with sharecroppers, he may pay for labor directly. A rancher who has capital
typically hires a foreman to recruit a labor squad from elsewhere (often unem-
ployed urban men from Alta Verapaz) to work for twenty days to a month for
$3.00–4.50 a day, depending on food provisions. If the rancher lives on the site,
he may hire local workers on a daily basis or by verbal contract for a set payment
per area cleared. Laborers generally prefer to be paid by the day, because quantitative contracts are often impossible to complete in the time allotted.[7] Ranchers
also find it hard to recruit piecemeal labor during planting and harvest times,
as few peasants like doing manual labor on the ranches. As Don Manuel Coc
from Atelesdale taciturnly remarked: "If I need money, I'll work on the fincas. If
not, I won't." With sharecropping arrangements, ranchers also run the risk that
tenants may refuse to leave or eventually claim usufruct rights. The most secure
means of planting pasture, therefore, is to purchase already cleared land outright
from peasant farmers at lower-than-market prices.

Though willing to buy land from anyone, ranchers have disproportionately targeted Q'eqchi' landowners because of geography. Having colonized Petén when there were no roads, Q'eqchi' pioneers tended to settle along rivers. With the introduction of roads years later, these settlement areas suddenly became prime ranching land, especially in lush and rainy villages like Agoutiville (see pp. 154–55).[8]

In this and many other cases, ranchers acquired parcels through trickery or coercion or by making farming impossible for their neighbors. As Don Sebastian Yaxcal related, the first man in the Agoutiville region who sold his land to a rancher and "brought this pestilence upon us" traded his parcel for a Nissan truck, and "he started going out womanizing in the truck, but it broke down six months later, and before the man knew it, he was suffering on squatted land in Petén . . . what a fool!" The second seller traded his twenty-one hectares for an old shotgun, a used chainsaw, and a decrepit truck. Now he is back in Agoutiville, stuck renting land from the ranchers at $37 a hectare per season. Yet another man traded his parcel for an old truck painted to look new, which lasted less than a week. Others received cash payments (starting at a little more than $140 per hectare) for land that is now worth ten times that.

When such deals fail to entice Q'eqchi' farmers to sell, ranchers employ more aggressive techniques such as letting their pasture fires "accidentally" burn out of control and into neighboring fields or "accidentally" letting their cattle get loose and destroy surrounding crops. The colonial archives hold proof that as early as 1520 in the Mexico City Valley, indigenous communities lodged complaints about Spanish livestock grazing on their communal lands despite government edicts forbidding cattle within four leagues of human settlement. Consider, for example, this village testimony from 1858: "We struggle to plant and care for our crops but they are ruined overnight by cattle trampling over them; cattle deliberately set out to pasture on our land or on the boundaries where the tenant farmers settle for the purposes of taking over" (Cambranes 1985: 68).

Ranchers erect barbed-wire fences, cutting farmers off from neighbors and blocking paths to farms. Sebastian Yaxcal complained, "Before, one went to work peacefully. No one would demand, 'Why did you walk through there?'" Women and elders lose nearby access to firewood and forest resources. As Mateo Pop from Atelesdale lamented, "What a shame about all that land sold. You can't even get firewood there." As another man observed, "For the poor man, there is no one who will investigate [these incidents] and take his side."

Agoutiville was once an extension of a larger village to the east, Yellowbeard Creek, settled in the 1880s exodus from highland Verapaz during the coffee boom. Over time, the hamlet of Agoutiville grew to a substantial settlement in its own right. Now numbering a hundred families, including six Ladino families, Agoutiville is quite active ritually (fig 5.3) and, correspondingly, is also among the minority of Guatemalan communities that maintained a customary land management system until the 1990s. Each family had two small parcels, one on the less arable red clay soils to the north and another on the fertile lands adjacent to the river. Beyond these cultivated areas, they conserved forests adjacent to the Sierra Cruz mountain range, including a sacred cave called Jagged Rocks where their village *Tz'uultaq'a* resides.

INTA, the government colonization program, awarded Sehalaw its land in the 1970s as a "collective agrarian patrimony"—meaning that the government only measured the village boundaries and left internal land distribution up to the village. After a road was constructed in the mid-1970s through Agoutiville that connected farther to the west with the Northern Franja Transversal and its associated oil pipeline, government agents returned to recommend that the village privatize its land—a decision the community now regrets. When the government shortly thereafter paved

FIGURE 5.3. Ritual procession, Agoutiville, 2003. Q'eqchi' elders and "mayordomos" greet members of the Agoutiville Catholic Church returning from a pilgrimage to see the Black Christ of Esquipulas as part of a three-day *mayejak* in the community. Photograph: Liza Grandia

	Cattle ranch
	Q'eqchi' parcels
	State forests
	Village center
▪▪▪	Road
∼∼	River

FIGURE 5.4. Cattle takeover of Agoutiville. The SW-to-NE line is a river, and the SE-to-NW line is a road. The village settlement is the large area where these lines cross. Drawing by Don Lorenzo Cac

the highway to Guatemala City ten kilometers away, this brought both poor Ladino settlers (either already or aspiring small cattle owners themselves) and investment ranchers to the area. Parcel by parcel they began buying up Q'eqchi' land.

Within six years, nine ranchers had acquired almost three-quarters of the village—including all the prime land near the roadside, close to the village, and along the river, as illustrated in figure 5.4. A rancher technically even owns the village soccer field and has been threatening to install pasture there. As Agoutiville leader Sebastian Yaxcal observed, "You don't yet see the illness of this village . . . but it's no longer a community. It's just a cattle ranch." Worse yet, many of the families who

moved to Agoutiville had lost their land once before; their previous village had some unusual natural hot springs, and a wealthy rancher seized the land and converted it into a private tourist business.

As residents progressively lost their land to cattle ranchers, many moved farther north. Far from being anarchic, lowland Q'eqchi' migration had a pattern and a reason.

Of course not every rancher abuses his peasant neighbors; absentee or investor-ranchers—including local urban elites, military officials, big ranchers from other departments, and businessmen and people from the capital—use the most aggressive practices (see Ybarra 2009 for additional case studies). In some neighboring communities, narco-traffickers use their vast pastures as illegal landing strips. They threaten people to surrender their land, saying to farmers, "You can sell me your land now, or your *widow* will have to sell it later." In some instances during the civil war, military officers misused their authority to coerce small landholders into selling.[9]

Yet the question remains, why do people who depend on land for their subsistence and who have suffered a difficult life as pioneers voluntarily sell what they have worked so hard to acquire? Certainly, the Q'eqchi' are not the only ones selling their land; Peteneros and Ladino settlers are also selling (though to a lesser degree, because the latter often aspire to own cattle). When an outsider offers them more cash than they have ever held at any time, even if it is far below the real value of the land, they can be tempted to sell. However, as Carmen Caal noted, "The cash is nice, but you won't ever have land again. With money, you feel like a king, but money is like water—it goes away before you know, and you are left with nothing." Although Carmen is aware that there is no longer free land left in Petén, many Q'eqchi' sellers hope they can acquire more land farther north or make do renting or borrowing. Others sell with a purpose in mind, such as educating a child, paying to heal an illness, opening a store or transport business, or moving to town.

The initial entry into a village requires some delicacy, but once a rancher has hired local people as cowboys, they will pass on information about land markets. By following inside tips on sudden tragedies (a sickness, death, lost crop, or accident), ranchers can get good deals. One rancher who gave me a ride near Tamalton pointed to a roadside house and ten-hectare parcel that he had bought for $1,177 because the owner's truck had broken down and he was desperate for parts; within a few months, the rancher was offered $4,575 for the same property. During a visit to the largest ranch in Agoutiville, I heard José Diaz's cowboy updating him on all the local purchasing opportunities. Acknowledging my presence, Don José joked with his cowboy not to introduce him to any more gringas or the people would start raising their prices.

As a rancher working east of Agoutiville declared publicly, "We are going to buy the whole community." With the steep rise in land prices, it certainly makes smart business sense to expand now and worry about pasture improvements later. As one local intellectual put it, "With cattle, the tendency is to appropriate more and more land." Titled land is generally three to four times more valuable than land owned in usufruct via improvements, and land with good road access is two to three times more valuable than fields accessible only by trails (cf. Kaimowitz 1995, which predicts that land prices will triple along newly paved roads and that anything within two to three kilometers of the road will at least double in price). In southern Petén, one small rancher from San Luis originally paid about $500 for four caballerías from FYDEP; someone recently offered him $26,000 for the parcel (a 500 percent increase in value in two decades). In northern Petén, the value of land has grown threefold from $1,300 to $3,900 per caballería in just a few years. Still, when compared with prices in southern Petén and Izabal (where a pastured caballería can be worth $65,000 to $260,000), land in northern Petén is still dirt-cheap. In fact, ranchers are selling their lands south of Petén to purchase four, five, ten times more in northern Petén, often inside the Maya Biosphere Reserve.

Ranchers prefer to sell to other ranchers because they can earn more for combined pastures than they would by breaking a ranch into smaller parcels. As Samuel Chun from Agoutiville observed, "They want to sell the whole lot and go off and buy somewhere else. Look at Victor Mejia. He made some big bucks on his ranch here and went to Petén to buy more." Another rancher near Agoutiville who had purchased almost one hundred farmers' parcels (an estimated two thousand hectares) wanted to sell the whole block for $1.5 million. One of the farmers who had sold to him remarked bitterly, "He's going to sell to someone even richer." With the exception of large holdings sold to returning refugees or other peasant groups through government programs or as a result of organized land occupations, cattle ranchers tend not to break up their properties voluntarily for resale to peasant farmers.

The fundamental problem with extensive land use for cattle is that as soon as fences are erected and pasture planted, employment opportunities quickly fall. Ranchers need to hire only some temporary labor to weed pasture (four to five days per hectare, twice a year), replace posts, or brand incoming cattle. Because this work is so unpleasant, ranchers struggle to recruit reliable workers, as peasant pioneers sell their labor only when convenient or necessary. Wages in Petén are roughly 50 percent higher than in the rest of the country, and workers also expect to receive a generous lunch or, if not, to be compensated another dollar a day.

If a rancher owns at least one hundred head of cattle, he can also afford to hire a permanent cowboy-administrator who will take charge of labor recruitment.[10] Above that threshold, the labor ratios decrease dramatically, as two or three cowboys are sufficient for a thousand head of cattle.[11] Petén's largest ranch, as of 2004, covered 4,500 hectares (one hundred "caballerías") with fifteen thousand to thirty-five thousand cattle at any given time but employed only six to seven cowboys and fifteen sharecropping families. Las Vegas, a large ranch in Izabal owned by a prominent Guatemalan family who dominates the sugar industry, covers seventy-five caballerías with fifteen thousand head of cattle but employs just twenty-two cowboys. Lorenzo Cac from Agoutiville village bluntly anticipates the labor contraction associated with cattle, saying, "What will happen here in fifteen years? They'll improve everything with new grasses and there won't be any work left. If someone doesn't have land and can't emigrate, he'll have to join a robbery gang."[12]

Beyond these highly successful ranchers, cattle is only marginally profitable for small- and medium-size ranchers, aside from the money to be made via enclosing and fencing property for future land speculation. Soil erosion, weeds, and drought are serious problems, as the karstic soils of Petén are easily degraded through overgrazing, compaction from cattle hooves, overexposure to the sun, and runoff. Productivity often falls after ten years of pasture use; although agronomists recommend fallowing and replanting pasture to protect soil fertility, ranchers use their fields continuously. Cattle also become ill from stagnant watering holes (fig. 5.5). Prices for most veterinary medicine and supplies are highly inflationary because they are acquired from transnational agribusiness and pegged to the dollar. Only three ranches in Petén sell registered breeds because producers cannot afford them. While some grasses do grow naturally, most are nutritionally poor (less than 0.5 percent protein), so ranchers find themselves needing to purchase expensive seeds with higher oil and protein content (Tucker 2000).

Infrastructure start-up costs for a medium-size ranch (fifty-six hectares) that would support a hundred head of cattle are at least $13,000 (three times Guatemala's per capita income). Thousands more dollars would be needed to purchase land and the first herd of cattle for fattening. The burden of all these inputs are comparatively worse for smallholder ranchers, most of whom will never pass a profitability threshold (cf. Edelman 1987 for similar conclusions about Costa Rican ranchers). Without external capital, it can take years to grow a herd from a few animals to a profitable size. Norman Schwartz (1990, 2001) estimates that ranchers need at least twenty hectares of pasture and thirty-five to forty head of cattle in order to turn a profit.

Those who do make something of the cattle business have access to other cash inputs with which to subsidize pasture improvements. Typically in

FIGURE 5.5. Cattle watering hole, 2003. A typical view of a Petén cattle ranch. Photograph: Liza Grandia

Petén, this money comes from illicit activities such as drugs and hunting, hauling and transportation work, or commodity agriculture. As Don Felipe Ba from Agoutiville put it, "[The ranchers] *already* have got money." Small ranchers frequently invest their profits in other small businesses, like dry-goods stores, as a way of maintaining cash flow, and most reported having a family member in the United States who sends them cash remittances. As Don Chepe Duarte explained on a visit to Guatemala, all he does is "work, work, work" in a Michigan meat-packing plant, and he looks forward to the day when he can retire quietly to the ranch he bought from a Q'eqchi' farmer.[13]

Some Q'eqchi' villagers are quite savvy about the external sources of wealth behind ranching, as this conversation between Samuel Chun and Mateo Cac, two young men from Atelesdale, reveals:

> *Samuel:* All the land here; it's owned only by Spanish-speaking people. The Q'eqchi' have very little. And, man, what good land!
>
> *Mateo:* One wonders what in the world the people [who sell] are thinking.

Samuel: Well, Roberto sold his land for his son's education. It served him, but imagine how much money he'll need now to buy land again!

Mateo: Oh, they've already sold. They'll never get it back.

Samuel: The people who sold, they didn't earn very much. Let's speak the truth here.

[Conversation continues about who sold what and for how much.]

Samuel: . . . What cash [the ranchers] are dropping along the route to Toquela village, something like Q2 million quetzals. [The buyers] are from Zacapa. I wonder, where does all that money come from?

Mateo: From cocaine. [Mateo proceeds to explain matter-of-factly to Samuel about the cocaine narco-trafficking in the region and its suspected linkages to the military.] (field notes, 2003)

While Samuel and Mateo understand the cash subsidies behind ranching, to other village farmers, ranching itself may appear to produce that wealth.

Prices are determined by a distant international beef market, so technological change comes slowly (Kaimowitz 1997). Precisely because cattle profit depends on the size of the herd, ranchers reinvest their profits in their ranches. Some might do so by intensifying production—for example, raising stocking rates, lowering mortality, hastening the fattening process with supplements, improving pastures, replacing posts with regenerative tree species, or investing in "double purpose" dairy cattle. At best, stocking rates might be improved from the present average of 0.7 to 1.4 head per hectare. Most ranchers, however, seek to expand their pastures, because, in the end, cattle ranching is an inherently extensive enterprise. It is also a splendid way to control and show "use" of large amounts of land with low overhead costs—especially if one's purpose is land speculation, oil or mineral extraction, logging, production of agrofuels, or narco-trafficking, rather than meat production.

ROPING IN THE Q'EQCHI'

Some Q'eqchi' leaders recognize the expansive threat of cattle ranching. As Sebastian Yaxcal observed, "The ranchers have their money but they don't have anywhere to put it . . . so they buy up the land of indigenous people like . . . how is the expression? . . . like hot bread!" Others reject the racist and sexist culture of cattle ranching and critique the tendency of Ladino ranchers to "solve their problems with machetes" or, worse yet, to protect their holdings with guns. Although Samuel and Mateo clearly understand the cash subsidies that support ranching, many other Q'eqchi' farmers imagine that cattle must be extraordinarily profitable and aspire to become ranchers themselves. They describe ranching as a passive activity of *ilok wakax*, or "watching the cattle," and often remark that cattle reproduce themselves with little labor required on the part of the owner.

Q'eqchi' intimacy with the cattle economy manifests in other ways. Q'eqchi' cattle owners may invoke traditional ceremonies and knowledge for taking care of their animals. If money permits, villagers may purchase a small steer for making *kaqik* beef stew to be served for major village celebrations. Having long worked as cowboys and field hands on cattle ranches, Q'eqchi' families seek to establish patron-client relationships by inviting ranchers to become godparents to their children. Especially in Petén (but less so in Belize), the characteristic white hat, blue jeans, boots, and large belt buckles of cowboys have become staples of the male Q'eqchi' dress-up wardrobe (fig. 5.6). When asked to name their favorite foods, malnourished Q'eqchi' schoolchildren's invariable (and understandable) response is red meat or cheese.

Because the 2003 national agricultural census did not disaggregate data by ethnicity, Q'eqchi' cattle ownership may be measured by the following proxy indicators:

- *Regional cluster sample survey of a thousand households:* In a Petén-wide survey asking a hypothetical question about how they might spend some extra money (*Wi wan nab'al aa tumin xb'an laa kanjel b'ar raj xb'en taa woksi'*), an equal percentage of Q'eqchi' respondents (20.5 percent) and Ladino migrants (19.8 percent) volunteered that they would invest in cattle (Grandia et al. 2001).
- *Municipal records:* Municipal branding registries through 2003 show that in areas that have been settled by the Q'eqchi' for several decades, the percentages of branding records issued to people with Q'eqchi' surnames were roughly half the percentage of Q'eqchi' people in relation to the whole population.[14]
- *Village survey:* When heads of household in Agoutiville were asked what they would do with the money if they suddenly won the lottery, nine of seventy-nine (11 percent) replied they would invest first in cattle, which is consistent with the branding registries in that region (Grandia 2006).
- *Soil-use study:* In a file of soil-use studies ("Estudios de Capaci-

FIGURE 5.6. Q'eqchi' cowboy fashion, 2003. A Q'eqchi' man and his son from Atelesdale display cattle-ranching fashions. Photograph: Liza Grandia

dad de Uso de la Tierra"), or ECUT, submitted to INAB in Petén between 1999 and 2003, 20 percent of Q'eqchi' landholders report having pasture on their land (compared to 60 percent of Ladinos).

Based on these sources, a surprising number of Q'eqchi' landowners in the lowlands—an estimated one-fifth—have pasture and/or own cattle (for more details, see Grandia 2006).

In many instances, outside agents including missionaries,[15] NGOs, colonization agencies, and multilateral donors were responsible for promoting cattle ranching as a land use to the Q'eqchi'. A recent multimillion-dollar IDB project recruited several Q'eqchi' communities in Petén into "sustainable cattle ranching" (Hamilton 2005). Years ago in Agoutiville, some villagers received a loan of $38,000 from the Spanish Cooperation Agency for fattening fifty steers, but most of the cattle died because villagers did not receive proper veterinary training. Of the eight people involved in this failed project, only two still have cattle. Just south of Atelesdale, the government land agency FONTIERRAS settled a mixed Q'eqchi' and Poqomchi' village on an old cattle ranch on the condition that villagers raise cattle in order to pay back their land loans. Lacking wells and sharing watering holes with the cattle, in 2003 almost everyone in the village had a visible skin disease from the dirty drums of lake water trucked in weekly by the municipality. Villagers struggle under the loan payments and said they felt compelled to accept the cattle project as a way "to prove it's true that they really need land." They are under the impression that if every family does not collaborate to plant pasture and tend the cattle one week a month, "the bank will see they didn't really need the land," as one villager explained. Across the border, too, many development agencies and missionaries have mounted cattle projects in Toledo, Belize, but almost all have failed because the high rainfall makes the animals susceptible to hoof disease.

Should the involvement of Q'eqchi' people with cattle surprise us, given their centuries-old entanglement with the ranching culture of regional economic elites? That is, of course, the essence of hegemony—that people learn to imitate their oppressors and participate in their own domination (Grandia 2009b). As James Scott argues, subordination elicits a combination of idealization (public emulation) and hatred (private critique). Subordinates often maintain fantasies that mirror reflections of the techniques of domination used against them, and thus, "the practice of domination, then, *creates* the hidden transcript [of resistance]" (1990: 27). For want of alternative investments, many affluent Q'eqchi' farmers, who might otherwise carry their objections to cattle into the public sphere, decide to invest in cattle. Hence, by 2007, Sebastián Yaxcal of Agoutiville, who was previously the most outspoken critic of the ranching invasion of his community, was privately planting pasture on his land in preparation for buying several steers himself.

Though not particularly profitable for small landholders, cattle ranching nonetheless creates a highly visible display of wealth on the landscape—and it *is* one ready means of investment in a region with few rural business opportunities aside from agriculture, small stores, and transportation (N. Schwartz, pers. comm., Jan. 7, 2003). As the richest investment rancher in Agoutiville, Jose Diaz explained: "Cattle is a way to save and protect one's money. . . . It's a reserve for the future. . . . I don't have much cash, because everything I've earned I've reinvested here in the ranch. It's really little what one earns because medicines are so expensive. The reason I do it is to avoid having money in the bank . . . plus I get to do what I really like." Because the vast majority of costs are up front and continued labor requirements are low, people perceive land purchased for cattle ranching to be a good investment for old age.

Many others see Q'eqchi' land as a good investment, following long-established patterns of land accumulation used by ranchers. In fact, cattle ranching in the Americas has long existed symbiotically with other plantation and extractive enterprises. Spaniards established some of the earliest cattle ranches in the Americas alongside their mining operations in order to feed workers. In the twentieth century, foreign fruit plantations once again raised cattle on their landholdings and helped modernize the Central American beef industry (Tucker 2000). While once portrayed as the end use for degraded tropical rainforests (Edelman 1995), cattle pastures *can* exist alongside and sometimes be transformed into more profitable enterprises. Mechanized soybean production, for instance, is replacing free-range cattle in much of the Amazon. Understocked cattle ranching is thus an excellent landholding pattern until synergistic investment opportunities arise.

One significant new development in Petén (especially in the southern municipalities of Sayaxché, San Luis, and Poptún), the Northern Transversal (Ixcán, Chisec, Fray, Chahal, and Izabal), and the Polochic Valley (El Estor) has been the conversion of cattle ranches into African palm (*Elaeis guineensis*) plantations. The Olmeca company introduced the crop to Guatemala in 1988. Planted as a monocrop, the trees are ready to harvest in three to five years and have a productive life of twenty to thirty years. Once devoted to smaller production of oil for the food and soap industries, the palm industry expanded dramatically in the 2000s with the goal of producing biodiesel. Before 2003, an estimated 9,000 hectares (200 caballerías) had been converted to African palm in southern Petén alone (field notes). By 2005, the company claimed to have 32,000 hectares in production, while private owners held another 18,000 hectares (Hernández 2005). By 2008, the area devoted to oil production had doubled to an estimated 83,385 hectares (Hurtado 2008b). Within the next decade, it may almost double again to 150,000 hectares, according to industry plans. Another oil crop recently introduced to Guatemala by the Colombian government on a much smaller scale is *Jatropha curcas* (Solano 2008).

Responding to a global demand for ethanol, the sugar industry is also expanding into these regions, albeit at a slower pace, having already saturated most production areas of Verapaz and the southern Pacific coast (Hurtado 2008b). Guatemala's sugar industry, which is controlled by the country's most elite families, is the fifth-largest exporter in the world and the second-largest in Latin America; under the terms of the DR-CAFTA, export potential can still grow (Solano 2008). While the sugar industry is dominated by Guatemalan companies, African-palm ventures have attracted the backing of transnational investors (Hurtado 2008b).

Although sugar and palm are portrayed as environmentally friendly bio-fuels, all these plantations displace food producers, which is why critics insist on calling them "agrofuels." They have displaced Q'eqchi' farmers in two ways. Some small landholders have sold or been forced to sell their property to the companies. In other cases, plantation and ranch owners have "reorganized" their lands, meaning they have evicted Q'eqchi' sharecroppers from previously idle lands that they plan to convert to African palm. Laura Hurtado (2008b) aptly describes this dual process as agrarian concentration and "re-concentration." Put more simply, the agrofuel industry is rehabilitating and revitalizing the latifundio plantation system for a twenty-first-century global economy.

While cattle ranchers tend to buy land farmer by farmer, palm plantations have purchased entire villages, sometimes including the homes, at less than market prices. For instance, one company acquired an entire village in Poptún for $500,000, plus $666 for each family's cinder-block residence (later converted to storage sheds). At $5,300 per caballería (forty-five hectares), in other words, the company paid less than one-fifth of current land prices (an estimated $27,000 per caballería, but $270,000 if located along an asphalt road). In a documentary video based on the Spanish-language version of this book, many villagers testified about losing their land wholesale. Angry at being "deceived" into selling his land, one said: "The owners of the African palm company told us they would buy our land and then we could ask for another piece of land. In the end, they bought the land and we gave them the titles. We were told that we were already given other land, but when we went to start farming there, they let us enter once. Then they told us we couldn't pass there anymore because it was private property. That was a dirty trick!" (ProPetén 2009). Many others describe being threatened with having their houses burned or family members killed. One man testified that when he refused the "rich men's" offer, they told him, "You'll be left alone in the middle [of all the farms sold.] And if you don't sell, when your son goes to work on the farm, he might not come back one night" (ibid.).

The agrofuel companies are buying small landholder parcels while the land titling process is still under way or even signing purchase agreements in antic-ipation of the World Bank survey project. Palm grower representatives also arrive at official government titling ceremonies and try to convince new own-ers to sell. Some palm companies have even hired legal staff to facilitate these transactions. A FONTIERRAS manager reportedly ordered the agency's staff to prioritize the legalization of parcels under negotiation with palm companies over peasant claims, some of which have already been in process for twenty to thirty years. The Guatemalan state has also exonerated palm planters from the soil-use studies required, at least nominally, of all other land purchasers (Hurtado 2008a). They have reduced what is a multiyear process for peasants to one of less than six months for palm companies.

Roughly half the palm crop is destined for export, but that may increase with European interest in purchasing the oil for biodiesel. Already 80 percent of Guatemala's sugar-based ethanol is exported to Europe. While potential export revenue for both is high—$157 million in 2008 for palm oil products (L. Solano, pers. comm., 2010)—the value of displaced local agriculture is higher still. Farmers in the Polochic region, for example, generate comparable revenue planting corn or okra as planting African palm ($6,148 versus $6,588 per hectare). Likewise, the traditional combination of corn and rice is competitive with sugarcane ($2,386 versus $2,643 per hectare). When analyzed in terms of labor opportunity, however, the traditional crops far outscore the agrofuels. Corn intercropped with vegetables such as okra and chili for national markets generates 284 labor days per hectare, while the production of basic grains for food security (corn, rice, beans) generates between 206 and 240 days per hectare. Palm and sugar require only 94 and 33 labor days per hectare, respectively (Alonso, Alonzo, and Dürr 2008) (conversions mine). Not only do agrofuels produce less employment, but the profits travel to Guatemala City and beyond, whereas the money earned from food crops circulates locally and strengthens the regional economy. If the territory devoted to palm and sugar were to increase by half in this valley, Q'eqchi' unemployment would go up by 15 and 22 percent, respectively (ibid.) Plantations prefer to hire energetic young men, so the displacement of subsistence crops often obscures even greater losses for women and older men.

Although potentially sustainable on a small scale (as in Colombia, for example), the vertically integrated agrofuel industry in Guatemala has created massive agrarian dispossession. Some companies are purchasing the land outright; others have created complex, twenty-five-year leasing agreements with peasants, promising them employment on the plantation as well as annual payments. As another man testified, "In the beginning they paid [fair wages], and then they stopped. One week we are paid, the next we are not." Many of those jobs never materialized, but the penalties are too high for peasants to break their contracts and reclaim their land. Others provide landowners technical assistance with converting their parcels to palm in exchange for exclusive purchase of their crops. Meanwhile, industrial farming practices are quickly eroding the quality of their land, dimming prospects for reclaiming it at the end of the lease (Hurtado 2009).

While regional and national elites dominate the cattle economy, foreign investors have quickly entered the agrofuel industry. In 2008, the IDB approved a $505,000 technical loan to develop plans for the palm industry through a "sustainable energy" component of the PPP (Solano 2008). The Central American Bank for Economic Integration and the World Bank's International Finance Corporation (IFC) supported smaller projects for palm and sugar (Alonso, Alonzo, and Dürr 2008). Though technically all Guatemalan companies, the six producers of African palm have alliances with and backing from Biogeos Imgeomega (a Colombian company), Unilever, Carlyle Group, Riverstone Holdings, and Goldman Sachs. Cattle ranchers had few pretensions to environmental sustainability, but these new plantations promise "renewable energy" and forest reserves around areas of "primary growth tropical forests," among many other mantras of World Bank–envisioned "green neoliberalism" (Goldman 2006) cited on the Web site of Texas-based Green Earth Fuels, a biodiesel producer supporting African-palm plantations across Central America. The problem is that displaced Q'eqchi' farmers then migrate into protected areas.

Worldwide, indigenous advocates estimate that net forest loss attributable to palm plantations is more than 20,000 hectares a day (7.3 million a year) (Tauli-Corpuz and Tamang 2007). Though touted as secondary forests, palm plantations are yet another iteration of colonial, monocrop farms that lack the "complex, self-regenerating system, encompassing soil, water, microclimate, energy, and a wide variety of plants and animals in a mutual relationship" of primary forests (ibid.: 6). Perhaps environmentally friendly on a small scale, when cultivated on an industrial level, they redirect water sources and transform the landscape into "green deserts," an evocative phrase invented by anti-plantation activists.

Another plantation project under way for northern Guatemala is a papaya cultivation project sponsored by the Ministry of Agriculture, beginning in 2003. This is an attractive crop for those interested in export production because Petén is free of the Mediterranean fruit fly. With start-up costs per hectare at $15,000, however, the project is clearly beyond the reach of small farmers. Unable to find local people to participate, the Ministry of Agriculture carried out its pilot papaya program with owners of the Olmeca company, which introduced African palm as a crop to Guatemala.

Meanwhile, transnational conservation organizations such as Conservation International are studying how they might tap into carbon-trading programs to fund their own biodiversity conservation activities in northern Guatemala. Some, like the World Wildlife Fund, are working with the agrofuel companies to tap into the Clean Development Mechanism under the Kyoto Protocol; four of them have together received about $6.5 million (Alonso, Alonzo, and Dürr 2008). Meanwhile, the National Forestry Institute runs a successful, small-scale reforestation subsidy program, PINFOR, which compensates landowners monetarily per hectare of tree saplings planted. Though not explicitly tied to carbon-sequestration schemes, the program might meet Kyoto Protocol standards. So far, funding has been a limiting factor, with cattle ranchers taking disproportionate advantage of the program, edging out many small farmers who want to participate. Moreover, the amount of land set aside for parks in the early 1990s has indubitably contributed to a rise in land prices outside reserves in both Belize and Guatemala. In addition, in Petén, the purchase of ranches by international human rights organizations in the mid-1990s for resettling civil war refugees returning from Mexico also fueled land speculation (Kaimowitz 1997). Prices are driven up further through new mechanisms for purchasing or placing easements on private land for biodiversity conservation through Guatemala's Association of Private Natural Reserves (in alliance with Conservation International, the Nature Conservancy, and the Mesoamerican Biological Corridor). Although they are helping indigenous communities register communal forests for conservation, this organization also includes some of Guatemala's most elite coffee producers, who may simply be reserving land for future investments or until global coffee prices stabilize.

As designed, none of these carbon-trading projects addresses the root cause of climate change, that is, putting underground fossil fuels into the atmosphere through combustion (Tauli-Corpuz and Tamang 2007). Guatemala is a small exporter (exporting enough to satisfy just eleven seconds of daily U.S. fuel consumption, according to my calculations), but its petroleum industry disproportionately undermines conservation because the most productive wells are located in Laguna del Tigre National Park. This has led to rampant land speculation along access roads and pipeline routes, some of which were constructed with IFC loans. Such speculation is reminiscent of conditions during the intense period of oil and mining discoveries and road building in the late 1970s, when national and military elites acquired large parcels in the northern lowlands, especially along the Franja Transversal, in the hopes of eventually claiming subsoil rights (Solano 2005). A new wave of petroleum and mining opportunities across the Q'eqchi' region once again seems to be fueling nearby land speculation. For example, south of Izabal, Canadian mining companies are renewing their nickel extraction operations, opposed by dozens of organized Q'eqchi' communities. Across the border in Toledo, Q'eqchi'-led NGOs have had to fight oil, logging, and other concessions granted by the Belize government on Q'eqchi' land.

Narco-traffickers, suspected of having ties to the Guatemalan military, have invested heavily in cattle as a front business in this same region, in part to hide illegal landing strips inside their vast ranches. Many of these narco-ranches, located along the Petén-Mexican border, also serve as conduits for smuggling undocumented immigrants into the United States. Over the last decade, narco-ranchers have acquired control of large sections of Sierra Lacandón National Park and almost all of Laguna del Tigre National Park, both in northwestern Petén; there has also been significant drug activity in southwestern Petén in the Sayaxché municipality. In 2006, some courageous journalists from Guatemala's national newspaper, *Prensa Libre*, published a series of exposés on the illegal registration of these holdings in the national property registry. Some of the largest properties they discovered measured as much as 120 caballerías each. All told, illegal properties in the Sierra Lacandón National Park alone amounted to an area double the size of Guatemala City. In response, a new Guatemalan drug squad began destroying more than five dozen landing strips inside these parks, identified by satellite imagery, but the battle rages on (Smyth 2005). Recently, some narco-ranchers have begun diversifying into African palm for both money laundering and territorial control around their holdings (*Prensa Libre* 2008).

A BEAST OF COLONIAL BURDEN

As a Q'eqchi' farmer eloquently stated: "We were utilized by coffee, cotton, cattle, and now palm and sugar cane. We already know what they have to offer" (Alonso, Alonzo, and Dürr 2008: 61). The business may vary, but the pattern is the same—cattle ranching segues easily into new industries controlled by foreign and national elites. Small and medium ranchers, however, may lack the kind of capital necessary to diversify their cattle holdings into these enterprises. Squeezed by the new terms of trade under the DR-CAFTA, they may themselves succumb to land speculation and sell out to larger landholders. Worse still, many of the aforementioned enterprises were financed with loans that must be paid back in foreign currency—further compelling government agencies to promote exports and sacrifice national food security.

Unfortunately for Q'eqchi' farmers, the new corporate cattle-plantation economy lacks the protective patron-client relationships of the old hacienda system (Helms 1982; Wolf and Mintz 1957; and, especially, Hurtado 2008a on the disintegration of the Verapaz *colonato* system). One Q'eqchi' laborer reflected that as plantations serfs, if they made a mistake, they were punished but allowed to stay, but today, "the companies just throw us out at once" (Alonso, Alonzo, and Dürr 2008: 80). While plantation owners once aimed to produce as much food as possible with maximum local labor, the new business model seeks to extract as much wealth from the land with as few people as possible.

The encroachment of this new plantation system onto Q'eqchi' land demonstrates how the latest tools of the transnational corporate economy, such as World Bank land administration programs, inadvertently reinforce traditional landed elites such as cattle ranchers whose tactics and operations have changed remarkably little since the colonial period. Both cattle ranchers and corporations will profit from uprooting the Q'eqchi'. The expansive nature of cattle ranching is a physically powerful way to claim large plantations for future investments. As a metaphoric beast of burden, the cattle industry drags feudal land arrangements into the contemporary global economic system (cf. Retort Collective 2005). The Guatemalan state continues to award favors to those loyal to the new neoliberal regime (Alonso, Alonzo, and Dürr 2008). Transnational investments are not antithetical to ranching; they can coexist and work well together. Roads and other infrastructure planned for transnational trade and economic integration under the PPP will only hasten voracious encroachment by cattle ranchers and other business investors onto Q'eqchi' lands.

6

The Neoliberal Auction

THE PPP AND THE DR-CAFTA

UNDER the guidance of Liberal-era caudillos, Guatemala's first railroad line was a quarter century in the making. Rufino Barrios initiated the project in 1883, and untold numbers of Guatemalan peasants sacrificed their lives laying its tracks. After it was completed in 1908, the Estrada Cabrera administration proceeded to award the Atlantic-Pacific line as well as 1,500 "caballerías" of land in Petén as a tax-free, ninety-nine-year concession to the International Railroad Company of Central America (IRCA), controlled by the United Fruit Company, which used it for transporting bananas to port. IRCA never used the Petén concession and abandoned the rail concession in 1968 when competition from the newly paved highway along the same route made it unprofitable. A state agency, Railroads of Guatemala (Ferrocarriles de Guatemala or FEGUA), assumed responsibility for the ailing railroad until 1997 when it awarded the line for fifty years to another private company, Guatemala Railways (Ferrovías Guatemala), a subsidiary of the Pittsburgh-based Railroad Development Corporation (RDC).

Why would the Guatemalan state continually give away its profitable enterprises to foreign investors but reabsorb them when the enterprises fail (i.e., privatize profits but socialize losses)? The history of the railroad reflects a deeply entrenched Liberal ideology, dating back to the nineteenth century, that foreign investment is Guatemala's most favorable path to "development" (defined only as economic growth). Foreign direct investment is once again on the upswing in Guatemala, having doubled from $2 billion in the early 1990s to $4.5 billion in 2005 (World Bank 2006d). Traditional liberal ideologies favoring privatization and foreign investment recrudesce today in two neoliberal programs: the Puebla to Panama Plan and the Dominican Republic–Central America Free Trade Agreement. Each was planned from the top down but then greenwashed and peoplewashed in order to appear more sustainable.

One local intellectual observed that these plans were for the rich, while "the rest of us are the dishwashers." As another Catholic leader succinctly remarked, "The PPP is a project of the devil" (field notes, 2002–4). Of course, the devil, as the saying goes, is in the details, which by design are often tediously dull. As Richard White observes:

> Planning is an exercise of power, and in a modern state much real power is suffused with boredom. The agents of planning are usually boring; the planning process is boring; the implementation of plans is always boring. In a democracy boredom works for bureaucracies and corporations as smell works for a skunk. It keeps danger away. Power does not have to be exercised behind the scenes. It can be open. The audience is asleep. The modern world is forged amidst our inattention. (1995: 64)

The full complexities of these neoliberal programs are beyond this book's scope, but this chapter demystifies some of the technicalities of the PPP and the DR-CAFTA. While it is important for anthropologists to engage with the legal complexities of such trade regimes, we must also understand the everyday realities of those disenfranchised by elites (see Nader 1980 on taking a "vertical slice" of power). Hence, interspersed in the chapter are ethnographic examples of how these trade and infrastructure agreements will exacerbate Q'eqchi' land dispossession by fomenting road construction and undermining regional food security.

PLANNED OUT

Although officially proposed by Mexican president Vicente Fox, the PPP was really the brainchild of the Inter-American Development Bank. This plan packages a series of legal initiatives (standardization of customs procedures and deregulation) with construction projects (roads, port development, electric grids, hydroelectric dams) meant to facilitate regional "economic integration." IDB analysts expect the PPP to increase annual trade from $5.1 billion to $8.5 billion within the decade. Covering 1 million square kilometers and affecting a population of almost 70 million people, the PPP represents an infrastructure plan for territorial restructuring unparalleled in Central America since the construction of the Pan American Highway, costing more than $25 bil-

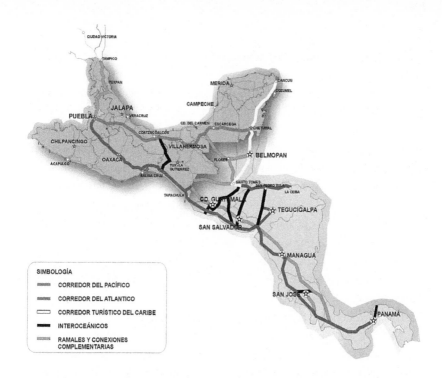

FIGURE 6.1. PPP highways. Source: IDB

lion over twenty-five years. The presidents of Mexico,[1] Guatemala, Honduras, El Salvador, Nicaragua, Costa Rica, Panama, and (informally) Belize signed a loose agreement in 2001, consenting to be administered by an unelected board of commissioners. Colombia joined the plan in 2007, and the Dominican Republic and Ecuador have requested observer status. Sensing benefit to U.S. corporations, Governor Jeb Bush proposed that Florida should also join (Barreda 2004).

Though ostensibly a Mexican–Central American initiative, geopolitical pressure for the plan originates farther north. With the bulk of the United States' population on its east coast, North American–based corporations face a shipping bottleneck. The world's cheapest labor markets in Asia, especially China, are located half a planet away from its largest consumer base (Hansen 2004). As an alternative to expensive trans-U.S. land shipment or the now-saturated Panama Canal, the PPP will establish a nine-thousand-kilometer network of highways, or "dry canals," to connect Atlantic and Pacific ports across the Central America isthmus (fig 6.1). These interoceanic corridors would include a Pacific route from Puebla to Panama and an Atlantic route from Yucatán to Belize to Honduras, as well as other east-west routes, and would cost an estimated $7.5 billion.

Administratively, the PPP is organized into eight sectoral commissions headed by each participating country, with Guatemala and Belize leading energy and tourism, respectively. Of the first $4.2 billion budgeted for PPP projects, 84 percent was devoted to transport, 10 percent to energy, 2 percent to communications, and 1 percent or less each for the commissions on sustainable development, human development, disaster prevention, tourism, and commerce regulation (AVANCSO and SERJUS 2003). Although the PPP includes much rhetoric about promoting Central American industry, most critics believe these transportation networks will facilitate resource extraction and transnational shipping and provide little local employment. Even the sectors that sound friendlier to people and the environment (e.g., human and sustainable development) are actually investing in hard, technocratic products such as information systems, networks, workshops, and public relations.

Many of these projects already existed; what the IDB did was to package them under the PPP umbrella, add some financial support ($1.6 billion from 2001 to 2011), and give it political spin. Other multilateral development banks and countries have quietly pledged funding, but due to negative publicity surrounding the PPP, they have avoided the vanguard protagonism of the IDB.[2] Though the PPP is not entirely synonymous with the IDB, without the IDB's leadership, the PPP would not exist. For instance, when the PPP faltered in 2003, the IDB announced a $4 billion line of credit for PPP projects. Since the IDB's own financial commitments to the PPP are relatively small, the institution has been working to leverage complementary private and government funds for these projects (what the United Nations labels "public-private partnerships"). Loans and public investment constitute more than 90 percent of the budget, which means that the Mexican and Central American people will be paying for these projects long into the future.

Ambitious in scope but with details shrouded in secrecy, the PPP immediately raised the suspicions of civil society groups after its official debut in 2001. The acronym invited alliterative reinterpretations by critics, for example, PPPetroleum; Projects, Privatization, and Poverty; Private Plans for Profit; and, my own version, Profits and Primitive Accumulation in the name of Progress. In Orwellian style, the presidents of Mexico and Central America renamed it the Mesoamerican Integration and Development Project or, for short, Mesoamerica Project in June 2008, but most critics continue to use the better-known name PPP.[3]

The IDB protests that opponents have mischaracterized the PPP yet refuses to provide specific program information (Barreda 2004). Whenever a project meets controversy, the IDB simply changes the budget or removes it from the official portfolio and shifts the blame to the national governments financing the effort. For example, in a 2002 meeting I had with an IDB-Guatemala representative, he denied any funding from his office for the controversial hydroelectric dams on the Usumacinta River but did not rule out the possibility that IDB-Mexico would provide funding. As controversy around the dams continued, the IDB removed the project from the PPP portfolio, but the Mexican government stepped forward to fund it. When IDB representatives attempt to deny their institutional responsibility for such projects, they disingenuously underestimate the sheer power of planning—that is, the symbolic importance of getting a project rolling and its capacity to take on a life of its own.[4] Precisely because the PPP is so substantively weak, "devoid of specificity, lacking flesh and bone . . . contradictory, uncertain, gelatinous" (Moguel 2004), it relies on the power of suggestion. After all, plans are "never innocent . . . [they] either reinforce or challenge existing social and economic arrangements" (Schmink and Wood 1992: 51). Perhaps that is why so many ideas for ill-conceived development projects reappear repeatedly on bureaucratic agendas (even across centuries) despite previous failures or public opposition.

Widespread dissent from civil society groups has led to the cancellation of several projects. In Mexico, Veracruz activists prevented a superhighway that would have cut through a cloud forest. El Salvadoran activists stalled a highway perimeter construction project around San Salvador (Call 2003a). In San Salvador Atenco outside Mexico City, local groups won the cancellation of a new airport. The hydroelectric dams on the Usumacinta River watershed have been put on hold at least temporarily. Despite these small victories and increasingly sophisticated critiques of neoliberalism among civil society groups, the sheer number of PPP projects (more than a hundred as of 2007) still poses a formidable challenge for opponents.

PEOPLEWASHING AND GREENWASHING THE PPP

In response to protests, the PPP, or at least its public face, has morphed over time. The original PPP "plan" emphasized hard infrastructure—highways, electrical grids, dams, ports. After viewing archived Internet pages using special software, John Richard Stepp and Ava Lasseter (2004: 28) describe the original PPP Web site as "filled with stark gray images of telecommunications, highways, bridges, trains, bulldozers and irrigations systems, yet not a single image of people or communities." After awarding a contract of almost a million dollars to Fleishman-Hillard International, the largest public relations firm based in the United States (Call 2003b), the revised PPP presented a Web site featuring smiling indigenous people, workers wearing safety hats, and green scenery, but not for long. The updated Mesoamerica Project Web site has returned to photos of infrastructure sans people.

Besides cosmetic changes, the IDB-PPP responded to public opposition primarily by co-opting the language of public "consultation" and indigenous participation. With the 2004 Declaration of La Ceiba, the PPP commissioners and presidents formally integrated the Advisory Group for Indigenous and Ethnic Participation. Their intent was not to change the direction of the PPP but to "promote joint venture schemes" between investors and consenting communities. Around this same time, the IDB launched a series of stylized public consultation forums, held in regional five-star hotels. Led by IDB representatives clad in safari shirts, khaki pants, and hiking boots, these meetings were highly scripted, with the usual mind-numbing PowerPoint presentations, and hardly participatory. The IDB arranged its Petén consultation at the luxurious Maya International hotel; when civil society representatives were permitted questions, they asked, "Why do you consult communities *after* the projects like the PPP are already defined?" Being asked to "participate" in consultations after the fact was insulting. They wanted local *decision-making* incorporated into project planning from the start.

The second response of the IDB-PPP has been to greenwash itself through the promotion of regional ecotourism and ethno-tourism through its murky association with Mundo Maya. Working through contracts with transnational NGOs such as Conservation International, the IDB aims to redistribute Tikal's heavy visitation load (about 125,000 people a year) to other Maya sites (IDB 2002). Government tourism data show that barely one-quarter of tourist dollars spent in Petén actually stays in Petén (Schwartz, pers. comm., 13 Sept. 2005); those who really profit from Tikal's tourism are tourist agencies, airlines, and hotels in Guatemala City. Unless they actively promote local ownership, Mundo Maya and a new Guatemalan initiative, Cuatro Balam, may further concentrate tourism in the hands of outside agencies and lead to the Cancúnization of Guatemala's archaeological sites.

The Mesoamerican Biological Corridor, a biodiversity project linked to the PPP, garnered considerable controversy. Launched in 1997 with $90 million of World Bank funding, the MBC aimed to connect Mesoamerican parks through new wildlife corridors. In response to immediate protests from indigenous peoples who feared that transnational conservation organizations would appropriate their lands, the MBC goal morphed into the fuzzier concept of "sustainable development" (Grandia 2007). Rather than coordinating with indigenous communities that manage communal forests and making them grassroots leaders for the corridor, MBC planners sought business partnerships. Additional funding from the IDB further transformed the MBC into an economic program compatible with the PPP, with new goals such as "the harmonization of biodiversity policies, valuation of natural resources and economic instruments, communication, sustainable production, and strategic information" (Casper 2004).

Although the MBC helped the IDB green the appearance of regional economic integration, the PPP's overall budgetary allocations remain virtually unchanged. All told, social and environmental projects amounted to less than 5 percent of the original PPP budget. At heart, the PPP is an outmoded modernization program of high-tech development projects incongruent with the poverty of the region, reminiscent of a scene witnessed by novelist and essayist Arundhati Roy: "Every night outside my house in New Delhi I pass this road gang of emaciated laborers digging a trench to lay fiber optic cables to speed up our digital revolution. They work by the light of a few candles" (2004: 30).

While poverty leaves many indigenous people vulnerable to *natural* disasters, geography seems to leave Q'eqchi' people vulnerable to *planning* disasters. Many PPP infrastructure projects will crisscross their land in northern Guatemala and southern Belize, including superhighways, electrical grids, and pipelines leading to expanded ocean ports. Hydroelectric dams have been especially troublesome for Q'eqchi' communities. One planned for the Sierra de las Minas mountain range has already displaced nearby Q'eqchi' villages. The proposed Xalalá dam on the Chixoy River threatens to inundate twelve communities, most of them Q'eqchi'.[5] Meanwhile, in the El Estor region, Q'eqchi' communities evicted from a nickel mining concession on their lands may bring their case before the Organization of American States Commission on Human Rights. Beyond immediate displacement caused by these PPP and related projects, many more Q'eqchi' communities face intense land speculation pressures around roads. Roads bring not only the hope of new economic opportunities but also the despair of dispossession.

> If I were to rate the acculturative forces I have seen at work in various communities I think I would suggest that one road is worth about three schools and about fifty administrators.
>
> —Ralph Beals, *Heritage of Conquest* (1952)

Inspired by ancient Maya trade routes, the Spanish conquerors hoped to reorganize a regional economic system under their command. Between 1697 and 1707, Spanish colonial authorities removed native populations along a royal route ("camino real") planned from Yucatán (Mérida specifically) down to Verapaz and on to Santiago (now Antigua) (G. Jones 1997; Sapper 1985). The north-south connection through Verapaz and Petén proved difficult, and dense tropical forest swallowed up Spanish attempts at road construction through this inhospitable region. Five hundred years later, international tourism investors are still trying to connect ancient Maya cities (now as archaeological sites) through PPP plans that, a first glance, look like Spanish dreams for overland, colonial trade routes (N. Schwartz, pers. comm. 2002).

Isolated during the colonial period, the Q'eqchi' region was integrated into *global* commerce before it entered the national economy through the late nineteenth-century German coffee trade, borne on mule trains to the Río Dulce and out to the sea. Not until President Ubico exploited indigenous labor for his infamous road-building projects of the 1930s did Verapaz have a road connection to Guatemala City. Q'eqchi' elders today still remember opening the road to Cobán in 1938 and later from Cobán to Sebol and into the northern lowlands, using just dynamite and sweat (A. E. Adams 2001). Not until a Verapaz landowner, Romeo Lucas, seized power in 1978 were more roads built from Verapaz into the northern forest (one of them conveniently passing Lucas's father's cattle ranch, Tuilá). The next great road builder in the Petén lowlands was neoliberal president Alvaro Arzú (1996–2000), who paved both the road from Guatemala City to Flores in 2000 (halving the travel time) and the connection between Flores and Cobán in 2002 (shortening a two-day trip to four hours). Subsequent presidents, Óscar Berger and Álvaro Colom, have continued PPP plans to improve or build at least four other major roads across the Q'eqchi' region (fig 6.2), including the following:

- A proposed highway through the Maya Biosphere Reserve to connect north-central Petén to Calakmul, Mexico

- Completion of the El Ceibo connection between Petén and Chiapas
- The paving of the 362-kilometer Northern Franja Transversal from Mexico to the Atlantic to be subsequently renamed the Northern Interoceanic Highway
- A partially constructed connection from southeastern Petén through the Toledo district to Belizean ports

In addition to these major projects, the Guatemalan government spent more than 100 million quetzals in 2006 alone on upgrading three overland routes between Alta Verapaz and Petén.

All these routes are arterial highways for passing quickly through the Q'eqchi' region, not the kind of feeder roads that would serve local farmers and catalyze agricultural development. Hidden from the international planners' view lies an organic transportation network built by Q'eqchi' people, including village paths worn by pedestrians and feeder roads built as the result of persistent village lobbying of municipal governments. One-fifth of Alta Verapaz residents lack access to vehicular roads, while another third suffer from weather closures (World Bank 2006d). "One gets the sense that you could walk the entire length and/or perimeter of Alta Verapaz on these footpaths and never have to pass through a town center or on a road open to vehicular traffic" (Collins 2001: 72).

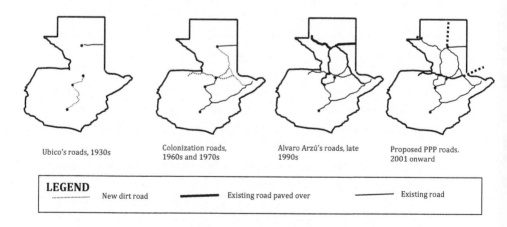

| Ubico's roads, 1930s | Colonization roads, 1960s and 1970s | Alvaro Arzú's roads, late 1990s | Proposed PPP roads. 2001 onward |

LEGEND
.... New dirt road ▬▬▬▬ Existing road paved over ———— Existing road

FIGURE 6.2. A century of road development in the Q'eqchi' lowlands

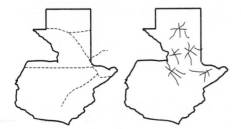

FIGURE 6.3. Planned pass-through roads versus organic feeder roads

Likewise, in Europe there have always been two kinds of road systems (cf. fig. 6.3). The first is made up of narrow, meandering streets used by pedestrians, farm carts, horses, and bicycles, which developed organically. The second is the network of planned, long-distance, straight paved roads dating back to at least Roman times. Mixing these two different road systems (e.g., too many donkey carts on paved roads or too many high-speed cars on local roads) can cause a transportation breakdown and defeat the advantages of each (Lohmann 2003: 4).

The importance of an organic road system (*eb li b'e*) manifests through colloquial expressions. In English, the method for doing something is described as a "way"; one thinks way ahead or way back; and the most powerful budgetary authority in the United States is the Ways and Means Committee (A. E. Adams 2001). Yucatec Maya also employ the concept of roads metaphorically, describing their fate and their work as their "road" and greeting each other by asking, "How is your road?" (Hanks 1990). In Q'eqchi', a leader is described as "the one that brings the way" or "the road bearer" (*aj k'ambol b'e*) (A. E. Adams 2001). To walk means to be "roaded" (the passive form of "road," *b'eek*). To wish someone well upon departure, one says, "Go slowly on the road" (*Timil timil sa' b'e*"). Even in Spanish and English, a routine Q'eqchi' greeting to a new arrival is "How was the road?" These sayings underscore traveling as a human phenomenon, often associated with acts of spiritual reverence. Indeed, along highland roads, Q'eqchi' travelers place crosses to demonstrate respect for the nearby *Tzuultaq'a*. Roads clearly hold cultural meaning beyond national economic development (see also Wilk 1984).

With the introduction of state roads on top of their network of organic roads, things get better *and* worse for the Q'eqchi'. For people in villages like Jaguarwood, traveling to Punta Gorda was once a "hell of a time"—a 2:00 A.M. departure and travel by canoe down the Sarstoon River followed by a rough sea journey. A new road built to Jaguarwood in the early 2000s enabled villagers to send their children to high school by bus. In Guatemala, roads bring improved teacher attendance and also access to medical services, especially lowering maternal mortality rates. For rural people, they decrease the costs of simple bureaucratic tasks such as acquiring birth certificates or national identification cards from municipal offices. In easing travel, they also afford rural communities a better chance to lobby for electricity or running water.

While roads allow farming families improved access to markets and better prices, they also bring intruders—NGOs, government bureaucrats, criminals, missionaries, the police, and the military. An intimate link also exists between roads and cattle development; ranchers value roads so highly that they sometimes build their own or bribe municipal authorities to build roads past their ranches under the guise of other projects. With roads, villages can become targets of urban-based development technicians who otherwise would not walk to these sites via muddy paths. They also bring increased state surveillance, especially evident during the Guatemalan civil war. As an Ixcán villager, Miguel Reyes, observed: "Always when there is an access road, this facilitates the army to corner people." Another villager, Gaspar, remarked, "To walk seven days with a load on your back, yes, the road was a relief, but then when you see the consequences, you say: 'On the one hand it comes to benefit us; but on the other hand it comes to harm us'" (Manz 2004: 88). When Don Lorenzo Cac was working as a bilingual schoolteacher in an isolated region near Agoutiville, he tried organizing a committee of five surrounding communities to petition for a road. Surprised to encounter resistance to the road, he discovered that the villagers were rightly worried that roads would bring more "castellanos" (Ladinos) who would take their land.

Given the double-edged impact of roads on their lives, what else may be smuggled into Q'eqchi' territory alongside new PPP infrastructure? First, there is a hidden process intended to "harmonize" laws in order to facilitate transborder trade. Though both activists and planners have focused their attention largely on infrastructure projects, the new legal frameworks behind them are also important. This includes, for example, efforts to homogenize customs and border procedures to speed the passage of business people and tourists but guard against emigration by local people. As the Mexican and Central American economies become more deeply linked, keeping those borders and roads open becomes more important. Mesoamerican activists astutely use civil disobedience to slow down commerce, routinely taking over roads and critical transportation infrastructure. For instance, in Guatemala in 2003, as part of a strike for higher wages, schoolteachers seized the airports in both Flores and Guatemala City as well as a petroleum refinery in La Libertad, Petén, and held them for several days. Across the border in Mexico, symbolically coordinated to fall on Columbus Day, October 12, 2002, more than sixty thousand protesters across Mexico blocked roads, seized airports, closed border customs, and raised a ruckus against the PPP at the U.S. embassy. Zapatista communiqués in 2003 pledged to impede PPP projects in southern Mexico as necessary (Chiapas-support.org).

With transnational corporate pressure on states to keep roads open, will the police and military continue to tolerate such disruptions? Or will the slowing of commerce be reinterpreted as an economic "terrorist" threat to capitalism? Since 2003, the Guatemalan congress has considered several new laws that would double the jail time for land occupations and treat protests against infrastructure as terrorist acts (UDEFEGUA 2008). Though these first legislative attempts at criminalizing social movements were unsuccessful, they remain in the realm of the politically imaginable. After all, the CIA overthrew the Guatemalan government five decades ago, in 1954, over a perceived threat to cheap bananas. U.S. military forces have once again been deployed to Guatemala, but this time under the guise of a "humanitarian" program called the New Horizons Plan, which includes road-building projects and natural disaster relief (NoPPP n.d.; Adams 2001). "The rise in U.S. military aid and influence to Central America is clearly essential to a strategy of expanding corporate trade," and new military facilities such as the International Law Enforcement Academy in El Salvador "demonstrate a move towards combating increased popular resistance with force" (Stansbury and de Sousa 2005).

The enclosure of public spaces for infrastructure projects turns them into property that then must be defended by state authorities (Illich 1983). Lewis Mumford presciently observed how certain energy technologies might become a Trojan horse for new forms of social control, arguing that infrastructure such as nuclear plants would "undermine democracy by their fostering of secrecy by and within the state" (Guha and Martinez-Alier 1997: 194). Building on insights from Amory Lovins, Laura Nader (1995) similarly suggests that "hard" technologies require standardization and, therefore, tend to rely on experts and centralized planning, while Arundhati Roy observes, "People have to understand that [dams] are just monuments to corruption and they are undemocratic. They centralize natural resources, snatch them away from people, and then redistribute them to a favored few" (2004: 23).

Certainly there is historical precedent in Guatemala for fears that military repression will be used to protect infrastructure. Perhaps the most egregious example from the 1980s was a series of military-led massacres of Achi' Maya people in the Chixoy River basin who refused to be relocated for the construction of the Chixoy hydroelectric dam funded by the World Bank and the IDB (Johnston 2005; Aguilera 1979; Elton 2004). While these massacres appear to have been ordered by the state in order to quell villagers' opposition to the dams, in other cases, the alignment of business interests with the military was subtler. When asked if the coffee planters had bribed the military to control troublesome workers during the civil war, one of the largest plantation owners in Alta Verapaz, Edgar Champney, said, "Maybe some did, but it wasn't common. There was no need because the alliances were natural, the army was on the side of the powerful. So money, no, but a bottle of whiskey, a woman, yes" (Grandin 2004: 116). The new "harmony" of free trade may also bring renewed police and military repression if state authorities insist on protecting corporate investors from social protest. As Guatemalan president Berger told CNN shortly before military and police attacked indigenous protestors during a 2005 conflict with the Glamis Gold mining company: "We have to protect the investors."

Aside from military repression and corruption, PPP megaprojects pose another implicit threat to democracy. Much of the infrastructure will be financed by loans, and as John Perkins's *Confessions of an Economic Hitman* (2004) reveals, U.S. intelligence agencies had a plan to indebt Third World nations with pointless infrastructure projects so as to be able to demand military favors later and/or trade for privileges when loans defaulted. Working with development agencies around the world, Perkins and other self-described EHMs (economic hit men) helped normalize the necessity of big infrastructure projects and trained a new generation of development workers who believe they are simply "doing good," blissfully unaware of these underlying geopolitical plans. In the vicious cycle of structural adjustment led by the IMF, Third World countries were compelled to request new loans so they could avoid default, obliging them to privatize state services. Some might argue that privatization makes little difference to the Latin American poor, as states never provided services to them anyhow. In areas such as telecommunications in Guatemala, privatization has, in fact, expanded services to citizens. Yet even under the most successful privatizations, citizens lose the historic possibility of holding governments accountable for meeting their needs. However corrupt or inefficient state agencies may have been, much of their ineptitude was not a result of being state-managed per se but because they were managed by elites who had succumbed to corruption and cronyism (Zibechi 2004).

Another hidden problem with the PPP is its prescription of technical initiatives as a means to development, thereby hampering the creativity of villagers, NGO directors, and government bureaucrats alike who come to assume they cannot solve basic problems without a formal project ("proyecto"). Likewise, the PPP presumes that Mesoamerican poverty stems from a lack of technical knowledge, infrastructure, and capital—not centuries of land and resource inequity, institutionalized racism, and other social factors considered to be more pressing problems at the grassroots. While many now scoff at Reaganomics (the idea that if you give tax breaks to the rich and free up capital, it will somehow trickle down and improve life for the poor), a similar fallacy is at work in the PPP and in modernization projects more generally—what I term the "infrastructure trickle down," meaning the false assumption that if you build something, development will magically appear. Yet, so many of these infrastructure projects are stillborn, because insufficient thought was given to the trickle—that is, their intended usage. How many schools have been built without parallel budgeting for teachers? Or clinics built without providing for nurses or medicines? Or ecotourism lodges built without teaching people the skills to run them? Or roads built without addressing the farmers' main problem of market prices?

Of course, when aptly designed by and for local users, infrastructure projects *can* be a powerful force for social transformation. Imagine if the Guatemalan government took just a fraction of the money it will borrow (plus the money it will pay in interest on those loans) for PPP highways and other infrastructure that facilitate accumulation and instead invested in many other smaller strategic projects that could strengthen democracy, education, and civil society in northern Guatemala. For example, grassroots and civil society groups in Petén have voiced the need for the following infrastructure projects:

- An office complex with low rents that civil society and grassroots groups might borrow on an ad hoc basis, as the costs of establishing independent offices (getting phone lines, Internet access, security, etc.) can be prohibitively expensive
- Cooperative storage silos for basic staples (corn, beans) so that prices will remain level during times of scarcity
- An extension of the central and municipal markets where local small producers could rent stalls on a daily basis and sell their foodstuffs directly to consumers in a rotating farmers' market
- A seed bank where farmers could preserve and share local and heirloom varieties.

- A public library/archive for the growing student population in the region that could be connected to a network of rotating tin-trunk rural libraries
- A regional museum for displaying locally discovered or repatriated archaeological pieces that would serve as a secondary attraction to Tikal (and therefore encourage tourists to stay longer than the regular day tours they take from the capital)
- A small air-conditioned warehouse for storing donated medicines to be redistributed to village clinics through grassroots health promoters and midwives
- A public meeting hall for conferences that are otherwise held in expensive hotels
- Training centers to help stimulate nonagricultural rural livelihoods (repair shops, stores, pharmacies, crafts, etc.) and prevent the unilineal cash flow from rural to urban areas
- An inexpensive, public boarding house so that rural students might attend high school and/or college in town

With public consultation, more ideas for small infrastructure might attract public and private funding.

These and other good ideas have been ignored because the ultimate purpose of the PPP may not actually be to serve the Mesoamerican people but to provide a construction program and legal framework for the influx of foreign corporations expected under the DR-CAFTA. "On rainforest frontiers, impatient entrepreneurs want property to settle down" (Tsing 2002: 127). Investors need predictable legal and property regimes "legible" to them (Scott 1998). The World Bank's land titling programs will conveniently clarify property regimes prior to their arrival. As Gustavo Soto from the Center for Economic and Political Investigation for Community Action (Centro de Investigaciones Económicas y Políticas de Ación Comunitaria) in Chiapas describes it: "The major corporations hope that the PPP will lower the costs of transportation, labor, and inputs, while freeing them of other costs of production (tariffs, taxes, regulations, etc.)" (NoPPP n.d.). By helping to make it as easy to do business in Guatemala as in Kansas, all these programs for attracting foreign investment are what Arundhati Roy characterizes as "imperialism by e-mail" (2004: 73):

> We all remember the East India Company. This time around, the colonizer doesn't even need a token white presence in the colonies. The CEOs and their

men don't need to go to the trouble of tramping through the tropics risking malaria, diarrhoea, sunstroke and an early death. They don't have to maintain an army or a police force, or worry about insurrections and mutinies. They can have their colonies *and* an easy conscience. "Creating a good investment climate" is the new euphemism for Third World repression. (Roy 2001: 180–81)

Corporations no longer need to build their own infrastructure; governments will go into debt in order to create a good investment atmosphere. Just as President Ubico utilized road infrastructure and state labor controls in the early twentieth century as part of the shift to Liberal bureaucratic modernization, with the PPP, the Guatemalan state is once again taking responsibility for providing labor and infrastructure for transnational investors. In that sense, the PPP is an infrastructural prelude to a brave new world of corporate trade.

THE HIDDEN PAGES OF THE CORPORATE AMERICA FREE TRADE AGREEMENT

One of the little-known facts lost amid the DR-CAFTA debates was that, since 1983, the United States and Central America had already lowered most of their tariffs through what was known as the Caribbean Basin Initiative, except for protections on "sensitive" commodities critical for Central American food security (e.g., white corn). If the United States *already* had a practically tariff-free relationship with Central America, and vice versa, then what was the purpose of negotiating a brand-new fifty-year trade agreement? After repeated failures to reach multilateral agreements at the level of the World Trade Organization (WTO) since the 1999 Seattle round, the United States began to shift its trade strategy toward bilateral and regional trade agreements. Following the events of September 11, the George W. Bush administration signaled a return to Monroe Doctrine geopolitics in order to unify the Western hemisphere under U.S. influence. While Central America is not particularly critical to the U.S. economy—representing just 1.6 percent of exports and 1.0 percent of imports—trade proponents hoped that a swift Central American agreement might establish a precedent for the Free Trade Agreement of the Americas (FTAA) with economic powerhouses like Brazil and Venezuela. Perhaps, too, by pushing the DR-CAFTA to extremes beyond both NAFTA and failed WTO agendas, the United States may have hoped to up the ante for negotiable terms in a trade agreement.

The power imbalances in this process were striking.[6] To give but a brief chronology of events: the Bush administration opened negotiations with the four poorest countries in Central America (El Salvador, Guatemala, Honduras, and Nicaragua). Costa Rica joined only after the end of the negotiations in January 2004. In a hasty afterthought in August 2004, the Office of the United States Trade Representative (USTR) added on (in its terms, "docked" on) a bilateral agreement negotiated with the Dominican Republic because it was similar in structure and content. Panama was excluded, as it is negotiating a special bilateral trade agreement with the United States, given the peculiar history of the Panama Canal. Compiling language from the failed WTO agenda in Cancun, the Chile-U.S. trade agreement (which took more than a decade to negotiate) and NAFTA (which took seven years to develop), the Bush administration rammed through DR-CAFTA talks in less than a year. At this speed, none of the Central American delegates had a chance to see the whole document in Spanish until after it was finalized.[7] The USTR also insisted that the treaty text remain secret until negotiations were complete, so neither U.S. nor Central American civil society organizations had an opportunity to participate. As if to admit that Central American countries did not come to the table with equal bargaining power, the USTR cunningly offered to train the El Salvadoran delegation in negotiation tactics. El Salvadoran activist Raúl Moreno, speaking at a 2005 World Social Forum panel, described the DR-CAFTA negotiations as akin to "letting a tiger loose on a pack of tethered mules." At a 2005 speech at the faculty club at the University of California, Berkeley, Guatemalan vice president Eduardo Stein admitted that the previous Portillo administration had failed even to send nominal representatives to all the meetings and mostly accepted whatever drafts the U.S. delegation presented.

Despite rhetoric about simplifying commerce and eliminating trade barriers, the DR-CAFTA contains hundreds of side agreements—from clauses protecting sectors like the El Salvadoran circus (Edelman 2004) to more consequential protections for industries controlled by national elites (e.g., the Guatemalan cement industry). The resulting 2,400-page agreement (longer than *Gone with the Wind* and the King James Bible combined) goes far beyond tariffs and trade to compel Central American governments to privatize essential services such as health, education, and water; transform their intellectual property laws in order to facilitate foreign investment; and undermine any environmental and social laws that might impede transnational business. Close examination reveals that the DR-CAFTA is not a free trade agreement, but a *corporate* trade agreement that transforms foreign investment from a privilege to an inalienable right.[8]

Following the mantra of neoliberalism, the DR-CAFTA promotes privatization as the only alternative to supposedly inefficient and corrupt state enterprises (Roy 2001), yet the speed at which state services are put on the auction block often results in unaccountable private monopolies seizing state assets (Zibechi 2004). With the privatization of Guatemala's electricity distribution, acquired by the Spanish firm Unión Fenosa in 1998, I observed that even under a supposedly efficient foreign company, the electric bills still arrived late, the meter readings were irregular and the rates incomprehensible, and customer service remained atrocious. My neighbors' bills showed that the urban and rural poor are taxed regressively to subsidize municipal lighting. When a village like Agoutiville goes without power for more than ten days and shopkeepers lose produce and meat to spoilage, they still must pay the monthly bill, in full.[9]

The DR-CAFTA facilitates such privatization endeavors by compelling governments to standardize and "harmonize" their laws, especially those related to intellectual property rights. Previously, some countries, such as Guatemala, prohibited the patenting of flora and fauna but now have to match their laws to U.S. standards and allow for corporate bioprospecting. Guatemala may also have to annul its policy against genetically modified corn, which could irreversibly contaminate the center of the world's global maize diversity and endanger international food security (Grandia 2005). There are as yet unsubstantiated reports of genetically modified varieties being planted in Petén, a region of extensive corn production with unique heirloom corn varieties that would be easily contaminated. The DR-CAFTA discriminates explicitly against organic, fair-trade initiatives by excluding these products from allowable quotas (Olson 2004). Although it ostensibly includes an environmental chapter, most of its points are simply best-practice recommendations and lack mechanisms for legal enforcement. As one El Salvadoran environmental activist observed, "They have added a bit of green sweetener to a truly toxic stew."

Undermining its own green rhetoric, the DR-CAFTA has a section akin to NAFTA's Chapter 11, allowing corporations to challenge any laws, including environmental ones, that they perceive as barriers to trade and foreign investment. Unlike the WTO, which permits only *governments* to initiate trade challenges, both NAFTA and the DR-CAFTA allow *corporations* the legal standing to bring lawsuits against sovereign governments. For instance, when California banned MTBE, a carcinogenic gasoline additive, because it was seeping into the state's drinking water, the manufacturer, Methanex, sued California for infringing on its trade rights under NAFTA and demanded $970 million in compensation. Dow Chemical recently used NAFTA's Chapter 11 to sue the Canadian government for allowing Quebec and Ottawa to ban the use of carcinogenic herbicides on residential lawns. Such suits are a direct threat to democracy because they prioritize the profits of foreign corporations over a country's own environmental, social, and labor laws. As an anti-CAFTA activist from San Luis Obispo's Sierra Club, Sue Harvey, emphasized, "People don't realize they're giving up the foundation of democracy for cheap lettuce."

Even before passage of the DR-CAFTA, corporations were already planning more such lawsuits. A subsidiary of Harken Energy (on whose board George W. Bush once served) said it would demand $58 billion from Costa Rica (whose entire GDP is only $37 billion) as compensation for hypothetical future lost profits if the company is not allowed to drill offshore in Costa Rica's protected Talamanca region—one of the planet's richest marine ecosystems and a United Nations Educational, Scientific and Cultural Organization World Heritage Site. One indirect side effect of such corporate claims to *future* profits will be legislative timidity and self-censorship on the part of national legislatures. For example, wary of violating the DR-CAFTA's intellectual property clauses, in December 2004, Guatemala rescinded a law allowing for increased availability of generic pharmaceuticals for the poor. Under threat of a NAFTA suit, a local Canadian government rescinded a law limiting cigarette packaging colors to black and white. In December 2008, a Canadian company, Pacific Rim Mining Corp., initiated a DR-CAFTA arbitration claim against El Salvador for $100 million of *future* lost profits if it is denied the opportunity to mine for gold and silver there (Mychalejko 2008).

Prior to that, the first state-investor claim under the DR-CAFTA actually came from the Railroad Development Corporation described at the beginning of this chapter. With a fifty-year lease for not only the railroad, but also port facilities and alternative uses of the right-of-way (e.g., for pipelines or fiber optics), the Pittsburgh-based RDC began rehabilitating the line in 1997 and reopened rail traffic in late 1999. Later alleging that the Guatemalan government had not fulfilled its promise to remove squatters from the right-of-way and to make timely payments for track rehabilitation, RDC filed a local arbitration suit in 2005 with support from the U.S. Embassy and the Guatemalan-American Chamber of Commerce (Wallach 2007). The Berger administration responded by trying to repossess its locomotives and railcars, arguing that these were not part of the original concession. After the DR-CAFTA went into effect in March 2006, the RDC filed an international arbitration case, suing for $65 million—$15 million for track investments and another $50 million in future lost revenues for damage to its reputation (NotiCen 2007). RDC president Peitrandrea argued that this constituted "an indirect expropriation of the company's assets and right to earn revenue." The company then hired Regina Vargo, the former head of the U.S. trade negotiation team for the DR-CAFTA and other trade talks in Latin America, to lead its legal case (RDC 2007).

Guatemalan economist Fernando Solis suspects that the rail company dispute is hardly a noble assertion of national sovereignty but rather a petty squabble among Guatemalan elites. The most powerful family dominating Guatemala's sugar industry (to which former president Berger belongs by marriage) had hoped to acquire the line and use it to expand sugar exports, already Guatemala's second-most-important source of foreign revenue. The three-person panel assigned to the case by the International Centre for Settlement of Investment Disputes has not reached a final verdict but did render a jurisdictional decision sympathetic to the company in January 2009. Should the RDC eventually win the arbitration, it will reap a sum that far exceeds its investments, while the sugar elite wins a railroad that will help it expand into northern Guatemala—both at the expense of Guatemalan taxpayers (NotiCen 2007). Guatemalan citizens can expect more raw deals under the DR-CAFTA, the worst perhaps being terms of trade in corn.

THE MAIZE PEOPLE

> Sown to be eaten [maize] is the sacred sustenance of the men who
> were made of maize. Sown to make money [corn] means famine for
> the men who were made of maize.
> — Miguel Angel Asturias, *Hombres de Maíz*

Nearly seven thousand years ago, the peoples of Mesoamerica began domesticating maize (*Zea mays*) from the grass weed "teosinte" (*Zea mexicana*) in the southern Mexican highlands. Over millennia, they transformed this weed into a resilient grain that would become the world's most astonishingly productive and versatile food crop, producing almost twice as many pounds per hectare as rice and wheat, truly one of humanity's greatest agronomic achievements. It quickly spread throughout Mesoamerica about four thousand years ago and became a staple food for many native peoples, including the Maya, who developed a culture centered around this sacred substance.

As reflected in their creation myth in the Popul Vuh, the Maya people believe they are "the people of corn" ("los hombres de maíz"). As the legend goes, the gods made three attempts to fashion humans. The first attempt with clay failed because the creatures were weak and could not think well; the second attempt with wood also failed because those creatures had no souls or reverence for their creator; not until the third attempt when the gods made people from maize were they satisfied. Today, Maya people, including the Q'eqchi', still believe they are made from maize, as Jaguarwood farmer Don Pablo Botzoc explained amid rustling corn stalks that seemed to whisper the secrets of the ancestors on a windy day when we visited his fields: "[The five colors of maize] are like our bodies: red for blood, yellow for skin, white for bones, black [blue] for our hair, and green [fresh corn on the cob] for the sky and earth."

Almost all Q'eqchi' people eat maize tortillas three times a day and claim that they cannot feel full without them. Even rice, yucca, spaghetti, or any other starchy carbohydrate is served with a stack of tortillas. While urban consumption is less, rural people eat roughly one pound of maize per capita per day.[10] Women's lives, in particular, are enmeshed with maize.[11] They spend hours each day cooking, shelling, washing, grinding, kneading, stirring, patting, and toasting this adaptable substance. Tortillas are the main food prepared from maize, but through many hours spent cooking and visiting with Q'eqchi' women in their homes, I have documented almost thirty Q'eqchi' names for different ways of cooking maize, not to mention dozens more recipes for maize with other foods (Grandia 2004a). Maize is a perfect carbohydrate and combines with beans to provide the full spectrum of protein; it is one of the most healthful subsistence diets in the world, but only when prepared with a special Mesoamerican technique. Maya women make a maize hominy called "nixtamal" by cooking dry maize kernels in lime water (calcium carbonate, derived traditionally from wood ashes or burning rocks); this softens and separates the husks from the kernels, making them easier to grind into a variety of foods, adds calcium, liberates the B vitamin niacin, and increases the lysine and tryptophan content of maize.

As with most Maya groups, for Q'eqchi' people, the maize cycle confirms and reaffirms religious holidays, kinship and friendships, and really the whole human life cycle. It is deeply significant to all Maya groups who believe themselves made from maize; indeed, the most repeated folktale in Q'eqchi' villages is a trickster story about the origins of maize and how a wild rabbit (in some stories, a fox or raccoon) discovered it inside the mountain by observing the leaf-cutting ants (see Grandia 2004b for the full tale). As it does in Spanish, the Q'eqchi' word for "cornfield" or "milpa" (k'al) has a double meaning—referring to both the physical field and the maize crop itself. To crop (k'alek), therefore, literally means to plant maize. The central feature of Q'eqchi' ritual life is paying respect for the planting of maize. Most Q'eqchi' rituals, whether performed as a community or within the family, involve a small ceremony known as a *wa'tesink*, literally "the giving to eat of tortillas." As reflected in the term *wa'tesink*, the word for "tortilla" or "wa" is deeply embedded in the Q'eqchi' language. "To eat" is *waak* (a passive construction that roughly means "to become one with tortillas"). In Q'eqchi' as well, the words for "first place," "second place," and so on (*xb'een wa*, *xka wa*) literally mean "the tortilla on top," "the next tortilla underneath," and so forth, referring to the stack of steaming hot tortillas prepared for every meal. *Wa uk'a'* (tortilla, drink) means "sustenance." Given the linguistic importance the Q'eqchi' ascribe to maize, it is little wonder that they should describe wheat bread brought by the Spanish as *kaxlan wa*, meaning "foreign tortilla."

Many Q'eqchi' settlers explained to me that their hope of planting enough maize to eat was one of their primary motivations for leaving the coffee plantations and migrating into the lowlands. Though subsistence was their goal, through government colonization programs, Q'eqchi' settlers gradually began to produce corn as a commodity on top of the maize they produced for themselves. (Although corn and maize are the same word in Spanish ["maíz"], in English, one can distinguish between maize as a subsistence food and corn as a commodity.) For both poor Q'eqchi' and Ladino colonists, commodity agriculture of corn and beans served as a way of capitalizing their homesteads and making a tenure claim of improving the land, which was necessary to gain title. New hybrid varieties allowed them to produce more per hectare and get their crop to market faster but are more vulnerable to weevils after harvest. Farmers had been limited by weather to one corn crop a year in the highlands but could produce two, even three corn crops annually in the lowlands.

Corn production soared. In 1970, Petén was responsible for just 1 percent of Guatemala's corn crop; by 1979, it was 10 percent; today, 17 percent of the country's corn and 25 percent of its beans come from Petén (which has just 5 percent of the total population) (Schwartz 2001). This, in turn, has allowed the Guatemalan elite to take advantage of the fertile, volcanic soils of the western highlands and the Pacific coast for export-agriculture of boutique vegetables (broccoli, snow peas, and baby squashes). Although the Ministry of Agriculture does not disaggregate its data by ethnicity, some gross extrapolations from 2002 census data and corn production figures suggest that Q'eqchi' people are responsible for an estimated 20 percent of Guatemala's excess corn production yet constitute only 7 percent of its population (Grandia 2006).

For settlers on the edge of subsistence, corn provides a perfect alternative to wage labor. Pioneer farmers can plant other food crops such as beans and roots among the corn stalks, thereby maximizing land use. Though the price is low (an average of $4.50–5.15 per quintal, but varies between $3.25 and $11.60), corn is a relatively stable crop, requires little supervision and weeding, is easily transportable and fairly imperishable, and can always be eaten or fed to animals if unsold (Shriar 2001). After saving enough for family food security, farmers can easily sell leftover corn to middlemen and use the proceeds to buy their basic household necessities, like medicines, shoes, clothes, tools, and daily comestibles (sugar, oil, coffee). In other words, household security—not cash accumulation—remains the milpa's underlying "moral economy" (Scott 1976; Edelman 2005).

One may anticipate the fate of the Q'eqchi' milpa under the DR-CAFTA by looking to Mexico's experience with NAFTA since 1994. Mexico was once largely self-sufficient in corn production, and farmers could demand decent prices for their products until NAFTA obligated Mexico to open its borders to cheap, subsidized U.S. corn. In the first three years, U.S. corn exports to Mexico tripled—well beyond the allowable trade quotas, which Mexico failed to enforce. Between 1994 and 2001, corn imports leaped from 2.5 million to 6 million tons, and prices plummeted by 70 percent. Mexican small farmers could not defend themselves against this predatory corn dumping (Gómez 2005; McElhinny 2004; Zahniser and Coyle 2004), and an estimated 1.5 million of them lost their livelihoods. Many migrated to the United States, according to a study by the National Autonomous University of Mexico (Universidad Nacional Autónoma de México) (Carlson 2007).

Similarly, throughout the DR-CAFTA negotiations, the United States pushed to open Central American markets to all food commodities but consistently refused to discontinue its own agricultural subsidies, especially for sugar. This illustrates an important, but little-understood point about trade agreements. Every country in the world historically has developed ways to protect its small farmers. Rich countries like the United States tend to use direct subsidies ($50 billion annually) as well as indirect subsidies (cheap water for irrigation, good roads for transportation, low fossil fuel costs) to help their own farmers. Because poor countries cannot afford such measures, they instead protect their farmers through tariffs, quotas, and fixed prices, especially for staple foods such as corn. So-called free trade agreements are, therefore, tremendously unfair because they force poor countries to lower their agricultural tariffs but allow rich countries to continue their agricultural subsidies.

As a supposed concession acknowledging its domestic sugar protections, the USTR will allow Central America to phase out tariffs on "sensitive" commodities over a twenty-year period. Although the USTR argued that the agreement would "equalize" trade, each Central American country negotiated separately on which food commodity to protect in the short to near term—Costa Rica (dairy), Nicaragua (beans), and Guatemala (corn)—yet there are virtually no import restrictions among countries in the Central American Common Market. That leaves U.S. companies a loophole, allowing them to export corn and other protected food commodities to the Central American country with the lowest tariffs and then ship them from there to a neighboring country and undercut prices. Even if Central American governments were to prevent this practice legislatively, smuggling remains a serious threat, given the region's porous borders.

Although the race to develop more ethanol fuel may divert a portion of both U.S. and Guatemalan corn production, the overall volume of U.S. corn production is so enormous that even small U.S. exports to Guatemala may wreak havoc on the Guatemalan corn market. In 2007, Guatemalan farmers earned about five dollars a quintal (one hundred pounds) in the countryside. Adding transportation costs and middlemen profits, that quintal eventually sold for about twelve dollars in the capital. By contrast, one hundred pounds of yellow corn was selling for a little more than four dollars on the Chicago Board of Trade. Given these dramatic price disparities, urban Central American consumers may be willing to change their tastes and switch to the cheaper yellow corn.

Although white and yellow corn imports will, in theory, be gradually phased in, so as to allow Guatemalan farmers to prepare for the deluge, Guatemalan production methods simply cannot be compared to those of U.S. agribusiness. With its arsenal of chemical, mechanical, and genetic inputs, U.S. corn yields are about five times those of Central America (178 versus 36 quintals per hectare, respectively). Obviously, mountainous countries like Guatemala face both geographic and economic constraints to mechanization. With sophisticated silo storage, U.S. corn growers can wait to sell until prices rise, whereas most Guatemalan farmers store corn in makeshift bins at home or in the field. Transporting it to market by mule or on their backs, they sell just enough to buy essentials such as shoes, medicines, and school notebooks. No one gets rich off of corn, but no one starves either. Selling corn is the main source of income for most Q'eqchi' farmers, so a drop in price is like a currency devaluation.

Urban consumers might ask, what is wrong with cheap corn? Ironically, low grain prices usually do not help consumers, because most grocery costs are in the processing, packaging, and marketing, not in the food itself (Pollan 2006). For example, a group of Petén peasants participating in an anti-CAFTA workshop calculated that purchasing the equivalent of one hundred pounds of corn ($10 in raw form) in small boxes of cornflakes would cost $445 (Valenzuela 2003). That is why food prices and profits for vertically integrated corporate agribusiness keep rising, even while global grain prices fall. The United States produces 39 percent of the world's corn, and just three corporations (Cargill, Archer Daniels Midland, and Zen-Noh) control 82 percent of U.S. corn exports. Since NAFTA (1994–2000), ConAgra and Archer Daniels Midland have tripled their profits (from $143 million to $413 million and $110 million to $301 million respectively). Unfortunately for Central America, on the eve of the DR-CAFTA's implementation, the U.S. Midwest had a bumper corn harvest, as shown in figure 6.4.

In the brave new world of "free trade," Central American farmers face an agricultural sector that is no longer dominated just by landowners and the state but by placeless and faceless transnational corporations commandeering mountains of corn (Edelman 2005; Mondragón 2005). The impact will fall disproportionately on Q'eqchi' corn farmers, in particular, as they dominate national corn production. With even a slight drop in prices, Q'eqchi' farmers may be compelled to sell their land, and there is no shortage of investors waiting to purchase it. Deprived of their livelihoods, displaced Central American corn farmers such as the Q'eqchi' may, like their Mexican brethren, become part of the next wave of "human exports" to the north (Bartra 2004).

GOING ONCE, GOING TWICE, SOLD
TO THE HIGHEST FOREIGN BIDDER

Unlike NAFTA, which passed with widespread support across both the Democratic and Republican parties, the DR-CAFTA generated unprecedented resistance in Central America and even in the United States. Without substantial political favors offered by the Bush administration and Republican maneuvers to extend the vote forty-seven minutes beyond the rules of the House of Representatives, the DR-CAFTA would likely not have passed by its razor-thin margin of two votes on July 27, 2005. The El Salvadoran legislature had to hold its vote after an all-night session. Honduras called a surprise, early morning vote after which members of congress had to flee the scene as protesters occupied

FIGURE 6.4. Corn harvest in Ralston, Iowa, 2005. The corn harvest in this one town is piled sixty feet high and weighs about 2.7 million bushels. By contrast, Guatemala's *entire* corn harvest the same year was 3.4 million bushels. Photograph: Mark Kegans

the building. Widespread protests in Guatemala prevented legislators from getting into the building for two days, until the military and police repressed the crowds, resulting in the death of at least one protester. Surveys indicated that at least 85 percent of Guatemalans wanted a constitutionally mandated referendum on the DR-CAFTA (Barreda 2006). After these coercive and secret ratifications, not a single Central American government managed to bring its constitution and national laws into conformance with the DR-CAFTA by the end of December 2005. Behaving like classic footdraggers (Scott 1985), the legislators went home for the holidays, delaying the DR-CAFTA's implementation until late spring 2006. Costa Rica delayed ratification until 2007 after citizens demanded a popular referendum, which passed by only a slim margin.

When the Office of the USTR began to push legislative changes beyond the original agreement (e.g., on public acquisitions and contracts, insurance policies, customs procedures, intellectual property rights, telecommunications, phytosanitary regulations, penal codes and labor laws, and pharmaceutical standards), some skeptics, such as Guatemala's vice president Eduardo Stein in late 2005, threatened to pull out, arguing, "It's an affront to Latin America when a government says it wants to be a 'partner' but then is only interested in our money and commodities" (Engler 2006). As newly elected South American democracies strengthen their own ties through the Common Market of the South (Mercado Común del Sur), negotiations for the Free Trade Agreement of the Americas have faltered over northern agricultural subsidies.[12] Like the fifth WTO round in Cancún in 2003, the sixth round in Hong Kong in late 2005 ended in disarray. The DR-CAFTA may very well mark the beginning of the end of pro-corporate trade agreements. That will prove little consolation, however, for Q'eqchi' farmers dispossessed by this particular neoliberal trade auction.

Beyond the continual displacement and suffering of the Q'eqchi', there are more unsettling lessons from new trends in corporate capitalism. Hiding behind the banner of "free marketism," corporations take advantage of trade agreements like the DR-CAFTA and infrastructure subsidies like the PPP to unshackle themselves from social and governmental control and acquire almost prebendal guarantees to profit. Freed from the reins of regulation, they can seize new kinds of property rights for themselves through negotiating tricks that are not all that different from those used by cattle ranchers to seize land from the Q'eqchi' with the aid of World Bank land-titling programs. That corporations have acquired so many extra-economic perks through the PPP and the DR-CAFTA raises profound questions about the very nature of capitalism.

Conclusion

COMMON FUTURES

> It could happen once; the like could happen again.
> *Pathih hun ten e; bey he u patal u lac e*
> > —Mayan proverb, from the Book of Chilam Balam

SHORTLY after the Spanish invasion of Mesoamerica, Catholic friars began teaching the Maya elite to read and write their own languages using a Latin alphabet. Nine of these manuscripts recorded by Yucatec Maya priests survived and are collectively known as the Book of Chilam Balam. Some of the texts were mixtures of colonial history and Maya prophecy, while others discussed Maya agronomy, astronomy, and medicine (Bricker and Miram 2002). The following passage is from Munroe Edmonson's translation of the sixteenth-century book of Tizimín, describing the arrival of foreigners in Maya lands:

And there was the beginning
And the construction of the god
House
That is in the middle of the city
Of Merida
Piling on work
Was the burden of the *katun* [a Maya time period of twenty years]
And there was the beginning
Of the noose.
And started was the fever of the nose

And limbs
Of the white lima bean
Grove lands,
Bringing with it their poison
And their ropes over the world—
Affecting children
And younger brothers
With the harsh lash,
With the harsh tribute.
And there was great theft of tribute:
There was the great theft of
Christendom (1982: 59–60)

Increased workloads. Religious conversion. Tribute demands. Corporate punishment. Poisoned soils. These have been the recurrent burdens of the Maya and other indigenous peoples subjected to colonial, Liberal, and then neoliberal plunder during the thirteenth *baktun*[1] (roughly 394 years in the Gregorian calendar). Marking the closure of a much longer calendrical cycle of more than five thousand years ending on the winter solstice, December 21, 2012 (13.0.0.0.0 in the Maya Long Count calendar), this period, according to ancient Maya prophecy, was to be an epoch of great strife and transformation.[2] In contrast to a Western Enlightenment paradigm characterizing history as linear and progressive, the Maya view time as cyclical. Hence, any prophecy depends on the unfolding of the past.

In that spirit, let us first review Q'eqchi' agrarian conditions over the last *baktun*. The three major periods of displacement and expropriation of the Q'eqchi' were (1) after the Spanish colonial invasion, (2) during the Liberal reforms of the 1870s that fueled Guatemala's coffee boom, and (3) through the counterrevolutionary colonization and development programs. During each of these historical moments, the Q'eqchi' people sought to escape the misery of plantation labor by migrating from their highland homeland of Alta Verapaz into the lowland hinterlands of both Guatemala and Belize and managed to stake substantial pioneer land claims. However, an agrarian squeeze caused by both demographic and distributional factors, compounded by a frontier property trap, prevents Q'eqchi' farmers from sustainable agricultural intensification. World Bank land legalization programs meant to stabilize the agricultural frontier are now exacerbating regional land speculation. Following an inherent expansionary logic, cattle ranchers were the first to appropriate Q'eqchi' land, but others have followed. In turn, this land concentration serves as a conduit for new transnational business investment under the PPP and the DR-CAFTA. Rather than closing the gap between economic classes, these trade and infrastructure programs seem to be giving a helping hand to "those who already have a centuries-old head start" (Roy 2001: 178).

Over time, these many consecutive colonizations (Bartra 2004) served to re-create the asymmetries of landownership in Guatemala. Layered upon colonial structures, new economic systems have maintained inequities dating back to the Spanish invasion of Mesoamerica. These historical repetitions help explain the central paradox of frontier colonization—that is, how, in a remarkably short period, Q'eqchi' settlers lose the land they worked so hard to claim, thereby replicating the agrarian inequities that compelled them to migrate to the lowland hinterland in the first place. It is as if, to borrow a phrase from historian David Noble, the Q'eqchi' people "confront a world in which everything changes, yet nothing moves" (1977: xvii). As the ancient Maya proverb in the epigraph prophesies, "It could happen once; the like could happen again" (Edmonson 1982: vi). To be sure, the continuities of Q'eqchi' dispossession were not accidental; they required reinforcements. Unveiling these repeated processes of enclosure reveals Guatemala's persistent, pervasive, and seemingly intractable issue of land inequity as a problem with a specific history and root causes that can be diagnosed and then treated politically (Bourdieu 1998).

THE HARD AND SOFT SIDES OF DISPOSSESSION

The recurring displacement of the Q'eqchi' over five hundred years suggests that enclosure is an ongoing process of both hard and soft dispossession that has as much to do with the control of labor as it does with the seizure of land. The Guatemalan national anthem emphasizes "better dead than to be enslaved" ("antes muertos que esclavos seremos"). The national bird, the quetzal, is said to die in captivity. Contrary to these symbols of freedom, throughout Guatemala's history, the oligarchy has maintained a lingering desire to enslave the indigenous majority as a dependent labor force. This dates back to a common colonial practice of assigning the labor of certain indigenous populations as just another kind of property for Spanish estate owners. When those labor concessions ("mandamientos") were abolished, landowners resorted to other methods, primarily debt peonage, for binding laborers to their plantations. The government aided them with coercive bureaucratic practices, such as issuing booklets to indigenous people, intended to ensure compliance with forced labor laws in the shift to a modern-state liberalism under the 1940s Ubico dictatorship.

What is striking about recurring Q'eqchi' dispossession is how often those in power, following Niccolò Machiavelli's sage advice to his prince, have sought to justify their appropriations via the "rule of law" (Mattei and Nader 2008). Long before the World Bank developed elaborate legal rationales for its "market-assisted" land reform, nineteenth-century Liberals had created a system of agrarian legislation so complex that it was virtually impossible for indigenous people to gain title to their lands individually, much less collectively. Bureaucratic techniques favoring foreign investment in Guatemala over the last century have been subtle and dull, and for that reason, all the more effective.

The World Bank's foray into land privatization in Guatemala may provide a hidden entrée to other kinds of privatizations under new transnational trade and infrastructure agreements. What makes the PPP so worrisome is not just the negative social and environmental impact of big infrastructure projects but the hidden legal agenda of border and trade harmonization. In addition to being an infrastructure portfolio for development, the PPP is also a far-reaching plan to develop a transportation and industrial landscape amenable to the foreign investments expected under new trade regimes.

In turn, the DR-CAFTA smuggles in an agenda of perks privileging the rights of transnational corporations over ordinary citizens through tortuous technicalities not easily understood by academics, much less the media, the general public, or elected legislators. Although this trade agreement includes hundreds of clauses that effectively violate the constitutions of Central American nations and the United States alike, these illegalities were hidden by soporific legalese. As Arundhati Roy observes:

> It's not war, it's not genocide, it's not ethnic cleansing, it's not a famine or an epidemic. On the face of it, it's just ordinary, day-to-day business. It lacks the drama, the large-format, epic magnificence of war or genocide. It's dull in comparison. It makes bad TV. It has to do with boring things like water supply, electricity, irrigation. But it also has to do with a process of barbaric dispossession on a scale that has few parallels in history. You may have guessed by now that I'm talking about the modern version of corporate globalization. (2001: 177)

Bland bureaucrats speak of "good governance" and the "rule of law"—not for the benefit of citizen rights, but to create a favorable climate for foreign investment, making it as easy to do business in Guatemala as in Kansas. Written out of sight of the public, these corporate subsidies quickly become naturalized, allowing the rich to claim that they made their profits simply by being more "efficient." Whatever chicanery, trickery, robbery, buccaneering, depredation, or plunder was initially responsible for concentration of wealth is easily hidden in dusty, legal tomes.

Like the English enclosures, which were supported by dozens of parliamentary acts, modern enclosures are obsessed with the "rule of law" or, as Ugo Mattei and Laura Nader (2008) describe it, with legalizing illegalities. Legal corruption and graft in the new privatizations seem habitual—indeed, almost structural (Zibechi 2004). As Arundhati Roy suggests, Rumpelstiltskin, the gnome who transforms straw into gold, has come back, but he has "metamorphosed into an accretion, a cabal, an assemblage, a malevolent, incorporeal, transnational multignome" (2001: 129)—and, one might add, he manages a slick legal team. Rumpelstiltskin LLP is no less ruthless today but has a shinier, happier face, scrubbed carefully by public relations managers.

While those in power have liberally exercised legal force against the Q'eqchi', they have also employed softer techniques of persuasion, such as the ideological degradation of the subsistence economy with descriptions such as "backward" or "primitive." This is due in large part to an autistic global economic system focused on quantitative variables such as the gross national product (GNP) and gross domestic product (GDP) that measure the amount of money circulating in an economy but fail to account for subsistence or informal economies as well as women's and household labor and do not subtract environmental degradation from the bottom line.[3] Rather than reforming an obviously flawed accounting system that reveals little about countries' real development (Waring 1988), neoliberal economists argue that these "externalities" must merely be quantified, commodified, and drawn into market calculations. The problems of privatization can be solved with more privatization, according to the Washington Consensus. Despite conservation rationales to the contrary, the rapid development of forested, frontier hinterlands such as Petén becomes irresistible to politicians leading nation-states that are judged by this narrow definition of "economic growth."

With the arrogance of aristocrats who complain about their servants, Guatemala's elite denigrate the backwardness of frontiers and the subsistence sector and criticize the supposed inbred laziness of Guatemala's indigenous people. Recognizing as "labor" only that which contributes to his profits, Verapaz's largest coffee baron, Erwin Dieseldorff, once declared: "Indians all have a mistaken understanding of 'free labor,' which they believe means 'we work only as needed to support ourselves, the rest of the time we can do as we wish'" (Grandin 2004: 31). The paradox is that although Guatemala's largest landowners strive to maintain strict control over indigenous labor, they have never allowed this labor force to become fully proletarianized. Structural forces in Guatemala may chip away at the subsistence economy but never entirely destroy it. In the Q'eqchi' region, plantation owners almost always allow their indigenous workers to continue planting staple grains by renting them land (albeit at high prices) or offering them sharecropping arrangements (albeit at unfavorable rates of exchange). This ensures that Q'eqchi' workers sell their labor to ranches and plantations at lower prices than they would without the food security of the milpa. As an Ixcán settler recalled about his previous life as a worker-serf: "They made us work hard. If they wanted to, they would pay us; if they didn't, then they wouldn't. They only gave us a little bit to eat, just so that we wouldn't die, right? Just to keep us alive so that we would continue working another day" (Manz 2004: 45).

The belt-tightening capacity of peasant producers (Chayanov 1986) within an inequitable agrarian system serves as an enormous subsidy for the rich. Small farmers toil to produce enough food so they can reproduce household labor that they then sell at incredibly cheap prices to plantation owners or ranchers. For peasants, being landless is a terrible thing, but having just a little bit of land may be even worse. As Norman Schwartz concluded, by "leaving [the Maya] with farms too small to sustain them throughout the year, the state virtually assured plantation owners of access to cheap labor" (1998: 9). The minifundio, or microparcel, functions for agro-capitalism in the same way that women's reproductive and home labor does for the reproduction of labor below cost. Should subsistence production (or women's free work) disappear entirely, employers would be forced to pay a higher living wage, or their workers would literally starve . . . or perhaps revolt. When caught between landholding and wage systems, small farmers get squeezed on both ends; in the United States, single women faced with leaving the welfare system for minimum-wage jobs might empathize, as they would earn too much to continue receiving government benefits but not enough to pay for day care and lift themselves out of poverty.

This hidden reliance on areas not formally valued in economic accounting systems reveals something paradoxical about capitalism. Partial self-provisioning by workers is good for capitalists because it allows them to pay lower wages. As discussed in the material feminist literature (Mies 1986; Waring 1988; Zaretsky 1975; Aronson 1980), the boundaries between public and private are constantly shifting, often to the disadvantage of the poor. As Friedrich Engels (1959) pointed out, labor is reproduced in the domestic sphere and then inserted into the capitalist market in a process that is remarkably similar to enclosure. Through the reproduction of labor, the drudgery of the domestic economy provides a permanent, unpaid subsidy of both physical and emotional support to the formal economy. The domestic economy also offers flexibility to modern capitalist systems, which need pay only for the direct support of workers while avoiding the indirect costs of labor maintenance when work is unavailable ("periods of enforced idleness") (Portes 1978; Meillassoux 1991). Domestic labor is thus separated from the market economy, "freely" available, like natural resources (Grandia 1996). Not surprisingly, early industrialization was coupled with strategies for indoctrinating women on how to use lowered family wages more efficiently. For example, new Taylorist principles of human management in the early twentieth century leaked into the domestic economy through the idea of "scientific housekeeping" (Hayden 1981). The grand duke of corporate capitalism himself, Henry Ford, encouraged his workers to plant suburban home gardens as a supplement to their factory incomes and, as late as the 1930s, sent inspectors on home visits to enforce this suggestion (Perelman 2000). In this sense, it could be said that capitalism simultaneously maintains and destroys the domestic economy by manipulating the mix of wage and non-wage labor (Kearney 1986; Meillassoux 1991; Perelman 1983).

Although corporate capitalism may significantly undermine these hidden extra-economic supports—be they civic structures, cultural heritage, natural resources, social networks, subsistence economies, women's labor, the inheritance of future generations, traditional knowledge, culture, and life itself—it can never destroy them completely, or the system would combust. In this sense, the Q'eqchi' folktales about *Laj Seleeq* (the magical slave dwarf that ranchers use to compel more work from their Q'eqchi' laborers) are prophetic, for they show the external help that capitalism needs.

A slightly different metaphor may help explain these paradoxical political economy dynamics. Like a parasite, capitalism (and especially its current corporate incarnation) seems to flourish by feeding off an external host—whether it be common resources, the environment, subsistence economies (i.e., "use value" economies), household reproductive labor in the domestic sphere, or broader social and cultural networks. Careful not to kill its host, the parasitic force of capitalism penetrates the social body just enough to prevent it from reacting and fighting back (cf. Farriss 1984). After all, the most successful parasites develop symbiotic relationships with their hosts, so as to remain undetected by the immune system. Parasites, too, are quintessentially opportunistic, as they often follow infection by some other disease. Following the U.S. military invasion of Iraq, petroleum corporations slipped quietly into the economic bloodstream, seizing control of Iraqi oil fields. In this and other examples, the state serves as a doctor of sorts—doling out pharmaceuticals and discouraging home remedies that oppressed peoples might use to cure themselves.

Thus, enclosure not only requires legitimacy based on the supposed rule of law but also relies on the hidden cannibalization of the household economy and previous economic systems. For the Q'eqchi', direct land appropriation by the cattle and plantation economy is the most obvious technique of enclosure, but there are subtler ways of making Q'eqchi' peasants increasingly dependent on wage labor so that their predicament mirrors those of industrialized consumer-citizens in the global North. Peasants may get trapped into wage labor via direct coercion (e.g., land dispossession and excessive taxation) as well as by indirect economic pressures that create "a gap between the peasantry's perceived needs and their ability to satisfy them" (Farriss 1984: 50). The all-too-familiar lure of consumer goods may appear innocuous on the surface but incrementally and inexorably deepens peasants' dependency on wage labor. The colonization of everyday life—of any aspect of humanity that lies beyond the market—creates new kinds of miseries for the poor: "Never before . . . have the wretched of the earth existed in such a bewildering and enraging hybrid state, with the imagery of consumer contentment piped direct" to them through media outlets (Retort Collective 2005: 173).

One of Hilary Kahn's Q'eqchi' informants, "Mariano," eloquently describes the slippery slope of consumerism:

> Because one day the time will come when they are not going to have corn. They will have to request corn from the United States and how much will that cost? . . . For this reason, things are getting worse because there is no corn. There is no rice. There are no beans. People are not working very hard. We're losing many things. It is not like before. Before, us Q'eqchi's did not use things like we use today, plastic things. Before, we used only ceramic pots. The women made pots and comals [clay griddles], all things. But today, we have electric frying pans, electric pots, all of this stuff. And it is expensive! And it is from the United States! Before, no! Before, they had to make their comals out of clay, pots from clay. And soap too. They made soap. Now, now we have to buy Zest and who the hell knows where that is from! (2002: 283–84)

The cost of consumer items is a constant subject of conversation and source of worry in Q'eqchi' households, as both male and female heads of household assess information about prices of new commodities. In villages with electricity, the monthly arrival of the bill always causes commotion, as this is one of the most burdensome and regular expenses poor households face. Family members pass around the paper to verify the ghastly numbers (usually equivalent to two or three days of wage labor). In Atelesdale, Antonio Tiul confessed he finally disconnected the lights ($5.40–$6.25 a month) so that he could continue to pay for water ($0.96) and cooking fuel ($7.74–$11.61 for a tank of propane) (2002 prices).

J. Eric Thompson, one of the first ethnographers to do research among Q'eqchi' people in the early twentieth century, once observed, "The Mayas display a curious lack of ambition for wealth, or even prestige" (1930: 86). Perhaps this was true a century ago, but today, young people discard the old ways, and the generational erosion of skills and material culture becomes an important pathway into increased monetization of the household economy. On my last visit to Agoutiville in 2007, I found the children of the Cac family listening endlessly to CD players and playing video games. They were clearly more interested in reggaeton than in what the outcome of the upcoming Guatemalan presidential elections might mean for the rural area. Their grandfather expressed ambivalence about their disinterest in his indigenous rural skills compared with the advantages of getting a Western education.

As detailed in chapter 1, Fray Bartolomé de las Casas converted Q'eqchi' proselytes by sending traveling merchants with Spanish tools and trinkets into Q'eqchi' territory (see also Wasserstom 1978). Once again, shoddy commodities may prove an efficient means of controlling Q'eqchi' labor—degrading what it means to be indigenous, indeed, to be human. Families bake under tin roofs inside windowless cinder-block houses, even though indigenous architecture made with free and local forest materials would be immensely cooler. Packets of monosodium glutamate–based seasoning are replacing local herbs. Expensive pharmaceuticals (often expired in the tropical heat) push aside home remedies. Instant ramen noodles were recently introduced in village stores across the region. Radios and electronics sold to people without electricity require expensive batteries that then decompose hazardously on village soils when discarded. Dangerous agrichemicals and Green Revolution corn hybrids replace pest-resistant heirloom varieties. Supplanting women's traditional woven skirts, which can last a decade, are cheap polyester dresses that fall into rags within weeks. Walmart just opened Petén's first big-box store,

Maxibodega, displacing dozens of small urban merchants who provide better-quality produce and goods.

All these growing cash needs are compounded in the inflationary tourism economy, leaving Q'eqchi' landowners vulnerable to speculators wanting to buy their parcels. The cost of the most commonly purchased dry goods (salt, soap, oil, sugar, junk food, boots, and metal tools) is roughly one-fourth to one-third higher in Petén than in the rest of Guatemala due to longer shipping distances from the capital. As a small experiment, I spent a typical day documenting 142 purchases made between 6:30 A.M. and 9:30 P.M. at the main dry-goods store in Agoutiville. Junk-food purchases (candy, chips, sodas) outnumbered whole foods and protein items almost nine to one. This is not to say that poor people do not deserve pleasures, but rather that small expenses add up and deepen their dependence on the cash economy.

Commenting that "money is like water," many Q'eqchi' families who sold their land expressed bewilderment about the quick disappearance of the cash. Another Q'eqchi' interviewee reflected:

> But the money they receive is so little, that it's all gone in a month or two. Money is . . . like a ripe banana: when you see a bunch of bananas, you start eating, and then the next day you have nothing. It's that way with money. You start spending it. You take a hundred to buy this and that, but you are not replacing it. It just goes, goes. When you have spent all the money, you can't expect any more. (ProPetén 2009: testimony 32)

To help pay for the increasing cost of the most basic family diet, Q'eqchi' parents are eager, even desperate to send their children to high school, as this will help them get professional jobs with steady incomes. Having themselves been denied education, these parents have become convinced that Western education and urban professions are prestigious and desirable. With the saturation of the northern frontier making land increasingly scarce, education becomes an escape hatch for the future. When asked how future generations would make a living, dozens of mothers and fathers with insufficient land to bequeath to their children and grandchildren responded overwhelmingly that they hoped their children would get an education and find employment outside of agriculture. Far more than for consumer items, Q'eqchi' parents will, therefore, sacrifice enormously to pay for their children's education—often selling their labor in exploitative day jobs (for example, weeding cattle pasture) they otherwise would never accept.

Vicente and Lorenzo Cac are good examples. After struggling in rental agriculture for years, both decided to seek unskilled wage jobs upon facing a cash crisis when their children reached high-school age and the cost of school fees and materials rose. Tears welled up in Vicente's wife's eyes when she explained that he works as a bank guard in the town of Morales, Izabal, and visits home at most only two days a month. His younger brother, Lorenzo, once worked as a teacher for the bilingual education program PRONADE, but his ninth-grade education no longer meets the new standards. Fiercely intelligent, he worked as a custodian and bookkeeper in a Rio Dulce restaurant for a period. Later, he took a better-paying job inspecting for drugs at the port authority, but he finds the work boring and dislikes the military atmosphere. He dreams of getting a decent NGO job that will allow him to use his organizing skills in Q'eqchi' communities, but for now he must take whatever work will help him get his youngest children through high school.

For poor people in an inflationary economy with no social security, putting their children through school is perhaps a wise gamble. Children, for now, can be expected to support their parents in their old age. In Agoutiville, Don Francisco Cac sacrificed to send his children through school, and two of them became professionals (a nurse and a schoolteacher). In return, they built him and his wife a comfortable house with a cement floor, which is the envy of the rest of the village. As Doña Maria Tiul remarked, "I sweated for my children," and she thought it only fair they should support her in her old age. Another mother from Agoutiville said, "I want my son to study so he can bring me out of poverty."

While one might sympathetically share this hope, it is not clear how so many children are going to graduate from elementary school, much less high school, when most rural Q'eqchi' villages are lucky if the schoolteacher shows up for an average of two or three days a week. The Guatemalan education system, moreover, devalues rural life and trains young people through rote memorization with the aim of producing diligent, urban workers rather than citizens who can think and live independently or perhaps start their own rural businesses. Nor is it clear how poor families, with an average of seven children, are going to provide expensive secondary education.

Even if a few families do manage to put some of their children through high school, as they have in Agoutiville, the lack of good jobs after students graduate is the next rude awakening. When I returned to Agoutiville in late 2004, a large group of young people had received their teaching diplomas, and their parents worriedly confessed that they were still unable to find work. After parents had struggled for years to put their children through school, they were faced with the ugly disillusionment of unemployment. Because there are few secondary educational and work opportunities in the rural area, attending high school usually takes young people away from the community. This has set in motion a brain drain of the countryside, as young indigenous people become convinced that the only alternative to rural poverty is to leave their villages altogether to become accountants, nurses, teachers, and other urban professionals.

Their children's lack of reciprocity is often the next rude awakening for parents. As more than one Q'eqchi' father lamented, "I sold my land to send my son to high school. Now he's married, wearing fine clothes, and living in town, but he's forgotten his parents, and here we are renting land again." In the same way that industrial capitalism secretly depends on the domestic economy for labor reproduction, the education of Guatemala's young people for a brave new corporate world clearly depends on subsidies from parents and the rural Q'eqchi' subsistence economy.

In the past, the penetration of capitalist relations into Q'eqchi' villages was impermanent and two-directional. Both before the Spanish invasion and during the colonial period, Q'eqchi' traders were known for moving goods between highland and lowland Maya cities. Despite, or perhaps because of, their isolation in the colonial period under the Dominicans, when the Verapaz region was suddenly catapulted into the global economy after independence, Q'eqchi' people quickly became involved in commodity markets. Before German planters took their land, small Q'eqchi' farmers reportedly experimented with growing coffee themselves in the mid-nineteenth century. When chicle, a resin used in chewing gum, became Guatemala's "white gold" in the early twentieth century (Schwartz 1990), many young Q'eqchi' men boarded Wrigley airplanes headed for Petén and learned to tap these trees. When Standard Fruit began buying bananas from small producers, Q'eqchi' farmers started growing bananas. As oil companies explored the forests for black gold, lowland Q'eqchi' settlers offered their labor as linemen. When the export economy called for spices, they grew cardamom, otherwise known as "green gold." When British markets demanded fair-trade chocolate, the Toledo Q'eqchi' quickly began planting cacao in impressive commercial quantities for Green & Black's, which sells this chocolate in a bar called "Maya Gold." Indeed, as Richard Wilk (1997) persuasively argues, Q'eqchi' people have regularly taken advantage of many other booms—growing pigs, beans, rice, sesame seeds, pumpkin seeds, chilies, pineapples, annatto, and even marijuana whenever the market demanded these commodities.

Yet, by never abandoning the security of the subsistence economy, Q'eqchi' people resiliently weathered the busts in these same commodity markets. Whenever these market forays failed, Q'eqchi' farmers returned to the safety of subsistence production in the frontier. The forests regenerated around their communities, hiding evidence of earlier market involvement (Wilk 1997). Put another way, *although Q'eqchi' people have long been involved in global markets, they never allowed markets to dominate their entire culture and society.* As Sol Tax so eloquently described in *Penny Capitalism* (1953), Maya people have long participated in face-to-face markets in which they could negotiate prices on their own terms. At the dawn of the twenty-first century, however, faceless transnational corporations are intervening in the Q'eqchi' peasant economy on an entirely different scale. Moving from the hacienda system, in which the "patrones" (bosses) personally knew their workers and often participated in fictive kinship relations such as godparenthood, the Q'eqchi' are now subject to a faceless corporate economy with little democratic, local accountability. As one Q'eqchi' ex–plantation worker remarked, "Before, if we committed a mistake, they kept us on the job. Now the [African palm] companies throw us out immediately" (Alonso, Alonzo, and Dürr 2008: 80) (translation mine).

Reflecting the boom-and-bust cycles of their participation in frontier markets, Q'eqchi' storytellers relate another premonitory tale about mythical forest figures, the Ch'ol men (*Ch'ol winq*). Some imagine them as more animal than human, rumored, for example, to be cannibals or to enjoy eating raw game meat such as paca ("tepezcuintle," better known as "gibnut" in Belize). Others envision Ch'ol men (and women) as the direct descendants of the ancient Maya, who have managed to survive unconquered by the Spanish or the Guatemalan state by residing in caves deep in the lowland forests. Some believe the Ch'ol men have shamanic powers and can even transform themselves into jaguars or other animals (Schackt 1981). Occasionally, they say, a Ch'ol man will make contact with a Q'eqchi' hunter, asking to trade bags of cacao for salt, but only if the farmer promises not to tell others (see also Wilk et al. 1987). In one version of the story I recorded in Belize, a Q'eqchi' farmer betrays his agreement with the Ch'ol man by bringing a friend to help him carry more sacks of cacao to sell at market. Seeing that the farmer is not alone, the Ch'ol man refuses to trade and disappears into the forest with his cacao. That night, the Ch'ol man appears to the farmer in his dreams. He is crying and tells the man, "We were working well together. You were getting money [from the cacao]. But it wasn't for anyone. It was just for you." The farmer also awakes crying, because he knows he made a mistake. In other versions of this story, the farmer dies for his betrayal or for trespassing in the wild cacao groves cultivated by the Ch'ol men (Grandia 2004b).

The march to market capitalism does not have to be unidirectional. Nor should people have to betray their ancestors to make a profit. A society can have markets without surrendering them completely to corporate power. The Guatemalan government need not abandon land administration completely to the whims of the market. The World Bank made serious mistakes in the first phase of the Land Administration Project in Petén, decimating the Q'eqchi' commons in the northern third of the country. However, the Guatemalan government still has time to reform the second phase of the project in the rest of Q'eqchi' territory and perhaps remediate the problems left from the first Petén phase. There is still an opportunity to rectify the historical injustices of Guatemalan land distribution and stop the immediate enclosure of Guatemala's diverse indigenous commons. The World Bank could reopen the Guatemala land project for a full evaluation and develop reforms that would mitigate its deleterious consequences for the Q'eqchi' people (for policy recommendations, see Grandia 2009c). I am currently working with Q'eqchi' peasant leaders and other civil society advocates to convince Bank managers to do so. Beyond such top-down advocacy to protect their material commons, the Q'eqchi' must also tackle the complex challenge of how to rebuild and strengthen their social commons from the bottom up.

AND YET . . .

> The law locks up the man or woman
> Who steals the goose from off the common
> But leaves the greater villain loose
> Who steals the common from off the goose.

> The law demands that we atone
> When we take things we do not own
> But leaves the lords and ladies fine
> Who take things that are yours and mine.

> The poor and wretched don't escape
> If they conspire the law to break;
> This must be so but they endure
> Those who conspire to make the law.

The law locks up the man or woman
Who steals the goose from off the common,
And geese will still a common lack
Till they go and steal it back.

        —English folk poem, circa 1764 (Bollier 2002a)

Perhaps what is so unsettling about the constant displacement of the Q'eqchi' over five centuries is that it was never inevitable. The depth and resilience of their peasant economy and their deep desire for autonomous subsistence drives settlers farther north each year in search of a piece of land where they may work with dignity. For Q'eqchi' colonists willing to move still deeper into the frontier to find land, separation from their means of production is postponed to another day. Not all Q'eqchi' settlers continue to migrate, but a significant number does. Repeated Q'eqchi' migration in an attempt to escape harsh working conditions as agricultural wage laborers and become independent farmers would seem to challenge the claim of postmodern scholars such as Michael Kearney (1996) that the "death" of the peasantry is a false social science metanarrative. Although Kearney might wish to "bury" peasant theory, curiously, the people in this category refuse to disappear (Edelman 1999) or abandon their aspirations for independent livelihoods.

Using a long-cherished tradition of escaping to the northern forest as a zone of refuge or a kind of Maya "Zomia" (Scott 2009), Q'eqchi' people have proved resilient in confronting the conquest and theft of their lands under the Spanish and then under the Guatemalan state. They have survived decades of coercive labor, followed by decades of civil war—and somehow managed to expand their territory almost fourfold. Perceiving it as the most expedient path to tenure security, many Q'eqchi' leaders advocated for private land titling. They initially welcomed the World Bank projects, hoping like indigenous peoples elsewhere that mapping land rights would provide them with more robust citizenship (cf. Li 1999). A spirit of frontier optimism beguiled them into selling their parcels to speculators with the hope of claiming more land farther north. They continued to resist proletarianization by invading national parks and resuming subsistence agriculture. Droughts and fires associated with this deforestation, however, now threaten the farming livelihoods they so wanted to maintain. The growing presence of Q'eqchi' squatters in protected areas reminds us that anti-dispossession movements are not always progressive or sustainable (Harvey 2003).

And yet . . . while it may appear that Q'eqchi' people are caught on a treadmill of recurrent agrarian inequity, their massive migration northward into the lowlands created the possibility that they would develop into a yeoman rural middle class. The local micropolitics matter, especially in small and eclectic contexts such as postcolonial Belize, where Maya leaders tenaciously fight the enclosures of indigenous land for state leases—stealing back the common for the goose, as suggested by the poem above. Resistance may rarely be successful, but sometimes there are surprises.

Without patron-client relationships mediating the worst aspects of the old plantation system, Q'eqchi' workers are becoming exhausted with their in-between position—neither fully independent farmers nor fully proletarianized laborers. Like their Mexican neighbors, they are reaching a moment in which they "cannot bear any more" ("el campo no aguanta más"), as the prophetic slogan of a new peasant campaign proclaimed when the last protections against NAFTA for Mexican farmers were phased out in December 2002. When speaking in Spanish, many Q'eqchi' men now prefer refer to themselves as farmers ("agricultores") rather than peasants ("campesinos"). Almost in the same breath, many men described their longing to work their milpas in peace *or* get a good job outside agriculture. They loathe their dependence on middlemen and bristle at the low commodity prices offered for the backbreaking work of corn production and the lack of viable markets for other agricultural products. Likewise, they despise the stress of finding itinerant work to fill the gaps in the corn economy. My Q'eqchi' friends told frequent stories about the unpleasantness of forcing themselves to seek wage work in order to pay for this or that crisis—health care bills, land costs, or education for their children. The common phrase "I looked for my cash" (*Xin sik in tumin* or "Busqué mi pisto") reveals their continued conception of wage work as a finite activity one must do before returning to the comforts and security of subsistence cropping.

When Q'eqchi' farmers occasionally hire out their labor, they prefer to work for their Q'eqchi' neighbors, even if that means lower wages (Siebers 1999). In villages like Macawville in northern Petén, where corn production has been especially abundant on newly cleared forestland, Q'eqchi' laborers arrive from as far south as highland Verapaz to work as harvest hands, because they would prefer to serve as field labor for a distant Q'eqchi' farmer than a non-Q'eqchi' person closer to home. Similarly, a landless friend from the Chisec region commutes two hours by bus to Sayaxché to rent a field from a fellow Q'eqchi' landowner (actually losing money in the process) instead of working for the cattle ranchers near his village. If they cannot afford paid laborers, Q'eqchi' subsistence farmers find other mechanisms such as shared-work exchanges for acquiring the help of other adult laborers (cf. J. R. Jones 1990). Q'eqchi' communal work groups are so successful that quite a few Ladino farmers in mixed-ethnic frontier communities lamented that their Q'eqchi' neighbors did not invite them to join.

Participation in the indigenous economy remains preferable to performing wage labor for outsiders.[4] Hence, plantation owners in the Q'eqchi' region may perceive NGO income-generating projects as a threat to "the constant stream of cheap labor [they are] used to" (Secaira 1992: 30). Efraín Reyes Maaz, a key Q'eqchi' organizer for the Guatemala Communist Party in Verapaz in the mid-twentieth century, advised a sharecropper on how to confront the plantation owner who was cheating him of his rightful wages: "If we are not worth anything to you, then plant the money you should pay us under the coffee bush and see what happens, see if it brings you a profit" (Grandin 2004: 121). Realizing the continued importance of their labor to the Guatemalan elite, and following this long tradition of labor organizing, Q'eqchi' peasant organizations are now demanding land in exchange for back pay and benefits plantations owners have withheld from them. As Norman Schwartz observes, "The second conquest of Petén resembles the first, but this time things may not settle down" (1990: 293).

I recall one stormy night in the Cac family home in Agoutiville. Rain poured noisily onto the metal roof, while lightning struck closer and closer. The grandfather, Don Francisco, prayed vigorously on his knees for hours beside his bed. The next morning, I asked him what had happened in the night. He explained that when demons draw near, the God of Thunder, *Qawa' Kaq*, hunts them down with his lightning bolts. If there is any silver lining to the sudden storm of corporate capitalism raining down upon Q'eqchi' settlers, many at least sense that danger is near, and the double threat of the PPP and the DR-CAFTA has animated democratic participation in the Guatemalan countryside. But can this bottom-up grassroots organizing to take back the commons keep up with the plans of men in gray suits and the tempo of the barbed-wire fences enclosing Q'eqchi' agricultural land? Were it not for plantations, pastures, projects, and other top-down development plans, Q'eqchi' farmers might be able to adjust gradually to the parks in their midst and help conserve their own village forests—both of which are necessary for regional climate stability—and, ultimately, maintain their own rural livelihoods. The speed with which these other enclosures are transforming the frontier landscape unfortunately leaves Q'eqchi' communities in conflict with protected area management.

> Any ecologist will tell you how dangerous and fragile a monoculture
> is. A hegemonic world is like having a government without a healthy
> opposition. It becomes a kind of dictatorship. It's like putting a plastic
> bag over the world, and preventing it from breathing. Eventually, it will
> be torn open.
>
> —Arundhati Roy (2001: 220)

In many ways, the Q'eqchi' story embodies the "double movement" described by political economist Karl Polanyi in his 1944 book *The Great Transformation*. For Polanyi, the problem of capitalism lies not with markets in and of themselves but in the ripping away of markets from the social and cultural limits previously placed upon them by the moralities of households, communities, and states. If left unharnessed, capitalism would appropriate more and more domains of life at the expense of the collective good (see also Edelman and Haugerud 2005). Polanyi rightly emphasizes the critical difference between *societies with markets* and *market societies* (cf. Hunn 1999). In and of themselves, markets are not a problem. Trouble begins when a society becomes so structured by raw economic relations that the demand for profit invades the entire social organism. While many political economists focus on state regulation of markets, Polanyi understood from reading anthropologists such as Bronislaw Malinowski that societies also protect themselves from markets by embedding them in culture and ritual.

Truly free markets (or, in Polanyi's terminology, "self-regulating markets") have never existed—nor could they ever exist. "Leaving the fate of the soil and people to the market would be tantamount to annihilating them" (Polanyi 1944: 131). Were all aspects of human life drawn into the "creative destruction" of capitalism, to borrow a phrase from Joseph Schumpeter, the whole system would implode. Contrary to the revolutionary teleology of Marx, Polanyi regarded social and economic change as a "double movement." He was confident that long before born-again capitalism could manage to destroy society, people would push back and seek to re-embed it through a "great transformation" that would bring renewed democratic governance—or be catapulted toward totalitarianism.[5]

By emphasizing the importance of tempo, Polanyi provides a dynamic framework for understanding social change, asking: "Why should the ultimate victory of a trend be taken as proof of the ineffectiveness of the efforts to slow down its progress?" (1944: 36). By retelling the story of capitalism as a back-

and-forth struggle over the embedding of the market, Polanyi helps us move past the twentieth-century dichotomy of capitalism versus Communism and refocuses our attention on the pace at which societies can decelerate, regulate, and harness the market through social, political, and cultural controls.[6] Some of the most egregious facets of corporate capitalism derive from specific and, hence, potentially reversible processes of dispossession. Polanyi's argument is most compelling in the deep connection he makes between the material and social commons—or, rather, between markets and democracy. In a vicious cycle, enclosures degrade the public commons (be they physical spaces for gathering or cyberspaces for sharing information), which are also the necessary organizing grounds for defending the material commons (sky, water, land, health, etc.) (Bateson 1998; Midnight Notes Collective 1990).

As the Q'eqchi' material commons erode, so, too, may the social commons. In the same way that the English enclosures destabilized village and community organization, this dispossession of the Q'eqchi' might conceivably undermine emergent movements for stronger indigenous citizenship. In both Guatemala and Belize, the breathtaking pace of economic and ecological change along frontiers combined with the shift to private land management poses many threats to community cohesion and neighborliness. Ruptures between the social and material worlds often manifest through violent land conflicts, but they can also be reflected in subtle ways in everyday village life.

At the end of my first six months in Petén in 1993, Consuela, the lady of a Q'eqchi' family with whom I stayed in Atelesdale, confessed that she was dreading my departure. Since her husband had accumulated a little income from an NGO project processing non-timber forest products, their economic status had risen, and he had ceased his participation in labor exchanges for planting corn. They still lived eight people to a one-room mud hut, but even small shifts in social standing can alter perceptions of reciprocity. Many of her former friends were too ashamed to visit because they were afraid of being perceived as moochers. While I lived there, people's curiosity about the gringa continued to bring visitors, but she worried that after I departed, their visits would cease and she would be doubly lonely. I was sobered by the idea that even a small development project might catalyze a process of household nuclearization that would initiate a fissure between her family and the social commons of the village. If a little extra income can isolate a friendly woman like Consuela from her friends, then what might something more consequential, like the privatization of village land or the public domain of an entire country, do to social and community relations writ large?

During the very same period in which structural adjustment decimated Third World nations, privatization also deeply undermined the social and political commons in the global North. By cutting taxes, liberalizing regulations, busting unions, and privatizing government services, Reaganomics and Thatcherism reduced government to absentee landlordism (Bello 1994; Harvey 2003; Klein 2001). They unraveled the social safety nets painstakingly earned by previous generations—ripping open and exposing new domains to exploitation for corporate profit, domains that democratic society had once decided should be protected from the market, such as education, health, social security, even the military. Not coincidentally, a decline of democratic participation accompanied these enclosures of our civic patrimony in the global North (Bollier 2002a).

Threats to certain resources, for example, water privatization, may immediately cause a social reaction (e.g., in Cochabamba, Bolivia) because so many other aspects of life depend on them. While such forms of enclosure of the environment and traditional inherited knowledge continue to threaten communities around the planet, new variations on this formula are less easy to resist because users and customary management systems are not yet clearly defined (Ostrom 1990). The 2008 global financial crisis revealed the dangers of derivatives, hedge funds, and other extreme fictionalized forms of money that threaten the abstract commons of financial stability. Experiments with carbon-trading markets have effectively given corporations a new kind of property: the right to maintain profits while causing planetary atmospheric harm (Lohmann 2006). In many new free trade agreements such as NAFTA and the DR-CAFTA, corporations audaciously demand new investment guarantees, arguing that any trade barriers that reduce their hypothetical future revenues constitute a form of property expropriation.

Yet, "multinationals have grown so blindingly rich, so vast in their holdings, so global in their reach, that they have created our coalitions for us" (Klein 2001: 84). If there is any welcome aspect to the blatant excesses of neoliberalism, it is the double movement of citizen mobilization. Even those caught irrevocably within an exploitative wage-labor system can always work to mitigate their dependence on capital through appeals to the moral economy, unionizing, foot-dragging, and other weapons of the weak (Scott 1985).

REMEDIES

In other words, *erosion of the commons is never inevitable*. They can always, always be defended and perhaps even rebuilt. While processes of privatization and enclosure are on the upsurge, so, too, is society's response to this cancer of profit—if the reader will allow a personal metaphor. As I learned from my own battle against lymphoma as I finished this manuscript, there are two ways to cure oneself of cancer. Because my tumor was spreading so aggressively, I accepted my oncologist's allopathic prescription for an onslaught of harsh chemotherapy and radiation treatments. In order to manage the side effects and rebuild my immune system, however, I turned to complementary and alternative therapies for help with putting my life together again—with less stress and better nutrition, exercise, herbal supplements, meditation, qigong, and other non-Western approaches to good health.

Social movements tend to be more experienced with the first kind of direct response—stand, organize, and fight. The second response—strengthening the social organism so that it can heal itself more naturally—is a bit more challenging. As Polanyi argues, the task of re-embedding markets goes beyond state regulation; it also requires social and cultural mobilization in order to strengthen the subsistence economy and other aspects of our lives that still remain outside the market. In contrast to frontal political struggles against enclosure, this second capillary process involves the slower, less dramatic, and often unrecognized work of restoring gift economies and revitalizing commons ethics that are the foundation of real social change—including such intangibles as a sense of security, hope, generosity, honesty, reciprocity, love, kindness, ritual, and concern for future generations (Bateson 1998). Albeit broad and amorphous, this second strategy gives us all a multitude of ordinary alternatives in the here and now . . . even without a full-fledged revolution. A summer garden. A bike ride to work. Cooking a simple pot of beans for lunch. Speaking to someone on public transportation. Introducing colleagues into a social network. Practicing random acts of kindness. Simple and ordinary gestures that protect certain aspects of our lives from the market can blossom with new meaning when seen as part of larger struggles against enclosure and the ugly tide of social atomization.

Commoditization and privatization not only threaten the cultural survival of indigenous peoples like the Q'eqchi' but also undermine public commons in the industrialized world if we are willing to shine the ethnographic mirror back on our own society, as Margaret Mead once did. Just as land dispossession hurls the Q'eqchi' down the slippery slope of wage labor, day by day, U.S. citizens also get caught up in ever expanding webs of commodification and the encroachment of corporations on almost every aspect of life. In this brave new world that depends so much on marketing and image, these new controls are cloaked in Orwellian rhetoric about choice, convenience, and comfort. While public-private divisions used to correlate fairly closely with commercial-communal struggles, these boundaries are swiftly changing. The newest commons is "private" life itself; hence, "the personal is political," as the feminist movement once declared.

To give but a few examples of the "poverty of affluence" (Wachtel 1983) and how capitalism continually pries open new arenas of private life (Luxemburg 1951): Parents today increasingly find two incomes necessary to get by. In turn, they hire out child care and call professional housecleaning services to clean their homes. Prenuptial agreements marketize marriage. Pregnant women hire doulas to fill the roles that mothers and grandmothers once played in assisting with births. Hardly anyone cooks anymore, instead purchasing meals on the run. The accelerated pace of professional specialization further prevents people from being do-it-yourselfers. Locked in sedentary jobs, we acquire gym memberships so we can exercise and go to spas for relaxation. With new communication tools such as cell phones, text messages, e-mail, and Facebook, we are ever more connected, but surveys show that people feel lonelier than ever. With social alienation on the rise, more consumer addictions fill the void. It's like drinking saltwater to quench a never-ending thirst.

Of course, the Corporate American Dream costs money—and not everyone has it. Simply by making life so expensive that it is impossible to survive without debt, credit becomes a controlling process (Nader 1997) that keeps people, and entire nations, dependent on their wages—and unlikely to rebel.[7] Witness, for example, how the massive debt crisis in the Third World led to harder forms of structural adjustment designed to produce more money for the GDP.[8] The United States itself has become a debtor nation, with personal savings rates falling below zero percent in 2005, equivalent to levels seen during the Great Depression. North Americans now spend one in seven after-tax dollars on debt payments, up from one in nine dollars in 1980 (Leland 2007). And the more people need to buy and become indebted, the more they will perceive their jobs as necessary and become ever more obedient workers, willing to sell their skins on the market whatever the going rate.

Lest the reader feel trapped, we should remember that even in the heart of empire, there are always cracks. Eighty years ago, in 1930, Mohandas K. Gandhi marched along one of those cracks to the sea and made salt, and this simple symbolic act was the beginning of the end of colonial rule across the planet. Despite the mantras of progress as privatization, throughout the Guatemalan countryside and even in U.S. middle-class suburbia, one still hears citizen demands for just prices and moral economies, for the right to health care, or for retirement security in one's old age (Gudeman and Rivera 2002). Even in the worst of times, hope remains for a new era of jubilation.

JUBILEE!

> You shall count off seven weeks of years, seven times seven years, so that the period of seven weeks of years gives forty-nine years. Then you shall have the trumpet sounded loud. . . .
>
> *That fiftieth year shall be a jubilee for you*: you shall not sow, or reap the aftergrowth, or harvest the unpruned vines. For it is a jubilee; it shall be holy to you: you shall eat only what the field itself produces.
>
> *In this year of jubilee you shall return, every one of you, to your property.*
>
> When you make a sale to your neighbor or buy from your neighbor, you shall not cheat one another.
>
> *The land shall not be sold in perpetuity, for the land is mine; with me you are but aliens and tenants.* Throughout the land that you hold, you shall provide for the redemption of the land.
>
> If anyone of your kin falls into difficulty and sells a piece of property, then the next of kin shall come and redeem what the relative has sold.
>
> . . . But if there are not sufficient means to recover it, what was sold shall remain with the purchaser until the year of jubilee; in the jubilee it shall be released, and the property shall be returned.
>
> . . . *the open land around their cities may not be sold; for that is their possession for all time.*
>
> — Leviticus (New Revised Standard Version) 25:8–34 (emphasis mine)

There are many movements afoot all across the planet to rope in the corporate capitalist bull running amok in the "china shop of human history" (Rieff 1993: 69). As discussed at World Social Forums, diverse grassroots organizations are pushing for more locally controlled economies within which to create "a world where many worlds fit." Seeking to avoid the misperception that they are just "anti-globalization," disparate movements in both the global North and South are now working to articulate what they are *for* (Klein 2001), not just what they are against. In citizen meetings in Latin America, this often means moving "de protesta hasta propuesta" (from protest to proposal) (Bell 2009)—for example, organizing seed exchanges, as Via Campesina does, at meetings to plan strategy for land reform. Reorienting debates over capitalism around questions of scale and plurality, new social movements have pushed past state-led socialism and offer different antidotes to capitalism that value local economies, reproductive work, and the subsistence sector.[9] These movements differ from earlier class-based organizing with their double insistence on economic autonomy and democracy, effectively arguing that citizenship trumps ownership (Bollier 2002a), as expressed by a manifesto signed by thousands of groups worldwide organized into a loose network named after the same phrase, "Our world is not for sale." Such movements would not tolerate Stalinist collectivization any more than freewheeling corporate capitalism. Like modern Luddites (cf. Midnight Notes Collective 1990: 8) with "commons sense" (Rowe 2001), they connect the economic with technological, political, social, and cultural issues. They want a kind of modernity that is different from free-trade Liberalism.

In a sense, they are calling for a grand global jubilee. Today, most people consider this word merely a synonym for "celebration." This association stems from a Judeo-Christian concept described in the book of Leviticus, which declared that once every fifty years there should be a period of jubilee—a year in which debts would be canceled, slavery abolished, sins forgiven, and private land returned to the commons.[10] This follows a Jewish tradition of the Shmitta, the seventh year of an agricultural cycle during which farmers must fallow the land. Like the repetitions of the Maya calendar, a jubilee year is then supposed to follow every seven sabbatical cycles, or forty-nine years. Though never implemented literally, the concept does cause us to think about how we might otherwise regularly level the playing field so as to give worth to the dignity of each person who enters this world (J. Grandia, pers. comm., 2006).

The tenacity of Q'eqchi' settlers in organizing land occupations to reclaim the territory stolen from them over the centuries by religious missionaries, coffee merchants, bureaucrats, and the current cattle-palm-military-corporate trade complex could be seen as part of this global jubilee. Their anachronistic desire to maintain independent livelihoods as peasant producers reflects a global yearning on the part of the poor for autonomy, respect, and dignity. Echoing themes articulated at the World Social Forum and other global summits by peasant movements such as Via Campesina, the Q'eqchi' people are asserting their right to remain farmers—albeit sometimes losing their hard-earned crop money to expensive soft drinks. After all, people do not always resist with coherency and twenty-twenty hindsight; they simply resist . . . often for deeply emotional reasons. As so many Q'eqchi' farmers said to me, "I was born working the land, and I shall die working the land." Although corn cropping is sometimes unprofitable, Q'eqchi' people still cultivate as much as their landholdings allow. Alongside petroleum pipelines, paved highways, and high-tech hydroelectric plants under the PPP, the moral economy of the Q'eqchi' milpa pulses ahead—like a weed pushing up through cracks in the pavement, to borrow a metaphor from Eugene Hunn (1999: 33).

Perhaps, too, over the years, I have been influenced by the hope of Q'eqchi' migrants that they will find a better life around the bend—or at least a piece of land to work with dignity. Certainly, living among the Q'eqchi' people for so many years gave me a deeper respect for the resilience of Maya culture and the abilities of people to find moments of delight in the crevices of an undeniably precarious pioneer existence. While this book has focused on the structural tragedies that have repeatedly dispossessed the Q'eqchi' over the past five hundred years, I deeply admire the way the Q'eqchi' people still carry on their daily lives with grace, dignity, good humor, and profound respect for one another, epitomized in the common Maya saying, "Each mind is a world unto its own" (Cada cabeza es un mundo) (cf. Haenn 2005).

I recall, especially, the common scene at daybreak in so many frontier Q'eqchi villages. Farmers in communities that had the courage and foresight to hold on to their parcels of earth sharpen their machetes in the light of kerosene lanterns before leaving for the fields in collective work groups. As howler monkeys awaken with thundering roars, girls scamper to wells to help carry water back home for their mothers. Sleepy boys chop some firewood before following their fathers to the fields. A mother crosses her yard to share some meat with her neighbor before it spoils in the heat of the day. After coaxing smoky embers of smoldering hearths into roaring fires, the village women pound out—with rhythmic slapping of palms—homemade maize tortillas for the morning meal. And so it is that my pioneering Q'eqchi' friends arise each morning in the shivery gray dawn of the restless tropical forest, reproducing every day an almost autonomous peasant economy.

GLOSSARY

Q'eqchi' words are in italics.

aj	masculine prefix or a word that signals occupation
alcalde	mayor
baldíos	no-man's-lands, not yet measured or registered by the state
caballería	measurement for 45 hectares or 64 manzanas; standard land grant in the colonization process
catechist	Catholic lay leader
chicle	tree resin harvested for export as main ingredient in chewing gum
Conservatives	people who wanted to uphold the power of traditional landed elites and favored protectionist trade policies
copal	tree resin harvested as incense for ceremonies
department	political jurisdiction like a U.S. state but without its own legislature
ejido	common lands administered by a municipality
encomiendas	landed estate concessions accompanied by a native labor pool
finca	plantation; ranch
hacienda	plantation (colonial era)
Ladino	person of mixed race or ethnicity (mestizo)
Laj Q'eq	Black Beast; immortal creature, half man and half horse
Laj Seleeq	magical dwarf creature who performs services for a rancher and can transform itself into different animals
latifundio	large landholding; plantation
Liberals	anticlerical modernizers who saw foreign investment and trade as the means for achieving Guatemala's development

manzana	land measurement, roughly equivalent to two acres
mayejak	ceremony to pay respect to the *Tzuultaq'a*
milpa	cornfield
minifundio	small or tiny landholding; usually insufficient for subsistence
mozos colonos	worker-serfs; sharecropping laborers bound to a plantation
municipality	equivalent to a county
reduction	"reducción" or "reduced" town; forcible recongregations of native peoples in the colonial period
Tzuultaq'a	Gods of the Hill and Valley
xate	palm frond harvested for export

ACDIP   Association of Indigenous Peasant Communities for the Integrated Development of Petén (La Asociación de Comunidades Campesinas Indígenas Para el Desarrollo Integral de Petén)

AVANCSCO   Guatemalan Association for the Advancement of the Social Sciences (Asociación para el Avance de las Ciencias Sociales en Guatemala)

CARE   Cooperative for Assistance and Relief Everywhere

CI   Conservation International (Conservación Internacional)

CNOC   National Coordinator of Peasant Organizations (Coordinadora Nacional de Organizaciones Campesinas)

CONAP   National Council for Protected Areas (Consejo Nacional de Areas Protegidas)

CONTIERRA   Presidential Dependency for the Resolution of Conflicts (Dependencia Presidencial para la Resolución de Conflictos)

DR-CAFTA   Dominican Republic–Central America Free Trade Agreement (Tratado de Libre Comercio de América Central–República Dominicana)

FONTIERRAS   Land Fund (Fondo de Tierras)

FYDEP   The Company for the Promotion and Development of the Petén (La Empresa para el Fomento y Desarrollo de el Petén)

IDB or IADB   Inter-American Development Bank (Banco Inter-Americano de Desarrollo)

INTA   Institute for Agrarian Transformation (Instituto para la Transformación Agraria)

LAP   Land Administration Project

MBC	Mesoamerican Biological Corridor (Corredor Biológico Mesoaméricano)
NGO	nongovernmental organization (organización no-gubernamental)
PPP	Puebla to Panama Plan (Plan Puebla Panamá)
RIC	Cadastral Information Registry (Registro de Información Catastral)
SATIIM	Sarstoon Temash Institute for Indigenous Management
USAID	United States Agency for International Development (Agencia de los Estados Unidos para el Desarrollo Internacional)
USTR	United States Trade Representative
UTJ	Legal and Technical Unit/Protierra (Unidad Técnico-Jurídico/Protierrra)

NOTES

Preface

Epigraph from Dowie 2009: xv.

1 The largest is Petén's Maya Biosphere Reserve (at 1.6 million hectares, roughly twice the size of Yellowstone), connecting an arc of parks in Belize, Mexico, and Guatemala known as the Maya Forest (La Selva Maya). With other smaller parks established in the mid-1990s in southern Petén, roughly half the department falls under some kind of protected status.

2 The Peace Accords do have a clause stipulating that by 1999 the government was to turn over one hundred thousand hectares within multiple-use zones to small and medium-size peasant groups (Hernández Alarcón 1998a). This apparently referred to community forest concessions already under negotiation and not to new settlements.

3 These concessions (called "agricultural polygons") are a hybrid tenure category awarding families private parcels in usufruct, with renewal depending on all the families conserving 20 percent of the forests on their land and collectively protecting nearby forests from other squatters.

4 Perhaps, too, my ambitious research plan of participant observation in six communities across two countries was meant to defy the common mispronunciation of my first name in Q'eqchi'—"Laizi," sounding like "lazy."

Introduction

1 The Midnight Notes Collective (www.midnightnotes.org) published some of the earliest writings on other fictions associated with the "new enclosures" (1990s). Along with many others among the netroots, David Bollier has produced a fascinating stream of commentary on the Internet commons (2002a) and other forms of "silent theft" (2001, 2002b). Vandana Shiva writes prolifically on the privatization of water, genes, and biotechnology. The ETC Group (formally Action Group on Erosion, Technology, and Concentration) warns that new patents on nanotechnology may create cross-sectoral monopolies never before possible. Building

on his previous studies in political economy (1983, 2000), Michael Perelman now writes on the enclosure of popular culture (2005). Massimo De Angelis edits a lively online journal, *The Commoner*, which offers perhaps the most innovative interpretations of enclosure and privatization today. The Tomales Bay Institute also manages a blog, onthecommons.org, featuring many of the aforementioned writers.

2   Polanyi (1944) argues that the creation of three "fictitious" commodities was critical to the ideological success of industrial capitalism. He refers to the idea (1) that *money* could represent economic power and value, (2) that the *labor* of human beings could be ethically bought and sold, and (3) that nature could be enclosed as *land* or private property. For Polanyi, these commodities are fictitious, not in the sense of being fake, but rather as socially contrived—having not been originally produced for sale. More important than their thingness as commodities were how they became equated with progress and the changes they wrought in human relations (see also Edelman and Haugerud 2005; Rasmussen 2001: 57).

3   Of 1,554 land conflicts registered with Guatemala's official human rights division in 2008, one-third were in the Q'eqchi' area (Alonso, Alonzo, and Dürr 2008).

4   Unless otherwise indicated, all currency is in U.S. dollars (Q7.75 = $1).

5   Hannah Arendt notes in *The Human Condition* that the etymological root of the word "deprive" is "prive," which means to forbid someone from having a public life (Hyde 2008).

6   Most orthodox Marxists tend not to draw attention to such extra-economic forces, perhaps to avoid diverting attention from the task of uniting the workers of the world against capitalism. In order to demonstrate the necessity for class revolution, Marx's main concern was to unveil how the inherent structural violence of capitalist wage relations exploited workers as much as overt, physical violence did. He assumed that after capitalism had taken hold, in the "ordinary run of things," businessmen would discover that the "silent compulsion" of market pressures was more effective than violence in exploiting labor (Perelman 2000) and capitalism would continue to spread by the force of its own internal logic (E. M. Wood 1999).

1. Liberal Plunder

1   In modern Guatemalan Spanish, the word "colonización" is understood as a specialized form of resettlement on unused or underused lands assumed to be unoccupied (see Morrissey 1978).

2   J. Eric Thompson (1972) emphasized that the Mopán, Manché Ch'ol, and Q'eqchi' were all distinct groups, but other lowland groups, such as the Chiapas Lacandón, the Belizean Succotz Maya, and the Guatemalan Itzá, are really a single ethnic group, separated only by artificial colonial and, later, national boundaries. James Nations (1979), however, distinguishes between Cholti and the Chol, whom the Spanish lumped together as "Lacandón." Nor should the western Chol (who continue to live in Chiapas) be confused with the Manché Ch'ol (who once lived to the east in the region between Motagua Valley and the Maya Mountains of

present-day Belize). For discussion of these pre-Columbian ethnic boundaries, see Stoll 1938, J. E. Thompson 1938 and 1972, Sapper 2000, and Wilk 1987.

3   Bartolomé de las Casas came to the New World as a farmer at age eighteen in 1502; he was so appalled by the massacres, torture, pillage, rape, and general plunder of the natives by the Spanish conquerors that he decided to take vows as a priest and joined the Dominican order in 1522 (Beaudry-Corbett and Hardy 2000). Drawing many of his ideas from Thomas Aquinas's theory of social rights, his most famous publication is *A Short Account of the Destruction of the Indies* (de las Casas 1992) (Morrissey 1978: 45).

4   Additional evidence of substantial and sustained Q'eqchi'-Ch'ol interactions include highland-lowland differences in regional dialects, cropping patterns, women's traditional dress, names for medicinal plants, and settlement patterns. See Grandia 2004c, Thompson 1938, and Levental 1997 for further discussion.

5   Established in Alta Verapaz in 1903, cardamom is known locally as "green gold" (as opposed to the "black gold" of coffee) (A. E. Adams 1999). Not a traditional spice for Mesoamerican cuisine, most is exported to the Middle East, where recent conflict led to a price collapse. Starting in 2002, this loss hit the Q'eqchi' area especially hard because it overlapped with a simultaneous drop in world coffee prices.

6   Due to rape or concubinage, four out of five children born to the first wave of German fathers in Verapaz were of mixed ethnicity (Schmolz-Haberlein 1996).

7   Liberals revived these labor drafts in 1829 but abolished them in 1837 in response to popular resistance. Conservatives used them infrequently from the 1840s, and they became a permanent feature of Liberal rule with the rise of the coffee plantation economy (McCreery 1983).

8   This practice is mirrored in today's custom of writing very standardized recommendation letters that simply confirm the dates the employee worked.

9   By December 1954, the U.S. government had hired a development consulting company, International Development Services (IDS), to advise the counterrevolutionary government on land reform. IDS continued to assist the military government through the 1960s with topographic maps, air-photo mosaics, and land-use and vegetation maps—ironically, the same activities that U.S.-based environmental groups currently perform for the Guatemalan government.

10   The very first U.S. donation of $14 million to Guatemala after the 1954 coup was used mostly to remove indigenous families from land Arbenz had expropriated from the United Fruit Company (Brockett 1998). By 1959, the United States had given $58 million to prop up the Castillo Armas regime, begin military training programs, and launch a "civic action" project in Petén (Doyle 2002). The average annual U.S. assistance to Guatemala grew from $1.2 million (1948–54) to $17.6 million (1955–65) (McPherson 1996).

11   For reasons associated with the Mexican Revolution, colonization projects in Chiapas started two decades earlier than most other Latin American efforts to settle their frontiers (Collier and Lowery 1994).

12   Many Ladino colonists in the north admitted having sold land in the south coast

colonization projects, because neither INTA nor FYDEP had any method for cross-checking their land registration systems.

13 General Lucas's father maintained Q'eqchi' concubines on his Tuilá ranch; hence, Lucas has an extensive Q'eqchi' family made up of half siblings in the greater Cahabón region. Despite this kinship connection, under Lucas's command, the Guatemalan military was responsible for massacring many Q'eqchi' and other Maya people.

2. Maya Gringos

1 There was a great deal of speculation among urban Guatemalan professionals, for instance, as to which presidential candidate (the right-wing military officer or the liberal centrist) the rural Q'eqchi' would support in 2007—virtually mirroring speculation during the U.S. election about how the folks on "Main Street" would vote.

2 Triangulating my migration research with municipal archives, census information, and a thousand-person survey designed and analyzed in partnership with the National Institute of Statistics (Grandia et al. 2001), I also interviewed approximately 350 settlers—listening to stories shared with tears, in whispers and triumphant tones, and with earnest clasping of hands.

3 In some cases, the migration and visitation flows between two villages are so strong that one becomes a satellite community for the other. In Petén, there are communities with numbered names (e.g., La Esperanza I and La Esperanza II) or named with Q'eqchi' diminutives (e.g., Machaca and Chinamachaca [Little Machaca]). Sometimes entire communities or large sections of communities will move en masse to set up a satellite village, but more commonly they are outlets for younger generations who cannot find land at home. This generational settlement pattern is probably how the Q'eqchi' were able to expand so rapidly across a large territory in the late nineteenth and early twentieth centuries.

4 In 1921, the average population of villages in El Estor was 101; in Izabal, 51; and in San Luis, 30.

5 Some Q'eqchi' women do feel a calling to become midwives and/or have received training from the Ministry of Health and NGO projects, but this is more the exception than the rule.

6 Witchcraft accusations cause healers to migrate frequently. Cahabón (where many of the migrants to Petén, Izabal, and Belize originated) is known to be the center of Q'eqchi' healers and witches (*aj tul*) (see also Parra Novo 1997).

7 Q'eqchi' people who lose their parents at any age will consider themselves orphans. In English, the term is generally limited to children who lose their parents, but a Q'eqchi' person might consider himself or herself an orphan if the loss of a parent occurs at age thirty, fifty, or even eighty!

8 David Carr (pers. comm., Nov. 4, 2003) kindly calculated these figures for me based on our 1998 survey data (Grandia et al. 2001).

9 Less flatteringly, Guatemalan anthropologist Goubaud Carrera described the

Q'eqchi' in 1949 as "the vainest people I have met outside of Guatemala's upper class" (quoted in A. E. Adams 1999: 52).

10 With so much historical intermixing with the Mopán, many lowland Q'eqchi' people expressed their puzzlement at these identity boundaries by repeatedly asking me whether "Maya" [Mopán] is a different language from Q'eqchi'.

3. Commons, Customs, and Carrying Capacities

1 The felicitous phrase "tragedy of enclosures" seems to have many discontinuous origins. Writing at the height of the nineteenth-century English enclosures, John Clare was the first to bring a poet's eye to the deleterious social and environmental impact of this process. Then, in 1975, S. V. Ciriacy-Wantrup and R. C. Bishop wrote about the "tragedy of the commoners." Joan Martinez-Alier crafted the phrase to support his elegant thesis about the ecology of the poor (1991). George Monbiot then published an article with this title (1994). Picked up by many global social movements, the phrase is now common.

2 For those interested in more details about the *mayejak* itself, see Wilson 1995 or Grandia 2004c.

3 In Guatemala, where the pressure to sell hybrid corn on the market is so strong, most farmers plant by area and calculate their harvests by the sack or quintal (one hundred pounds). In Belize, however, elder Q'eqchi' farmers conceptualize field size relative to the number of corncobs to be planted (approximately 142 cobs per hectare) and somatic measurements for stacking crop yields: a *moqoj* (the length of extended arms measured fingertip to fingertip, approximately six feet tall, twelve feet long, and six feet wide) or a *b'aar*, roughly half a *moqoj*.

4 The calendar may vary by one or two months according to regional differences in rainfall.

5 Because the word for "milpa" in Q'eqchi' literally means "cornfield," when asked by outsiders what they plant in their milpas, Q'eqchi' farmers may answer literally, "corn." If one visits the milpa, however, the farmer may have many other crops interspersed among the corn stalks (field notes, March 2003; N. Schwartz, pers. comm., Nov. 2009). This illustrates the continued importance of participant observation as the fundamental ethnographic method, because there is often a difference between what people say they do and what they actually do.

6 Q'eqchi' farmers recognize the necessity of a good fallow for preventing weed infestation and maintaining soil fertility. Depending on soil quality and farmer preference, the same field may be cropped twice but then must be left fallow longer. Typical fallow period ratios are 1:3 or 2:5 years, but there is great variability (see Cowgill 1962; Carter 1969; Secaira 1992; Fagan 2000). Fewer farmers reuse the burned milpa field twice (the 2:5 ratio), because productivity the second year is about 35 percent less than the first yield (Schwartz 1990). Beyond short fallows, Anne Osborn (1982) writes that Maya elders in Toledo reported to her that their ancestors once maintained a long fallow system of approximately fifty years.

7 Peteneros historically planted their two annual corn crops in a 2:1 ratio, sowing

more for the first (burned) milpa and leaving the second (mulched) milpa largely for home consumption (see also Collins 2001). William E. Carter (1969) observed at that time a shift toward marketing the second crop in the Izabal region.

8   See Hatse and De Ceuster 2001b for a study of highland Q'eqchi' traditions.

9   For more details on sustainable lowland cropping, see Nations and Nigh 1980 on Lacandón agriculture in neighboring Chiapas.

10 Juanita Sundberg (1998) places the blame on conservation NGOs, which are certainly easy targets for criticism, but critics must also take into account all the donor, corporate, and government pressures that shape NGO behavior.

11 The use of a Spanish term for private land underscores the cultural foreignness of the concept.

12 Atran et al. 2002 claims, for example, that Q'eqchi' people do not believe in forest spirits, yet they do, as evidenced by dozens of folktales narrated about them (Grandia 2004b). Scott Atran and his research team missed those beliefs because they apparently asked Q'eqchi' people about "duendes" (an unfamiliar Spanish term used by Itzá people to describe forest spirits) instead of using the term for "forest spirits" in the Q'eqchi' language.

13 Hecht, Rosa, and Kandel (2002) proposes a concept of "matrix ecology" that would place a conservation value on mosaic landscapes in places such as El Salvador, which has forest fragments, coffee plantations, agroforestry orchards, secondary growth, woodlots, abandoned fields and pastures, home gardens, and hedgerows.

14 Grünberg (2000) presents satellite data showing that cattle ranching still has the greatest impact on deforestation patterns but that the importance of smallholder clearing is increasing geometrically.

15 See Sutherland, Carr, and Curtis 2004: 8 for another analysis of data collected in Grandia et al. 2001 that confirms this trend.

16 Given high rates of birth and mortality, some people could not readily state their family size. More than once when I asked a father about this, he would reply, "Goodness, who knows?" (Saber Usted) and turn to his wife to ask, "How many children *do* we have?"

17 The main rumors are that birth control pills cause cancer or excessive weight changes, make women permanently infertile, or result in deformities in future children. Unfortunately, those most reluctant to use family planning methods are also those most at risk for maternal deaths associated with late pregnancy. Many women, even if they do not show signs of menopause, assume that they have already had all the children they are going to have after a certain point. One older woman joked with me, saying, "My plant has dried up," but had a baby the next year.

18 See Wasserstom 1978 for a historical analysis of how colonial exploitation, not the culture, of the Tzotzil Maya of Chiapas is to blame for environmental degradation in Chamula.

19 Likewise, while many environmentalists worry about the carbon emissions of swidden agriculture, few question the carbon emissions associated with the air travel of wealthy ecotourists who come to see the ancient Maya ruins of Tikal.

4. Speculating

Epigraph from Dowie 2009: 191.

1 See, for example, a historic 1998 edict issued by the Catholic Church: "The clamor for land is without a doubt, the loudest, most dramatic and most desperate cry heard in Guatemala today. It springs from the hearts of millions of Guatemalans who not only are anxious to possess land, but who also want to be possessed by the land" (cited in Manz 2004: 16).

2 For further critiques of these projects, see Garoz and Gauster 2002; Deere and León 1999; Saldívar and Wittman 2004; Sydow and Mendonça 2003; Worby 2000; World Bank 2006a; Grandia 2006.

3 Donors divided their funds as follows: the Netherlands (in Zacapa and Chiquimula), Germany (in Alta and Baja Verapaz), the European Union (in Sacatepéquez), Sweden (technical assistance and in the south coast), Norway (cartography), France (general), and the United Nations Development Program (research and financial administration) (Garoz and Gauster 2002).

4 Although UTJ was reorganized as RIC after 2005, I refer to the agency as UTJ because most of my field research took place between 2002 and 2004.

5 For similar conclusions, see a USAID report in Lastarria-Cornhiel 2003.

6 In 1989, land taxes represented just 2.2 percent of the tax base, while income taxes accounted for 22.1 percent and imports/exports for 24.9 percent. Such a skewed tax system hurts a small farmer trying to produce food exports for the international market more than a large landholder with idle fields. The powerful agribusiness sector, represented by CACIF, has thwarted four major attempts since the mid-1980s to raise property taxes (Gould 2001).

7 A project official told Kevin Gould (2009: 135) that Petén was ideal for the pilot phase because "it is scientifically demonstrated that the Maya disappeared [from Petén]—in other words, there are no great grandkids [to make claims]." Itzá, Ch'orti', Mopán, Pocomchi', and Q'eqchi' peoples born and raised in Petén might beg to disagree.

8 The subcontractors are allowed discretion up to a 10 percent margin of error in the allocation of encroachments claimed illegally outside parcel boundaries.

9 Many military officials and members of the economic elite were awarded parcels illegally in absentia; some were not even aware they had been given parcels in Petén (Schwartz 1987).

10 After all, every other aspect of their relationship to government was and is individualized—from birth registries to vaccine cards to national identification cards.

11 Demonstrating its importance to rural life, the verb "to be counted in a census" has been incorporated into the Q'eqchi' lexicon—"Did you get counted yet?" (*Ma ak xat censaak?*).

12 Q'eqchi' communities represent at least 90 percent of ACDIP's membership, but just 40 percent of Petén's overall population.

13 Some believe that the Candelaria network of caves in Chisec could be the actual

archaeological site of the underground world depicted in the Maya origin story of the Popul Vuh because they both have seven entrances.

14 Their Petén counterparts were certainly aware of these problems. In fact, many key staff members, in their private educational lives, are or were working on independent master's theses documenting the dispossession caused by the project. Although Gould (2009) did ethnographic research within the Petén UTJ project, curiously, he did not write about the doubts many of the technicians reveal in conversations outside the office.

5. From Colonial to Corporate Capitalisms

1 Q'eqchi' people tell stories of another immortal servant to the wealthy, known as *Laj Q'eq*, which translates roughly as "the Black Beast." Half man, half horse, this creature is said to have been brought to Guatemala by German coffee planters. It walks as fast as a car, works like a machine, and can throw even the fattest person over its shoulder. Late-night travelers swear to have witnessed the outline of such a beast by the light of the moon, smoking a cigarette underneath a tree on a nearby plantation. A voracious eater, *Laj Q'eq* requires copious amounts of food every day—dozens of eggs plus meat and more meat and handfuls of avocados. Only the rich can afford to maintain one, but, in return, *Laj Q'eq* will do great labor for the owner. Echoing Q'eqchi' experience, corporal punishment appears to be the only way to control *Laj Q'eq*.

2 Webster's II New Riverside University Dictionary has a similar etymology in English for the word "cattle," which derives from the Latin term *capitale*, meaning "property."

3 Contrary to common misconceptions, the guerrilla insurgency and civil war actually started in eastern Guatemala between 1966 and 1968 and not among Maya people of the western highlands (Schwartz 1990). Ranchers took advantage of the chaos to expand their pastures, and military commanders established their own ranches in these eastern conflict zones on land they received from the government (Williams 1986).

4 A report published by an Argentine firm, Latinoconsult, was influential in the 1960s and 1970s in arguing not only that cattle ranching was the best land use for Petén but that it would be more profitable if FYDEP awarded large concessions to ranchers (Kaimowitz 1995).

5 Beef is said to have high income elasticity—in other words, the demand for beef increases disproportionately in relation to even small improvements in per capita income (Edelman 1995).

6 Another proxy measure would be membership lists of ranchers' associations as used by David Kaimowitz (1997).

7 This is a classic trick of debt peonage, to offer a daily wage for tasks that are impossible to complete in a day (Cambranes 1985).

8 River access saves ranchers considerable investments in wells or watering holes and transportation to market.

9   The infamous massacre of Q'eqchi' peasants at Panzós in 1978 was a result of land conflicts caused by the expansion of cattle ranching into the Polochic Valley (Secaira 1992; Williams 1986: 147).

10 Ranchers prefer to hire a married man as a cowboy because his wife will care for other domestic animals, such as barnyard fowl, and might cook for the owner when he visits. Absentee ranchers with fewer head of cattle may share a cowboy with a neighboring cattle owner. A cowboy's typical wage is $130 a month, plus rights to plant a subsistence corn plot and consume milk from the cows; some ranchers do pay government benefits for health insurance and social security but most generally do not.

11 Norman Schwartz (1990: 108) has the same estimate of one cowboy per five hundred head of cattle.

12 Certainly, cattle rustling, extortion, kidnappings, and armed robberies are on the rise across Guatemala, leaving absentee owners increasingly reluctant to visit their properties. Much of the prestige and pleasure of having a ranch is being able to visit on the weekends and show off one's possessions to friends and family. These trips also facilitate management decisions about when to sell and what inputs are needed (in lieu of those magical *Seleeq* dwarves, described earlier). When co-owners José Díaz and Jorge Vargas clearly would have preferred to rest in hammocks after lunch, their conscientious cowboy insisted that several steers needed vaccinations and "cattle fatten only when beheld by the eyes of the owner."

13 After taking advantage of public libraries in Michigan to learn about the latest techniques in cattle raising, he is experimenting with the use of feed supplements for a few weeks before slaughter (a mix of molasses, soy, and corn) in order to improve the meat grade (known as "feedin' 'em cut" in the U.S. Midwest) (D. Grandia, pers. comm., 2005).

14 Although many ranchers are no longer registering their branding designs because of banditry, it was still a reliable source of information in 2003.

15 See Tucker 2000: 327 on the involvement of Quaker and Seventh Day Adventist missionaries in the Costa Rican cattle sector.

6. The Neoliberal Auction

1   The Mexican states included in the plan are Chiapas, Oaxaca, Guerrero, Quintana Roo, Yucatán, Campeche, Tabasco, and Veracruz.

2   Other lenders include the World Bank, the European Union, the Andean Development Corporation, the Central American Integration Bank, USAID, and bilateral aid agencies from Japan and Spain that are well known for funding infrastructure. The World Bank was clearly involved in early planning documents but retreated upon early public outcry to the PPP.

3   Some Central Americans view the PPP as "Mexican imperialism" and point to the incongruity of its name, which equates a Mexican state (Puebla) with a Central American country (Panama) (Bartra 2004).

4 One of Kevin Gould's (2009: 99) interviews provides a fascinating insider perspective on how IDB managers plant ideas and get projects moving behind the scenes: "We need projects to come from the countries. So what we do is we put some people down there in this [policy institution] and their job is to foment projects ... not design projects, but get the conceptual idea for projects and to sell it in the country, and then [the country representatives] come to the bank and say, 'Hey, we need this project,' and [together we] get it into the pipeline and get it started."

5 Organized into the Association of Communities for Development and in Defense of Territory and National Resources (ACODET), they called a historic referendum against the project in April 2007. Of the 19,911 participants from 144 communities, 90 percent voted against both the Xalalá dam and a petroleum exploration license awarded in the region (Kern 2007). In part because of the vocal opposition of the communities, this particular dam project received no bids in November 2009, even though it expects up to $150 million in annual profits (Comer 2009).

6 I was deeply involved in lobbying against the DR-CAFTA, so much of the information in this section comes from conferences, talks, conversations, and gray literature circulated among activists.

7 Activists testified to this at the 2005 World Social Forum.

8 This includes changes to government contract rules. No longer can Central American countries give preference to home industries; for any contract that exceeds $117,000 (eventually to be lowered to $58,550), governments will have to open bidding to transnational corporations.

9 Frustrated that the company ignored their complaints, communities in San Marcos, a western highland department, organized a movement, FRENA, to denounce high electricity bills and advocate for municipal management of electricity as an essential public service. One of its leaders, Evelinda Ramírez, was assassinated on January 13, 2010, on her way home from meetings with government officials in the capital (NISGUA 2010).

10 The national per capita consumption of corn is 100 kilograms (295 pounds) per year, based on a per capita corn consumption of 454 grams (1 pound) in the rural areas and 102 grams in urban areas. On average, corn provides 65 percent of carbohydrate and 71 percent of protein needs (Fuentes Lopez et al. 2005).

11 Women also help the men with certain stages of corn cultivation, and female-headed households grow corn for themselves. Overall in Guatemala, though, corn cultivation remains primarily a male-led task and corn processing a female-led task. Spiritual beliefs about corn are also deeply gendered, with the earth seen as a "mother" into whom a seed is planted. Traditional Q'eqchi' couples continue to practice sexual abstinence before planting, and some Q'eqchi' men will offer sacrifices inside caves, which are symbolic of the womb of the earth.

12 Nevertheless, the IDB is pushing forward with what it is calling the South American Regional Integration Initiative. There are also compelling similarities between the MBC/PPP and the Proyecto BioPacífico/Plan Pacífico, both funded by the IDB.

Conclusion

Epigraph from Edmonson 1982: vi.

1   The base of the Maya calendar is a *winal*, or 20 days (equivalent to the number of fingers and toes on the human body). Eighteen *winals* make a *tun* (360 days plus a 5-day *wayeb'* complete a solar year). Twenty *tuns*, in turn, form a *katun* (7,200 days), and twenty *katuns* constitute a *baktun* (144,000 days).

2   As for the outcome of the chaos, the prophecies remain ambiguous; there may be a positive shift to a new way of life—or an apocalyptic future.

3   Nor have Marxists paid much attention to these "extra-economic" variables since they do not fit into a model of class struggle. Like the classical political economists who realized that "self-provisioning did not have to be restricted on account of its failure, but rather because of its success" (Perelman 2000: 370), Marx shared an antagonism to small-scale, independent producers (whether peasants or other small family businesses), exemplified by his infamous comment in the *Eighteenth Brumaire* describing peasants as "potatoes in a sack."

4   This is similar to Sol Tax's study (1953) of the western highland Maya economy, which showed that indigenous town residents clearly preferred trading over seasonal labor on plantations, market production over trading, and autochthonous farming above all.

5   Writing from the context of World War II, Polanyi viewed humanity as being at a crossroads. Under conditions of "cataclysmic" change, societies could either opt for re-embedding the market within society through deepened democracy (for example, Franklin Roosevelt's New Deal as a response to the Great Depression) or be propelled toward fascism (Germany's response to its economic crisis after World War I).

6   As Samir Amin (1977) pointed out in his dependency critiques (and as the rise of Islamic fundamentalists further reminds us), one can be anti-capitalist without being socialist (Harvey 2003: 172).

7   Consumption as a controlling process (Nader 1997) is not a new phenomenon, but it is accelerating. As described in Mintz's *Sweetness and Power* (1985), the transformation of sugar from a luxury commodity to an everyday necessity in the working-class diet was a critical factor in the cultural shift from mercantilism to industrial capitalism. The more people want to buy, or must buy, the more dependent they become on their wages and the less likely they are to question the conditions of employment.

8   Marx himself anticipated that public debt (e.g., treasury bonds) and the international credit system would become "the most powerful levers of primitive accumulation," working like an "enchanter's wand" to turn nonexistent money into capital (1976: 919).

9   Harking back to dependency theory, they emphasize that the global South was not merely *un*developed but *under*developed as a consequence of the *over*development (or, more precisely, the greed) of the global North. Shattering a key myth of modernity, they make a connection between increased poverty and the accelerating accumulation of wealth.

10 On the Gulf Coast of Alabama in Mobile Bay near where my parents live, local people ring bells announcing a jubilee whenever a red tide kills the fish and anyone may gather them for free (J. Grandia, pers. comm., April 2007).

BIBLIOGRAPHY

Adams, Abigail E. 1999. "Word, Work, and Worship: Engendering Evangelical Culture between Highland Guatemala and the United States." PhD diss., University of Virginia. 329 pages.

———. 2001. "The Transformation of the *Tzuultaq'a*: Jorge Ubico, Protestants and Other Verapaz Maya at the Crossroads of Community, State and Transnational Interests." *Journal of Latin American Anthropology* 6(2): 198–233.

Adams, Richard N. 1965. *Migraciones Internas en Guatemala: Expansión Agraria de los Indígenas Kekchíes hacía El Petén*. Guatemala City: Centro Editorial Jose de Pineda Ibarra, Ministerio de Educación.

———. 1993. "Draft: Notes on Ethnicity in the Army of Liberal Guatemala, 1870–1915." 16 pages.

Adams, Tani Marilena. 1982. *Mining Guatemala and Nickel: Transformation of a Region and the Organization of an Industrial Workforce by a Foreign Enterprise in Guatemala*. December, unpublished manuscript. Antigua, Guatemala: Centro de Investigaciones Regionales de Mesoamérica, Archives.

Agrawal, Arun, and K. Sivaramakrishnan, eds. 2000. *Agrarian Environments: Resources, Representations and Rule in India*. Durham, N.C.: Duke University Press.

Aguilera Peralta, Gabriel. 1979. "The Massacre at Panzos and Capitalist Development in Guatemala." *Monthly Review* 31(7): 13–23.

Aguirre Beltrán, Gonzalo. 1979. *Regions of Refuge*. Washington, D.C.: Society for Applied Anthropology.

Alonso Fradejas, Alberto, Fernando Alonzo, and Jochen Dürr. 2008. *Caña de Azucar y Palma Africana: Combustibles para un Nuevo Ciclo de Acumulación y Dominio en Guatemala*. Guatemala City: CONGCOOP y Magna Terra Editores.

Alonso Fradejas, Alberto, and Susana Gauster. 2006. *Perspectivas Para la Agricultura Familiar Campesina de Guatemala en un Contexto DR-CAFTA*. Red ComAgri: Construyendo una Red Latinoamericana de la Agricultura, Desarrollo y Comercio. Guatemala City: CONGCOOP, Mesa Global, Alianza Social Continental Action Aid, and IDRC.

Alvarado Pinetta, Edgar, and Federico Alvarado Gonzalez. 1981. *La Agricultura en*

Guatemala. Cámara del Agro de Guatemala and Asociación de Amigos del País. Guatemala City: Editorial Académica Centroamerica, S.A.

Amin, Samir. 1977. *Imperialism and Unequal Development*. New York: Monthly Review Press.

Andreasson, Stefan. 2006. "Stand and Deliver: Private Property and the Politics of Global Dispossession." *Political Studies* 54: 3–22.

Anthony, David. 1990. "Migration in Archaeology: The Baby and the Bathwater." *American Anthropologist* 92(4): 895–914.

Arendt, Hannah. 1973. *The Origins of Totalitarianism*. New York: Harcourt Trade.

Arizpe, Lourdes, M. Priscilla Stone, and David C. Major, eds. 1994. *Population and Environment: Rethinking the Debate*. Boulder, Colo.: Westview Press.

Aronson, Naomi. 1980. "Working Up an Appetite." In *A Woman's Conflict: The Special Relationship between Women and Food*, edited by Jane Rachel Kaplan, 203–29. Englewood Cliffs, N.J.: Prentice-Hall.

Arriola, Luis Alfredo. 2005. "Agency at the Frontier and the Building of Territoriality in the Naranjo-Ceibo Corridor, Petén, Guatemala." PhD diss., University of Florida, Gainesville. 324 pages.

Asturias, Miguel Angel. 1993. *Men of Maize*. Translated by Gerald Martin. UNESCO Colleción Archivos. Pittsburgh, Pa.: University of Pittsburgh Press.

Atran, Scott, Douglas Medin, Norbert Ross, Elizabeth Lynch, John Coley, Edilberto Ucan Ek', and Valentina Vapnarsky. 2002. "Folkecology, Cultural Epidemiology, and the Spirit of the Commons: A Garden Experiment in the Maya Lowlands, 1991–2001." *Current Anthropology* 43(3): 421–50.

AVANSCO and SERJUS (Asociación para el Avance de las Ciencias Sociales en Guatemala and Servicios Jurídicos y Sociales). 2003. *Amenazas y Oportunidades del Plan Puebla Panamá*, 1st edition. Guatemala City: AVANCSO and SERJUS.

Bac, Rigoberto. 2000. *Aatinaqo Sa' Q'eqchi' Mayab': Hablemos en Q'eqchi'*. Guatemala City: Academia de Lenguas Mayas de Guatemala.

Balzac, Honoré de. 2004. *Le Pére Goriot*. Translated by Ellen Marriage. Mineola, N.Y.: Dover Publications.

Barreda, Carlos. 2006. "DR-CAFTA Imposition and Poverty in Guatemala." In *Stop CAFTA Monitoring Report: DR-CAFTA in Year One*, September 12, Stop CAFTA Coalition, 19–25. www.stopcafta.org.

Barreda Marín, Andrés. 2004. "The Dangers of the Plan Puebla Panama." In *Profound Rivers of Mesoamerica: Alternatives to Plan Puebla Panama*, edited by Armando Bartra, 131–208. 3d ed. Mexico City: Instituto Maya, El Atajo, and Mexico Solidarity Network.

Bartra, Armando, ed. 2004. *Profound Rivers of Mesoamerica: Alternatives to Plan Puebla Panama*. 3d ed. Mexico City: Instituto Maya, El Atajo, and Mexico Solidarity Network.

Basurto, Xavier, and Ostrom Elinor. 2009. "The Core Challenges of Moving Beyond Garrett Hardin." *Journal of Natural Resources Policy Research* 1(3): 255–59.

Bateson, Mary Catherine. 1998. "Can the Commons Exist without Common Decency

and Common Sense?" *Whole Earth Review*, Fall. http://findarticles.com/p/articles/
mi_moGER/is_n94/ai_21260233/.

Beals, R. 1952. "Notes on Acculturation." In *Heritage of Conquest: The Ethnology of
Middle America*, edited by Sol Tax, 229–32. Glencoe, Ill.: Free Press.

Beaudry-Corbett, Marilyn, and Ellen T. Hardy, eds. 2000. *Early Scholars' Visits to
Central America: Reports by Karl Sapper, Walter Lehmann, and Franz Termer.*
Translated by Theodore E. Gutman. Occasional Paper 18. Los Angeles: Cotsen
Institute of Archaeology, University of California, Los Angeles.

Bell, Beverly. 2009. May/June. Interview. *Multinational Monitor* 30(3): 35–38.

Bello, Walden. 1994. "Adjusting America." In *Dark Victory: The United States, Structural Adjustment and Global Poverty*, edited by Walden Bello, Shea Cunningham,
and Bill Rau, 86–104. London: Pluto; Oakland, Calif.: Food First.

Berkey, Curtis. 1994. "Maya Land Rights in Belize and the History of Indian Reserva-
tions: Report to the Toledo Maya Cultural Council." Washington, D.C.: Indian
Law Resource Center, May 1. 45 pages.

Bertrand, Michael. 1989. "La Tierra y Los Hombres: La Sociedad Rural en Baja Verapaz
Durante Los Siglos XVI al XIX." In *La Sociedad Colonial en Guatemala: Estudios
Regionales y Locales*, edited by Stephen Webre. Antigua, Guatemala: Centro de
Investigaciones Regionales de Mesoamérica y Plumsock Mesoamerican Studies.

Biermann, Benno M. 1971. "Bartolome de las Casas and Verapaz." In *Bartolome de
las Casas in History: Toward an Understanding of the Man and His Work*, edited
by Juan Friede and Benjamin Keen, 443–84. DeKalb: Northern Illinois University
Press.

Blaikie, Piers, and Harold Brookfield. 1987. *Land Degradation and Society.* London:
Methuen.

Bobrow-Strain, Aaron. 2004. "(Dis)Accords: The Politics of Market-Assisted Land
Reforms in Chiapas, Mexico." *World Development* 32(6): 887–903.

———. 2007. *Intimate Enemies: Landowners, Power, and Violence in Chiapas.* Durham, N.C.: Duke University Press.

Bollier, David. 2001. "The Cornucopia of the Commons." *YES! Magazine*, Summer, 4.

———. 2002a. "Reclaiming the Commons." *Boston Review: A Political and Literary
Forum*, Summer. http://bostonreview.net/BR27.3/bollier.html.

———. 2002b. *Silent Theft: The Plunder of Our Common Wealth.* New York: Routledge.

Bonfil Batalla, Guillermo. 1996. *México Profundo: Reclaiming a Civilization.* Austin:
University of Texas Press.

Borras, Saturnino M. 2005. "The Underlying Assumptions, Theory, and Practice of
Neoliberal Land Policies." Land Research Action Network, September 5. www.
landaction.org. 27 pages.

Bourdieu, Pierre. 1998. *Acts of Resistance: Against the Tyranny of the Market.* New
York: New Press.

Bourque, Martin Robert. 1989. "Local Solutions to Regional Problems: The Use of Velvet Bean in San Luis, Petén, Guatemala." Master's thesis, University of California,
San Diego, Latin American Studies. 91 pages.

Brandon, Katrina, Kent H. Redford, and Steven E. Sanderson. 1998. *Parks in Peril: People, Politics, and Protected Areas.* Washington, D.C.: Island Press.

Bricker, Victoria Reifler, and Helga-Maria Miram, eds. and trans. 2002. *Encounter of Two Worlds: The Book of Chilam Balam of Kaua.* New Orleans, La.: Middle American Research Institute, Tulane University.

Brockett, Charles D. 1998. *Land, Power, and Poverty: Agrarian Transformation and Political Conflict in Central America.* Boulder, Colo.: Westview Press.

Brown, Cecil H. 2006. "Glottochronology and the Chronology of Maize in the Americas." In *Histories of Maize: Multidisciplinary Approaches to the Prehistory, Linguistics, Biogeography, Domestication, and Evolution of Maize,* edited by J. E. Staller, R. H. Tykot, and B. F. Benz, 648–64. New York: Elsevier.

Caal Xi, Dario. 1992. La Tierra en la Cosmovisión Maya y Sus Incidencias en la Vida, Política, y Económica. Seminario Taller Sobre la Tenencia de la Tierra, Tierra Sagrada, Loq'laj Ch'och. Pastoral Social, Diocesis de Verapaz, Cobán, Guatemala. July 13–26.

Cabarrus, Carlos. 1974. *La Cosmovisión K'ekchi' en Proceso de Cambio.* Cobán, Guatemala: Centro San Benito.

Cahuec del Valle, Eleuterio, et al. 1997. *Historia y Memorias de la Comunidad Etnica Q'eqchi': Volumen II,* edited by Guillermina Herrera. Guatemala City: Universidad Rafael Landivar y UNICEF.

Call, Wendy. 2003a. "PPP Focus Moves South as Mexican Backing Loses Momentum." In *Citizen Action, PPP Spotlight #1,* vol. 2003, edited by Americas Program. February 20. www.americaspolicy.org.

———. 2003b. "Public Relations Firm to the Rescue of Plan Puebla-Panama." In *Citizen Action, PPP Spotlight #4,* vol. 2003, edited by Americas Program. September 10. www.americaspolicy.org.

Cambranes, Julio C. 1985. *Coffee and Peasants: The Origins of the Modern Plantation Economy in Guatemala, 1853–1897.* South Woodstock, Vt.: CIRMA/Plumsock Mesoamerican Studies.

Campbell, Anthony Gerald. 2003. "The Struggle for Livelihoods through Community in North Izabal, Guatemala (1970–2002)." PhD diss., University of Southampton, School of Modern Languages. 167 pages.

Carlson, Laura. 2007. "NAFTA Free Trade Myths Lead to Farm Failure in Mexico." In *Americas Program Policy Report,* December 6, edited by Center for International Policy (CIP). http://americas.irc-online.org/am/4794.

Carr, David L. 2004. "Ladino and Q'eqchí Maya Land Use and Land Clearing in the Sierra de Lacandón National Park, Petén, Guatemala." *Agriculture and Human Values* 21:171–70.

Carr, H. Sorayya. 1996. "Precolumbian Maya Exploitation and Management of Deer Populations." In *The Managed Mosaic: Ancient Maya Agriculture and Resource Use,* edited by Scott Fedick, 251–61. Salt Lake City: University of Utah Press.

Carter, William E. 1969. *New Lands and Old Traditions: Kekchi Cultivators in the Guatemalan Lowlands.* Gainesville: University of Florida Press.

Casasola, Oliverio. 1968. *Grandezas y Miserias del Petén.* Guatemala City: Talleres Tipográficos Zapa.

Casper, Angela. 2004. "Plan Puebla Panamá: Iniciativa Mesoamericana de Desarrollo Sostenible: Perfiles de Proyectos Prioritarios, Componente Ambiental." BID-IMDS/P. February 9. 21 pages.

Catholic Church, Bishops of Guatemala. 1988. "A Pastoral Letter, 'The Cry for Land.'"

Central Intelligence Agency. 1968. Intelligence Memorandum, "Guatemala: The Problem of Poverty." Available through George Washington University, National Security Archive Microfiche NSA 00370.

Chacón Véliz, M. A. 2003. "Challenges of Public Participation in Land Dispute Resolution with Geographic Information Systems in Guatemala." PhD diss., State University of New York, Department of Geography. 304 pages.

Chapin, Mac. 2004. "A Challenge to Conservationists." *World Watch Magazine* November/December: 17–31.

Chayanov, Aleksandr V. 1986. *The Theory of Peasant Economy.* Madison: University of Wisconsin Press. (Orig. pub. 1925.)

Chevalier, Francois. 1963. *Land and Society in Colonial Mexico: The Great Hacienda.* Berkeley: University of California Press.

Ciriacy-Wantrup, S. V., and R. C. Bishop. 1975. "'Common Property' as a Concept in Natural Resources Policy." *Natural Resources Journal* 15(4): 713–27.

Clare, John. 1984. *The Oxford Authors: John Clare.* New York: Oxford University Press.

Collier, George Allen, with Elizabeth Lowery Quaratiello. 1994. *Basta!: Land and the Zapatista Rebellion in Chiapas.* Oakland, Calif.: Food First Books.

Collins, Darron Asher. 2001. "From Woods to Weeds: Cultural and Ecological Transformations in Alta Verapaz, Guatemala." PhD diss., Tulane University. 393 pp.

Comer, Carrie. 2009. "Not with Bullets or Machetes: Popular Resistance to Xalala Dam Finds International Law on Its Side." *The Dominion: News from the Grassroots,* issue 59, April 5. http://www.dominionpaper.ca/articles/2497.

Comisión de Apoyo y Acompañamiento Para la Legalización de la Tenencia de la Tierra. 2002. "Diagnóstico Sobre la Situación Socioeconómica y el Estado en el Proceso de Regularización y Legalización de Tierras de Comunidades Ubicadas en los Deparatamentos [sic] de Quiché, Alta Verapaz e Izabal que Son Apoyadas por las Instituciones Miembros de la Comisión de Tierras." Catholic Relief Services. July. 84 pages.

Conklin, Beth, and Laura Graham. 1995. "The Shifting Middle Ground: Amazonian Indians and Eco-Politics." *American Anthropologist* 9(4): 695–710.

Corzo, Amilcar Rolando. 2003. "Proyectos de Desarrollo y Conservación en El Departamento de Petén, Guatemala, Centroamérica, Una Revisión Histórica." Flores, Petén: Fundación ProPetén, y Centro Universitario de El Petén, USAC. May.

Cowgill, Ursula. 1962. "An Agricultural Study of the Southern Maya Lowlands." *American Anthropologist* 64(2): 273–86.

Coy Caal, Jorge Leobaldo. 2002. "Análisis de la Tenencia de la Tierra en Cuatro Comunidades de la Franja Transversal del Norte." Master's thesis, Universidad de Rafael Landívar, Cobán, Guatemala.

Crosby, Alfred W. 1972. *The Columbian Exchange: Biological and Cultural Consequences of 1492*. Westport, Conn.: Greenwood Publishing.

Danaher, Kevin. 1994. *50 Years Is Enough: The Case against the World Bank and the International Monetary Fund*. Boston: South End Press.

Danien, Elin C., ed. 2005. *Maya Folktales from the Alta Verapaz*. Philadelphia: University of Pennsylvania Museum Press.

De Angelis, Massimo. 2004. "Separating the Doing and the Deed: Capital and the Continuous Character of Enclosures." *Historical Materialism* 12(2): 57–87.

de Borhegyi, Stephen F. 1954. "The Cult of Our Lord Esquipulas in Middle America and New Mexico." *El Palacio* 61(12): 387–401.

de la Cruz Torres, Mario. 1982. "Monografía del Municipio de San Antonio, Senahú." *Guatemala Indígena* 7(3–4): 1–176.

de las Casas, Bartolomé. 1992. *A Short Account of the Destruction of the Indies*. Translated by N. Griffin. New York: Penguin Classics. (Orig. pub. 1552.)

de Soto, Hernando. 2000. *The Mystery of Capital: Why Capitalism Triumphs in the West and Fails Everywhere Else*. New York: Basic Books.

DeChicchis, Joseph. 1986. "The Kekchi and Their Language in Guatemala and Belize." Antigua, Guatemala: Centro de Investigaciones Regionales de Mesoamérica, Archives, October 4. 31 pages.

Deere, Carmen Diana, and Magdalena León. 1999. *Mujer y Tierra en Guatemala*. Autores Invitados No. 4. Guatemala City: Asociación para el Avance de la Ciencias Sociales en Guatemala (AVANCSO).

Deininger, Klaus. 2003. "Land Rights for Poor People Key to Poverty Reduction, Growth: Summary of a World Bank Policy Research Report." Washington, D.C.: Center for International Private Enterprise. 3 pages.

Deininger, Klaus, and Hans Binswanger. 1999. "The Evolution of the World Bank's Land Policy: Principles, Experience and Future Challenges." *World Bank Research Observer* 14(2): 247–76.

del Cid, Mario, and David Ricardo Garcia. n.d. "Cuevas Candelaria: Desmitificando La Participación Comunitaria en la Conservación del Patrimonio." Counterpart International, Chisec, Guatemala. 15 pages.

Demarest, Arthur A., Prudence M. Rice, and Don S. Rice. 2004. *The Terminal Classic in the Maya Lowlands: Collapse, Transition, and Transformation*. Boulder, Colo.: University Press of Colorado.

Dillon, Brian D. 1985. "Preface to Karl Sapper's Book." In *The Verapaz in the Sixteenth and Seventeenth Centuries: A Contribution to the Historical Geography and Ethnography of Northeastern Guatemala*, by Karl Sapper, translated by Theodore E. Gutman. Los Angeles: Institute of Archaeology, University of California, Los Angeles.

Doukas, Dimitra. 2003. *Worked Over: The Corporate Sabotage of an American Community*. Ithaca, N.Y.: Cornell University Press.

Dowie, Mark. 2009. *Conservation Refugees: The Hundred-Year Conflict between Global Conservation and Native Peoples*. Cambridge, Mass.: MIT Press.

Downing, Theodore E., Susana B. Hecht, Henry A. Pearson, and Carmen Garcia-

Downing. 1992. *Development or Destruction: The Conversion of Tropical Forest to Pasture in Latin America.* Boulder, Colo.: Westview Press.

Doyle, Kate. 2002. *Death Squads, Guerrilla War, Covert Operations, and Genocide: Guatemala and the United States, 1954–1999.* Washington, D.C.: National Security Archive, George Washington University.

Dozier, Craig L. 1969. *Land Development and Colonization in Latin America: Case Studies of Peru, Bolivia, and Mexico.* New York: Frederick A. Praeger.

Early, John D. 1982. *The Demographic Structure and Evolution of a Peasant System: The Guatemala Population.* Boca Raton: University Presses of Florida.

Edelman, Marc. 1987. "From Costa Rican Pasture to North American Hamburger." In *Food and Evolution: Toward a Theory of Human Food Habits,* edited by Marvin Harris and Eric B. Ross. Philadelphia: Temple University Press.

———. 1995. "Rethinking the Hamburger Thesis: Deforestation and the Crisis of Central America's Beef Export." In *The Social Causes of Environmental Deforestation in Latin America,* edited by Michael Painter and William Durham, 25–62. Ann Arbor: University of Michigan Press.

———. 1999. *Peasants against Globalization: Rural Social Movements in Costa Rica.* Stanford, Calif.: Stanford University Press.

———. 2004. "Farm Politics and CAFTA." LASA (Latin American Studies Association) Annual Meeting, Las Vegas.

———. 2005. "Bringing the Moral Economy Back In . . . To the Study of 21st-Century Transnational Peasant Movements." *American Anthropologist* 107(3): 331–45.

Edelman, Marc, and Angelique Haugerud. 2005. *The Anthropology of Development and Globalization: From Classical Political Economy to Contemporary Neoliberalism.* Malden, Mass.: Blackwell.

Edmonson, Munroe S. 1982. *The Ancient Future of the Itza: The Books of Chilam Balam of Tizimin.* Texas Pan American Series. Austin: University of Texas Press.

Elton, Catherine. 2004. "Berger's Dam Plans Face Difficult Test." *EcoAméricas,* September, 6–8.

Engels, Friedrich. 1959. "Excerpt: The Origin of the Family, Private Property and the State." In *Karl Marx and Friedrich Engels: Basic Writings on Politics and Philosophy,* edited by Lewis S. Feuer, 392–95. New York: Anchor Books.

Engler, Mark. 2006. "CAFTA's Corpse Revived." *Nation,* March 1. www.thenation.org.

Fagan, Christopher T. 2000. "Cultural and Economic Constraints to Farming in a Core-Zone Community of the Maya Biosphere Reserve, Guatemala." Master's thesis, Duke University. 54 pages.

Falla, Ricardo. 1980. "Chisec: Tierras, Caminos y Petroleo en la FTN." April. 126 pages.

Farriss, Nancy M. 1984. *Maya Society under Colonial Rule: The Collective Enterprise of Survival.* Princeton, N.J.: Princeton University Press.

Fay, Chip, and Genevieve Michon. 2003. "Redressing Forestry Hegemony: Where a Forestry Regulatory Framework Is Best Replaced by an Agrarian One." International Conference on Rural Livelihoods, Forests and Biodiversity. Bonn, May 19–23.

Federici, Silvia. 2004. *Caliban and the Witch: Women, the Body, and Primitive Accumulation.* Brooklyn, N.Y.: Autonomedia.

Fedick, Scott, ed. 1996. *The Managed Mosaic: Ancient Maya Agriculture and Resource Use.* Salt Lake City: University of Utah Press.

Ferguson, B. G., J. Vandermeer, H. Morales, and D. M. Griffith. 2003. "Post-agricultural Succession in El Petén, Guatemala." *Conservation Biology* 17: 818–28.

Fernside, Philip. 1986. *Human Carrying Capacity of the Brazilian Rainforest.* New York: Columbia University Press.

Foucault, Michel. 1977. *Discipline and Punish: The Birth of the Prison.* New York: Pantheon Books.

Fuentes López, Mario Roberto, Jacob van Etten, José Luis Vivero Pol, and Ávaro Ortega Aparicio. 2005. *Maiz para Guatemala: Propuesta para la Reactivación de la Cadena Agroalimentaria del Maíz Blanco y Amarillo.* Guatemala City: FAO, Organización de las Naciones Unidas para la Agricultura y la Alimentación.

Fuentes-Mohr, A. 1955. "Land Settlement and Agrarian Reform in Guatemala." *International Journal of Agrarian Affairs* 2: 26–36.

G. Donovan Holder and Associates. 1999. "Review of Agriculture in Southern Region of Belize." Environmental, Social and Technical Assistance Project and the Ministry of Economic Development. May. 306 pages.

García Márquez, Gabriel. 1970. *One Hundred Years of Solitude.* New York: Harper & Row.

Garoz, Byron, and Susana Gauster. 2002. *FONTIERRAS: El Model de Mercado y el Acceso a la Tierra en Guatemala, Balance y Perspectivas.* Guatemala City: IDRC Canada.

Gobierno de Guatemala. 1964. "Ante-Proyecto de Desarrollo Integral, Sebol-Chinaja." Dirección General de Asuntos Agrarios, Guatemala City. October 16.

Goldman, Michael. 2006. *Imperial Nature: The World Bank and Struggles for Social Justice in the Age of Globalization.* New Haven, Conn.: Yale University Press.

Gomez Lanza, Helio. 1983. *Desarrollo Histórico de la Verapaz y la Conquista Pacífica.* Publicaciones Especiales, Segunda Epoca, No. 1. Guatemala City: Ministerio de Educación.

Gómez, Rossana. 2005. "Liberalización, Un Modelo que Arraiga la Dependencia." Universidad de San Carlos de Guatemala, Dirección General de Investigación (DIGI). 18 pages.

Góngora Zetina, Mirtala Concepción. 1984. "La Tenencia de la Tierra en el Departamento de El Petén y Su Legislación." Licenciatura thesis, Universidad de San Carlos, Guatemala. 154 pages.

Gould, Kevin A. 2001. "Land Titling in an Agricultural Frontier, Petén Guatemala." Master's thesis, University of Florida, Gainesville. 140 pages.

———. 2006. "Land Regularization on Agricultural Frontiers: The Case of Northwestern Peten, Guatemala." *Land Use Policy* 23(4): 395–407.

———. 2009. "Marking Land, Producing Markets: The Making of a Guatemalan Rural Land Market." PhD diss., University of British Columbia. 214 pages.

Gould, Kevin A., D. R. Carter, and R. K. Shrestha. 2006. "Extra-legal Land Market

Dynamics on a Guatemalan Agricultural Frontier: Implications for Neoliberal Land Policies." *Land Use Policy* 23(4): 408–20.

Gramsci, Antonio. 1971. *Selections from the Prison Notebooks.* New York: International Publishers.

Grandia, Liza. 1996. "From Dawn 'Til Dawn: Valuing Women's Work in the Petén, Guatemala." BA thesis, Yale University. 183 pages.

———. 2000. "Cuantas Personas Quiere que Vivan en Petén?" In *Nuevas Perspectivas de Desarrollo Sostenible en Petén,* edited by Facultad Latinoamericana de Ciencias Sociales, 137–56. Guatemala City: FLACSO.

———. 2004a. "From the Q'eqchi' Kitchen: Recipes of Traditional Corn, Forest, and Milpa Foods from the Sarstoon-Temash Villages." Punta Gorda, Belize: Sarstoon Temash Institute for Indigenous Management. 23 pages.

———. 2004b. "Stories from the Sarstoon Temash: Traditional Q'eqchi' Tales by the Elders from Crique Sarco, Sunday Wood, Conejo, and Midway Villages (Toledo District, Belize)." Punta Gorda, Belize: Sarstoon Temash Institute for Indigenous Management. 78 pages.

———. 2004c. "The Wealth Report: Q'eqchi' Traditional Knowledge and Natural Resource Management in the Sarstoon-Temash National Park." Punta Gorda, Belize: Sarstoon Temash Institute for Indigenous Management. 96 pages.

———. 2005. "An Honest Mistake?" Common Dreams.org, April 5. http://www.commondreams.org/views05/0405-22.htm.

———. 2006. "Unsettling: Land Dispossession and Enduring Inequity for the Q'eqchi' Maya in the Guatemalan and Belizean Frontier Colonization Process." PhD diss., University of California, Berkeley. 553 pages.

———. 2007. "Between Bolivar and Bureaucracy: The Mesoamerican Biological Corridor." *Conservation and Society* 5(4): 478–503. Special issue, *Engaging Neoliberal Conservation,* edited by Jim Igoe and Dan Brockington.

———. 2009a. "Milpa Matters: Maya Communities of Toledo v. Government of Belize." In *Waging War, Making Peace: Reparations and Human Rights,* edited by B. R. Johnston and S. Slyomovics, 153–82. Walnut Creek, Calif.: Left Coast Press.

———. 2009b. "Raw Hides: Hegemony and Cattle in Guatemala's Northern Lowlands." In *Geoforum* 40: 720–31. Special issue, *Land, Labor, Livestock and (Neo)Liberalism: Historical and Contemporary Transformations in Pastoralism and Ranching,* edited by Nathan Sayre.

———. 2009c. *Tz'aptz'ooqeb': El Despojo Recurrente al Pueblo Q'eqchi'.* Autores Invitados No. 20. Guatemala City: AVANCSO (Asociación para el Avance de las Ciencias Sociales en Guatemala with Siglo XXI Editores) with Oxfam–Great Britain.

Grandia, Liza, Norman B. Schwartz, Amilcar Corzo, Oscar Obando, and Luis H. Ochoa. 2001. *Salud, Migración y Recursos Naturales en Petén: Resultados del Módulo Ambiental en la Encuesta de Salud Materno Infantil 1999.* Guatemala City: Macro Internacional, USAID, Instituto Nacional de Estadística.

Grandin, Greg. 2004. *The Last Colonial Massacre: Latin America and the Cold War.* Chicago: University of Chicago Press.

Grieb, Kenneth J. 1979. *Guatemalan Caudillo: The Regime of Jorge Ubico, Guatemala, 1931–44*. Athens: Ohio University Press.

Grünberg, Georg. 2002. "Territorio Etnico y Paisaje Sagrado de los Maya Q'eqchi' en Petén, Guatemala." URACCAN/Cooperación Austríaca, Managua, Nicaragua, November 18. 8 pages.

Grünberg, Georg, Johannes Kranz, and Juliana Stroebele-Gregor. 2006. "When Difference Matters: Communication and Development with Indigenous People in Latin America." First World Congress of Communication and Development, Rome. October.

Grünberg, Wolfgang, William Shaw, and D. Phillip Guertin. 2000. "Resultados Preliminares de un Modelo sobre los Riesgos de Deforestación en la Reserva de la Biósfera Maya, Guatemala." In *Nuevas Perspectivas de Desarrollo Sostenible en Petén*, 159–68. Guatemala City: FLACSO.

Gudeman, Stephen, and Alberto Rivera. 2002. "Sustaining the Community, Resisting the Market: Guatemalan Perspectives." In *Land, Property and the Environment*, edited by J. F. Richards, 355–81. Oakland, Calif.: Institute for Contemporary Studies.

Guha, Ramachandra. 1997. "Radical Environmentalism and Wilderness Preservation: A Third World Critique." In *Varieties of Environmentalism: Essays North and South*, edited by R. Guha and J. Martinez-Alier, 92–108. London: Earthscan Publications.

Guha, Ramachandra, and Juan Martinez-Alier. 1997. *Varieties of Environmentalism: Essays North and South*. London: Earthscan Publications.

Haenn, Nora. 2005. *Fields of Power, Forests of Discontent: Culture, Conservation, and the State in Mexico*. Tucson: University of Arizona Press.

Hamilton, Roger. 2005. "Environmentally Friendly Cattle? A National Park's Checklist of Fauna Normally Does Not Include Cattle, but There Are Exceptions." *IDB America Magazine*, July. 3 pages.

Handy, Jim. 1988. "National Policy, Agrarian Reform, and Corporate Community during the Guatemala Revolution, 1944–1954." *Comparative Studies in Society and History* 30(4): 698–724.

Hanks, William F. 1990. *Referential Practices: Language and Lived Space among the Maya in Yucatan*. Chicago: University of Chicago Press.

Hansen, Tom. 2004. "Plan Puebla Panama and the 'Washington Consensus.'" In *Profound Rivers of Mesoamerica: Alternatives to Plan Puebla Panama*, edited by Armando Bartra, 359–414. 3d ed. Mexico City: Instituto Maya, El Atajo, and Mexico Solidarity Network.

Hardin, Garrett. 1968. "The Tragedy of the Commons." *Science* 162(3859): 1243–48.

———. 1998. "Extensions of 'The Tragedy of the Commons.'" *Science* 280(5364): 682–83.

Harvey, David. 2003. *The New Imperialism*. Oxford: Oxford University Press.

Hatse, Inge, and Patrick De Ceuster. 2001a. *Cosmovisión y Espiritualidad en la Agricultura Q'eqchi'*. Textos Ak' Kutan No. 18. Cobán, Alta Verapaz, Guatemala: Centro Ak' Kutan, Centro Bartolome de las Casas.

———. 2001b. *Prácticas Agrosilvestres Q'eqchi'es: Mas Allá de Maíz y Frijol, Un Aporte Para la Revalorización y el Fortalecimiento de la Agricultura Tradicional Q'eqchi'.* Textos Ak' Kutan No. 19. Cobán, Alta Verapaz, Guatemala: Centro Ak' Kutan, Centro Bartolome de las Casas.

Hayden, Dolores. 1981. *The Grand Domestic Revolution: A History of Feminist Designs for American Homes, Neighborhoods, and Cities.* Cambridge, Mass.: MIT Press.

Hecht, Susanna B. 1984. "Ranching in Amazonia: Political and Ecological Considerations." In *Frontier Expansion in Amazonia*, edited by Marianne Schmink and Charles Wood, 366–98. Gainesville: University of Florida Press.

———. 1993. "Of Fates, Forests and Futures: Myths, Epistemes, and Policy in Tropical Conservation." Thirty-second Horace M. Albright Conservation Lectureship, University of California, Berkeley, Department of Enviornmental Science, Policy and Management. 31 pages.

Hecht, Susanna B., Herman Rosa, and Susan Kandel. 2002. "Globalization, Forest Resurgence and Environmental Politics in El Salvador." PRISMA (Salvadoran Program for Research on Development and the Environment), San Salvador. 26 pages.

Helms, Mary W. 1982. *Middle America: A Culture History of Heartland and Frontiers.* Washington, D.C.: University Press of America.

Hernández Alarcón, Rosalinda. 1998a. *¿A Quién Servirá el Catastro? Las Dificultades para Convertir el Censo Territorial en un Recurso para Atender la Añeja Demanda de Tierra en Guatemala.* Investigación Interactiva No. 2. Guatemala City: Inforpress Centroamericana.

———. 1998b. *The Land Issue in the Peace Accords: A Summary of the Government's Response:* Investigación Interactiva No. 2. Guatemala City: Inforpress Centroamericana.

Hernández, Herberth. 2005. "Un Aceite que se Lleva Las Palmas." *Prensa Libre*, Guatemala City, September 5.

Howard, Michael. 1977. "An Account by the Count Perigny of the Kekchi of the Alta Verapaz." *Belizean Studies* 5(4): 27–31.

Hunn, Eugene S. 1999. "The Value of Subsistence for the Future of the World." In *Ethnoecology: Situated Knowledge/Located Lives*, edited by Virginia D. Nazarea, 23–36. Tucson: University of Arizona Press.

Hurtado Paz y Paz, Laura. 2008a. *Dinámicas Agrarias y Reproducción Campesina en La Globalización: El Caso de Alta Verapaz, 1970–2007.* Guatemala City: F&G Editores with Grupo Pop Noj, Seva Foundation, ProPetén, and Action Aid.

———. 2008b. "Plantations for Agro Fuels and Loss of Lands for the Production of Food in Guatemala." Guatemala City: ActionAid. August. 29 pages.

———. 2009. "Agrofuels Plantations and the Loss of Land for Food Production in Guatemala." In *Agrofuels in the Americas*, edited by R. Jonasse, 77–88. Oakland, Calif.: Food First Books.

Hyde, Lewis. 2008. "The Gift." Clark University President's Lecture. Worcester, Mass., September 19.

IDB (InterAmerican Development Bank). 2002. "Initiative Launched to Promote

Sustainable Tourism in Mayan Region of Central America, Press Release," January 16. 3 pages.

IDS (International Development Services). 1961. "The Sebol Project: A Proposed Extension of the Rural Development Program in Guatemala." Guatemala City: Planning Division of the Dirección General de Asuntos Agrarios. October. 119 pages.

Igoe, Jim. 2004. *Conservation and Globalization: A Study of National Parks and Indigenous Communities from East Africa to South Dakota*. Case Studies on Contemporary Social Issues. Belmont, Calif.: Wadsworth/Thompson Learning.

Illich, Ivan. 1983. "Silence Is a Commons: Computers Are Doing to Communication What Fences Did to Pastures and Cars Did to Streets." *CoEvolution Quarterly*, Winter.

INE (Instituto Nacional de Estadistica). 2002. "XI Censo Nacional de Población y VI de Habitación." Vol. data CD. Guatemala City.

———. 2004. "IV Censo Nacional Agropecuario 2003." In *Tomo I, Características Generales de las Fincas Censales y de Productores Agropecuarios*, edited by Ministerio de Agricultura Ganadería y Alimentación, MAGA. Vol. data CD. Guatemala City.

INE (Instituto Nacional de Estadistica) et al. 1999. *Encuesta Nacional de Salud Materno Infantil 1998–1999*. Guatemala City: Macro Internacional, Measure/ DHS+. 167 pages.

Johnston, Barbara Rose. 2005. "Chixoy Dam Legacy Issues Document Review: Chronology of Relevant Events and Actions." Center for Political Ecology, Santa Cruz, Calif. March 17. 89 pages.

Jones, Grant. 1986. "The Southern Maya Lowlands during Spanish Colonial Times." In *Handbook of Middle American Indians*, edited by R. Wauchope. Austin: University of Texas Press.

———. 1997. "Historical Perspectives on the Maya-Speaking Peoples of the Toledo District, Belize." Affidavit, Appendix B.4, Petition to the Inter-American Commission on Human Rights submitted by the Toledo Maya Cultural Council, on behalf of the Maya indigenous communities of the Toledo District. February 24. 10 pages.

Jones, Jeffrey R. 1989. "Human Settlement of Tropical Colonization in Central America." In *The Human Ecology of Topical Land Settlement in Latin America*, edited by Debra A. Schumann and William L. Partridge, 43–85. Boulder, Colo.: Westview Press.

———. 1990. *Colonization and Environment: Land and Settlement in Central America*. Tokyo: United Nations University Press.

Kahn, Hilary Elise. 2002. "Morality in Motion and In-Sightful Ethnography: The Q'eqchi' Mayan People of Livingston, Guatemala." PhD diss., State University of New York. 322 pp.

Kaimowitz, David. 1995. "Land Tenure, Land Markets, and Natural Resource Management by Large Landowners in the Petén and the Northern Transversal of Guatemala." Latin American Studies Association conference, Washington, D.C., September 28–30.

———. 1997. "Livestock and Deforestation in Central America in the 1980s and 1990s: A Policy Perspective." EPTD Discussion Papers, no. 9. Bogor, Indonesia: Center for International Forestry Research (CIFOR). 68 pages.

Kaplan, Robert D. 1994. "The Coming Anarchy." *Atlantic Monthly* 273(2): 44–76.

Kearney, Michael. 1986. "From the Invisible Hand to Visible Feet: Anthropological Studies of Migration and Development." *Annual Review of Anthropology* 15: 331–61.

———. 1996. *Reconceptualizing the Peasantry: Anthropology in Global Perspective.* Boulder, Colo.: Westview Press.

Kern, Kimberly. 2007. "Ixcan, Guatemala says NO to Xalala Dam." Press release, NIS-GUA (Network in Solidarity for the People of Guatemala), Washington, D.C., and Guatemala City. May 2.

King, Arden. 1974. *Cobán and the Verapaz: History and Culture Process in Northern Guatemala.* Middle American Research Institute, Publication 37, New Orleans, La.: Tulane University.

King, Peter. 1989. "Gleaners, Farmers and the Failure of Legal Sanctions in England 1750–1850." *Past and Present* 125: 116–50.

Klein, Naomi. 2001. "Reclaiming the Commons." *New Left Review* 9: 81–89.

Kramer, Karen L., and James L. Boone. 2002. "Why Intensive Agriculturalists Have Higher Fertility: A Household Energy Budget Approach." *Current Anthropology* 43(3): 511–17

Lastarria-Cornhiel, Susan. 2003. "Guatemala Country Brief: Property Rights and Land Markets." U.S. Agency for International Development and Development Alternatives. Document no. BASIS IQC lAG-I-00-98-0026-0. March. 29 pages.

Leland, John. 2007. "Couple Learn the High Price of Easy Credit." *New York Times,* May 19, A1, A14.

Leventhal, Richard. 1997. "Maya Occupation and Continuity in Toledo." Affidavit, Appendix B.4, Petition to the Inter-American Commission on Human Rights submitted by the Toledo Maya Cultural Council, on behalf of the Maya indigenous communities of the Toledo District. February 24. 10 pages.

Li, Tania Murray. 1999. "Marginality, Power and Production: Analysing Upland Transformations." In *Transforming the Indonesian Uplands: Marginality, Power and Production,* edited by Tania M. Li, 1–46. Amsterdam: Harwood Academic Publishers.

Locke, John 1980. *Second Treatise of Government.* Indianapolis, Ind.: Hackett Publishing. (Orig. pub. 1689.)

Lohmann, Larry. 2003. "Re-imagining the Population Debate." The Corner House Briefing Paper 28. Dorset, U.K. 20 pages.

———. 2006. *Carbon Trading: A Critical Conversation on Climate Change, Privatisation and Power.* Uppsala, Sweden: Dag Hammarskjöld Foundation.

Lovell, George W., and Christopher Lutz. 1995. *Demography and Empire: A Guide to the Population History of Spanish Central America, 1500–1821.* Boulder, Colo.: Westview Press.

Luxemburg, Rosa. 1951. *The Accumulation of Capital*. New York: Monthly Review Press. (Orig. pub. 1913.)

Machiavelli, Niccolò. 1950. *The Prince and the Discourses*. New York: Modern Library.

Macz, Nery, and Jorge Grünberg. 1999. *Manual de Comunidades de Petén*. Guatemala City: CARE Guatemala.

MAGA (Ministerio de Agricultura, Ganadería y Alimentación). 1999. "Informe de Gestión, 1997–1999 MAGA." Under the direction of Mariano Ventura Zamora, Guatemala City. 25 pages.

Malthus, Thomas Robert. 2004. *An Essay on the Principle of Population; And, A Summary View of the Principle of Population*. Whitefish, Mont.: Kessinger Publishing. (Orig. pub. 1798.)

Manger-Cats, Sebald. 1966. "Land Tenure and Economic Development in Guatemala." PhD diss., Cornell University, Agricultural Economics Department. 265 pp.

Manz, Beatriz. 1988. *Refugees of a Hidden War: The Aftermath of Counterinsurgency in Guatemala*. Albany, N.Y.: State University of New York Press.

———. 2004. *Paradise in Ashes: A Guatemalan Journey of Courage, Terror, and Hope*. Berkeley: University of California Press.

Martinez-Alier, Joan. 1991. "Ecology and the Poor: A Neglected Dimension of Latin American History." *Journal of Latin American Studies* 23(3): 621–39.

Martínez Peláez, Severo. 1992. *La Patria del Criollo*. Mexico D.F.: Ediciones en Marcha.

Marx, Karl. 1976. *Capital: A Critique of Political Economy, Volume 1*. New York: Penguin Books.

Massey, Douglas S. 1990. "Social Structure, Household Strategies, and the Cumulative Causation of Migration." *Population Index* 561(Spring): 3–26.

———. 2001. "A Theory of Migration." In *International Encyclopedia of the Social and Behavioral Sciences*, vol. 14, edited by Neil J. Smelser and Paul B. Baltes. New York: Elsevier.

Mattei, Ugo, and Laura Nader. 2008. *Plunder: When the Rule of Law Is Illegal*. Malden, Mass.: Blackwell Publishing.

Mauro, Annalisa, and Michel Merlet. 2003. "Access to Land and Recognition of Land Rights in Guatemala." Analyses and Perspectives. Paris: International Land Coalition (IFAD Secretariat). 38 pages.

McCay, Bonnie J., and James M. Acheson, eds. 1987. *The Question of the Commons: The Culture and Ecology of Communal Resources*. Tucson: University of Arizona Press.

McCreery, David. 1983. "Debt Servitude in Rural Guatemala, 1876–1936." *The Hispanic American Historical Review* 63(4): 735–59.

———. 1994. *Rural Guatemala, 1760–1940*. Stanford, Calif.: Stanford University Press.

McElhinny, Vincent. 2004. "Update on the U.S.–Central America Free Trade Agreement (CAFTA): Implications of the Negotiation." IDB–Civil Society Initiative. Washington, D.C.: InterAction. 40 pages.

McPherson, Alan. 1996. "First Things First: Guatemala, United States Assistance, and the Logic of Cold War Dependency." *Ex Post Facto* 5: 58–78.

Meillassoux, Claude. 1991. *The Anthropology of Slavery: The Womb of Iron and Gold*. Chicago: University of Chicago Press.

Mendes Pereira, João Márcio. 2005a. "From Panacea to Crisis: Grounds, Objectives and Results of the World Bank's Market-Assisted Land Reform in South Africa, Colombia, Guatemala and Brazil." Rio de Janeiro: Land Research Action Network. October. www.landaction.org.

———. 2005b. "The World Bank's Contemporary Agrarian Policy: Aims, Logics and Lines of Action." XXC Congress of the Latin American Sociology Association (ALAS), Porto Alegre, Brazil, Land Research Action Network. August 22–26. www.landaction.org.

Micklin, Michael. 1990. "Guatemala." In *International Handbook on Internal Migration*, edited by Charles B. Nam, William J. Serow, and David F. Sly. New York: Greenwood Press.

Midnight Notes Collective. 1990. "Introduction to the New Enclosures." *Midnight Notes* 10: 1–9.

Mies, Maria. 1986. *Patriarchy and Accumulation on a World Scale: Women in the International Division of Labor*. London: Zed Books.

Millet, Artimus. 1974. "The Agricultural Colonization of the West Central Petén, Guatemala: A Case Study of Frontier Settlement by Cooperatives." PhD diss., University of Oregon. 164 pp.

Mintz, Sidney Wilfred. 1985. *Sweetness and Power: The Place of Sugar in Modern History*. New York: Penguin Books.

Moguel, Julio. 2004. "The Good and the Bad of the Plan Puebla Panama: How Indigenous Rights Were Obfuscated and the Debate Shifted to Alleged Development Issues." In *Profound Rivers of Mesoamerica: Alternatives to Plan Puebla Panama* edited by Armando Bartra, 319–34. 3d ed. Mexico City: Instituto Maya, El Atajo, and Mexico Solidarity Network.

Monbiot, George. 1994. "The Tragedy of Enclosure." *Scientific American*, January.

Mondragón, Héctor. 2005. "Colombia: Agrarian Reform, Fake and Genuine." Land Research Action Network. September 5. www.landaction.org.

Morrissey, James Arthur. 1978. "A Missionary Directed Resettlement Project among the Highland Maya of Western Guatemala." PhD diss., Stanford University. 826 pp.

Municipio de Poptún. n.d. "Historia del Municipio de Poctun." 6 pages.

Mychalejko, Cyril. 2008. "Canadian Company Threatens El Salvador with Free Trade Lawsuit Over Mining Project." Upside Down World, December 19. www .upsidedownworld.org.

Nader, Laura. 1972. "Up the Anthropologist: Perspectives Gained from Studying Up." In *Reinventing Anthropology*, edited by Dell H. Hymes, 285–311. New York: Pantheon Books.

———. 1980. "The Vertical Slice: Hierarchies and Children." In *Hierarchy and Society: Anthropological Perspectives on Bureaucracy*, edited by Gerald Britan and Ronald Cohen. Philadelphia: Institute for the Study of Human Issues.

———. 1990. *Harmony Ideology: Justice and Control in a Zapotec Mountain Village*. Stanford, Calif.: Stanford University Press.

———. 1995. "Energy Needs for Sustainable Human Development from an Anthropological Perspective." In *Energy as an Instrument for Socio-economic Development*, edited by José Goldember and Thomas B. Johansson, 42–48. New York: United Nations Development Programme.

———. 1996. *Naked Science: Anthroplogical Inquiry into Boundaries, Power, and Knowledge*. New York: Routledge.

———. 1997. "Controlling Processes: Tracing the Dynamic Components of Power." *Current Anthropology* 38(5): 711–36.

Nations, James D. 1979. "Population Ecology of the Lacandon Maya." PhD diss., Southern Methodist University. 375 pages.

———. 2001. "Indigenous Peoples and Conservation: Misguided Myths in the Maya Tropical Forest." In *On Biocultural Diversity: Linking Language, Knowledge, and the Environment*, edited by Luisa Maffi, 462–71. Washington, D.C.: Smithsonian Institution Press.

———. 2006. *The Maya Tropical Forest: People, Parks, and Ancient Cities*. Austin: University of Texas Press.

Nations, James D., and Daniel Komer. 1983. "Rainforests and the Hamburger Society." *Environment* 24(4): 12–20.

Nations, James D., and Ronald B. Nigh. 1980. "The Evolutionary Potential of Lacandon Maya Sustained-Yield Tropical Forest Agriculture." *Journal of Anthropological Research* 36: 1–30.

NoPPP (Network Opposed to the Plan Puebla Panama), ed. n.d. *Plan Puebla Panama: Battle over the Future of Southern Mexico and Central America*. Burlington, Vt.: ACERCA (Action for Community and Ecology in the Region of Central America).

NISGUA (Network in Solidarity with the People of Guatemala). 2010. "Urgent Action: Leader Evelinda Ramírez Reyes Killed." Listserv announcement, February 2. nisgua@lists.riseup.net.

Noble, David. 1977. *America by Design: Science, Technology, and the Rise of Corporate Capitalism*. New York: Oxford University Press.

NotiCen. 2007. "Guatemala's Only Railroad Shuts Down Amid Hints of a Conspiracy under Cover of CAFTA." *NotiCen: Central American & Caribbean Affairs*, September 20.

Oliver, Arnold J. 2004. "Guatemala and the Forgotten Anniversary." Common Dreams.org, June 18.

Olson, R. Dennis, and Carlos Galian. 2004. "Agriculture." In *Why We Say No to CAFTA: Analysis of the Official Text*, edited by Raúl Moreno, translated by Karen Hansen-Kuhn, 2–6. Institute for Agriculture and Trade Policy/ART, Bloque Popular Centroamericano, and Alliance for Responsible Trade, Hemispheric Social Alliance. March.

Orwell, George. 1950. *1984*. New York: Signet Classic.

Osborn, Anne. 1982. "Socio-anthropological Aspects of Development in Southern Belize." Punta Gorda, Belize: Toledo Rural Development Project. April.

Ostrom, Elinor. 1990. *Governing the Commons: The Evolution of Institutions for Collective Action.* New York: Cambridge University Press.

Ostrom, Elinor, Joanna Burger, Christopher Field, Richard B. Norgaard, and David Policansky. 1999. "Revisiting the Commons: Local Lessons, Global Challenges." *Science* 284(5412): 278–82.

Pacheco, Luis. 1992. *La Religiosidad Contemporanea Maya-Kekchi.* Cayambe, Ecuador: Talleres Abya-Yala.

Parra Novo, José C. 1997. *Persona y Comunidad Q'eqchi': Aproximación Cultural a la Comunidad Q'eqchi' de Santa María Cahabón.* Textos Ak' Kutan No. 3. Cobán, Alta Verapaz, Guatemala: Centro Ak' Kutan, Centro Bartolomé de las Casas.

Peckenham, Nancy. 1980. "Land Settlement in the Petén." *Latin American Perspectives*, Spring/Summer: 169–77.

Pedroni, Guillermo. 1991. *Territorialidad Kekchi: Una Aproximación al Accesso a la Tierra: La Migración y la Titulación.* Debate No. 8. Guatemala City: FLACSO (Facultad Latinoamerica de Ciencias Sociales).

Perelman, Michael. 1983. *Classical Political Economy: Primitive Accumulation and the Social Division of Labor.* London: Rowman and Allanheld.

———. 2000. *The Invention of Capitalism: Classical Political Economy and the Secret History of Primitive Accumulation.* Durham, N.C.: Duke University Press.

———. 2005. *Manufacturing Discontent: The Trap of Individualism in a Corporate Society.* Ann Arbor, Mich.: Pluto Press.

Perera, Victor. 1993. *Unfinished Conquest: The Guatemalan Tragedy.* Berkeley: University of California Press.

Perkins, John. 2004. *Confessions of an Economic Hit Man.* San Francisco: Berrett-Koehler.

Pielemeier, Jason. 2004. "Land Stewardship in Q'eqchi' Lowland Communities." NISGUA Report on Guatemala 24(3).

Piven, Frances Fox, and Richard A. Cloward. 1993. *Regulating the Poor.* 2d ed. New York: Vintage Books. (Orig. pub. 1971.)

Polanyi, Karl. 1944. *The Great Transformation.* New York: Rinehart and Company.

Pollan, Michael. 2006. *The Omnivore's Dilemma: A Natural History of Four Meals.* New York: Penguin Press.

Portes, Alejandro. 1978. "Migration and Underdevelopment." *Politics and Society* 8(1): 1–48.

Prensa Libre. 2009. "Narcos Obligan a Finqueros a Venderles sus Propiedades." *Prensa Libre*, Guatemala City, December 7.

Presidencia de la República. 1950. "Primera Colonia Agrícola de Poptún: El Arevalismo Hace Llegar al Petén Los Beneficios de la Revolución." Tipografía Nacional. Departamento de Publicidad. February.

ProPetén. 2009. *Li Qana'aj: Li B'e Re Xtawb'al li Qaxe' (Territorio: El Camino a las Raíces).* Edited by Producciones Comunitarias de Alto Impacto. DVD, 39 minutes. Guatemala: ProPeten, Pop No'j, Seva, El Observador (Oxfam producer).

Rasmussen, Derek. 2001. "Reconciliation-to-Forgive v. Reconciliation-to-Forget." *Cultural Survival Quarterly* 25(1): 56–60.

RDC (Railroad Development Corporation). 2007. "Press Release: RDC Files Notice of Intent to Submit Claims for Arbitration under CAFTA against the Republic of Guatemala." Pittsburgh, Pa., March 13. 2 pages.

Reep, Edwin Charles. 1997. "Revolution through Evolution: The Dynamics of Evangelical Christian Belief Systems in Senahu, Alta Verapaz, Guatemala." PhD diss., University of Georgia. 201 pages.

Reina, Ruben E. 1967. "Milpas and Milperos: Implications for Prehistoric Times." *American Anthropologist* 69(1): 1–20.

Resende, Marcelo, and Maria Luisa Mendonça. 2005. "The Counter-Agrarian Reform of the World Bank." Land Research Action Network. July 12. www.landaction.org.

Retort Collective (Iain Boal, T. J. Clark, Joseph Matthews, and Michael Watts). 2005. *Afflicted Powers: Capital and Spectacle in a New Age of War.* London: Verso.

Rieff, David. 1993. "Multiculturalism's Silent Partner." *Harper's Magazine,* 287(1719): 62–72.

Rodríguez de Lemus, Guillermina. 1967. *Despertar de un Gigante: Petén Ante Mis Ojos, 1955–1965.* Guatemala City: Editorial San Antonio.

Romero, Sergio. 2008. "The Linguistic Construction of Everyday Christianity: Social History and Pastoral Q'eqchi.'" Thirteenth European Maya Conference, Paris, December 1–6. European Association of Mayanists, WAYEB.

Ross, Eric. 2000. "The Malthus Factor: Poverty, Politics and Population in Capitalist Development." Dorset, U.K.: The Corner House Briefing Paper 20. July. 20 pages.

Rosset, Peter. 2004. "O Bom, O Mau e O Feio: A Política Fundiária Do Banco Mundial." In *O Banco Mundial e A Terra: Ofensive e Resistência na América Latina, Africa e Asia,* edited by Monica Dias Martins, 16–24. Saõ Paulo, Brazil: Editora Viramundo.

Rosset, Peter, Raj Patel, and Michael Courville, eds. 2006. *Promised Land: Competing Visions of Agrarian Reform.* Oakland, Calif.: Food First Books.

Rousseau, Jean-Jacques. 1994. *Discourse on the Origins of Inequality.* Translated by Franklin Philip. Oxford: Oxford University Press. (Orig. pub. 1755.)

Rowe, Jonathan. 2001. "The Hidden Commons." *YES! Magazine,* Summer, June 30. http://www.yesmagazine.org.

Roy, Arundhati. 2001. *The Algebra of Infinite Justice.* London: Harper Collins, Flamingo.

———. 2004. *Checkbook and Cruise Missile: Conversations with Arundhati Roy.* Cambridge: South End Press.

Saldívar Tanaka, Laura, and Hannah Wittman. 2004. "Acordo de Paz e Fundo de Terras Na Guatemala." In *O Banco Mundial e A Terra: Ofensive e Resistência na América Latina, Africa e Asia,* edited by Monica Dias Martins, 101–20. Saõ Paulo, Brazil: Editora Viramundo.

Sapper, Karl. 1897. *Northern Central America with a Trip to the Highland of Anahuac: Travels and Studies of the Years 1888–1895.* Brunswick, Germany: F. Viewig.

———. 1985. *The Verapaz in the Sixteenth and Seventeenth Centuries: A Contribution to the Historical Geography and Ethnography of Northeastern Guatemala.*

Translated by Theodore E. Gutman. Occasional Paper 13. Los Angeles: Institute of Archaeology, University of California.

———. 2000. "Fray Bartolome de las Casas and the Verapaz." In *Early Scholars' Visits to Central America: Reports by Karl Sapper, Walter Lehmann, and Franz Termer, Occasional Paper 18*, edited by Marilyn Beaudry-Corbett and Ellen T. Hardy, translated by Theodore E. Gutman. Los Angeles: Cotsen Institute of Archaeology, University of California, Los Angeles.

Sawyer, Donald R. 1984. "Frontier Expansion and Retraction in Brazil." In *Frontier Expansion in Amazonia*, edited by Marianne Schmink and Charles Wood, 180–203. Gainesville: University of Florida Press.

Sayre, Nathan. 2008. "The Genesis, History, and Limits of Carrying Capacity." *Annals of the Association of American Geographers* 98(1): 120–34.

Schackt, Jon. 1981. "A Kekchi Account of an Encounter with the Chol Indians." *Belizean Studies* 9(3): 21–24.

———. 1984. "The Tzuultak'a: Religious Lore and Cultural Processes among the Kekchi." *Belizean Studies* 12(5): 16–29.

———. 1986. *One God—Two Temples: Schismatic Process in a Kekchi Village*. Oslo: Department of Social Anthropology, University of Oslo.

Schlesinger, Stephen, and Stephen Kinzer. 1982. *Bitter Fruit: The Story of the American Coup in Guatemala*. Garden City, N.Y.: Doubleday.

Schmink, Marianne, and Charles Wood, eds. 1992. *Contested Frontiers in Amazonia*. New York: Columbia University Press.

Schmolz-Haberlein, Michaela. 1996. "Continuity and Change in a Guatemalan Indian Community: San Cristobal–Verapaz, 1870–1940." *Hispanic American Historical Review* 76(2): 227–48.

Scholes, France V., and Eleanor B. Adams, eds. 1960. *Relaciones Historico-Descriptivas de la Verapaz, El Manche y Lacandon en Guatemala*. Guatemala City: Editorial Universitaria.

Schwartz, Norman B. 1987. "Colonization of Northern Guatemala: The Petén." *Journal of Anthropological Research* 43: 163–83.

———. 1990. *Forest Society: A Social History of Petén, Guatemala*. Philadelphia: University of Pennsylvania Press.

———. 1995. "Colonization, Development, and Deforestation in Petén, Northern Guatemala." In *The Social Causes of Environmental Deforestation in Latin America*, edited by Michael Painter and William Durham, 101–30. Ann Arbor: University of Michigan Press.

———. 1998. "Socio-Ethnographic Evaluation of Land Tenure and Land Legalization Problems in Protected Areas (Core, Multiple Use and Buffer Zones; Archaeological Parks), Municipal Commons (Ejidos), and Areas Outside Protected Areas." 136 pages.

———. 2001. "Pobreza Planeada o Accidente Histórico? La Lógica Capitalista, Los Asentamientos Fronterizos y Las Condiciones Rurales en Petén." Keynote address at the II Encuentro Internacaional Sobre Desarrollo Sostenible de Petén: Los Retos de la Economía Rural, Flores, Petén, November 29–December 1. 36 pages.

Scott, James. 1976. *The Moral Economy of the Peasant: Rebellion and Subsistence in Southeast Asia.* New Haven, Conn.: Yale University Press.

———. 1985. *Weapons of the Weak: Everyday Forms of Peasant Resistance.* New Haven, Conn.: Yale University Press.

———. 1990. *Domination and the Arts of Resistance: Hidden Transcripts.* New Haven, Conn.: Yale University Press.

———. 1998. *Seeing Like a State: How Certain Schemes to Improve the Human Condition Have Failed.* New Haven, Conn.: Yale University Press.

———. 2009. *The Art of Not Being Governed: An Anarchist History of Upland Southeast Asia.* New Haven, Conn.: Yale University Press.

Secaira, Estuardo. 1992. "Conservation among the Q'eqchi'-Maya: A Comparison of Highland and Lowland Agriculture." Master's thesis, University of Wisconsin. 146 pages.

———. 2000. "La Conservación de la Naturaleza, El Pueblo y Movimiento Maya, y la Espiritualidad en Guatemala: Implicaciones Para Conservacionistas." PROARCA/CAPAS/AID, Iniciativa de Uso Sostenible de la Unión Mundial para la Naturaleza (UICN), el Fideicomiso para la Conservación de Guatemala (FCG), y the Nature Conservancy (TNC). September. 99 pages.

SEGEPLAN (Secretaria General del Consejo Nacional de Planificación Económica). 1993. "Plan de Desarrollo Integrado de Petén. Vol. 1, Diagnostico General de Petén." 1st ed. Corregida. Agrar-und Hydrotechnik (AHT) y APESA. Guatemala.

Shaw-Taylor, Leigh. 2001. "Parliamentary Enclosure and the Emergence of an English Agricultural Proletariat." *Journal of Economic History* 61(3): 640–62.

Shriar, Avrum. 1999. "Agricultural Intensification and Resource Conservation in the Buffer Zone of the Maya Biosphere Reserve, Petén, Guatemala." PhD diss., University of Florida. 346 pages.

———. 2001. "The Dynamics of Agricultural Intensification and Resource Conservation in the Buffer Zone of the Maya Biosphere Reserve, Petén, Guatemala." *Human Ecology* 29(1): 27–48.

Siebers, Hans. 1999. *"We Are Children of the Mountain": Creolization and Modernization among the Q'eqchi'es.* Amsterdam: CEDLA.

Smith, Adam. 2007. *An Inquiry into the Nature and Causes of the Wealth of Nations.* Lausanne: Metalibri Digital Library. (Orig. pub. 1776.)

Smith, Nigel J. H. 1993. "Colonization Lessons from a Tropical Forest." In *Tropical Rainforests: Latin American Nature and Society in Transition, Jaguar Books on Latin America, Number 2,* edited by Susan E. Place, 139–50. Wilmington, Del.: Scholarly Resources.

Smyth, Frank. 2005. "The Untouchable Narco-State: Guatemala's Military Defies the DEA." *Texas Observer,* November 18.

Solano Ponciano, Luis Eduardo. 2000. "Efectos Económicos y Sociales de la Actividad Petrolera en la Franja Transversal del Norte y Petén Durante el Periodo, 1974–1998." Universidad de San Carlos, Guatemala City. 245 pages.

———. 2005. *Guatemala: Petróleo y Minería en las Entrañas del Poder.* Guatemala City: Inforpress Centroamericana.

———. 2008. "Reconversión Productiva y Agrocombustibles: La Nueva Acumulación Capitalista en el Agro Guatemalteco." *El Observador: Análisis Alternativo Sobre Política y Economía* 3(14): 31–61.

Stansbury, Burke, and Andrew de Sousa. 2006. "More CAFTA Failure for the Bush Administration: Thousands Protest Free Trade Agreement in El Salvador." Press release, Stop CAFTA Coalition. www.stopcafta.org. 2 pages.

Stavenhagen, Rodolfo. 2006. "Indigenous Peoples: Land, Territory, Autonomy, and Self-Determination." In *Promised Land: Competing Visions of Agrarian Reform*, edited by Peter Rossett, Raj Patel, and Michael Courville, 208–20. Oakland, Calif.: Food First Books.

Stepp, John Richard, and Ava Lassater. 2004. "The Plan Puebla-Panamá." *Anthropology News*, December: 28–29.

Stocks, Anthony. 2002. "The Possibilities for Q'eqchi' Community Conservation in Chisec Municipality, Alta Verapaz, Guatemala." American Anthropological Association conference, Chicago. 22 pages.

Stoll, Otto. 1938. *Etnografía de la República de Guatemala*. Translated by Antonio Goubaud Carrera. Guatemala City: Tipografia Sanchez y de Guise.

Strasma, John D., and Rafael Celis. 1992. "Land Taxation, the Poor and Sustainable Development." In *Poverty, Natural Resources, and Public Policy in Central America: U.S. Third World Policy Perspective*, edited by S. Annis, 143–70. Washington, D.C.: Transaction Publishers (Overseas Development Council).

Sundberg, Juanita. 1998. "NGO Landscapes in the Maya Biosphere Reserve, Guatemala." *Geographical Review* 88(3): 388–412.

Sutherland, Elizabeth G., David L. Carr, and Siân L. Curtis. 2004. "Fertility and the Environment in a Natural Resource Dependent Economy: Evidence from Peten, Guatemala." *Poblacion y Salud en Mesoamerica* 2(1): 1–12.

Sydow, Evanize, and Maria Luisa Mendonça, eds. 2003. *The Destructive Agrarian Reform Policies of the World Bank*. Saõ Paulo, Brazil: Social Network for Justice and Human Rights.

Taracena Arriola, Arturo. 2002. *Etnicidad, Estado y Nación en Guatemala, 1808–1944. ¿Por Qué Estamos Como Estamos?* Antigua, Guatemala: Centro de Investigaciones Regionales de Mesoamérica.

Tauli-Corpuz, Victoria, and Parshuram Tamang. 2007. "Oil Palm and Other Commercial Tree Plantations, Monocropping: Impacts on Indigenous Peoples' Land Tenure and Resource Management Systems and Livelihoods." United Nations, Permanent Forum on Indigenous Issues, sixth session, New York, May 7. E/C.19/2007/CRP.6. 19 pages.

Taussig, Michael. 1980. *The Devil and Commodity Fetishism in South America*. Chapel Hill: University of North Carolina Press.

Tax, Sol. 1953. *Penny Capitalism: A Guatemalan Indian Economy*. Washington, D.C.: Government Printing Office.

Tercer Precongreso de Pueblos Indígenas, Comunidades Locales y Afrodesendientes de Mesoámerica: Sobre Áreas Protegidas y Derechos Territoriales. 2010. "Declaració de Yucatán." Mérida, Yucatán. March.

Thompson, E. P. 1966. *The Making of the English Working Class.* New York: Vintage Books.

——. 1971. "The Moral Economy of the English Crowd in the Eighteenth Century." *Past and Present* 50: 76–136.

——. 1991. *Customs in Common.* New York: New Press.

Thompson, J. Eric S. 1930. *Ethnology of the Mayas of Southern and Central British Honduras.* Anthropology Series. Vol. 17. Chicago: Field Museum of Natural History.

——. 1932. "A Maya Calendar from the Alta Vera Paz, Guatemala." *American Anthropologist* 34(3): 449–54.

——. 1938. "Sixteenth and Seventeenth Century Reports on the Chol Mayas." *American Anthropologist* 40: 584–605.

——. 1972. *The Maya of Belize: Historical Chapters since Columbus.* Belize City: Benex Press.

TMCC and TAA (Toledo Maya Cultural Council and Toledo Alcaldes Association). 1997. *Maya Atlas: The Struggle to Preserve Maya Land in Southern Belize.* Berkeley, Calif.: North Atlantic Books.

Todorov, Tzvetan. 1984. *The Conquest of America: The Question of the Other.* New York: Harper & Row.

Tsing, Anna Lowenhaupt. 2002. "Land as Law: Negotiating the Meaning of Property in Indonesia." In *Land, Property and the Environment,* edited by John F. Richards, 94–137. Oakland, Calif.: Institute for Contemporary Studies.

——. 2005. *Friction: An Ethnography of Global Connection.* Princeton, N.J.: Princeton University Press.

Tucker, Richard P. 2000. *Insatiable Appetite: The United States and the Ecological Degradation of the Tropical World.* Berkeley: University of California Press.

UDEFEGUA (Unidad de Protección a Defensoras y Defensores de Derechos Humanos de Guatemala). 2008. "La Tendencia Creciente de la Criminalización del Movimiento Social Guatemalteco." *El Observador: Análisis Alternativo Sobre Política y Economía* 3(14): 22–30.

Valenzuela, Ileana. 2003. "Memoria Cuarto Taller, Proyecto GSAPP." October 8. 9 pages.

Vargas Foronda, Jacobo. 1984. *Guatemala: Sus Recursos Naturales, El Militarismo, El Imperialismo.* Mexico City: Tipografía, Diseño e Impresión, S.A.

Wachtel, Paul. 1983. *The Poverty of Affluence: A Psychological Portrait of the American Way of Life.* New York: Free Press.

Wagner Henn, Regina. 1996. "Los Alemanes en Guatemala, 1828–1944." In *Historia General de Guatemala,* vol. 5: 267–82. Guatemala City: Asociación de Amigos del País, Fundación para la Cultura y el Desarrollo.

Wainwright, Joel. 2008. *Decolonizing Development: Colonial Power and the Maya.* Malden, Mass.: Wiley-Blackwell.

Wallach, Jason. 2007. "Ex-USTR Negotiator Vargo Key in CAFTA Case,." *Upside Down World,* March 28. www.upsidedownworld.org.

Waring, Marilyn. 1988. *If Women Counted: A New Feminist Economics.* San Francisco: Harper & Row.

Warren, Kay B. 1978. *The Symbolism of Subordination: Indian Identity in a Guatemalan Town.* Austin: University of Texas Press.

———. 1998. *Indigenous Movements and Their Critics: Pan-Maya Activism in Guatemala.* Princeton, N.J.: Princeton University Press.

Wasserstrom, Robert. 1978. "Population Growth and Economic Development in Chiapas, 1524–1975." *Human Ecology* 6(2): 127–43.

Weaver, Frederick Stirton. 1999. "Reform and (Counter) Revolution in Post-independence Guatemala: Liberalism, Conservatism, and Postmodern Controversies." *Latin American Perspectives* 26(2): 129–58.

Weber, Max. 1978. *Economy and Society: An Outline of Interpretive Sociology.* 4th ed. Berkeley: University of California Press.

West, Paige, James Igoe, and Dan Brockington. 2006. "Parks and People: The Social Impact of Protected Areas." *Annual Review of Anthropology* 35: 251–77.

White, Richard. 1995. *The Organic Machine.* New York: Hill and Wang.

Whitmore, Thomas, and B. L. Turner III. 2001. *Cultivated Landscapes of Middle America on the Eve of Conquest.* New York: Oxford University Press.

Wilk, Richard R. 1981. "Pigs Are a Part of the System: A Lesson in Agricultural Development." *Belizean Studies* 9(2): 20–24.

———. 1984. "Rural Settlement Change in Belize, 1970–1980: The Effect of Roads." *Belizean Studies* 12(4): 1–10.

———. 1987. "The Kekchi and the Settlement of Toledo District." *Belizean Studies* 15(3): 33–50.

———. 1997. *Household Ecology: Economic Change and Domestic Life among the Kekchi Maya in Belize.* DeKalb: Northern Illinois University Press. (Orig. pub. 1991.)

Wilk, Richard, Manuel Cab, Mateo Cab, and Laura Kosakowsky. 1987. "The Prisoner and the Chol Cuink: A Modern Kekchi Story." *Belizean Studies* 15(3): 51–57.

Wilk, Richard, and Mac Chapin. 1990. *Ethnic Minorities in Belize: Mopan, Kekchi and Garifuna.* SPEAR Reports 1. Belize City: Cubola Productions.

Williams, Robert G. 1986. *Export Agriculture and the Crisis in Central America.* Chapel Hill: University of North Carolina Press.

Wilson, Richard. 1995. *Maya Resurgence in Guatemala: Q'eqchi' Experiences.* Norman: University of Oklahoma Press.

Wittman, Hannah, and Laura Tanaka Saldívar. 2006. "The Agrarian Question in Guatemala." In *Promised Land: Competing Visions of Agrarian Reform,* edited by Peter Rosset, Raj Patel, and Michael Courville, 23–39. Oakland, Calif.: Food First Books.

Wolf, Eric R., and Sidney W. Mintz. 1957. "Haciendas and Plantations in Middle America and the Antilles." *Social and Economic Studies* 6(3): 380–411.

Wood, Charles. 1981. "Structural Changes and Household Strategies: A Conceptual Framework for the Study of Rural Migration." *Human Organization* 40(4): 338–43.

Wood, Ellen Meiksins. 1999. *The Origins of Capitalism.* London: Monthly Review Press.

———. 2002. *The Origin of Capitalism: A Longer View.* London: Verso.

Worby, Paula. 2000. "Security and Dignity: Land Access and Guatemala's Returned Refugees." *Refuge* 19(3): 17–24.

World Bank. 2006a. "Implementation Completion Report (SCL-44320) on a Loan in the Amount of US$23 Million to the Republic of Guatemala for a Land Fund Project." World Bank, Environmentally and Socially Sustainable Development Sector Management Unit, Central American Country Management Unit, Latin America and the Caribbean Regional Office. Report no. 34615, March 21. 38 pages.

———. 2006b. "Integrated Safeguards Datasheet Appraisal Stage." Report no. AC1728, Washington, D.C., November 2. 7 pages.

———. 2006c. "Project Appraisal Document on a Proposed Loan in the Amount of US$62.3 Million to the Republic of Guatemala for a Land Administration Project in Support of the Second Phase of the Land Administration Program (APL)." Washington, D.C. Report no. 37995-GT, December 15. 114 pages.

———. 2006d. "Republic of Guatemala Country Environmental Analysis: Addressing the Environmental Aspects of Trade and Infrastructure Expansion." Report no. 36459-GT. 87 pages.

Wright, Charles. n.d. "The Use of Land by Maya Indians, Section 1, General Overview of Activity by Mayas in Central America." In Papers, housed at the Belize National Archives BAD/CHW/9. Belmopan.

Wright, Ronald. 1992. *Stolen Continents: The Americas through Indian Eyes since 1492.* Boston: Houghton Mifflin.

Ybarra, Megan. 2008a. "Informe Antropológico sobre el Lugar Sagrado, Cuevas 'Xch'ool Tzuultaq'a' de Muqb'ilha' I y Candelaria Camposanto, Chisec, Alta Verapaz." Prepared for the Guatemalan Ministry of Culture, Cobán, Alta Verapaz. August. 38 pages.

———. 2008b. "Sostenibilidad Legal y Cultural de Patrimonios Agrarios Colectivos en Comunidades Q'eqchi'es." Independent report, October. 33 pages.

———. 2009. "Violent Visions of an Ownership Society: The Land Administration Project in Petén, Guatemala." *Land Use Policy* 26(1): 44–54.

———. 2011. "Slashed and Burned: The Debate over Privatization of Q'eqchi' Lands in Northeastern Guatemala." *Society and Natural Resources* 24(10): forthcoming.

Ybarra, Megan, Oscar Obando Samos, Liza Grandia, and Norman B. Schwartz. 2011. "Tierra, Migración y Vida en Petén: 1999–2009." 73 pages.

Zahniser, Steven, and William Coyle. 2004. "U.S.-Mexico Corn Trade during the NAFTA Era: New Twists to an Old Story." Electronic Outlook Report from the Economic Research Service, U.S. Department of Agriculture, Document no. FDS-04D-01. 20 pages.

Zaretsky, Eli. 1975. *Capitalism, the Family, and Personal Life.* New York: Harper & Row.

Zarger, Rebecca K. 2009. "Mosaics of Maya Livelihoods: Readjusting to Global and Local Food Crises." *NAPA Bulletin* 32: 130–51.

Zibechi, Raúl. 2004. "Privatizations: The End of a Cycle of Plundering." Americas Program. Interhemispheric Resource Center, November 1. www.americaspolicy.org. 8 pages.

INDEX

Acalá people, 30, 32, 35, 36

ACDIP (Asociación de Comunidades Campesinas Indígenas . . . Petén), 133, 136, 233n12

Achi' people, 182–83

ACODET (Association of Communities for Development . . . Resources), 236n5

Adams, Richard, 66

African palm. *See* palm oil industry

Agoutiville community: agrarian privatization effects, 98; anthropological methodology, 22–26; cattle ranching incursion, 153, 155, 156–57, 158, 161–63; consumerism example, 207; customary land management, 93*f*, 99*f*; education examples, 208–9; electrical outage, 188; map, xviii; profile of, 23*f*, spiritual practices, 75; testimonies from, 7, 61-62, 98, 102-3, 106-7, 134-35, 153, 157-60, 163, 181, 208, 214; textbox, 154–55; titling program speculation, 141

Agrarian Reform Law (1952), 46

agribusiness, corn production, 193–95, 196*f*

agricultural polygons, 227n3

agroforestry training program, xv. *See also* fruit orchards

agrofuel industry, 164–68. *See also* palm oil industry

Aguacate community, 92

Aguirre-Beltrán, Gonzalo, 6

Alonso Fradejas, Alberto, 140

Alta Verapaz: cardamom crops, 229n5; civil war violence, 64; climate characteristics, 22; German-controlled coffee plantations, 38–40; Germany's donor projects, 233n3; land concentration statistics, 118; map, xxvii; migration patterns, 61; population statistics, 34–35, 35; resistance activity, 136, 137–38; road system, 178, 179; traders, 71. *See also* Cobán

Amin, Samir, 237n6

Andean Development Corporation, PPP support, 235n2

APROBASANK (Sa Qa Chol Nimla K'aleb'aal), 137–38

Arbenz, Jacobo (and administration), 45, 46–47

Archer Daniels Midland, 195

area measurements, equivalents, xxvi

Arendt, Hannah, 17, 228n5

Arévalo, Juan Jose (and administration), 45–46

Armas, Carlos Castillo, 47, 229n10

Arzú, Alvaro (and administration), 178

Asociación de Comunidades Campesinas Indígenas . . . Petén (ACDIP), 133, 136, 233n12

Associated Peasant Businesses, 132

Association for Harmony in Our Community (APROBASANK), 137–38

CAFTA; PPP (Puebla to Panama Plan)

economic accounting systems, 202–4, 237*n*3

ecosystem diversity, overview, 21–22, 26, 92, 103

ecotourism, xv, 137, 176, 232*n*19

Ecuador, 173

Edmonson, Munroe, 198

education/schools: bilingual educators, 72; coffee planter perspective, 44, 65; expectations for, 207–9; Jaguarwood community, 99, 100; road system benefits, 180–81; Rockridge community, 7; Spanish colonial era, 35

egalitarianism ethic, 72–74. *See also* customary land management

Eisenhower, Dwight D. (and administration), 47

elders, 73, 93, 94, 100, 102

electrical service, 7, 11, 188, 206, 236*n*8

El Estor, 230*n*4

El Salvador, 173, 175, 182, 187, 195, 232*n*13

La Empresa para el Fomento y Desarrollo de El Petén. *See* FYDEP

enclosure movements, overview: British experience, 13–18; in capitalism debates, 12–13; Christianity-based conquest, 5, 30–36, 206, 229*n*3; commerce-based conquest, 36–45, 52, 229*n*7; Cuc family story, 7–12; ideological reconditioning, 15–16, 129, 131–32, 160–63, 202–4; justification for, 4-5, 17; as labor control, 200–201; market-assisted reform, 16–18; processes of, 4–5; as recurrent pattern, 5–7, 26, 199–200; summarized, 31*t*. *See also specific topics, e.g.,* cattle ranching; colonization, state-led; corporate capitalism; land dispossession; legitimization of enclosures; titling programs

Engels, Friedrich, 204

environmental stewardship. *See* customary land management

epidemics, 34–35

equity emphasis. *See* customary land management

escape agriculture, 76–77. *See also* migration *entries*

Esquipulas, 76

Essay on the Principle of Population (Malthus), 84–85

ETC Group, 227*n*1 (Intro)

ethanol industry, 164–67

ethnicity. *See* Maya ethnicities

European Union, 233*n*4, 235*n*2

Explotaciones Míneras Izabal, 42

expropriation of land. *See* land dispossession

Fagan, Christopher T., 105

fallow fields, 83, 90, 94, 158, 231*n*6

family planning, 111–13, 232*n*17

family size, milpa size correlation, 111

fees/tributes, requirements, 34–35, 36, 42, 73

fencing, 9, 151, 153

Ferdinand V, 40

fertility rates, 79, 106, 108

fertilizers, 83, 94, 97, 98

fictitious commodities, Polyani's, 4, 228*n*2 (Intro)

field selection process, customary land management, 92–94

financial crisis (2008), 217

Fleishman-Hillard International, 176

folklore, 36, 144–45, 190–91, 204, 210–11, 214, 234*n*1. *See also* ceremonies; spiritual beliefs/practices; *Tzuultaq'a*

Fomento y Desarrollo de El Petén. *See* FYDEP

FONTIERRAS, 10, 121–22, 128, 133, 162–63, 166

Ford, Henry, 204

forest camps, commercial extraction, 51–53

forest use: access loss, 153; with bioculture mosaics, 106, 137–38, 232*n*13; in conservation planning, 105–6, 168;

ary land management; FYDEP; land dispossession; migration *entries;* San Luis; spiritual beliefs/practices; titling programs

pharmaceutical industry, 189, 205

PINFOR, 168

Pocomchi' people, 30, 233*n*7

Polanyi, Karl, 4, 12–13, 228*n*2 (Intro), 237*n*5; double movement concept, 215-21.

Poor Laws, England, 86

Poptún, 165; National Agrarian Colony, 45–46

population growth: and deforestation patterns, 83, 84*f*; as environmental degradation element, 108–9; family size considerations, 111–13, 232*nn*16–17; fertility rates, 79; Malthusian/Neo-Malthusian theory, 85–88; momentum problem, 109–10

population statistics: cattle growth compared, 150*f*; classic Maya civilization, 113; European impact, 34–35; Jaguarwood fluctuations, 89; Petén villages, 230*n*4; Q'eqchi' ratios, 4, 21, 79; from 1700s through 1990s, 85*f*

Popul Vuh, 190–91, 233*n*13

PPP (Puebla to Panama Plan): overview, 27–28, 172–74; as democratic threat, 181–86; greenwashing strategies, 176–77; harmonization agendas, 181–83, 201; ideological foundation, 171–72; as imperialism, 185–86; palm industry subsidies, 167; planning approach, 174, 175, 184–85, 236*n*4; protests against, 174–75, 176, 177, 181–82, 235*n*3, 236*n*5; revisions of, 175–77; road construction plans, 177–81

precolonial period, Q'eqchi' commerce, 30, 52

Presidential Dependency for the Resolution of Conflicts (CONTIERRA), 121–22, 136

prices, land: buyer tactics, 9–10, 153, 156;

carbon-trading program impact, 168; titling program impact, 6, 55, 139–43, 157, 234*n*14

primitive accumulation, defined, 12. *See also* enclosure movements, overview

private property, as fictitious commodity, 228*n*2 (Intro)

private property approach: agrarian productivity effects, 96–101; and carrying capacity question, 114–16; as commons enclosure, 3–5, 227*n*1 (Intro); cultural permeations, 129, 131–32; customary land management compared, 95–96, 97*f*; environmental degradation consequence, 85, 87–88, 101–8, 130–31; family size considerations, 111–13, 232*nn*16–17; ideological themes, 15–16, 19; as inequity foundation, 117–18, 141; land management impact, 94–99; and population growth question, 108–13; sales obstacles, 122–24. *See also* titling programs

privatization philosophy, as commons erosion, 11, 183, 215–18, 237*n*5. *See also* corporate capitalism; DR-CAFTA; PPP (Puebla to Panama Plan); titling programs

ProPetén, xvi, 24, 52, 97–98. *See also* Conservation International; Remedios program

prophecy for 2012, Maya, 199, 237*n*2

protected areas: agricultural concessions, xiv, 227*n*3; burning of biological station, xi, xiv–xv, 130; carbon-trading projects, 168; conflict statistics, 228*n*3; environmentalist perspectives, 83–85, 115–16; frontier optimism problem, 107–8; FYDEP program, 51–55; Jaguarwood's forest use, 89; and land tenure security expectations, 130–31; maps, xii–xiii; market-oriented elements, 20–21, 88; Mesoamerican Biological Corridor proposal, 176–77;

as migration obstacle, 6–7; mosaic landscapes, 106, 137–38, 232*n*13; parcel inheritance problem, 107; Peace Accords rumor, xiii, 227*n*2; petroleum reserves, 169; as recurring land dispossession, xvi–xvii; road construction plans, 178; Rockridge community, 9; size of, xii–xiii; and titling programs, 124–29. *See also* Atelesdale community; customary land management; Macawville community

Protestants, 21, 69, 73, 74–75, 89

Punta Gorda town, 61, 100

Qawa' Kaq, 214

Laj Q'eq, 234*n*1

Q'eqchi' people, anthropological methodology, 22–26. *See also specific topics, e.g.,* Agoutiville community; customary land management; folklore; land dispossession; migration *entries;* protected areas; spiritual beliefs/practices; titling programs, United States and Q'eqchi' comparisons

quetzals, currency equivalent, xxvi

quintal, pounds equivalent, xxvi

railroads, 38, 171, 189–90

Railroads of Guatemala, 171

Ramírez, Evelinda, 236*n*8

ranching. *See* cattle ranching

reductions, Spanish colonial era, 33. *See also* conquest

re-embedding capitalism, 215–16, 218, 237*n*5

reforestation, milpa system benefits, 94

Registro de Información Catastral (RIC), 121–22, 125–26, 128*f*

religion. *See* Catholic Church/Catholicism; spiritual beliefs/practices

religious brotherhoods, during colonial era, 34–35

Remedios program, xiii–xv

reproductive health care, 73, 111–13, 230*n*5

resilience factors: cultural cohesion, 79–80; egalitarian social structure, 72–74; kinship networks, 77–79; as recurring theme, 221–22; spiritual practices, 74–76; subsistence agriculture, 76–77

resistance activity, 34–35, 44–45, 136–37, 147, 236*n*8. *See also* citizen mobilization opportunities

Reyes, Miguel, 181

RIC (Registro de Información Catastral), 121–22, 125–26, 128*f. See also* Legal and Technical Unit/Protierra; World Bank

rituals. *See* ceremonies

Riverstone Holdings, 167

road construction: agrarian market opportunities, 100; Belizean court case, 139; for cattle ranching, 69, 147–48; double-edged impact, 180–81; and harmonization agendas, 181–83; history overview, 178–79; Liberalism-led programs, 38–39, 43; as migration influence, 61–63; Northern Franja Transversal, 49, 154–55; organic system, 179–80; Petén, 53, 54; under trade agreements, 7, 172–74, 175

Rockridge community, xviii, 7–11; testimonies from, 7-12, 79

Rousseau, Jean-Jacques, 15

Roy, Arundhati, 177, 182, 185–86, 201

rule of law, 201-2, 205. *See also* legitimization of enclosures

sacred areas: Agoutiville community, 154; as cultural heritage, 137–38, 233*n*13; identification of, 74-75; Jagged Rocks cave, 154; private property ideology, 131; rituals, 236*n*11; Rockridge community, 10; Tamalton community, 69, 70*f. See also Tzuultaq'a*

San José municipality, 65

time, Mayan perspective, 199, 237*n*1

violence, during enclosure processes, 14–16, 17, 33–34, 42, 47–48, 228*n*6, 230*n*13. *See also* legitimization of enclosures

wages: agrofuel industry, 166; cattle ranching, 152, 157, 235*n*10; currency equivalents, xxvi; and debt servitude, 41–42, 234*n*7; as fictitious commodity, 228*n*2 (Intro); as migration influence, 65; road construction, 61–62; as subsistence inefficiency, 15. *See also* labor practices

Waka' site, 52

Walmart, 206–7

water access, 9

wealth, magic explanations, 144–45, 234*n*1

White, Richard, 172

Wilk, Richard, 80, 92, 209

witchcraft accusations, 62, 70, 73, 130, 230*n*6

worker-serf, 26, 40, 43, 65, 203. *See also* mozo colono

World Bank: agrarian reform programs, 6, 7, 18–21; cattle ranching reinforcement, 170; dam projects, 183; Mesoamerican Biological Corridor, 176–77; land market theory, 122-24; migration portrayal, 81–82; park preservation philosophy, 88; population growth question, 110, 112–13; PPP support, 174, 235*n*2; subcontractors, 125-27, 135, 139-140, 233*n*8; titling programs, 119–21, 125–26, 142–43, 185. *See also* cadastre; RIC; UTJ (Unidad Técnico-Jurídico/Protierra)

World Parks Congress, xi

World Social Forum, 3–4, 187

World Wildlife Fund, 168

Xalalá dam, 177, 236*n*5

xate harvesting, xv, 51, 52, 62, 103, 131

Yat, Melchior, 44

Ybarra, Megan, 135

Zen-Noh, 195

Zero Population Growth, 86

Zotz National Park, 131